PHILIP II
THE FIRST MODERN KING

PHILIP II. AT THE AGE OF TWENTY-FOUR
From a portrait by Titian in the Corsini Gallery, Rome

PHILIP II
THE FIRST MODERN KING

BY

JEAN H. MARIÉJOL

PROFESSOR AT THE UNIVERSITY OF LYONS

TRANSLATED FROM THE FRENCH

BY

WARRE B. WELLS

HARPER & BROTHERS
PUBLISHERS : NEW YORK

First Published . . *1933*

PRINTED IN GREAT BRITAIN

CONTENTS

5

LIST OF ILLUSTRATIONS

THE LIFE AND REIGN OF PHILIP II OF SPAIN

CHAPTER I

THE HEIR OF CHARLES V

OF all the Sovereigns of Spain, the most famous, and perhaps even to this very day the most popular among the Spanish people, is Philip II, whose reign and life I propose to study here.

His father, the Emperor Charles V, whom history in general scarcely recognizes under the name of Charles I, King of Castile and Aragon, was a cosmopolitan monarch, Flemish, German, Italian as much as Spanish, the last of the great Emperors of the Middle Ages, overburdened and distracted in all directions by his duties as the head of Christendom. Out of the forty years of his reign, Charles spent only thirteen in all in Spain, and most frequently he made short stays there merely for the purpose of extracting from the Cortes the subsidies which he required for the defence of his Empire.

Philip II, on the other hand, was a monarch essentially Spanish. He took up his residence in the Peninsula immediately after his accession, and refused ever to leave it, even for the purpose of reducing the rebellious Low Countries to obedience. Who dare say whether even the Spain of to-day will cease to revere this sixteenth-century king who personified a nation of soldiers and ardent Catholics, and, even though it might be at the price of the severest suffering on their part, satisfied his subjects' passion for glory and their zeal for proselytism?

Philip was born in Valladolid on May 21st, 1527. A little earlier, Pope Clement VII had come to the reckless decision to form a Franco-Italian Holy League against the Spanish hegemony in Italy. In this same month of May, the Imperial army of the

9   B

Milanese, driven to mutiny through lack of pay, barely able to feed itself by marauding, and reinforced by ten thousand lansquenets who were nearly all Lutherans, marched on Rome, that Babylon glutted with gold won from the exploitation of the Christian world. The Imperial troops stormed the city, besieged the Pope in the Castello San Angelo, and for a whole week pillaged, massacred, raped, sacked and profaned the monasteries and churches.

The scandal of this orgy of robbery, bloodshed and sacrilege stirred the Catholic world so deeply that Charles V countermanded the fêtes in honour of the birth of his first son, and ordered public prayers for the deliverance of the Sovereign Pontiff. But the Emperor was himself in no hurry to deliver the Pope. It was only at a very high price, and after long negotiation, that Charles gave Clement back his liberty. All this cast a shadow over the cradle of the Prince. It was, so to speak, a token, if not of conflict, at least of possible disagreement, based on the most profane grounds, between the Courts of Rome and Madrid, which were supposed to be whole-heartedly devoted to the defence of Catholicism.

At the baptismal font the baby boy received the name of Philip in memory of his grandfather, Philip the Fair, who reigned in Castile, conjointly with his grandmother, Joan the Mad, from 1504 to 1506, after the death of Isabel the Catholic.

About Philip's infancy, apart from official records, little is known. When he was less than one year old, on April 19th, 1528, he was recognized as heir-apparent by the Cortes of Castile. But the Cortes of Aragon, more wedded to formalism and also less well domesticated, declined to recognize him until he reached the age of fifteen.

Together with his younger sister, Doña Maria, Philip spent most of his time in Castile, in Madrid, Ocaña, Toledo, Aranjuez, Avila and other places reputed for their healthy climate, under the authority of his mother, the Empress Isabel. His first governor, Don Pedro González de Mendoza, in his letters to Charles V, describes, as though they were worthy of note, traits of the four years old boy which are mere features of any childhood, suitable for a nursemaid's admiration.

At the same time, it is interesting to hear that Philip had no love to lose for Doctor Villalobos, his father's learned medical attendant. Villalobos was an enemy of the plentiful platters of the people of the North and a partisan of Spanish sobriety, and he refused to let Philip eat anything he liked. Philip was so naughty (*travieso*), says the good governor, that the Empress lost her temper and whipped him with her own hand in the presence of her ladies, who wept at the sight of such cruelty. He was fond of riding, on mounts suitable to his age. One day, in company with the Empress, he went out in Toledo on a little mule, which he insisted on mounting without assistance, and, with the Marquis de Lombay and de Mendoza on either side of him, rode through the streets full of people, saying things that made his mother laugh, and highly delighted to find himself a member of a cavalcade.

Philip grew up under a new governor, Don Juan de Zuñiga, Grand Commander of Castile, who, like Mendoza, chose very quiet mounts for him, in particular a nag which was big, but extremely gentle. This was when he was nine years old. He went through the little misfortunes of childhood, such as measles, about which Villalobos and his colleague Escoriaza kept the Emperor supplied with copious details. He became taller and stronger, though he always remained rather frail of body. By the age of thirteen Philip was such a good horseman that he could spend six hours on horseback, " as though they were only two hours, whereas to me ", reports Zuñiga with all the exaggeration of the courtier, " they seemed like twelve ". He hunted at least twice a week, with the long-bow, with the net, with the falcon, to hounds ; started hares, and stalked stags.

As tutor Philip was assigned Juan Martínez Siliceo, a sometime student at the Sorbonne and reader at the University of Salamanca, and it is through the medium of this master of his that we learn some details about his education. While Philip was still quite young he was set at his Latin, an indispensable language, as Zuñiga puts it, for the future Sovereign of countries speaking so many different tongues. But, at the age of nine, he had a hard job of it assimilating grammar, which demanded too great an effort either of memory or of application from him. Within three months, however, he had succeeded in learning the conjugations and the other elements of the language. This was more than half of rudimentary knowledge of it, and, once this first stage was passed, Philip could be put to the reading of any author.

" If Your Majesty approves," Siliceo wrote to Charles V, " the first will be the Cato." This was the usual name of the *Catus*, one of the treatises of Varro, a contemporary of Cicero's, about the education of children (*de Liberis Educandis*). This treatise, in Siliceo's opinion, was " very clear in what it says and contains maxims very necessary for human life ". With all respect to Siliceo, his choice of this little work is astonishing. It would certainly teach the boy words, but not all of them were words which he would be in the habit of using.

11

" The midwife brings the child into the world, the nurse feeds him, the pedagogue trains him, the master teaches him." What, again, was the boy to make of advice such as this ? " The nurse must be young : in older women the milk is, in fact, as bad as the blood ; for the milk, as the doctors say, is the yeast of the blood." One is irresistibly reminded of " conversation manuals ". Besides, the text was not quite as clear as the sometime Sorbonne student believed. Geography—the geography of Antiquity—and the mythology of the gods, great and small, had to be explained to the boy. Would it not have been better to put the Vulgate into the hands of this Christian prince ?

After four years of Latin Philip was so far advanced, Siliceo further tells us, that within six months he was able to read the historians, however difficult they might be, without requiring too much help from his masters. He could speak Latin fairly well, for all his studies were carried on in this language, and he was beginning to write it. Two scholars, Honorato Juan and Ginés Sepulveda, were charged with talking and arguing in Latin in his presence, or with him. In March, 1540, Philip went to the University of Alcalá to listen to all the readers, except the Hebrew reader, and was attentive for three hours.

It is probable that, until he was thirteen years of age, Philip did not apply himself seriously to anything but Latin, since both his governor and his tutor were equally afraid of overdriving him. He was so fond of hunting, writes Siliceo, that he divided himself between hunting and study, " which two things, taken in moderation, procure health of body and augment that of the mind ".

For this pleasant balancing of means of education Philip was, apparently, so grateful to his master that in 1540 he had Siliceo nominated Bishop of Carthagena and, six years later, promoted Archbishop of Toledo. But Charles V, though he was ready to gratify his son in this respect, had no very great opinion of Siliceo. When the Emperor learnt that his son had chosen Siliceo as his confessor, he wrote to Philip : " He is a worthy man, as everybody knows, but I hope that he will take better care of your conscience than he has done of your studies, and that he will not show himself as accommodating in this direction as he has been in the other." This reproach is significant. It testifies to the Emperor's anxiety because Philip, as early as the age of fourteen, showed some disposition towards gallantry. His father, in this letter of 1541, draws his attention to the dangers of a dissolute life for body and soul.

Siliceo, the future Primate of Spain, devoted himself enthusiastically to introducing the test of " pure blood " (*sangre limpia*) into his diocese. This test, inspired by popular prejudice and inaugurated from the foundation of the Inquisition, excluded from certain benefices, from the military Orders, from the tribunal of the Holy Office, and from colleges, confraternities and well-endowed monasteries any descendants of Moors, Jews, heretics, or persons who had been condemned to any penance by the Inquisition. The result of this was that, by a startling contradiction, a convert might become a bishop or a cardinal—or even Pope—but he was forbidden to become a poor student or an illiterate monk in a rich monastery ; and that a man might aspire to the Archbishopric of Toledo, but not to being accepted as a choir-boy in the cathedral. But Siliceo was not charged with teaching Philip logic.

Did he teach Philip anything at all but Latin ? We cannot say. The Venetian ambassador, Badoaro, who was in Brussels at the time of Charles V's abdication in 1556, reports to Their Serene Highnesses the Seignury of Venice that the new King, then in his thirtieth year, " is fond of study and reads history. He is well informed about geography, and knows something about sculpture and painting ; he paints and models himself, and finds pleasure in it. He talks very little, and always in his own language (Spanish) ; as for Latin, he can speak it very well for a prince ; he understands Italian, and knows a little French. In short, he is a prince in whom are assembled many parts worthy of esteem."

Whence did Philip acquire his knowledge, apart from Latin ? He probably learnt Italian and what little French he knew during his youth in Spain. Geography he picked up in the course of the journeys which he made before his accession in Italy, Germany, the Low Countries, and England. History he acquired from books, and especially from the Instructions of Charles V and the daily interviews which they had in Brussels, in 1549-50. He learnt how to deal with men and affairs on the world-stage. He was the leading figurant or spectator upon it during his father's reign ; and, on Charles V's abdication, he became the star actor upon it. His education through the medium of the eyes must have been completed outside Spain ; for Italy, Flanders and Germany were richer in works of art and in full process of expansion under the sun of the Renaissance.

It was at Augsburg, whither the Emperor took him in August, 1550, that Philip saw Titian at work on his painting " The Trinity ", or, as it is called, " La Gloria " of Charles V, and it was between Titian's arrival there in November of that year, and his return to

Venice in the following June, that the great painter drew the sketch of Philip of which he later made use to depict the Infante on one occasion in warrior garb and on another occasion in Court costume. One would like to believe that it was through this meeting, and in response to the spectacle of great works of art, that the taste for art of which Badoaro speaks awakened in Philip. Titian was his favourite painter, as he had been his father's, and Philip, at once pious and sensual as he was, never tired of asking Titian for religious pictures and " poesies ", as he called mythological studies in the nude.

Quite early Philip was put to another schooling : in government. When the French, hoping to profit by the defeat which Charles V had suffered at Algiers, invaded the Roussillon in 1542, the Infante Philip marched to the relief of the fortress of Perpignan, and was lucky enough to raise the siege without striking a blow. It was on his way back, at Monzon in August of that year, that he was recognized as heir apparent by the Cortes of Aragon.

Charles V, once more compelled by his rupture with François I of France to leave Spain and proceed to Italy and Germany, entrusted the regency to his son, now aged sixteen. As Philip's advisers—though at the same time the Emperor recommended him to trust nobody—Charles left him the best of the Spanish generals, the Duke of Alba, who masked a keen spirit of domination under his smooth tongue and his affectation of humility, and the cleverest and most confidential of his Secretaries of State, Francisco de los Cobos, who was so given up to pleasure that he was ruining himself, body and soul. This was intended to serve as a lesson to Philip (1).

Much later, in 1581, the leader of the insurgents in the Low Countries, William of Nassau, Prince of Orange, accused Philip of having, while he was still a boy, married Doña Isabel Osorio, a girl belonging to the Castilian aristocracy, at a time when arrangements were in progress for his marriage to the Portuguese Infanta, Doña Maria. It is not credible that so docile and respectful a son as Philip should have contracted a clandestine marriage, without the knowledge of the Emperor-King, his father, just when he was on the point of wedding the Portuguese princess. But so the rumour ran, and an official history mentioned it for the purpose of discrediting it. Cabrera, the historiographer of Philip III, in his record of the life and reign of Philip II, refers to the death, in 1588, of Doña Isabel Osorio, " who," he says, " claimed to be the wife (la mujer) of the King Don Philip ; and, if she raised herself so high, it was because she loved him so much ".

Charles V's letter of 1541 about the sexual precocity of his son, his advice in 1543, which smacks of a reprimand, and finally the very definite accusation of the Prince of Orange, permit us to believe that in 1542, on the eve of the Portuguese marriage which was celebrated during the following year, Philip was Doña Isabel Osorio's lover.

The rather odd explanation of the dead woman's claims which Cabrera gives—that she regarded herself as Philip's wife because she loved him so much—probably means that this lady of noble birth never chose, as other mistresses of the King did, to marry a man who would serve as a cloak for her fault, which she did not consider a fault. She felt that, by remaining faithful to him in body and heart, she had acquired a just title to call herself his spouse.

She bequeathed an income of eight thousand ducats and sixty thousand ducats' worth of furniture and silver to her " nephew ". It was a fine heritage, of which Philip's generosity had doubtless laid the foundation. The aunt may well have been the mother. The Spaniards, like the Italians, employed this word " nephew " to designate a filial relationship which the rank of the parents made it impossible to avow (2).

It was, perhaps, in order to break off this affair at the beginning that Charles V decided to marry his son. He offered Philip his choice between Marguerite of France, daughter of François I, a match which would strengthen the peace between the Courts of Spain and France, and Jeanne d'Albret, who would bring as her dowry the part of Navarre which Ferdinand of Aragon had not filched from her grandfather, Jean d'Albret, in 1513. But it had been traditional in Spanish policy, since the time of the Catholic Sovereigns, to multiply matrimonial alliances with Portugal in order to multiply chances of succession which would enable the dynastic unity of the Peninsula to be achieved. In accordance with this calculation, or as a matter of taste, Philip preferred a Portuguese Infanta, Doña Maria, his first cousin, to the French or Béarnese princesses, whose hands, for that matter, he was not sure of winning.

To meet her and welcome her at the frontier Philip sent the Duke of Medina Sidonia and Cardinal Tavera, Archbishop of Toledo, to whom he added his dear Siliceo, then Bishop of Cartagena. The Duke, who was one of the richest nobles of Andalusia, made a magnificent display of loyalty, as the aristocracy always did in connection with great official ceremonies. He travelled in a superb litter in the ancient style, whose front and rear shafts rested upon mules caparisoned in gold, and he was followed by three thousand retainers and gentlemen, all well mounted and bearing his livery or his arms. He conducted the Infanta to his palace in Badajoz, where he staged a splendid reception for her (3).

At Salamanca, where her marriage was to be celebrated, Doña Maria made a solemn entrance. The Rector and professors of this famous University, and the judges and *regidores*, went to meet her outside the walls. She traversed the city, decorated for the occasion, on a mule in rich trappings, with a saddle of silver, beneath a canopy held aloft by the city magistrates, and dismounted at the palace of the Duke of Alba, where she granted the honour of kissing her hand to the ladies presented to her by the Duchess of Alba, who had been chosen as her Lady of the Bedchamber (*camarera mayor*).

Philip took up his position wherever he could get a glimpse of Doña Maria. She cannot have been other than pleased by this assiduous attention of his; but she pretended, coquettishly, that she wanted to avoid it. Knowing that he was standing at a window in the house of Doctor Olivares, she hid her face with her fan as she passed. A famous jester of the Count de Benevente's, however, with becoming boldness pushed this screen aside, and enabled her betrothed to have a good look at the Infanta.

The intertwining of all these marriages between the two Courts, however politic it might be, had the unfortunate result of transmitting, and even aggravating, family taints—and they were many. The youth of the couples was another source of degeneracy. On November 15th, 1543, the wedding-day of Philip and Maria of Portugal, the bridegroom was sixteen and a half, and the bride a little less. They were scarcely more than eighteen when their son was born, on July 8th, 1545; and the mother died as a result of her childbirth.

Charles V, who was fearful about the effects of too much sexual indulgence upon the health of his son, had recommended Philip —probably to no purpose—to suspend marital relations with his wife at the least sign of trouble. The Emperor reminded Philip that the son of the Catholic Sovereigns, the Infante Don John, married too young to the Archduchess Margaret of Austria, daughter of the Emperor Maximilian, had died worn out by love. So it is understandable that the death of Doña Maria did not unduly affect Charles V, that inhibiter of conjugal joys. The son who had just been born to Philip, the Emperor thought, assured the future of the dynasty. This son was the unhappy Don Carlos.

The mother could be replaced. There were so many eligibles among the princesses of Christendom! The Emperor is reported to have gone so far as to say, when he heard of the death of Tavera, the Archbishop of Toledo : " My son will find another wife more easily than such a good counsellor as Tavera." He was in no embarrassment about marrying his son again, and perhaps he was in no hurry to do it.

Never had Charles V seemed more powerful than during the few years which followed. He was at peace, since the Treaty of Crépy, signed on September 18th, 1544, with François I, who was ill and old before his time. He was freed from the nightmare of a Turkish invasion of Hungary by a truce of five years with Suleiman the Magnificent. He had persuaded the Pope to convene at Trent, in Imperial territory, a general Council which would accomplish —or at least so Charles believed—the reform of the Church in her head and in her members, and the re-establishment of religious unity. Victor at Mühlberg, on April 24th, 1547, over the Protestant princes of Germany, who were weakened by their divisions, the Emperor felt himself capable of reducing the enemies of the Imperial power to obedience ; and, despite the ill will of the Pope, who transferred the Council to Bologna, he kept on seeking a remedy for anarchy in dogma.

It was while Charles was bending his efforts in this direction at Augsburg, where he had assembled the Diet, that he fell seriously ill. Fearing that he was going to die, he drew up a kind of political testament for his son, in which he addressed him as though he were already dead. He recommended to Philip trust in God and the defence of the faith, the continuation of the Council, due deference to the Holy See, and the selection of good ecclesiastics for the churches, dignities and benefices in his gift.

He charged Philip to use all possible means of avoiding war, which brought so many scourges in its train and was the cause of the exhaustion and ruin of his hereditary States. There had been conquests enough ; it sufficed to preserve the results achieved. He exhorted Philip to live in good understanding and concord with Ferdinand, the King of the Romans, and the sons of this uncle of his. Though Charles had to leave his son the burden of the campaigns against the Turks, it was not the Emperor's wish that Spain and Italy should be made to contribute to them needlessly and unfairly. Only the Low Countries, which Charles contemplated uniting with the Germanic *corpus* as a new " circle ", should participate with their revenues in the defence of the Empire. In any event, it was necessary for Philip to observe the truce concluded with the Sultan and execute the engagements entered into with the Infidels in good faith. To fail in this respect would give the King of France opportunity to fish in troubled waters.

It was necessary for Philip to maintain good relations with the princes of the Empire, but he should not pay too dearly for their goodwill. Whenever the need arose, all the soldiers that were required could be bought for hard cash in Germany. Nor was it expedient to pay reservists in the Swiss cantons and raise levies there, except in default of lansquenets. But it was important for Philip to maintain the hereditary pact concluded with these cantons by the Houses of Austria and of Burgundy, to pay them the sums provided for in the conventions punctually, and to interest them in the defence of the neutrality of the Franche-Comté. At the same time he should guard against their pretensions on the borders of the province, in particular to the rock-salt mines. Fortifications at Gray, at Dôle, and at the castle of Joux would provide for this.

On various pretexts Pope Paul III, contrary to the interests of the Christian world, had transferred the Council assembled at Trent to Bologna. Let Philip settle his differences with the Court of Rome " with the submissiveness of a good son of the Church " ; but let him not tolerate any derogation of, or prejudice to, his sovereign rights and pre-eminences and the common weal in Naples, Sicily, and Castile.

From the free States of Italy, including even Ferrara, despite its French attachment, there was nothing to be feared, and the alliance with Genoa assured the policing of the Mediterranean.

France—there was the enemy, and a perfidious one. Assuredly it was desirable to maintain the peace with her, " because so demand the service of God, the general good of Christendom, and the interests of the Kingdoms, States and successions " which Charles's son would inherit. But the new King of France, Henri II, would want to go back on the existing treaties. It was essential to yield nothing to him. It was much better " to preserve the whole to-day than to expose oneself to having to defend the fragments some day, at the risk of losing them ". " It would be well ", the Emperor added, " to leave our claims relative to the Duchy of Burgundy in suspense." Philip, however, should not omit to affirm Spain's rights to this province as occasion served. It would be prudent to fortify the Spanish frontier and maintain galleys in the Mediterranean.

The question of Savoy-Piedmont must be settled on political grounds, and on political grounds alone. The French had been occupying these Duchies since 1536, and their legitimate masters were fugitives and had taken service in the Imperial army. Interested as the Emperor was in their fate, he was of no mind to resume the war against Henri II in order to re-establish them in their States. Since they absolutely refused to cede the smallest particle of their territory to the King of France, even at the price of a matrimonial alliance, there was nothing to be done but wait until Divine providence should enable them to re-enter into the enjoyment of the rights of their ancient House.

Philip should continue to help them, but he should declare himself incapable of increasing, or even maintaining, the pensions which had been assigned to them. The best service he could render them was to take care, when the time came for negotiation with France, that such negotiation should be as much as possible advantageous to the Dukes of Savoy-Piedmont, and as little as possible prejudicial to the Spanish possessions in Italy.

Still in the interests of general peace, Charles advised his son to keep on good terms with the English, and refrain from involving himself in their differences with France. At the same time, he should have no dealings with the Tudor King Edward VI which, directly or indirectly, might do damage to the Holy Catholic Faith, or to the authority of the Holy See. As for Scotland, there was nothing to be hoped from her, apart from a treaty for the security of commerce and navigation.

In the case of Denmark, Charles was in favour of observing the agreement reached with the *de facto* Sovereign, Christian III, and of non-intervention on behalf of his own brother-in-law, the legitimate King, Christian II, who was dethroned and imprisoned, or of his two nieces, the daughters of his sister, Isabel of Austria, one of whom was the wife of the Elector Palatine, and the other, Christine, was Dowager Duchess of Lorraine.

Since Philip could not be everywhere at once, for the well-being and security of his kingdoms he should choose his governors with the greatest care, and suppress any abuse of power, " whatever might be the rank of the guilty parties ". The Emperor's recommendations about the New World show how near to his heart lay the fate of the natives. It was essential, in the Indies, to assure the service of God, the obedience due from subjects, and a " just government "—" the only efficacious means of making good the losses in population and in all other respects which they have suffered, and also of putting an end to the oppression of the early conquerors and the behaviour of those who have abused their authority to multiply exactions ".

The Council of the Indies was expressly designed to exercise this police function and take care that the Indians were subjected only to reasonable taxes, such as were least prejudicial to their interests. These were humane sentiments, which do honour to this great monarch.

the river-valleys of Lombardy, could give his son's investiture the requisite degree of grandeur, and, at the same time, link the new kingdom directly by sea with the garrison towns of Tuscany, the Two Sicilies, and Spain herself.

Two men upon whom Charles could depend, Ferrante Gonzaga, Governor of the Milanese, and the Duke of Florence, Cosimo de Medici, lent themselves to the Emperor's plot against the Republic. Alleging that Philip had not brought enough soldiers with him to do him fitting honour, Gonzaga required billets in Genoa for two thousand horse and two thousand foot ; and Cosimo, who was coming to render his homage, also proposed to be escorted by a guard of similar strength, in order to overawe the *fuorisciti*, the Florentine refugees in Genoa. But Doria and the Seignury, warned about the plot by Pope Paul III, politely excused themselves from entertaining troops for a service which the local militia could very well render (4).

From the Admiral's own palace, where he was staying, and in the very midst of all the fêtes which were organized in his honour, Philip, so it was said, surreptitiously fomented disturbances, which aimed at enabling him to step in, by common consent, as master. But the Admiral cut through all these contrivings. In the end Philip was obliged, after a fortnight's stay in Genoa, to depart disappointed from the city whose gardens, villas and marble palaces he had admired from the summit of Cargnano hill. It was a crown which he was losing ; but, despite his soreness, skilled in dissimulation as he already was, he made magnificent presents to his host's family before his departure.

He went on his way to Milan, paying a passing visit to Pavia and the battle-field where the dash of François I's troops had been shattered by the strategy of the Spanish leaders and the steadiness of the Spanish troops. The Milanese had been assigned by Charles V to his son. Accordingly the capital of this appanage of his gave its Sovereign a triumphal reception.

The Princess of Ascoli, the governor's wife, to delight the eyes of this young prince whom she knew to be susceptible to feminine beauty, gave a great ball at which the ladies of Milan appeared in their most sumptuous finery. He was so grateful to her for it that he made her a gift of a diamond ring worth five thousand ducats, presented her daughter with a ruby necklace worth three thousand, and gave other persons of the Court largesse less lordly. The total value of all his gifts came to nine thousand five hundred ducats—nearly half the twenty thousand which Milan had voted him.

Among other Italian princes who came to do Philip honour at Genoa was Octavio Farnese, grandson of Pope Paul III. Farnese solicited the good offices of the Infante in order to obtain the restitution of Piacenza, which Charles V had seized after Pier Luigi, son and feudatory of the Pope—a monster of depravity—had been assassinated, if not with the complicity, at least with the connivance, of the Spanish governor of the Milanese, Ferrante Gonzaga. Philip made Farnese an ambiguous reply, sweetened by compliments.

To Mantua, to Trent, to Munich, to Heidelberg, deputies of princes and cities flocked to meet the Emperor's son. In July, 1549, Philip made his entrance into Brussels, where his father, who had not seen him for six years, was awaiting him impatiently. The States-General of the Low Countries recognized him as Charles's heir apparent. From July to October, Philip went from province to province, visiting the capital cities in company with his father and his aunts, the Queens Dowager of Hungary and France, Eleonore and Marie, receiving homage, attending fêtes and taking part in tourneys.

After the enthusiasm of the early days, signs of discord made their appearance. With the people of the Low Countries Philip had not, like his father, the capacity, or even the desire, to become on friendly terms. He knew very little French, and he knew no Flemish at all. He spoke nothing but Spanish, and he remained cold and distant in the midst of an expansive aristocracy and a commonalty bursting with the joy of life. He was not fond of showing himself in public, and shut himself up as much as possible in company with his favourites and his retainers.

Constitutionally delicate, living on a diet and spending a good deal of time in bed, Philip avoided violent exercise. He hunted and rode as little as possible. In Milan he had appeared in the lists to advantage ; but in Brussels tourneys were not a graceful game. He triumphed in a few courses, and, perhaps thanks to the indulgence of a jury presided over by his aunts, he received a magnificent ruby awarded " *a la lanca de las damas* ". But, in an encounter with an uncourtly jouster—who may have been the son of his former governor, Zuñiga—Philip was unhorsed and lay unconscious for some little time.

At Augsburg, whither his father brought him, in August of the following year, to present him to his brother Ferdinand and the members of the Diet, Philip's contact with the German aristocracy was even more frigid. He did his best to make himself liked and, knowing that in Germany power of attraction was measured by drinking capacity, he drove himself to make a good showing at

23

table. But he did not get up from it disposed to take off his hat to his distinguished boon-companions. Even with the help of libations, his Spanish haughtiness found difficulty in relaxing.

His father had conceived the loftiest ambitions for Philip. Nearly twenty years earlier, Charles had his own brother Ferdinand made King of the Romans. He provided himself with this auxiliary at a time when the Lutheran princes and the cities won over to the Augsburg confession formed a league at Smalkelde against his religious intolerance. Philip at that time was only three years old. Now that he was twenty-two, his father found it quite natural to substitute son for brother as his own coadjutor. After Mühlberg and the Interim of Augsburg, Charles thought himself master in the Empire and in Christendom, and, in order to perpetuate this great power of his, he dreamt of assuring his son's succession to it.

But the Emperor could not persuade his brother Ferdinand to divest himself of his title of King of the Romans in favour of the Infante. The two brothers' sister, the Queen Dowager of Hungary, exerted her arts of persuasion, which were considerable, upon Ferdinand, and even her tears, but without success. Ferdinand's son, Maximilian, summoned from Spain, refused to forgo his chances of succession to his father either. Maximilian, brought up among the Germans and in German ways, had just been elected hereditary King by the Diet of Bohemia, and had thus acquired a seat in the College of Imperial Electors.

Driven to desperation, Charles V fell back upon the idea of associating Ferdinand with himself as Emperor, and nominating Philip and Maximilian conjoint Kings of the Romans. But the Electors rejected this tetrarchy of two Augustuses and two Cæsars, comparable with the one organized by Diocletian, as being contrary to the traditions of the Germanic Holy Roman Empire. Charles contrived, however, by dint of promises and cajolery, to induce his brother to grant Philip the reversion of the title of King of the Romans when Charles handed over the Imperial dignity to Ferdinand. Maximilian was not to become King of the Romans until after Philip had become Emperor.

But the opposition of the Electors and the Diet, and the victorious taking-up of arms by Maurice of Saxony against the victor of Mühlberg, followed by the Emperor's frantic flight across the Alps in 1552, brought this scaffolding of dynastic substitutions crashing to the ground.

Meanwhile, in July of the previous year, Philip had returned to Spain to exercise in Castile, with the title of Regent, the very wide and indeed absolute powers with which Charles V had invested him, without consulting the Cortes. Now it was a question of marrying Philip again and increasing his chances of paternity. Charles V had come to believe that subjects feel more sure about the morrow when they see a Royal House with a quiverful of children.

The Prince did not take kindly to the idea, which his father once more suggested to him, of espousing either Marguerite of France, Henri II's sister, or Jeanne d'Albret, the heiress of Navarre. Again Philip's choice fell upon a Portuguese princess—his own mother's sister. It looked as though there were no women to his taste except in Portugal ; or perhaps he wanted, through this new alliance, to strengthen the rights of his dynasty to the Portuguese succession when the time came.

But, just two years after Philip's return to Spain, while the dispensation necessary for the marriage of a nephew with his aunt was being sought at Rome, Edward VI, King of England, died, and his sister, Mary Tudor, succeeded him. This daughter of Henry VIII's was as passionately devoted to the Roman Church as her brother, that little crowned theologian, had been to the form of Anglicanism most closely approximating to Calvinistic dogma. She re-established Catholicism as the State religion, and forbade her subjects to practise any other form of worship under pain of death.

Charles V, who could not reconcile himself to compromising with Protestants in Germany, when he was persecuting them furiously in the Low Countries, was delighted to learn of this change of regime in England and of Mary's declaration of war on heresy. He envisaged the advantages which he might derive from it for the aggrandisement of his House. He put his son forward as a suitor for the hand of the Queen of England.

The years 1552 and 1553 had been disastrous to Charles's fortunes. He had been driven to flight by Maurice of Saxony. He had failed, after a siege of three months, to retake Metz, one of the French-speaking Three Bishoprics, in fief to the Germanic body politic, which Henri II had occupied with the consent of the Protestant Princes of Germany. He was old and ill, he was tired of living, tired of trying. What a revenge for the ruin of his Imperial pretensions, for his defeat at Metz, this English marriage would be !

Mary was thirty-eight, and Philip was twenty-six ; but this difference in age could not stand against the advantages of such an alliance. Philip, as responsive to the call of ambition as his father, and always a respectful and docile son, agreed to marry this old maid, skinny, pimply, sickly, and go and live—for how

25

long he could not tell—in a country which had no love for Spaniards and of whose language and customs he was entirely ignorant.

" As a son ever obedient," he wrote to Charles V, " it is not for me to have any other will. . . . And thus it is my purpose to place myself in Your Majesty's hands, so that everything may be done as Your Majesty sees fit and pleases." Charles V saved his son the trouble of making his own advances. Once the Emperor had been assured by his ambassador in London, Simon Renard, that the Queen would gladly accept this proposal of marriage, he wrote to her gallantly that, if only he were the right age, he would have liked to marry her himself, " and that would have given me quite as much satisfaction " (5).

It was the Emperor who wrote the love letters. He distributed rich presents to the Queen's counsellors and to the great nobles of her kingdom. He delegated the Count of Egmont as matrimonial plenipotentiary. He accepted, without changing a word, a marriage contract drawn up in such terms that the English Government's distrust of this foreign consort was displayed in it without any ambiguity.

Philip was to have the title of King of England during the lifetime of the Queen, but no longer. Mary retained the full and complete disposal of the benefices, offices, revenues and fruits of her kingdoms, and she had no power to grant them, or give the usufruct of them, to any person other than native-born subjects of the said kingdoms. She was to bear all her husband's titles, both those which he now possessed, and those which he might acquire later. He was to bring her a dowry of sixty thousand pounds, levied upon all the States, territories and patrimonial lordships of the Emperor, his father.

The children born of this marriage were to inherit the States of their mother, and would receive in addition the Low Countries and Burgundy, which were to be annexed to them. If the Infante Don Carlos died without an heir, then the whole succession to Charles V and Philip was to pass to the children of Mary Tudor.

Other clauses of the marriage contract specified the obligations of the husband. While no foreigner—in other words, none of Philip's subjects—could be invested with any office in England, he was obliged to take a certain number of English nobles and vassals into his service. He was to have no right to take the Queen out of the kingdom, without her consent, or any of the children born of the marriage, without a vote of Parliament. He was forbidden to remove the Crown jewels out of the kingdom. On the other hand, he was bound to provide its fortresses and ports with means of defence and take good care of them. He was to maintain the existing treaties between England and France. England was not to be involved, directly or indirectly, in war between the Empire and the King of France.

Charles V accepted everything and demanded nothing. He counted upon the youth of the husband to persuade the wife, who was likely to be malleable in proportion as she was mature, to get round the articles of the contract. When it was read in Parliament, Lord Windsor, who was not noted for his brains, demanded : " What guarantees have we that these words are anything more than words ? " He was showing himself wiser than the wise. Mary Tudor, before her marriage, declared that " her kingdom was her first husband ". She had not yet seen her second, who showed himself more attractive than her first.

One of the outstanding features in the character of the English at this time was hatred of foreigners and more especially of the Spaniards, those limbs of the Inquisition and monopolists of trade in the South Seas. The idea of this marriage was repugnant to them from every point of view. When the Count of Egmont arrived to make the formal proposal, in December, 1553, the people of London attended his disembarkation in glacial silence. Insurrection broke out, but it was drastically suppressed, and Jane Grey, an innocent victim, paid with her head for the ambition of her father-in-law, the Duke of Northumberland (6).

Philip could now come to England for his bride. It was not without apprehension that he sailed from Corunna. He was afraid of sea-sickness, of the French corsairs from La Rochelle, of an attack by the fleet of Henri II, of the hostility of the English, of assassination, of poison. So one must not laugh too much when the historian of Charles V, Sandoval, Bishop of Pampeluna, compares Philip with Isaac, agreeing without a murmur to be sacrificed by his father Abraham.

As soon as he disembarked at Southampton, Philip did his best to win sympathy. Except that he remained covered in the presence of the great nobles who came to meet him, he showed himself, contrary to his custom, approachable and affable. He sent many of his travelling companions back to Spain, lest their number should wound the susceptibilities of the English.

Mary's welcome of him at Winchester reassured him. She was impatient to be united to him. The marriage was celebrated on July 25th, 1554, the feast-day of Saint James, patron saint of Spain. Before Bishop Gardiner of Winchester pronounced the sacramental formula of union, a special delegate, Figueroa, read an Act of

Charles V, dated June 23rd, which, in order to make the husband the wife's equal on this solemn occasion, invested Philip with the titles of King of Naples and Duke of Milan. On August 18th London gave the Sovereigns a reception which was not hostile.

Philip took his first steps. He appeared in public, and even made up his mind to take off his hat to those of the leaders of the aristocracy who were worth the trouble. He had casks of gold carried to the Tower of London, by way of demonstrating that the Spaniards were not a swarm of locusts ready to fall upon a rich harvest. He distributed rich presents to influential members of the House of Lords and the House of Commons, because he knew— so his favourite, Ruy Gómez de Silva, who had accompanied him to England, tells us—that in that country, " more than in any other country in the world, nothing is to be done except for hard cash ". Gómez adds : " As we have very little of it . . . I do not know, if we came to have none at all, [how] we should get off with our lives ; we certainly should not with our honour, for they would give us kicks by the thousand."

Gómez's comparison between the English and the Spaniards is also worth recalling : " There are among them (the English) great robbers who steal before your very eyes (*a ojos vistas*). We Spaniards have this advantage over them, that we do it by guile, while they do it by force " (7). The balls at which men of the two nations met gave them an opportunity of getting to know one another better.

Philip, intolerance incarnate, left the responsibility for measures of repression against the Protestants to Mary. With a fanatical hatred, aggravated by her resentment over the miseries of her past life, she persecuted the bishops and the faithful who had made themselves conspicuous for their anti-Catholic zeal during the reigns of Henry VIII and Edward VI. Her Chancellor, Bishop Gardiner of Winchester, and the Bishop of London condemned to the stake those of their colleagues who refused to recant the errors of the past two reigns, or did not recant them in time.

She was especially vindictive towards Cranmer, Archbishop of Canterbury, who, during the lifetime of Henry VIII, had caused her to be declared illegitimate. Even though he dishonoured himself orally and in writing by a disavowal of his whole conduct, she demanded that he should be burned alive, and thus gave him a glorious opportunity to denounce the Pope at the foot of the stake as " Antichrist ", and to thrust into the flames that hand of his which, through fear, had signed the recantation of his lifelong doctrine.

While Mary devoted herself to persecuting those enemies of God who had once been his own too, Philip allowed his confessor, Alfonso de Castro, to preach against these first executions of heretics. They were opposed to the true Christian spirit, which demanded not revenge upon the sinner, but that he should be enlightened about his errors and brought to repentance. All this was—if Castro was correctly understood, and if he did not deliberately distort his master's sentiments on his own account—a piece of political calculation which could not deceive anybody. Even those Englishmen who might consent to retrace their steps from the Calvinism of Edward VI to the Anglicanism of Henry VIII suspected a government which recalled Cardinal Pole to England as Papal Legate.

This great Catholic, who had been obliged by the earlier persecution to live outside his own country for a long time, was received with enthusiasm by the Royal couple. Philip got up from table to go and meet him, and Mary fell into the arms of this cousin of hers. At the request of Parliament itself, Pole pronounced absolution for the past and reconciliation with Rome at a plenary session of the two Houses, in the presence of the King, the Queen, the Lords and the Commons, all on their knees.

But, after this act of repentance, the Lords and the Commons, despite all the efforts and even the threats of the Papal legate, refused to repeal the laws which had long protected the Kingdom and the Crown of England against the encroachments of the Court of Rome. Philip's situation was in no way improved. The Commons did not want him to be crowned King. The most they would admit was that if the Queen, who was said to be pregnant, should die, Philip should be regent of the kingdom during the minority of the Royal child, as long as he stayed in the kingdom, and that in case of absence he might depute the regency to whom he pleased.

The Court could not secure the Commons' assent to Philip's keeping the Crown for his lifetime if the Queen died childless. This recalcitrant Parliament had to be dissolved. The ceremony of absolution marked the apogee of the Catholic reaction's power and the beginning of its decline.

The Queen said, and believed, that she was pregnant; but a year after her marriage it had to be recognized that this was a false hope. To this disappointment of hers was added the grief of losing her young husband, with whom she had fallen passionately in love. Charles V was demanding his son back. The people of Castile were complaining about the continued absence of both father and son; and the Emperor had made up his mind to hand over all his crowns, whose burden was proving too much for him, to his heir apparent.

Charles had postponed taking this step during the lifetime of his mother, Joan the Mad, who, though she was incarcerated at Tordesillas, theoretically continued to reign with him, inasmuch as the Castilian Cortes had consistently refused to regard the mad-woman as dead. Lest he should bequeath to his son the difficulties against which he had had to contend himself, the Emperor waited until his mother actually did die before deciding upon his abdication.

However much Mary might try to keep Philip, her husband had no choice—whatever his desires may have been—about leaving a wife of whom he was not over-fond, and a country which was positively hateful to him. But Mary parted from him with a broken heart. She accompanied him as far as Greenwich, whence he set out for Dover. From there he reached Calais, in September, 1555.

The prayer which Pole drafted to ease Mary's pain has the commonplace phraseology of a Churchman, but still it is warmed by the emotion of a pitying soul. The grief of the wife, even as it is interpreted by the priest, breaks out in expressions of ardent love. " O my Lord Jesus Christ, true spouse of my soul, my true King and my Master . . . Thou Who didst choose me for spouse and consort a man who, more than all others, in his own acts and in his guidance of mine, reproduced Thy image . . . this Thy image whom Thou didst send into the world in holiness and justice."

But can we be quite certain that this young husband of hers, whom Pole, carried away by his sympathy, did not hesitate to compare with his God, had not cast only too fond an eye at his sister-in-law, Elizabeth Tudor ? Elizabeth at this time was twenty-two years of age, and her beauty was in striking contrast with the tarnished features of Philip's wife.

Mary Tudor detested this other daughter of Henry VIII's, whose mother, the beautiful and seductive Anne Boleyn, had induced the King of England to repudiate his legitimate wife, Catherine of Aragon, in order to wed her, and to break with Rome just because Rome was unready to pronounce a divorce. Mary would have been only too glad to implicate Elizabeth in the plot which cost Jane Grey her life, at the time of her accession ; but she could not succeed in extracting from the depositions of Wyatt, the leader of the uprising, any grounds for a charge of high treason.

So Mary spied upon her half-sister to find her at fault. She summoned her to her presence, interrogated her about her religion,

30

and, although she could discover nothing with which to reproach her, dismissed her without a single friendly word. Mary could not contrive to find Elizabeth guilty, and still she could not make up her mind to be reconciled with her. The Queen was angry with her high officers of State, like the first Lord Howard of Effingham, Admiral of the Fleet, who went to call upon Elizabeth and kiss her hand. At one time Mary went so far as to imprison her sister in the Tower of London, that ante-chamber to the scaffold.

Unquestionably Philip must have paid some attention to this beautiful girl, with her charm heightened by her misfortunes, so proud in her disgrace, and ever dearer to the people of England in proportion as Mary Tudor ceased to be dear to them. Charles V and his ambassador in London, Simon Renard, considered Elizabeth's popularity so dangerous to the Queen that they thought it would be well to get rid of her. They suggested to Philip—if, indeed, the idea did not occur to himself—that she should be married to the Duke of Savoy, Emmanuel Philibert, one of the Emperor's best lieutenants. This would mean establishing in London, in case the throne should fall vacant, a Prince-Consort who would be an enemy of France.

But Mary refused her consent, which would have involved recognizing her sister's rights in the marriage-contract. Philip, whether from susceptibility or far-sightedness, insisted upon seeing Elizabeth before he left England. He begged his wife to treat her with consideration and, secretly, he made the same recommendation to the leading nobles of England before his departure. Was he thinking that, some day, he might capitalize these marks of sympathy and aspire to Elizabeth's hand, if she succeeded Mary Tudor, whose state of health was precarious?

Despite his influence over his wife, which counterbalanced the opposition of the people of England to him, Philip had not induced Mary to declare war on France. But she accepted the fine rôle of arbiter in the differences between France and Spain. In accordance with the motto of her father, Henry VIII: "He whom I defend is master," her representatives at the conference at Marck —a village between Ardres and Gravelines—playing an odd part as mediators, took the side of Spain so enthusiastically that Henri II broke off the negotiations (8).

On the other hand, the new Pope, Paul IV Carafa, a Neapolitan and a deadly enemy of the Spaniards, provided a counterpoise to England's goodwill towards them. Charles V, who had learned the lesson of experience and was tired of warfare, was afraid of an alliance between the Holy See and France. Five months after

31

Philip's leaving England, Charles hastened to sign the Truce of Vaucelles, which assured each of the two Powers in arms, for a period of five years, the benefits of the *status quo*.

The Emperor proposed to hand over the rest of his States to his son, and he wanted to give him time to find his feet and settle down. After the Kingdom of Naples and the Duchy of Milan, of which he had dispossessed himself at the time of Philip's English marriage, the time had come for him to renounce his other crowns. Very solemn was the ceremony of his abdication in the Low Countries and the Duchy of Burgundy, at an assembly of the States-General before which Charles V appeared on October 25th, 1556, accompanied by his Court, his sisters, the Queens Dowager of Hungary and France, and Philip.

One of his counsellors, Messire Philibert de Bruxelles, set forth that " a cruel and merciless disease ", which made his life " one long martyrdom ", compelled the Sovereign, old before his time— he was only fifty-six—to hand over his States to his son. Then Charles V arose and, leaning with one hand on a stick, and with the other hand on the shoulder of William of Nassau, Prince of Orange, one of the greatest nobles of the Low Countries, he recalled the hard labours of a reign which he had begun at the age of fifteen, his forty journeys from one end of his monarchy to the other, across the Mediterranean and the Ocean, and his crusades in Africa and all his wars. Now that his mother was dead and his son was fit to rule, there was no longer any reason why he should retain the reins of government, which his hands, growing weaker day by day, were powerless to hold.

He had no doubt that his subjects would be as faithful and devoted to the son as they had been to the father. He exhorted them to stand firm in the Catholic religion. He begged them to forgive him if, through error and without intent, he had committed any injustice towards them. He turned towards the new Sovereign. " Preserve," he bade him, " an inviolable respect for the Catholic religion ; maintain the Catholic faith in all its purity. . . . Make no invasion of the rights and privileges of your subjects. . . ."

Exhausted by fatigue and emotion, he sank back on to his throne. Philip knelt down before his father, and sought to kiss his hand. The Emperor took him in his arms, weeping as he clasped him. The whole assembly burst into tears.

Philip offered his excuses, on the ground that he did not know French or Flemish, for being unable to express, as well as he would like, " the heart, the will, and the deep love " that he had for his States of Flanders, and he begged the deputies to believe what the Bishop of Arras, Granvelle, would say to them in his name. Granvelle bore ample witness to this great Royal love of Philip's. Marie, Queen Dowager of Hungary, who had governed the Low Countries for the past twenty years in the name of her son, the Emperor, justified the great expenses incurred during her regency on the ground of necessity. The Advocate Maes acted as the spokesman of the gratitude of the States to all those who had ruled over them, and protested their fidelity to their new Sovereign.

Two days after the Emperor's abdication, Philip, in solemn assembly of the States-General, swore to observe the laws, privileges and liberties of the country, and in their turn the representatives and deputies of the Seventeen Provinces swore him fealty and obedience. A few weeks later, on January 16th, 1557, Charles V, in the presence of the nobles and grandees of Spain who were then in Brussels, signed his renunciation of the Kingdoms of Leon, Castile, and Aragon, with all their dependencies. At the request of Ferdinand himself, who wanted to prepare the Electors for this great change, he postponed his resignation of the Imperial dignity until the following March ; but he delegated full powers to his brother, and made him wear the Imperial insignia.

Charles V stayed in the Low Countries for the spring and summer, and it was only in September that, in company with his son, his son-in-law, Maximilian, and his sisters, Marie and Eleonore, he made his way to Zeeland and embarked for Spain at the port of Flushing. He landed at the port of Laredo, near Santander, and crossed the north of Spain by easy stages. It was not until February that he reached the monastery of Yuste, in Estremadura, which he had chosen as his place of retirement.

There, in a house attached to the monastery of the Hieronymite monks, lodged in a room one of whose windows looked out upon the church and the high altar, and the other upon a garden full of flowers and orange-trees, he found peace at last, though in a climate which he had thought was more equable and temperate. He heard Mass, meditated and prayed, refusing to take part in the affairs of Spain and the world, but still maintaining his interest in them. There he died, on September 21st, 1558.

CHAPTER II

THE GLORIOUS BEGINNING OF THE REIGN

THE VICTORY OF SAINT QUENTIN—THE TREATY OF CATEAU-CAMBRÉSIS

ON his accession Philip II was in his thirtieth year. The ambassador, Giovanni Michieli, who resided in England until 1557, says of the young King, whom he saw there : he " is the living image, the faithful portrait, of the Emperor his father ; he resembles him altogether, in complexion, in appearance, in features ; he has the same mouth, the same pendent lip, with all his other physical characteristics ; but he is of less stature, that of the Emperor being medium, while his is small. At the same time, he is very well made and very fit, as far as those can judge who have seen him in tourneys, with or without arms, on foot or on horse-back."

Another ambassador, Michael Soriano, also says that Philip " is small of stature, but he is so well made, so well proportioned, and dresses with such good taste and chooses his clothes so cleverly that one could not imagine anything more perfect ". He adds : " The constitution of this prince is very delicate, and accordingly he lives with great regularity, and habitually nourishes himself with very substantial meats, eating neither fish, nor fruit, nor anything which might engender ill humours. He sleeps a great deal, takes little exercise, and his pastimes are all quiet."

The two of them agree in saying that he had got rid of that Spanish haughtiness and severity of his which, at the time of his first journey, made him hateful to the Italians, the Germans, and the Flemish. The advice of the Emperor and his aunt Marie had borne fruit. " There is nobody," says Michaeli, " however lowly he may be, who does not find him easily approachable and a patient listener. He is generous ; he grants much more than he leads one to hope."

Both of them, too, recognize that he did not seem to show that loftiness, that magnificence of spirit, or that breadth of vision which might be expected in so powerful a prince, or that ambition, that desire for glory and domination which the Emperor his father had displayed. " He seems quite different in this way from His Imperial Majesty. His aim and object are peace and quiet." He is neither ambitious nor warlike. " The Emperor found pleasure in affairs of war, and understood them thoroughly. The King understands them but poorly, and he does not enjoy them. The one engaged in great enterprises eagerly ; the other avoids them " (1).

Nevertheless, in the very first year of his reign this pacifist was provoked to war by the very Power which, as a fervent Catholic, he was most prone to revere. Charles V had accepted the Truce of Vaucelles in disadvantageous conditions in order to allow his son time to breathe and initiate himself into the administration of all his States. But he reckoned without the new Pope, Paul IV Carafa, who had numerous grudges to wipe off.

Scion of a leading Neapolitan family, which had declared itself against King Ferdinand of Aragon, and elected Sovereign Pontiff at the age of eighty, this old man, ascetic and arrogant, one of the great Popes of the Counter-Reformation, apart from his nepotism, considered himself, as Vicar of Christ, much superior to the kings of this earth. Formerly Archbishop of Naples, he had never forgiven Charles V for excluding him from the Royal Council and interfering with him in the administration of his diocese. Apart from these personal grievances, he was indignant over the Emperor's policy of religious compromise in Germany and his tendency to forget the suzerain rights of the Holy See over the Kingdom of Naples.

More responsive to these grudges of his than to his spiritual mission, Pope Paul IV set himself to spur on the French against the Spaniards, that breed of Jews and Moors, those dregs of the earth, as he called them. He pretended to offer himself as mediator in connection with the Truce of Vaucelles ; but at the same time he charged his nephew, Carlo Carafa, a former condottiere promoted Cardinal, with the duty of negotiating a treaty with Henri II which would transfer the Duchy of Milan and the Kingdom of Naples to two of the King of France's younger sons. Undeterred by the suspension of hostilities between France and Spain, he succeeded in luring Henri into the Italian trap (2).

As soon as he was assured of this foreign support, the Pope excommunicated the Colonnas, partisans of Spain, and confiscated their property ; re-built the walls of Rome ; threw into prison Garcilaso de la Vega, Charles V's former ambassador, who was keeping the viceroy of Naples, the Duke of Alba, informed about his doings ; and finally, in open consistory, accused Philip II of lacking in the obedience which he owed to him as vassal of the Holy See in Naples. He summoned Philip to appear before him for judgment, though he made the concession that, in view of the importance of the trial, he would act only in accordance with the Cardinals.

Philip, surprised at this summons, assembled theologians and jurists, and asked them whether there was any means of putting an end to the unjustifiable proceedings of the Pontiff other than prayer and petition. His consultants replied that laws Divine and human authorized him to defend himself by force of arms.

He informed his sister Doña Juana, whom he had nominated Regent in Castile, of the decisions which had been reached and the measures which were to be taken. " Since I wrote to you about the proceedings of the Pontiff and the information which has been received from Rome, we have further heard that he proposes to excommunicate the Emperor, my Lord, and myself, and to pronounce interdict and cessation *a divinis* in our Kingdoms and States." According to the advice of responsible and learned persons whom Philip had consulted, no account need be taken of these prohibitions of His Holiness's.

The King advised his sister that he was about to write to the grandees of Spain, to the cities and universities, and to the heads of Orders in Castile—and in the Kingdom of Aragon—that there was to be no observance of " either interdict, cessation, or any other censures, because all of them are and will be of no value, null, unjust, and without foundation". Let roads and ports be well guarded, so that nothing could be " intimated " from Rome, and let there be " stern and exemplary punishment " of any persons who should carry such intimation.

The Dominican Melchior Cano, one of the greatest theologians of Spain, also declared that resistance to the unjustified aggression of the Sovereign Pontiff was just and legitimate. If the King desired to free the Royal authority from any limitation, he had only to renounce the subsidies to the Spanish Church, and he could obtain more from his own States than was granted him by the Roman Curia.

The Duke of Alba prepared means of bringing the Pontiff to reason. This Viceroy of Naples was a Castilian of very high degree, a loyal soldier and a man who obeyed orders without question. He had learned in the school of Charles V how to distinguish between religion and the Church, the spiritual and the temporal.

He assembled troops. Summoned by Paul IV to disband them,

he replied with vigorous remonstrances against the Pope's own preparations for war upon the Emperor and the King, "those most obedient and true defenders of the Apostolic Holy See". If the Pope continued to show himself the step-father of those whose father he ought to be, Alba vowed that, with the help of God, in the name of his Lord and by the blood that ran in his veins, he would march on Rome and take drastic measures on his way. He left the responsibility for the violent acts which might be commit ed by his soldiers to the Pope, since, born to be a shepherd, he had turned himself into a wolf.

And invade the Papal States in fact Alba did. He carried Anagni by assault and put it to fire and sword, in order to satisfy and pay his army, in accordance with the practice of the generals of the period, and pushed on to Tivoli, at the very gates of Rome. In every town he entered, Alba put up notices on the church doors that he would hand it back to the new Pope elected by the Sacred College.

The Cardinals and the Romans, frightened by the proximity of this terrible enemy, urged Paul IV to make peace. But the indomitable old man did not think that the time had yet come for that. The Duke of Alba was led by a Spanish Cardinal, a cousin of his, to fear a repetition of the abominations of 1527. So he contented himself with blockading Rome and besieging the port of Ostia, through which it received supplies. Contrary to his expectations, the citadel held out until November 19th, 1556, and Rome did not suffer from hunger. In the following January the Pope learnt that the Duke of Guise was crossing the Alps with the French forces. Then he consented to sign a suspension of arms with the Spanish general, in order to give the relieving army time to arrive.

Already Paul IV saw himself master of the Kingdom of Naples, which he proposed to share with Henri II ; but he did not make the necessary effort. He did not raise the contingent of his own which should have joined the French invaders, and he did not revictual them at cost price, as he had promised to do.

The Princes of Italy remained faithful to Spain. The Duke of Parma was won over to Philip's side by the restitution of Piacenza. The Duke of Florence, Cosimo II—who was also disquieted by the pretensions of Catherine de Medici to the succession to the Medicis of the elder branch—was won over by the cession of Philip II's rights over the territories of the former republic of Sienna. Venice maintained neutrality. The Duke of Ferrara, Hercules d'Este, wanted his son-in-law, the Duke of Guise, to instal himself in the Milanese, close to his own territory, for the purpose of helping him

Finally, in March, 1557, he crossed the Channel and endeavoured to persuade England to take part in the struggle. The amorous Mary Tudor did not want to refuse anything to her husband ; but the Privy Council raised the objection of the terms of the marriage contract. Perhaps England would have remained neutral if a proscribed man, Sir Thomas Stafford, sailing from the mouth of the Seine with two vessels, had not disembarked with some thirty other Englishmen and a Frenchman at Scarborough Castle, and summoned the people to revolt. Parliament deemed the King of France responsible for this act of aggression or privy to it, and declared war on him (5).

With the seven thousand English, of whom the Earl of Pembroke was given the command in the Low Countries, Philip disposed of an army of about fifty thousand men. He put at its head the Duke of Savoy, Emmanuel Philibert, one of Charles V's best lieutenants, who, expelled from his country with his father by François I in 1536, had no chance of recovering his heritage except at the price of the best service he could render and at the point of the sword. Philip did not like him, because he had threatened to resign from the Council of Regency of the Low Countries if the Sovereign, in his search for revenue, refused to reckon with the general misery ; but the King could not fail to take the Duke's military value into account, especially during the lifetime of the best judge of it, Charles V.

The French army numbered only eighteen thousand foot and six thousand horse, with an artillery train of sixteen pieces. (Let me say here, once and for all, that the figures of effectives borrowed from De Thou by Prescott are, like those of the budgets of the period, always merely approximate. They are of value only for the purpose of comparison, so far as they permit us to estimate the proportions of the forces in the two camps.) But the aristocracy and nobility, who flocked to arms at the news of invasion and organized themselves in companies of irregulars, constituted a strong body of heavy cavalry, and the Gascon infantry were the equal of the Spanish in dash and steadiness. The French might have stood up to the enemy, or at least checked them in their advance, if they had been better led. The old Constable de Montmorency, Henri II's bosom friend and, in his absence, generalissimo of the army, was a good courtier and a brave soldier, but an indifferent leader. He could neither foresee danger, nor provide against it.

Emmanuel Philibert, skilfully concealing his intentions, went and laid siege to Marienbourg. When he had attracted de Montmorency in this direction, he suddenly turned by forced marches against Saint Quentin, the best fortress on the frontier, but badly garrisoned and in poor repair. He might have carried it by assault if Coligny, Admiral of France, Montmorency's nephew, had not thrown himself into it with a handful of reinforcements and organized the defence. Coligny, however, warned his uncle that, with the resources which he had at hand, he could not hold out long.

The Constable hastened up with all his forces, but did not succeed in introducing sufficient help into the fortress. He found himself so close to the besieging army that, as he was too weak to give battle to it, he ordered a retreat; but he ordered it too late to escape. Obliged to turn and fight, he was, in the course of this change of front, hotly charged by the Count of Egmont's lancers. The irregular companies withstood them for a time successfully, but finally, overwhelmed by the ever-increasing masses of the enemy infantry and cavalry, they gave ground. The Constable himself, despite his sixty-one years, fought with all the ardour of a young man, until a pistol bullet broke his thigh and he was forced to surrender.

Elsewhere on the battle-field, panic spread from the camp-followers to the German lansquenets in Henri II's service. Only the Gascons, drawn up in a square, withstood all the cavalry charges, and cannon had to be trained upon them to blast breaches in their lines through which the Spaniards could penetrate. Then it was a massacre rather than a battle. The victors, so it was said, lost only eighty men, and the vanquished fourteen thousand. More than three hundred gentlemen were taken prisoner, and the number of common soldiers who surrendered was so great that Philip ordered all those who were too poor to pay ransom to be released, on condition that they did not serve against him for a year.

He was not present on this memorable occasion, called after Saint Laurence, in honour of the saint whose feast fell on that day, August 10th, 1557. But he appeared in camp the next day, armed from head to foot. All he liked about fighting was military display.

The Duke of Savoy wanted to march straight on Paris; but Philip, either from lack of decision or lack of money—those two curses of his whole reign—ordered the small fortresses in the valley of the Oise to be occupied and, in the first place, Saint Quentin to be reduced. Coligny, summoned to surrender, held out behind his bad ramparts for another fortnight, when he was taken prisoner, arms in hand, in the breach.

The assailants, infuriated by a resistance which the weakness of

41

the fortress made outrageous to any besieger according to the ideas of the time, and moreover accustomed to sack as the price of victory and as a supplement of pay and pleasure, killed, pillaged and raped to their heart's content. The next day, the King entered the town and had the women and the nuns escorted into the principal church or under the Duke of Savoy's protection in camp ; but he could not prevent the soldiery from robbing these unfortunate women of their very chemises and treating them even worse (6).

While Philip's father, in his retreat at Yuste, was impatiently awaiting news of his triumphal entrance into Paris, this royal manager was devoting himself to cleaning up the town, repairing the fortifications, and drawing up the list of prisoners. He gave Henri II time to organize his defence. In Paris Queen Catherine de Medici went in person to ask the civic councillors to provide the funds, which were voted without debate, for recruiting ten thousand infantry. Henri II raised soldiers everywhere, summoned his veterans from Piedmont, and sent Guise the order to bring back the army which he was frittering away in Italy.

Meanwhile Philip was having difficulty in wresting from the States-General of the Low Countries, assembled at Valenciennes, an annual subsidy of eight hundred thousand crowns. He obtained an immediate vote of one million two hundred thousand florins only on condition that he suppressed all existing contributions, and left the receipt and spending of the subsidy, parades for verification of numbers, distribution of pay, etc., in the hands of agents of the States. He was obliged to accept all these measures of distrust, but he did not forget them (7).

France was ready for the counter-stroke. Guise, appointed Lieutenant-General of the kingdom, assumed the command of all the forces. From Champagne, where he had concentrated them, he marched straight on Calais, that French town which the English had held for two hundred and eleven years (1347–1558). Mary Tudor, out of a spirit of economy, had recalled Pembroke after Saint Quentin. Out of a spirit of economy, she maintained a garrison of only five hundred men in this last foothold of her continental possessions, and provisioned them parsimoniously.

Guise made his way at low tide to the foot of the citadel, which, standing on the Rysbank, commanded the entrance to the port and to the fortress, and, taking it by assault, turned its heavy guns against the town. The Spaniards, setting out from Gravelines, edged along the coast to bring help, but they were repulsed. The bombardment made a breach in the ramparts, and the Governor of Calais, Wentworth, in order to avoid a massacre in case of successful attack, capitulated on January 6th, 1558, on terms which the victor dictated to him.

The garrison and the inhabitants, men, women and children, five thousand souls in all, were given their freedom to withdraw to England, safe and sound, with their clothes, but without anything else. The victorious troops gorged themselves with booty— a fair revenge for the sack of Saint Quentin. Mary made hasty preparations to save Guines, another fortified place ; but the sea, usually so kind to the English, treated them badly this time and wrecked the ships which were bringing reinforcements. The vessels which Philip sent from Antwerp and Dunkirk arrived at Dover when it was too late. Guines, left to its own resources, resisted until a fortnight after the surrender of Calais, and obtained an honourable capitulation.

In May Guise turned eastwards and took Thionville, after a twenty days' siege. Marshal de Thermes, whom he had charged with barring the Spaniards' way into Picardy, seized Dunkirk and gave it up to pillage ; but he was surprised near Gravelines on July 13th, by an army of fifteen thousand foot and three thousand horse, commanded by the Count of Egmont and supported by an English squadron broadside on to the coast. It was another rout like Saint Quentin : two thousand soldiers killed and three thousand prisoners, among them Marshal de Thermes himself.

But Guise, who was not far away, was able to prevent the enemy from exploiting their victory. Henri II appeared in the midst of his troops and took command of them. On his side, Philip II rejoined Emmanuel Philibert's army, which had reinforced that of Egmont. The two kings, encamped behind the Authie and the Somme, stood face to face as though they were about to engage in decisive battle. But neither one nor the other of them was disposed to risk everything on one throw of the dice : Henri fearing, if he lost, to expose his capital and his person ; and Philip fearing, if he won, to owe the glory to the merits of his lieutenants. Both of them were short of money, and they had already entered into negotiations, which they expected to lead to the end of the conflict.

In the lists of diplomacy Philip had all the advantage. He would never have suffered a favourite or a mistress to make up his mind for him. With him reasons of State always excluded personal considerations. Whatever interest he might have in signing peace —and the state of his finances made it necessary that he should— he allowed nothing of this necessity to appear on the surface.

Even though they were without funds, Philip's plenipotentiaries took as lofty a tone as though they could carry on the war for ever. Granvelle, who was handling foreign affairs, would not even consider the alternative which Cardinal de Lorraine went to Péronne to submit to him—namely, that Savoy and Piedmont should be restored to Emmanuel Philibert against the cession of the Milanese to France, or that Piedmont should be left to France, if Philip wanted to keep the Milanese.

What a difference between this firm determination of Philip's to defend his own interests and those of his allies, and the vacillations of Henri II ! He, too, until November, 1558, was in favour of proceeding by way of exchanges. But he missed the presence of Constable de Montmorency, still a prisoner since Saint Quentin, to whom he was as attached as he was to his old mistress, Diane de Poitiers ; and he was suspicious of the Guises, those cheerful partisans of war.

He was anxious about the progress of the Reformation, which was gaining recruits in the upper classes. A nephew of the Constable's himself, d'Andelot, Colonel-General of the French infantry, had embraced the religion of the pure Gospel with all the ardour of a passionate soul. The first Prince of the Blood, Antoine de Bourbon, King of Navarre, had rallied to it—not without calculation. Married to Jeanne d'Albret, and less concerned about his conscience than about his wife's rights, he hoped, thanks to French diplomacy, to recover the part of Navarre on the other side of the Pyrenees, and, with the aid of the future strength of the new Church, to assure himself a great position in France.

Henri II's need of peace, his affection for the Constable, and his hatred of the heretics had so much effect upon the King of France that he entrusted the duty of negotiating peace with the Spaniards to two of their prisoners, Constable de Montmorency and Marshal de Saint-André, whose interest it was to conclude it as soon as possible. To them he added Cardinal de Lorraine, who could hardly be left out, and the preliminaries opened at the abbey of Cercamp, in Cambrésis. Two supernumeraries, Jean de Morvilliers, Bishop of Orléans, and Claude de l'Aubespine, Lord of Hauterive, Secretary of Finance, acted as secretaries and countersigned the minutes.

By contrast with this very ill-assorted group of defenders of the French cause, the Spanish plenipotentiaries—the Duke of Alba, the Prince of Orange, Ruy Gómez de Silva, the Bishop of Arras, Granvelle and his assistant Viglius der Zuychem, Counsellor of State—had no other object than that of rounding off the successes of the war by a profitable peace.

44

Side by side with them sat the representatives of England, the Bishop of Ely, the Earl of Arundel, and Nicholas Wotton, former ambassador to France, whom Mary had specially charged with reclaiming Calais. To follow the negotiations, the Duke of Savoy had delegated Count de Stropiano and the president of Ast i and the King and Queen of Navarre had delegated the Bishop of Mende, Nicolas d'Angu, and Jean-Jacques de Mesmes, Lord of Roissy. The Dowager Duchess of Lorraine, Christine of Denmark, first cousin to Philip II, whose son, the reigning Duke, had married one of Henri II's daughters, Claude of Valois, presided over the conference and acted as mediator.

The French were at sixes and sevens. Cardinal de Lorraine and the Constable negotiated separately. The former complained about the latter to the Court, sometimes as a partisan of peace at any price, " because, being here as a prisoner, he cannot speak as he would do if he were a free man ", sometimes insinuating that the roughness of his character and his conversation thwarted the efforts of diplomacy. As for the King of France, he did not waver in his affection for the Constable and his desire for a " good peace ". What he meant by this was a peace which would give him back his bosom friend. Since he had no love for the Guises, he considered them sufficiently recompensed for the taking of Calais by the marriage—at length consummated on April 24th, 1558, after a long engagement—of their niece, Mary Stuart, Queen of Scots, to the Dauphin François.

The Spaniards, who presented their demands with a united front, proposed to give nothing away, short of a breakdown in the negotiations. They obeyed the directions of Granvelle, who corresponded directly with Philip II, suggested procedure to him, and scrupulously carried out his orders (8).

This clever native of the Franche-Comté, then Bishop of Arras, and a little later Cardinal, had been trained while quite young in the handling of affairs by Chancellor Granvelle, his father, one of Charles V's principal Ministers. He let French ardour wear itself out against English tenacity. Mary Tudor demanded the retrocession of Calais, and Philip could scarcely avoid taking his wife's part. But when she died, on November 16th, 1558, he had no reason to care about Calais any longer.

It is true that for a moment he hoped that Elizabeth, the new Queen of England, whose beauty had not left him cold, would accept his hand. A month after his sister-in-law's accession, Philip added to his congratulations to her an assurance of fraternal friendship which foreshadowed a more intimate offer.

45

Very clumsily, Henri II had allowed his son and his daughter-in-law to add the arms of England to those of Scotland on their escutcheon, as though they were calling Elizabeth's rights in question. Philip might reckon that the Queen of England, thus challenged, would consent to marry him, from fear and out of calculation, in order to assure the aid of the Spanish forces. He saw many difficulties about such a marriage : the threat of a fresh war with France, the expense which it would involve in England, the complaints of his Spanish subjects about his continued absence, the necessity of returning to Spain to put his finances in order.

Nevertheless, he resigned himself, as he put it, in the interests of Christendom and religion, to marrying Elizabeth. Two months after Mary's death, he instructed Count de Feria, his ambassador in London, to inform himself discreetly whether a proposal of marriage would have any chance of success, given the secret conditions which he attached to it : that the new Queen of England should give a formal assurance that she would profess Catholicism, and that she should secretly ask the Pope for absolution for her past errors and a dispensation for her marriage. Philip thought, in short, that he was making a great sacrifice, and he would not agree, as Charles V had done in the contract of marriage with Mary Tudor, to deprive Don Carlos of the inheritance of the Low Countries in favour of any son born of the new marriage.

Elizabeth replied courteously that she realized all the value of such an alliance, but that the friendship of His Catholic Majesty was as efficacious a protection for her as his love would be. A true daughter of Henry VIII's, she denied the Pope's authority to give her as his wife to her sister's husband. As a matter of fact, she was beginning to react against the intolerance and the Catholicism of her sister. Her preferences tended towards a moderate Anglicanism, as far removed from Edward VI's Calvinism as from Mary's Papistry.

The fate of Calais was henceforth settled. As a concession to the *amour-propre* of the English, it was decided that they should cede the town and its dependencies to Henri II for eight years, on the condition that, if the King of France neglected to restore it to them at the end of the period, he should pay them an indemnity of five hundred thousand crowns, without prejudice to their rights, which would remain intact. But this guarantee masked a definitive cession, for it was agreed that, if one of the two parties attacked the other, it would lose its title. By way of compensation, the Spaniards demanded that the Dauphin and Dauphine of France, by their adherence to the treaty, should *ipso facto* recognize Elizabeth's rights to the Crown of England (9).

In conformity with their engagements to him, the Spaniards also maintained the claims of the Duke of Savoy inflexibly. Philip was determined to close Italy to the French. To make sure of the passes over the Alps which he could not guard himself, it was important for him to establish a prince there, as his neighbour and his ally, who would have an interest in defending them against his enemies. This rôle of guardian of the frontier was one which could be filled to perfection by Emmanuel Philibert, a great soldier, the victor of Saint Quentin, and, so it seemed, the natural enemy of the Kings of France, who had reduced him to living in exile from his States, as a condottiere, for more than twenty years.

But the Duke was a politic man. If he had helped Spain, by way of helping himself back to his heritage, he did not want France to remain hostile to him, lest he should be obliged to rely all the time on the Power which had restored him, to the great prejudice of his independence. So he sought a reconciliation with Henri II. In default of one of Henri's daughters, Claude of Valois, who was intended for the young Duke of Lorraine, the Duke accepted instead the King's sister, Marguerite of France, Duchess of Berry, who was past her youth, being now thirty-five.

In consideration of this family alliance, the French, who first proposed to restore his patrimony to the Duke only on condition that they kept twelve towns and fortresses in Piedmont as a pledge for the faithful execution of the treaty, reduced their claim to the five towns which he offered to leave them : Turin, Chieri, Pignerol, Chivas and Villaneuva d'Asti. The three hundred thousand écus of Marguerite's dowry and the revenues of the Duchy of Berry, her appanage, were to be regarded as compensation for his leaving these towns to them.

The King of Navarre was sacrificed. The occupation by the Spaniards of the part of Navarre on the other side of the Pyrenees was as difficult to justify as that of Savoy and Piedmont by the French. Charles V, so we read in a codicil to his testament, felt doubtful whether his grandfather, Ferdinand the Catholic, had good grounds for depriving Jean d'Albret of it, and he left this case of conscience to his successor. Philip does not appear ever to have been troubled by it. Length of possession, or in other words prescriptive title, constituted a good enough claim for him.

The plenipotentiaries of Henri II might well have had scruples about sacrificing the rights of a French prince. But Henri II was not fond of his cousins, the Princes of the Blood, and least of all of the first of them, Antoine de Bourbon, King of Navarre, who had recently compromised himself at Pré-aux-Clercs in the demon-

47

strations of the Parisian Reformists. The King of France was afraid, perhaps, of the establishment of a great vassal State astride the Pyrenees, even though it were at the cost of Spain. The congress at Cercamp listened courteously to the long plea of M. de Mesmes, Lord of Roissy, about the rights of the d'Albrets to the retrocession of Spanish Navarre. The French plenipotentiaries maintained the same thesis ; but this was merely a matter of form, as Cardinal de Lorraine admitted, unofficially, to the Duke of Alba, who, deaf though he was, could always hear anything favourable to his own country.

With the questions of Calais, Savoy-Piedmont and Navarre thus settled, the peace—a one-sided peace—was made. France abandoned her claims in Italy and, except for the Marquisate of Saluces, all her trans-Alpine possessions. Spain left it to the Emperor to reassert his claims to the Three Bishoprics, Metz, Toul and Verdun. She handed back the fortresses, with the exception of Hesdin, which she had taken : Saint Quentin, Ham, Le Catelet, Thérouanne. France ceded to her Marienbourg, Thionville, Damvilliers, Montmedy, and finally the countship of Charolais, that fragment of the heritage of Charles the Bold, a patrimonial possession of Philip II's.

The congress had been transferred from the abbey of Cercamp, which proved uncomfortable, to Cateau-Cambrésis, a castle of the Archbishop of Cambrai's, which as a matter of fact was found to be scarcely more habitable. It was here that, after six months' negotiation, the articles of the treaty were finally signed, between France and England on April 2nd, and between France and Spain on April 3rd, 1559.

Meanwhile arrangements were being made for the marriage of Philip, widower of Mary Tudor, to Elizabeth of Valois, elder daughter of Henri II. She was not yet fourteen, and Philip was nearly thirty-two. First intended for the Infante Don Carlos, she was now, in accordance with similar political calculation, given to his father, as a pledge of lasting agreement between the two Courts.

Philip was a lucky Sovereign. His soldiers had won the war, and his diplomats had won the peace. Master of Italy, he had not abused his victory. He had compelled the Duke of Alba to kneel down before the Pope and beg his pardon for having beaten him. He had given Sienna to the Duke of Florence, restored Piacenza to Octavio Farnese, and re-established the Duke of Savoy in his States. In a separate treaty, annexed to the main treaty, he had secured the retrocession of Corsica to Genoa ; of Casal, the fortress of Montferrat, to the Duke of Mantua; and of the principality of Orange to William of Nassau.

By way of compensation for the territorial advantages given to his allies, he undertook to examine, and settle with all justice, the claims and titles of the Dauphin, of Diane de Poitiers, and of some other lords of less importance, to certain fiefs in the Low Countries. In return for definite concessions, he offered a vague assurance of his goodwill. By a stroke of the pen Henri II lost whole territories, whole conquests, " which were not so little, seeing that they were estimated as equivalent to one-third of the Kingdom of France " (10). It was not much to keep Calais and its dependencies, and the Three Bishoprics, Metz, Toul and Verdun. But Henri had the satisfaction, which to him was considerable, of getting his Constable back; of marrying his sister, Marguerite of France, to a reigning prince; and of uniting his daughter with the most powerful monarch in Christendom.

Two months later, the Duke of Alba and the Duke of Savoy arrived in Paris for the wedding ceremonies. It had been expected that Philip would come himself; but, on thinking it over, he announced that the Kings of Spain did not go to fetch their wives, but waited for their wives to be brought to them. It was another way of asserting the hierarchy of greatness. The Duke of Alba was charged with marrying the princess by proxy.

We know what sad event clouded these nuptials. Henri II decided to celebrate them by great fêtes, and to take part himself in the tourney which was one of their outstanding features. Under the eyes of Diane de Poitiers, whose white and black colours he carried, and of Catherine de Medici—of his legitimate wife and the other woman—he rode several courses, broke lances, displayed his strength and skill. He wanted to round all this off by a striking show, and ordered Montgomery, his captain of the Guard, to tilt against him.

The two adversaries entered the lists, launched their horses against one another at full speed, and drove their lances against one another as they met. Montgomery's weapon broke off short, and the shaft of it, which remained in his hand, penetrating the visor of the royal helm, wounded Henri in the right temple and the left eye. He was carried unconscious to the Tournelles palace, where he died, on July 10th.

Elizabeth of Valois's marriage to Philip had already been celebrated on June 22nd. By order, so it was said, of the dying King of France, that of Marguerite to the Duke of Savoy took place on July 9th, at midnight, by the light of torches, in the little church of Saint Paul.

CHAPTER III

THE SPANISH MONARCHY

THE KING—THE GOVERNMENT—AND THE COURT

PHILIP II, now at peace with France, was in a hurry to return to Spain, where his presence was necessary and his subjects were clamouring for him. He organized the administration of the Low Countries ; listened—in no good humour—to the complaints and grievances of the States-General, assembled at Ghent ; dismissed the deputies, and proceeded to embark at Flushing. On September 8th, 1559, he landed at Laredo, between Bilbao and Santander (1).

From Spain, from which he never stirred again, he was henceforth to govern, as Charles V had done—but as a roving Sovereign —his three patrimonial heritages of Castile, Aragon, and Burgundy. Apart from these, his monarchy was immense : a dynastic body with unequal members, scattered over four out of the five continents—and Oceania, in the sixteenth century, was almost unknown.

There were in Europe Castile and Aragon, the Kingdoms of Naples and of Sicily, the Milanese and the garrison-towns of Tuscany, the Low Countries and the Franche-Comté. There were in Africa five ports and fortified places : Oran, Mers-el-Kebir, Melilla, the Peñon of Velez, and La Goulette. There were in America the vice-royalties of Peru and Mexico. There was to be in Asia, a little later, the archipelago of the Philippines.

This vast empire, built up in the course of centuries through successions, marriages, conquests and discoveries, consisted, like all historical formations, of diverse parts and populations. Amid the variety of its peoples, its languages and its institutions, the Catholic King—the title of the Sovereign of Spain—stood out as the living symbol of dynastic unity, of general interests and common activity.

Except for the independent State of Portugal—ruled, at the time of Philip II's accession, by a national dynasty—all the rest of the Hispanic peninsula belonged to the great-grandson of Isabel

50

of Castile and Ferdinand of Aragon. But the two kingdoms united by the marriage of that King and that Queen had not merged into one whole. They continued to live apart, with their own laws, their own social and political regime, and their own body of officials and judges. They had not even any extradition treaties which enabled one of them to surrender fugitive malefactors to the other.

Neither one nor the other of them was unified in itself. In Castile, the territories conquered or reconquered from the Mussulmen between the eighth and the fifteenth centuries, Leon, Old and New Castile, Murcia, and finally Granada, certainly seemed sufficiently soldered together to convey the impression of a single State : the Crown of Castile, a name which makes one think of the gems of a diadem. They had common Cortes which sat together to deliberate about common charges and common interests.

But what a petty national assembly it was ! Charles V had excluded the aristocracy and the clergy from it, on the ground that, since they were exempt from taxes, they were not qualified to vote on the subsidies (servicio) which they did not pay. Thirty-six procuradores, delegated by the councils of eighteen towns, alone represented the whole population of Castile.

To the north the Customs frontier did not reach as far as the natural barrier of the Pyrenees. The Basque provinces (vascongadas), Biscay, Alava, and Guipúzcoa, and the Kingdom of Navarre, filched by Ferdinand the Catholic in 1513 from its legitimate possessor, Jean d'Albret, constituted free zones which traded directly with France and enjoyed a large measure of autonomy. Navarre and the Basque provinces had their fueros or franchises which dated back to the beginning of the Middle Ages and limited the authority of the Sovereign. They had elective representative bodies, Cortes in Navarre, General Juntas in the Basque provinces ; courts of law without appeal outside the territory, an independent administration, and no other taxes except a free gift.

In Navarre, the King of Castile, represented by a viceroy, struck money and enjoyed the revenue of his estates. These were about all the rights he had. If he wanted the nobles to serve him for longer than three days, he had to take them into his pay.

The three Basque provinces, Biscay, Alava and Guipúzcoa, arrogated to themselves the right to disobey the orders of the Sovereign if they were contrary to their fueros. The Deputado General, the elective civil and military head of Alava, who resided at Vittoria, took oath, when he assumed office, in the presence of the General Assembly (Junta), upon an old knife : " May this

knife cut my throat if I do not defend the *fueros* of the country ! ”
The Guipúzcoans had obtained from Isabel's predecessor, Henry IV
of Castile, recognition of their right to resist any noble who, on
the ground of a simple decree of the King, not previously approved
by the Junta, attempted any encroachment upon their privileges.

With these frontier territories the Kings of Spain found it expedient to compromise. Philip did not want to run the risk of
provoking complaints and a state of discontent which might have
dangerous repercussions outside—for example, in France. Nor did
he touch the Constitution of Aragon until towards the end of his
reign, and then only after he had been more or less compelled to
do so. Whereas in Castile his will was law, dominated the privileged
classes, and reduced national representation to the expression of
complaints and desires and to the voting of subsidies, which were
not a free gft, he suffered the organization of Aragon to thwart
the royal power in all directions.

It was not the same thing in his States of the Crown of Aragon
as in Castile. The three members of the Crown, Aragon, Valencia
and Catalonia, although they were united by an indissoluble link,
preserved their own individualities and had their different Cortes,
and it was with each one of them that the King had to negotiate.
Even when he summoned them all together and the deputies of
the two Kingdoms of Aragon and Valencia and of the Countship
of Catalonia sat in the same place, they arrived grouped by nationalities, deliberated separately, took no interest except in their own
affairs, and did not interfere in those of their neighbours. These
general Cortes were merely a juxtaposition of individual Cortes,
and the individual Cortes granted *servicio* only if the King was
present and begged for it, so to speak, in person.

In the Kingdom of Aragon, especially, a body of institutions
hampered the Royal authority. The Cortes here was composed
of four orders : towns, clergy, nobility and aristocracy. The
presence of the privileged orders made it better fitted to resist
royal demands than was the case in Castile, where the nobility
and the clergy, wealthy, educated and independent-minded, were
not allowed to give the thirty-six representatives of the towns the
backing of a serious element of opposition, and were themselves
deprived of the moral support of the urban population. Unanimity
of the deputies of every one of these four orders was necessary if
the vote of the order in question was to be effective.

Aragon was noted above all for its *justicia mayor*, whose jurisdiction was both superior to, and parallel with, ordinary jurisdictions. This supreme magistrate was not, as learned patriots later

imagined, a kind of tribune or ephor, created to prevent encroachments by the royal prerogative. He was nominated by the King for life, and there was no law which prevented him from holding other high civil or military office in the King's name at the same time. But it is true that, in his capacity as *justicia mayor*, it was his duty to resist abuses of power, from whatever quarter they might proceed.

It is a remarkable fact that an institution should have made its appearance during the Middle Ages, and maintained itself for centuries, which was capable of guaranteeing the privileges of the nation against the omnipotence of the Prince, the liberty of the individual against the tyranny of the majority, and the rights of private persons against abuses of feudal, ecclesiastical, and royal jurisdiction (2). Despite the encroachments of Ferdinand the Catholic and Charles V, this institution, at the time of Philip II, still possessed much authority and prestige, and it was supported by the traditionalist spirit of the Aragonese.

The Kings of Aragon found other hindrances in their Italian possessions. Brought to a standstill to the west, on the frontier of the Kingdom of Valencia, by the conquests of the Castilians from the Moors of Granada, they had sought a new sphere of expansion at sea. They became masters of the archipelago of the Balearics. Their Catalan mariners, driven back from the Eastern Mediterranean by the growth of Turkish power, remained dominant in the Western Mediterranean. At the end of the thirteenth century, after the massacre of the Sicilian Vespers in 1282, the Aragonese dynasty substituted itself in Sicily for the Angevin princes of French stock. In the fourteenth century it installed itself in Sardinia, despite the opposition of the islanders and the Genoese. In the fifteenth century it established itself in the Kingdom of Naples, which an Aragonese prince seized from the successors of Charles of Anjou, and which Ferdinand the Catholic, Isabel's husband, snatched in turn from one of his own cousins, the heir of the conqueror.

But he and his successors reigned here by the title of vassals of the Holy See. Every year, on the feast-day of Saints Peter and Paul, they paid homage to their suzerain with the gift of a white palfrey. They had not repudiated this not very costly duty ; but there were other failings with which a Pontiff jealous of his rights could reproach them.

The Viceroy of Naples, taking advantage of the hatred between the bourgeoisie and the nobles, influenced elections to the States, and, disposing of an armed force of three thousand veteran Spanish soldiers and a thousand local lancers, exercised absolute power over this divided people. The clergy themselves came and offered him their services. At the outset they had embraced with enthusiasm the decrees of the Council of Trent, which forbade laymen from encroaching upon ecclesiastical jurisdiction or subjecting clerics to taxes. But the clergy were less keen about reform, also ordered by the Council, of the abuses which had been introduced by the relaxation of discipline, the worldly life of prelates, and the exploitation of the sacraments. In reply to the Pope's injunction, signified by the Nuncio, to create seminaries for the training of young priests, they pleaded lack of funds and put themselves under royal protection (3).

It was an opportunity of withdrawing them from the interference of Rome and reducing them to a state of tutelage which the Sovereign was quick to seize. A *capellano maggiore*, a kind of theological consultant, was charged with the duty of expunging anything in the Papal briefs which seemed to exceed the Pope's spiritual sphere or encroach upon that of the temporal Sovereign.

Sicily was not so completely domesticated. The supreme courts, the Great Court and the Court of Conscience, were composed of removable magistrates, who could be dismissed at will ; but there were also officials who were nominated for life and were in a large measure independent. Opposition to royal authority was not concentrated in the Parliament, in which the three orders were represented. It was diffused in the privileges of the towns, the barons and the clergy ; in the jealous rivalry of Palermo and Messina ; in the mischievous agitation of life magistrates, and in the anarchical spirit of a populace torn by faction. This opposition gave much trouble to the representative of the King of Spain in the country, and sometimes presented him in such a bad light in Madrid by denunciations of all kinds that it ended by securing his recall or dismissal. Happily the Church provided a counterpoise. The King, by virtue of ancient rights, regarded himself here as the natural Legate of the Pope and, despite the protests of the Holy See, invested himself with a body of privileges and rights comprised under the name of *Monarchia Sicula*.

The Spanish Sovereigns claimed similar prerogatives elsewhere. The Council assembled at Trent in 1545, twice reassembled and twice dissolved, held its last sessions in 1562-3, during the early years of Philip II's reign. It disappointed the hopes of monarchs who, like Catherine de Medici and the Emperor Ferdinand, counted upon it to rally the dissident at the price of a few concessions—prayers in the common tongue, Communion in the two elements, and even marriage of priests—in return for the shelving of irritant dogmatic questions : justification by works or by faith ; real, substantial and bodily presence of Christ in the Eucharist, etc. These hopes of Catherine's and the Emperor's collided with the compact opposition of the Italians and the Spaniards, who were hostile to any compromise.

The Council fixed the articles of faith in inflexible formulæ, and anathematized the faithful who did not adhere to them absolutely. To the demand put forward by the Sovereigns for the reform of the Church in its head and in its members, it replied by a project for the reform of princes. In this project it claimed for ecclesiastical tribunals the right to judge clerics ; prohibited secular magistrates from interfering in any suits dealing with spiritual affairs, matrimony, benefices and heresy, even if the Church judges consented to hand them over ; and threatened with excommunication any Sovereigns who, except in case of war against the Infidels or in case of extreme necessity, levied any duty, tax, toll or subsidy upon the clergy.

These clerical pretensions raised such a storm of protest that this attack upon the lay power was transformed into a mere exhortation to Sovereigns to maintain the rights of the Church. Even in this milder form, the Court of France, though it accepted the dogmatic decisions, refused to publish the decrees of the Council as laws of the State, since it deemed the parts of them relating to discipline to be encroachments upon the rights of the King and contrary to the liberties, customs, privileges and franchises of the Gallican Church.

Philip was much more subtle. His ambassadors, Vargas at Rome and Count de Luna at Trent, exploited the services which the refusal of the Spanish prelates and theologians on the Council to compromise about dogma rendered to the Court of Rome. Accordingly the Papal legates gave Count de Luna precedence over the ambassadors of France, and were slow to meet the latters' vigorous protests. Once, in solemn prayers, the legates omitted to mention the King of France together with the Emperor and the Catholic King.

Philip did not altogether ignore the opportunity of letting the Pope feel his power, but he did not, like Charles IX of France, oppose him principle by principle, thesis by thesis. He caused the *canones de fide* and the *decreta de reformatione* to be published in all his States, without any distinction between matters of faith and matters of discipline. Nevertheless, despite the Popes and the Council, he still maintained all the prerogatives of his Crown.

On this question of their sovereign rights, as restrictive of Pontifical intervention, the Catholic Sovereigns were always inflexible. In his famous Augsburg Instructions Charles V expressly ordered his son never to yield anything in connection with the infeudation of the Kingdom of Naples and the monarchy of Sicily, or in connection with the royal right of presentation to ecclesiastical benefices in Castile./

Philip II obeyed his father's instructions to the letter. He made merely a formal concession to Paul IV, on the occasion of their conflict of 1556-7, when he humiliated himself by proxy, so to speak, in the person of the Duke of Alba. Though it was with more respect for the forms than his predecessor, he was just as careful to defend himself against the manœuvres of Rome in this sphere of his privileges.

The differences between the Holy See and Spain, which had ended in war in 1556, under Paul IV, continued under this Pontiff's successors. Pius IV, Pius V, and Gregory XIII also protested, though with no stronger arms than mere representations, against the Spanish Government's spirit of independence—sometimes in such terms that Philip was obliged to remind Pius V of Christ's words : " Render unto Cæsar the things that are Cæsar's." But, wherever Philip could give way without compromising any particle of his rights, he was scrupulous about showing his deference for the head of the Church.

This was a matter of sincere piety ; it was also a matter of political prudence. If Philip was to keep Italy at peace, it was essential for him to handle her princes and peoples tactfully. His titles were so diverse that every State, every situation, called for different treatment. In Tuscany his position was that of a suzerain. To secure the alliance of Cosimo II de Medici, Duke of Florence, he had ceded him the city and territory of the former Republic of Sienna—less that republic's castles, places and lands, Porto Ercole, Orbetello, Talamone, Monte Argentario and Porto San Stefano—on condition of faith and homage, and in exchange for the town and estates of Piombino and the iron and alum mines dependent upon it, except Porto Ferraio and the adjacent territory.

Suzerain in part of Tuscany, in Genoa Philip played the rôle of protector, although his legal status was simply that of ally of the Republic. Genoa put her fleet of galleys at his disposal, and made available to him the extensive credit of the Bank of Saint George, a State within the State, which administered Corsica. Charles V said of Genoa : " It is my bedchamber." It was more —the port of the Milanese, a Spanish possession.

In the Milanese Philip was a vassal of the Holy Roman Empire.

The Duchy of Milan was a fragment of the former Kingdom of Italy, and in this fragment of it, as in all the rest of it which theoretically formed a part of the Germanic *Corpus*, the Imperial authority had gone on weakening since the time of Frederick II until it had ceased to be anything more than nominal. Charles V, that ghost of the Middle Ages, had assumed the iron crown of the Lombard Kings at Pavia for the last time, and he had taken advantage of the extinction of the House of Sforza to lay hands on the Milanese, despite the pretensions of France to the heritage of the Visconti. He made his son Duke of Milan by Imperial investiture. The grants of Charles V's successors as Emperor, Ferdinand I, Maximilian II, and finally that of Rudolph II, in February, 1579, confirmed this alienation of the Milanese (4).

The Milanese, like Navarre, was one of those frontier countries where the Sovereign had to respect the feelings of the people. Philip did not interfere with the Senate which Louis XII, during the French occupation, had organized on the model of the Parliament of Paris and invested, like it, with the right of remonstrance. He consented to submit the complaints of burghers about the billeting and maintenance of troops to a *Consulta*, consisting of the heads of city companies, which acted with the Governor. Lest riot should degenerate into insurrection, he had to abandon the idea of introducing the Spanish Inquisition into this Duchy.

But, above all, he had to reckon with the archbishops, who during his reign were the great adversaries of his lieutenants. The Archbishop of Milan, Carlo Borromeo, nephew of Pius IV and one of the originators of the Council of Trent, a saintly ascetic, passionately devoted to reform of morals and to the rights of the Church, claimed the right to interfere in the amusements and private life of laymen, as he was entitled to do in the conduct of clergy. To defend ecclesiastical jurisdiction he armed his retainers. The Senate arrested one of them and had him whipped. The Governor, the Duke of Albuquerque, had the episcopal palace guarded by his soldiers. The Archbishop excommunicated the Governor and the Senate. Albuquerque, worried by religious scruples or badly supported by the King, demanded absolution from this censure from Pius V, and he obtained it, but at the price of a disavowal which diminished his power.

Velasco, who succeeded him as Governor of the Milanese, however, stood up to another Borromeo, who was also Archbishop, and he was so stoutly defended by the King's ambassador at Rome, the Duke of Sesa, that Clement VIII conceded him the rights of it and forbade the Archbishop to excommunicate him.

The Milanese was a point of departure and a point of arrival. It commanded the routes which led from the valley of the Po to the valley of the Danube, and linked Spanish Italy with the patrimonial States of the House of Austria across the Central Alps. To the west it bordered upon the mountainous region of Piedmont, through which ran a kind of military road, continuing through the friendly territory of Savoy and Lorraine, that Philip II's troops followed on their march towards the Franche-Comté and the Low Countries.

In the plain, wide open to invaders, the masters of Milan who had succeeded one another had multiplied means of defence. Charles V recommended his son—this was at the time when Henri II held Savoy—to take care to maintain six great fortresses and six others of less importance, and to provide them with good Spanish garrisons, in order to check the first thrust of the French troops and give time for reinforcements to arrive.

But it was not in Italy that Philip was to test the strength of his gallant *tercios* in defence and in attack. How was he to foresee, in 1548, that the principal battle-field of ambition would also be that of religion?

Far away, very far away, without direct communication with Spain except by sea, opposite England, between France and Germany, lay that region, mostly flat, which was known as the Low Countries. It was the heritage of Charles the Bold, minus the Duchy of Burgundy, and plus Gelderland, an amalgam of lay and ecclesiastical lordships : around the Zuyder Zee, Holland, Gelderland, the Bishopric of Utrecht, Over-Ijssel, Friesland, and Groningen ; at the mouth of the Meuse and the Scheldt, Zeeland ; in the valleys of the Scheldt and the Meuse, Flemish Flanders and French Flanders (Lille, Douai, Orchies), Brabant, Artois, Malines, Hainault, Tournai and its district, Namur ; and, further to the east, detached from the compact group of the other acquisitions, Limbourg and Luxemburg.

Upon these seventeen provinces, differing in customs, institutions and language, some of which were in the tenure of the Crown of France, while others, at least nominally, formed part of the Germanic Holy Roman Empire, the Dukes of Burgundy had worked and succeeded in making one State out of them. By the Treaty of Cambrai in 1529, Charles V had secured France's renunciation of her suzerainty over Artois, Flanders, and Tournai. To safeguard the future, he had strengthened their links with Germany and constituted them, together with the Low Countries, into a " circle ", the " circle of Burgundy ". This " circle " was comprised within the public peace of the Empire, and, in accordance with the Transaction of Augsburg of 1548, was to be defended by the Emperor against any aggression.

This new member of the Germanic *Corpus* contributed to the subsidies for the maintenance of the Imperial Chamber and for the war against the Turks ; but it was dispensed from observance of the " recesses ", in other words the decisions taken by the Diets, and freed from the jurisdiction of the Imperial Chamber, except in case of violation of the public peace or of refusal to pay the contribution against the Turks. The Sovereign of the Low Countries, however, was alone responsible for these breaches of engagement, and it was from him alone that a reckoning for them could be demanded. By this means Charles V contemplated achieving a twofold object : interesting the Empire in the security of the Low Countries, and excluding it from any intervention in their internal affairs. His pragmatic sanction of Brussels, in 1549, proclaimed the new State inalienable and indivisible.

Out of Burgundy, properly speaking, there remained to him only the Franche-Comté. On the death of Charles the Bold, Duke of Burgundy, who left only a daughter, Louis XI of France had seized the duchy as a fief fallen into disinheritance, and taken over the Comté (later the Franche-Comté) as the dowry of Marie of Burgundy, daughter of Charles the Bold, whom he announced his intention of marrying to the Dauphin Charles. But Charles VIII married Anne of Brittany instead, and restored her dowry to the heiress of Burgundy.

The Comté remained isolated. Maximilian of Austria, who married Marie of Burgundy, in order to protect it against French aggression ; François I of France, in order to prevent the passage of a hostile army through it ; and the Swiss Cantons, in order to preserve peace along their frontiers in a territory rich in rock-salt mines, had all, at one time or another, proposed to create a state of neutrality in it. Charles V found it sufficient for its defence to incorporate it in the Empire, in the same way as the Low Countries. He agreed, with bad enough grace, to accept a *de facto* condition which meant neutrality, but without adopting that expression, which he deemed derogatory to his Sovereign rights.

If he was himself prepared to let his claims to the Duchy of Burgundy lie dormant, in order not to perpetuate war with France, nevertheless in his Instructions of 1548 he bade his son never forget them. As his aunt, Margaret of Austria, had begged him to do in her will, he insisted upon keeping " the Franche-Comté in hands " at least, " so as not to wipe out the name of the House of Burgundy " (5).

The Franche-Comté and the Seventeen Provinces had but one Sovereign ; but he governed all and every one of them by different title and in accordance with different laws. They were deeply attached to their liberties, privileges and customs ; and, passionately particularist as they were, they resented and indeed resisted, as we shall see, any attempt, whether well-meant or not, at unification and uniformity.

> " *A Castilla y a León*
> *Mundo neuvo dió Colón.*"

" To Castile and Leon Columbus gave a New World."

Since Columbus, seeking for the Western route to the Land of Spices in the service of Isabel, had bumped into a continent without realizing the extent of his good fortune, navigators, explorers and soldiers had pioneered, conquered and created an immense Spanish empire there. The Antilles were the first land to be occupied, and a capital, San Domingo, was founded in the island of Hispaniola. In these West Indies, as they were called to distinguish them from the Indies of Asia, the conquistadors found gold and learnt of the existence in this New World of countries where it was plentiful and there were great civilized nations.

From Havana, capital of the island of Cuba, a hidalgo, Hernán Cortés, set out in search of wealth and adventure, which he associated in his own mind with pagans to be converted. He disembarked near what is now Vera Cruz, and, with a few hundred soldiers and sailors and a few thousand native auxiliaries, overthrew the rich, powerful, and idolatrous empire of the Aztecs. He took, lost, and re-took Mexico City, their capital, and by dint of executing, massacring and burning overcame all resistance within three years. He and his lieutenants extended the boundaries of New Spain southwards as far as Guatemala and northwards as far as California.

Crossing the isthmus of Darien, Vasco Núñez de Balboa saw before him the infinity of the Pacific Ocean, and thus established beyond dispute that America was not an extension of Asia. Starting from this region of Darien, two adventurers, Pizarro and Almagro, attacked another immense empire which was said to be bursting with gold. Here reigned a dynasty which claimed to be of solar origin, the Incas, lords of the soil and the sub-soil, of men, of labour and of property : a theocracy on a basis of communism. By guile, by force, by superiority of armament, here, as in Mexico, a few hundred Spaniards exterminated the ruling caste and made millions of subjects submit to their yoke.

But the conquistadors fought over the spoils of precious metal, arms in hand. Almagro was put to death by a son of Pizarro's, and Pizarro was assassinated in his capital, Lima. The rivalry of their heirs, revolts of the Indians, massacres and disturbances were threatening to go on for ever when Charles V, determined to bring them to an end, dispatched an ecclesiastic of great renown as a peacemaker, in the person of Pedro de la Gasca. After exhausting all means of persuasion, in April, 1547, he had the leaders of the two rebellious parties, Carbajal and Pizarro, arrested, and exiled one of them and beheaded the other.

During this struggle, other soldiers of fortune, acting with or without orders, had explored, subjected, exploited and pillaged the territories to the north and south of the empire of the Incas : New Granada, even richer in gold than Mexico or Peru ; Bolivia, where silver mines were discovered in 1545 at Potosi ; Venezuela, and, farther away, Chile and Argentina. The whole of South America, with the exception of Brazil, belonged to the Spaniards.

Discoverers and conquerors would gladly have arrogated to themselves possession and exploitation of these new lands. But the Catholic Sovereigns, whatever engagements they might have entered into in order to fan the spirit of enterprise, could not tolerate the constitution overseas of vassal sovereignties more extensive than their own States in Europe. This was what Ferdinand the Catholic said in so many words to Christopher Columbus's son, who, by virtue of the agreement of April 17th, 1492, claimed the admiralty, the vice-royalty and the general administration of the seas, coasts, islands and mainland which his father had discovered. The litigation between the Columbuses and the Crown was settled in 1536 by a compromise. Don Luis Columbus (III), Admiral of the Indies, ceded all his pretensions against the Duchy of Veragua and an annual income of ten thousand ducats (6).

Charles V refused to grant Hernán Cortés the administration of New Spain, and appointed a viceroy there in 1535. In Peru, as soon as order was re-established, he instituted a second vice-royalty.

At the beginning of the conquest, the soldiers who fought and the colonists who went to seek their fortunes in America massacred the natives in droves and employed those who survived upon exhausting work in the mines and the fields. Was it legitimate to treat these new Christians as slaves ? Isabel the Catholic did not think so. But what other means was there of attracting Spaniards to these new lands ? Two of the governors sent to the West Indies, Ovando and Bobadilla, conceived the idea of making a grant to colonists of one or more lots of Indians, soil and souls.

export to America. These included Bayonne, Corunna, Avilés, Laredo, and Bilbao on the Atlantic coast, and, in the Mediterranean, Carthagena and Malaga. But on their return the merchant ships had to go straight to Seville, where the agents of the *Casa de Contratación* collected the King's fifth share, the *quinto*, from the cargoes of gold, silver and precious stones.

Since the Government was not in a position to safeguard the navigation of isolated merchant ships at all points, the risks and perils of the sea, without any legislative intervention, reduced the number of privileged ports more and more. From 1574 onwards there were only two of them left, Seville (San Lucar) and Cadiz, which handled the export as well as the import trade. For some time vessels of large tonnage had been unable to get up the Guadalquivir as far as Seville any longer, and they had to stop at San Lucar, on the estuary of the river. It was even necessary, on account of the difficulty of crossing the bar, to divert some of the traffic to Cadiz, not far away, but outside the estuary. With trade thus unified, the protection of merchant ships became easier, and it was definitely organized from 1550 onwards (8).

They were forbidden to navigate unescorted. They sailed every year at a fixed date, and were convoyed by war vessels to the West Indies. There they dispersed to go and load or unload in New Spain, in Honduras, and in Tierra Firme (South America). At the end of three months they rejoined the armada, which meanwhile had been keeping an eye on the corsairs in the Antilles and chasing them as requisite, at Havana, and it escorted them back to the Guadalquivir.

Around these points of arrival smuggling was very active. In order to escape the *quinto*, shipowners and bold mariners, at the risk of prison and even of their lives, ran the precious cargoes from America ashore at well-chosen spots on the coast, remote from the vigilance of the Customs officers.

The *Casa de Contratación* remained established at Seville, where there was organized an association of merchants who monopolized the outward and homeward traffic between Spain and the Indies.

During the early years of the reign of Philip II, the Spaniards rounded off the cycle of their colonization in the known world. They occupied, this time in Asia, on the other side of the Pacific, an archipelago which Magellan had sighted and where he had touched in the course of his famous voyage around the world in 1521. Philip ordered the viceroy of Mexico to colonize these islands, which were named the Philippines after him.

A flotilla sailed from the Mexican port of La Natividad, and frontier fortresses ; one thousand infantry in Navarre ; one thousand light horse in Andalusia ; two thousand five hundred infantry, with a few cavalry and artillerymen, in the other fortresses of the kingdom and in the Balearic Islands ; two thousand infantry, a hundred and sixty cavalry, and eighty gunners in the fortresses in Africa (9).

But the real Spanish army, the army which for a century and a half was regarded as the best in the world, had no resemblance either to feudal levies, or to town train-bands, or to crusaders, or to a coast defence force. It was a professional army which dated from the struggle between the French and the Spaniards, at the beginning of the sixteenth century, for the conquest or defence of the Milanese and the Kingdom of Naples. Its principal force was the infantry, organized by two Castilians, Gonzalo Ayora and Gonzalo de Cordova—by the former in accordance with the lessons of the past and the present, by the latter on experimental principles of his own.

With their heads protected by helms, and their chests and arms by breast-plates and braces, these soldiers, divided up into units as numerous and as mobile as the Roman legions, were an excellent fighting force in the hands of good leaders. Their dash in attack was irresistible. When they were surprised in open country, they met their assailants with the point of their pikes and mowed them down by volleys of fire, with the arquebusiers shooting from cover behind the bearers of bucklers (round shields). It was perhaps from this method of drawing up in three ranks that these regiments gained the name of *tercios* which they made famous.

They were professional soldiers, accustomed to living far away from their own country, to which some of them never went back. They kept garrison in the annexes of the monarchy, in Italy and the Low Countries, when they were not fighting there or elsewhere. They grew old under the flag and often died under it. These *soldados viejos*—which did not mean retired veterans, but men broken to the use of arms—represented traditions of military honour, of bravery, of contempt for death, and it was they who trained the new recruits (*bisoños*).

In Spain the infantry, the queen of battles, contrary to the ideas of other countries, was the arm which inspired military vocations. The proudest hidalgos considered themselves honoured to serve among men on foot. Poets and writers, such as Lope de Vega and Cervantes, took up the musket on occasion for the service of God and the King. " There is no better soldier," declares Cervantes, " than those who transplant themselves from the sphere of study to the battle-field. Nobody has ever turned himself from a student into a soldier who has not been one to excess."

But this school of heroism was not always one of virtue and discipline. There were to be found in it violent, coarse natures, greedy for plunder and carnage. The sacking of towns, murder and rape counted among their most pleasant pastimes. The question of pay, when it fell too far into arrears, provoked furious mutinies. The soldiery deposed their officers and devastated town and countryside to pay themselves, even in friendly territory. The Kings tolerated these acts of violence on the part of their defenders as the ransom of their glory.

For ruling this immense empire of his, the past had bequeathed to Philip II an organization in which he made only such changes as a new situation imposed upon him. He was not, like Charles V, both King of the Spains and Emperor of Germany, a cosmopolitan monarch whom his twofold, complex duty thrust along all the roads of Europe and overseas to Africa. Philip established himself for good in the Hispanic peninsula, and refused ever to leave it, no matter what necessity might summon him outside. He made it the centre of his monarchy and fixed his capital there, Madrid, almost at the geometrical centre of this centre.

For every one of his States, and even for every group of important affairs, there were as many Councils which sat with him and assisted him. As an Imperial Council, so to speak, his father had had a Council of State, composed of two or three leading Ministers of different nationalities, who accompanied him wherever he went and issued his sovereign commands from wherever he happened to be.

This Council persisted; but, when Philip made Spain the seat of the monarchy and Castile the seat of government, it became a purely Castilian Council. Only Spaniards were admitted to it: the Duke of Alba, *mayordomo mayor* of the King's household; his cousin, Don Antonio de Toledo, Master of the Horse; the Duke of Feria, former ambassador in London and commander of the Spanish Guard; Ruy Gómez de Silva, Chamberlain and favourite of the King, who created him Prince of Eboli; the Duke of Francavilla, Ruy Gómez's father-in-law; and the Duke of Medina-Celi, Don Juan Manrique, the Queen's majordomo.

The most eminent of the collaborators of Charles V and Philip II, Cardinal Granvelle, who had been left in Brussels in the service of Margaret of Parma, the new Governor of the Low Countries, was only nominally a member of this Council. Two Italian princes, Octavio Farnese, Charles V's son-in-law, and Ferrante Gonzaga, his most devoted servant and the one of whom he was fondest, were only admitted to the Council of War, a kind of annexe to the Council of State, together with plain colonels : " a Council of the plebs ", as they called it in joke.

Castile had its own Council, which was both an administrative council and the supreme court of justice. The Chancellery of Germany had disappeared together with the Imperial dignity. The Chancellery of Aragon turned back into the Council of Aragon, and Italy, hitherto attached to it, had a new Council to herself, the Council of Italy.

Charles V had instituted, in 1524, a Council of the Indies, charged with the judicial and political administration of the New World. Until 1580 the Low Countries had three resident Councils, corresponding with a keeper of the seals and a secretary resident in Madrid. Philip II ended by associating with himself, but only in 1580, a supreme Council of Flanders.

Apart from the Council of State, whose competence extended over the whole monarchy, there were other Councils which were not confined to nationalities, such as the Council of the Chamber, which the King consulted about nominations ; the Council of War, whose name sufficiently explains its functions ; the Council de la Hacienda or of Finance ; the Council of Orders, which administered the estates and the revenues of the Military Orders of Santiago, Calatrava, Alcantara, and Manresa ; the Council de la Cruzada, which administered a tax intended to defray the expenses of war against the infidels and against heretics ; and finally the Council of the Inquisition.

In all, there were thirteen Councils, of which five were National Councils : Castile, Aragon (constituted in 1559), Italy (1559), the Indies (1524), the Low Countries (1580), to represent the monarchy towards the monarch, and eleven governors and viceroys to represent the monarch towards the people : Aragon, Catalonia, Valencia, Navarre, Naples, Sicily, Mexico, Peru, the Milanese, the Low Countries, and the Franche-Comté (10).

Except for the Council of Castile, which was also Supreme Court of Justice, the Councils were consultative committees designed to study affairs and draft advice. Philip reserved the power of making decisions to himself ; but, before making them, he insisted on being properly informed. To this end he surrounded himself with a numerous personnel, who devoted themselves to giving him the benefit of their interested advice. Hence, under a personal government which seemed to reduce everything to the action of a single man, arose all the profusion and complexity of a bureaucracy.

By virtue of the rank and birth of the great lords who sat.upon it, the Council of State was an aristocratic body, which was called upon to discuss the most important affairs of the monarchy and might claim to play the rôle of a governing organism. Its members bore the high-sounding title of Ministers of State. But it was absolutely dependent on the Sovereign, who summoned it only when he chose, under any form he pleased, and treated its advice exactly as he liked. It had neither pre-eminence over the other Councils, nor any competence on its own account, nor any regular organization. This meant just so many ways of keeping it in hand.

The Council of Castile, largely recruited from professional jurists, had a definite jurisdiction. When the King was absent, it transacted on its own authority the affairs which fell within its competence. The formula : " Seen and approved by His Majesty," was nothing more than a formula.

On the other hand, the Council of State could decide nothing on its own account. Moreover, the King, who was its president *de jure*, in fact did not preside over it except on rare occasions. There were complaints about his deliberate abstention. The reasons for it which he one day gave to Antonio Pérez, then his favourite Secretary of State and his confidant, are characteristic.

" Let them talk ", he said in reply to these criticisms. " They understand nothing about what is expedient in this respect. Every office—for royalty is an office—has its own principles and its own rules, and among others one of the most important, perhaps the most important, is whether kings ought to hold councils in their own presence."

On this subject the Emperor, his father, had once told him, as man to man, that a king ought not to be present at the deliberations of Councils of State. It was a good thing for him to preside over councils of war in the field, for in the extreme dangers (*aprietos*) of war the presence of a prince keeps his finger on the pulse, acts as a moderating influence, strengthens the more courageous and inspires the less courageous. But in the case of Councils of State quite a different consideration had to be borne in mind : " that in the presence of a prince councillors do not disclose their intentions and their objects so fully, which is a point of great importance for the success of the decisions taken by kings. But this is to be understood in the sense that the prince should have a gleaner (*cardillo*), a person completely in his confidence, who reports all that takes place to him."

When councillors vote in the presence of a prince, they hold themselves in and speak as though they were in church, whereas, when they are alone, they start disputing, get warmed up, spur one another on, and reveal their real feelings ; and from them the Prince can draw for himself the best advice he could possibly receive. " And what is of no less importance is that, if the Prince is present, he may be obliged to disclose what he really thinks and cross swords with his subjects ; whereas, as the veneration of men for a man is not of the same nature as that which they pay to God, it is necessary that men should contribute to it, in the same way as ornaments serve to make a prelate revered."

This was Philip's way of keeping himself informed without compromising his dignity. He was careful to keep divisions in the Council of State alive, since he profited by them. The Duke of Alba and Ruy Gomez fought for the upper hand in it. The opinion of either one of them was always opposed to that of the other. " The result of this," Michael Suriano reports in 1559, " is great slowness and difficulty in the negotiation and transaction of affairs, whether public or private ; for whoever is for the Duke of Alba puts himself in the bad graces of Ruy Gómez and vice-versa." But what did this matter to this King who was never in a hurry ?

In affairs of State, War and Government, the King deferred especially to the advice of the Duke of Alba, who was regarded as the most experienced of all his councillors in these matters. In grants of favours and the distribution of honours, he was readier to entrust himself to Ruy Gómez's views.

" Both of them cut a fine figure and are adorned with rare gifts ; but, just as the Duke of Alba has more experience, so Ruy Gómez has more affable and ingratiating manners, and in every-thing he shows much penetration. The Duke of Francavilla, Don Juan Manrique and Count de Feria are good men ; the most experienced among them is Don Juan Manrique, who trained himself in affairs during the time he spent in Italy " (as Viceroy of Naples). The Bishop of Cuenca, the King's confessor, also sometimes attended meetings of the Council, as did Don Luis de Avila y Zuñiga, Charles V's comrade in arms in his campaigns of 1546 and 1547 against the Protestants of Germany, who wrote his history (11).

The Councils were not the King's only official source of in-formation. Sometimes he summoned Juntas to deliberate—tem-porary and occasional meetings of persons chosen in the different Councils, or even from outside the Councils. In proportion as he grew older, his passion for exercising power in person became ever keener. He was quite ready to seek the advice of his subjects, great or small, but he proposed to settle everything according to his own lights.

The Junta which was the last, and the most influential, of these extraordinary Councils, the Council of the Junta, as it was called, which sat in 1585 and was composed of three or four Ministers of State and the heir apparent to the Crown, the Infante Philip, was a Council that closely resembled that of the French monarchy at the time of Louis XIV. But it deliberated only at night, as though the Sovereign did not like to admit his advancing age and the decline in his capacity for work.

His secretaries were not all mere office-boys. There were some of them, Secretaries of State, secretaries of the *Despacho universal*, who played a leading rôle in his system of personal government. They received and opened letters which were not addressed directly to the King ; they drafted replies, and, after royal revision, annotation and modification, dispatched them in their definitive form. As for dispatches from ambassadors and viceroys, relating to the great interests of the monarchy, they handed them over to the King, who examined them and communicated them to the Council of State as they stood, if he judged it expedient, or in a truncated and mutilated form, if he did not suppress them without communicating them at all.

But here again, as in the Council of State, the King's jealousy about his power led him to play one influence off against another. The most powerful of his Secretaries of State, at the beginning of his reign, was Antonio Pérez, the illegitimate son of another Secretary of State, Gonzalo Pérez, whom he succeeded in his office. He had as his colleague Zayas, an easy-going and lazy man who left the bulk of the work to him. Philip, who liked him for his brains and his capacity for work, ended by getting tired of entrusting his whole confidence to a single man. For this and other reasons, he listened to and encouraged another secretary, Mateo Vázquez, whose tale-telling ultimately led to Pérez's dismissal.

Finally there was a personage who, in Spain, always had a known, avowed and official influence—the confessor. Was it not quite natural that he should give his advice about peace and war, since a decision on these matters exposed the Sovereign to responsibilities beyond the grave ? Charles V's doctor, Villalobos, declared, like a good courtier, that, if the Kings of France gave way so readily to their appetite for conquest, it was because they had no confessors capable of showing them the injustice of their claims. He could not, or would not, recognize that a theological consultant, despite

72

his cassock, might be subject to national and political passions, or even to personal considerations. A King's confessor, exerting himself to serve the interests of the Prince and the aggrandizement of the State, as well as to safeguard morals and maintain his own credit, might let himself yield to the temptation to reconcile opposites by a triumph of casuistry—that growth which was so peculiarly tenacious in Spanish soil.

Of all the kingdoms of the peninsula, Castile may be chosen as the most typical example of the encroachment of the royal power upon the privileges of the nobility, the clergy and the towns. Philip ruled them "with a rod of iron", declares the Venetian ambassador, Francesco Morosini.

The Catholic Sovereigns had extended to almost the whole of the kingdom the system, inaugurated in the thirteenth century by Alfonso X of Castile, of *corregidores* nominated by himself, who presided over the town councils (*ayuntamientos*) and dispensed justice. Wherever they could, the Sovereigns abolished the elective choice of municipal *regidores*, *alcaides*, and judges. The revolt of the *Comuneros* was the last manifestation of the local spirit of independence, and its suppression marked the definitive triumph of royal authority in the towns. From 1538 onwards, Charles V no longer summoned the nobility and the clergy to the Cortes. The national assembly was thus decapitated, for these privileged orders were, by birth and position, in the habit of adopting a higher tone, and expressing themselves in more emphatic terms, than the municipal magistrates, who were almost all officers of the King.

Philip degraded the Cortes still more. He influenced the election of deputies, and demanded that they should vote the *servicio* before setting forth their complaints and their wishes. In addition, he took his time about replying to their petitions. His father used to reply "Yes" or "No." Philip confined himself to a vague : "We shall see."

The Catholic Sovereigns had requested from the Court of Rome the right of presentation to vacant ecclesiastical benefices, and Charles V obtained this right, without any reservations, from his old tutor, Adrian of Utrecht, who became Pope Adrian VI. The Kings of Spain nominated learned and pious priests, devoted to their Prince and their country, and generally chosen outside the ranks of the aristocracy. They held this Church of Spain, which was thoroughly Spanish, in their hands by means of the Inquisition, a tribunal religious as well as political, composed of monks who watched jealously over offences against God and the King and kept the bishops themselves in a state of tutelage.

73

As the clergy were prodigiously rich, the Sovereigns, in their capacity as defenders of the faith, and sworn enemies of the infidel and the heretic, extracted immense sums from them. Accordingly Philip II had no interest in restricting the amount of property held in mortmain, upon which he drew as far as he could to meet pressing necessities of State.

"I estimate," wrote Lucio Marineo Siculo, an Italian man of letters in the service of Ferdinand and Isabel, "that the revenues of the whole of Spain are divided into three almost equal parts, of which one belongs to the King, the second to the Grandees, and the third to the clergy." The Castilian aristocracy were the wealthiest of all the grandees. The family of the Mendozas, divided into twenty-three lineages, surpassed all the others in the extent of its estates and the great number of its entails and its vassals. The head of the house, the Duke del Infantado, was a magnificent lord whose residences were bursting with tapestry, jewels, and gold and silver vessels. During the reign of Philip II, in 1574, it was estimated that he could mobilize twenty relatives or allies, each one capable of furnishing twenty companies of three hundred noble members.

The Catholic Sovereigns, Ferdinand and Isabel, had set about weakening this power. At the expense of the Military Orders, they assured themselves means of attaching the nobility to themselves and recompensing them for their services. They prevailed upon Pope Alexander VI Borgia to grant them the Grand Masterships of the Orders of Santiago, Alcantara, and Calatrava during their lifetime. Leo X invested Charles V with these Grand Masterships, and Adrian VI granted them to the Kings of Spain in perpetuity.

This meant the right to dispose of a million souls, one-third of the population of Castile, and of a revenue of one hundred and fifty-five thousand ducats. By a new favour, Sixtus V allowed Philip II to incorporate in his crown the Order of Montesa of Aragon, the fourth and last of the Spanish Military Orders (12).

The Sovereigns reduced the great officers of the Crown of the Middle Ages, the Constable and the Grand Admiral, to the rôle of decorative figurants. Others commanded the army and the fleet. "Everything is changed," wrote Salazar in the seventeenth century; "what was once an office is now merely a dignity."

The nobility were divided into two classes, the titled and the simple nobles or hidalgos. But there were ranks even inside the higher class. The most highly qualified of the titled formed, as it were, an aristocracy within the aristocracy, *la grandeza*. The

" grandees " enjoyed privileges which distinguished them from other lords. They were entitled to keep their hats on and remain seated in the presence of the King.

Under Ferdinand and Isabel this honour was probably enjoyed by all dukes, marquises and counts. Charles V restricted it to a small number of families, fifteen in all. The King, who could confer on his servants the dignity of duke, marquis, or count, could also promote them to *la grandeza*. Philip II granted this distinction no more than seven or eight times.

He treated the grandees as Charles V had recommended him to do in his Instructions of 1543. Philip was then quite young, and his father, who was setting out for Germany, entrusted him with the regency in his Kingdom of Castile. Fearing in view of his poor health that he might die in the course of the campaign, the Emperor drew up some general rules of policy for his sixteen years old son. Philip was not to employ the grandees inside the kingdom, for fear, no doubt, lest, already powerful as they were through their birth, their wealth, and the number of their vassals, they might become even stronger if they held high offices of State. But it was a good thing to confer military commands upon them for purposes of war abroad, since nobles who had a taste for arms did not readily serve except under the orders of leaders with distinguished titles.

It was also expedient to give the grandees expensive embassies and diplomatic missions abroad. There they would contribute by the display they made to exalting the glory of the Sovereign. But in Spain it was essential to keep them in idleness on their estates, aloof from public affairs and the exercise of power, in order in this way to diminish their activity and their prestige.

This was the system which Philip II pursued. The chiefs of the Spanish armies were leaders of the aristocracy or princes related to the Royal Family or to the Habsburgs of Vienna : the Duke of Alba, Velasco, Don John of Austria, illegitimate son of Charles V ; Farnese, son of his illegitimate daughter ; the Archdukes Ernest and Albert of Austria. Philip's choice of Don Luis de Requesens y Zuñiga as the Duke of Alba's immediate successor in the governorship of the Low Countries almost created a scandal. Requesens had been ambassador in Rome, and belonged to one of the leading families of *la grandeza* ; but he was only a younger son of it, " *un caballero particular de una espada y una capa*", a mere gentleman who had nothing but his cloak and sword, as the Duke of Alba's private secretary wrote disdainfully.

As much might be said about the Marquis of Santa Cruz,

Spain's greatest sailor, but also merely a younger son of a leading family. Philip II, moved by similar considerations, made the mistake of replacing him by Medina-Celi, one of the grandest of the grandees, but a man of no ability. In Navarre, in Aragon, in Valencia, in Milan, in Naples, in Sicily, in the two viceroyships in the New World, were posted grandees such as the Duke of Albuquerque and the Duke of Medina-Sidonia, or nobles of the first rank, such as Don Garcia de Toledo, a member of the Manrique family, and one of the leaders of the nobility of Aragon, Lanuza.

But, apart from the high commands by land and sea, the governorships, and the Council of State, where of necessity places had to be found for the grandees, the King most frequently chose hidalgos with no fortune or even persons of obscure birth as his principal Ministers. Prelates and jurists, often of quite humble origin, monopolized the administration of the State.

In proportion as Philip grew older, he showed himself more and more ill disposed towards the aristocracy. In 1591 he dismissed Diego Zapata de Mendoza, Count of Barajas, from the presidency of the Council of Castile, and replaced him by the lawyer Jimenez Ortiz. In the Council of the Junta of 1585, side by side with Princes of the Blood, sat Don Juan Idiáquez and Cristóbal de Moura, who were its leading spirits. Both of them were creatures of Philip II's—ancestors, not descendants.

The nobility maintained its place—an important place—in the King's personal entourage. The Habsburgs had given monarchical ceremonial a scope which it had never known before. At the time of Ferdinand and Isabel the Catholic, the Court, where administrative action began and ended, was a little world of dignitaries, familiars, and domestics. The Sovereigns had no Guard. The protection of the royal person by night belonged from time immemorial to the twenty-four *Monteros de Espinosa*, recruited from among the noble families of Espinosa, twelve of whom slept outside the door of the royal bedchamber, while the remainder kept watch in the palace.

It was only after Isabel's death that Ferdinand, rendered suspicious by his quarrel with Philip the Fair, husband of Joan the Mad, and by the disaffection of the grandees of Castile, surrounded himself with a hundred halberdiers and a hundred mounted estradiots. This was a temporary and occasional measure of precaution.

The Court, which frequently moved from one capital city to another, or from one castle to another, was accompanied by artisans and tradesmen to assure its subsistence and maintenance :

76

butchers, pastry-cooks, fishermen, water-carriers, armourers, harness-makers, blacksmiths. There were embroiderers and seamstresses, too ; but they were all indispensable servitors in a country where travellers were obliged to carry provisions with them to avoid dying of starvation in the inns, which were often lacking in wine and victuals.

It is true that there were solemn occasions, State entrances, marriages, receptions of ambassadors, when Royalty asserted itself by splendour of retinue and luxury of attire. The aristocracy, who as a rule lived on their estates, flocked to the scene and spared no expense in order to shine side by side with the Sovereigns. Every great lord brought with him a numerous suite of pages and gentlemen richly equipped at his own expense. The whole nobility, following the Sovereigns' example, made a display " of great wealth and great enthusiasm in spending it ".

But these costly ceremonies, at which everybody threw money away with both hands, came only at very rare intervals. The Venetian ambassador Quirini said of the Spaniards that they were spendthrift on ceremonial occasions and lived sadly for the rest of the year. This remark was as true of the Sovereigns as it was of the nation. On the morrow of these fêtes they reverted to leading a simple, sober and economical life. The upkeep of their household and that of the Infantes and Infantas cost them barely fifteen hundred thousand maravedis.

The dynasty of the Habsburgs of Spain, however, introduced habits of luxury and magnificence commensurate with its rank and its pretensions in Christendom. When Philip, then still an Infante, rejoined his father in the Low Countries in 1549, Charles V, who proposed to put him forward as a candidate for the Imperial dignity, ordered that his household, in order to make it more imposing, should be organized along the lines of that of the former Dukes of Burgundy, which was sumptuous to the last degree. Even after the failure of his father's claims on his behalf, Philip did not discard that environment of grandeur which had not succeeded in attracting the German princes to him.

A muster-roll quoted by Gachard, dated 1558, while Philip was still in the Low Countries, gives details of a household establishment very different from that of the Catholic Sovereigns : five majordomos, eleven grooms of the bed-chamber, six doctors and surgeons, four wax-chandlers and apothecaries, fourteen household officers and varlets, eight pantlers, seventeen cup-bearers with their assistants ; sixty pages with their governor and their chaplain ; five sauciers, six upholsterers, nineteen officers and attendants for the service of the King, and so on in proportion ; twelve trumpeters, two drummers, twelve lackeys, falconers, huntsmen, sixty grooms, a master of litters, quarter-masters, any number of artificers, and one solitary painter, Christian of Antwerp.

At a pinch one may find an explanation for all these officers, these aides, these servants, these craftsmen, excessive in number though they may appear ; but what is one to say about the thirty-seven princes, great lords and dignitaries, Flemish, Italian, and Spanish, except that they were attached to the King solely to serve him as a retinue and increase the pomp of his progresses ? As though all these high and mighty personages were not enough to maintain monarchical prestige, more than eighty gentlemen of the buttery, as many gentlemen of the household, and some fifty *coutilliers*, all of them doubtless on the pay-roll, swelled the number of supernumeraries, useless officers and redundant servitors (13).

In addition to the twenty-four *Monteros de Espinosa*, to protect the Sovereign there were now a Spanish guard, a German guard, and a Burgundian guard. This last consisted of a hundred mounted archers, further armed with pistols. It was the old and noble guard of the Dukes of Burgundy, says the Archer Enrique Cock in his narrative of the royal progress to Saragossa in 1585, a bodyguard recruited in the Low Countries among the sons of families of good birth, " faithful escort of all the royal journeys . . . brave defenders in everything that touched the King and his family, to whom the keys for opening and closing the royal palace were handed over every day ". In the morning they relieved the *Monteros de Espinosa* of their nocturnal mounting of guard, and transferred the duty back to them at night (14).

Ferdinand and Isabel had a choir in which a few *mozos de capilla* (choir-boys), under the direction of a choir-master, raised their young voices. An orchestra of wind and string instruments accompanied the singing : *altos de sacabuches* (a kind of trombone), *cornetas* (horns), trumpets and cymbals.

But the spirit of magnificence of the Habsburgs coincided with the great awakening of religious music in Spain. In both his great and his small choirs Philip II may have had the pleasure, which he would have enjoyed extremely, of listening to the motets of Vitoria and Morales, disciples and rivals of Palestrina. He also induced musicians from the Low Countries to come to Spain, and usually recruited singers among his Northern subjects, whose voices he probably found less harsh than those of the Spaniards.

Philip's Court was costly. It comprised no less than fifteen hundred persons, of whom nine-tenths were Spaniards and the remainder Flemish, Burgundians, English, Italians, and Germans. The Cortes of Castile deplored these unnecessary expenses, which it had to defray. The assembly held at Valladolid in 1558 complained about having to pay the salaries of so many singers, chamberlains, etc.

With such a profusion of servitors of all ranks, and with three Guards, it was easy to organize great processions. Queens and princesses naturally took part in them ; but, since Kings had resumed the ruling of the State after the death of Isabel, apart from these exceptional occasions the royal ladies scarcely ever appeared in public. There was no comparison with conditions in France, where Queens had their own circle, received ambassadors, and lived in the midst of Court ladies and gentlemen.

The Court of Spain was an assembly of dignitaries—councillors, generals, jurists, monks, and priests—to which the grandees of Spain and their ladies came only when they were invited, unless the exercise of their duties happened to keep them there. It lacked the constant presence of a feminine element, which had nothing else to do but appear in public, adorn itself, make itself attractive—the indispensable company of the Valois in their palaces and their châteaux, and the charm of all their fêtes.

The Queens of Spain lived in seclusion, under the administration of a *camarera mayor*, and in strict observance of a system of etiquette exacting in its minuteness. When they went out, it was in a closed litter. They danced only with their husbands, though they might give themselves the pleasure of watching their ladies and maids of honour dance.

When Doña Juana, the King's sister, arrived at Toledo with Elizabeth of Valois, who was going to make a solemn entrance there, she left her litter only to withdraw to the upper part of the palace, where she isolated herself with her ladies and slept in a kind of dormitory. To get an exact idea of the life of a Queen of Spain at the time of Philip II, we can take no better example than that of Elizabeth of Valois, the one among all his wives whom the King seems to have loved most dearly.

When he returned from the Low Countries to Spain, he was anxious to see the young Queen, that child of fourteen, whom Catherine de Medici wanted to keep a little time longer, because she was not yet marriageable. But Philip insisted on her presence. Her departure was first fixed for November 8th or 10th, and then delayed, with Philip's consent, only until December 10th or 12th. It was certainly an odd time of year to choose for crossing the

Pyrenees by Saint Jean-Pied-de-Port and the pass of Roncevalles, over three thousand feet in altitude.

The first Prince of the Blood, Antoine de Bourbon, King of Navarre, was to accompany the Princess and hand her over to her husband. He had accepted—or requested—this mission in order to have an opportunity of pressing his claims to Spanish Navarre upon the King of Spain by word of mouth ; but this was a method of negotiation which Philip II, always slow to make up his mind, did not like. Would it become him to treat as a Sovereign a man whom he could only, and would only, recognize as Prince of Béarn ? It was perhaps for this reason that he decided to send Don Iñigo Lopez de Mendoza, Duke del Infantado, and another Mendoza, the Cardinal-Archbishop of Burgos, to meet Elizabeth.

Meanwhile, the Queen and her suite had arrived on January 2nd, 1560, in rain, wind and snow, at the monastery of Roncevalles, the last place on the French side of the frontier, and there they waited for the ceremony of " *tradición* " to take place. Philip had regulated its details with the minute care which he took about everything. His representatives, making additions on their own account to what formalism and etiquette demanded, wanted Antoine to proceed on to Spanish soil, mid-way between the monastery and the hamlet of Espinal, where they had halted. The King of Navarre refused to hand Elizabeth over in open country under a winter sky. It was not without difficulty that the Mendozas were induced to proceed to Roncevalles themselves and receive the Queen there.

Infatuated with national pride and prejudice as they were, they waxed indignant at the moment of parting, when she embraced her relative, the Prince of Béarn, and could not keep back her tears at the thought of leaving her family and her country. The Archbishop of Burgos sternly reminded her of her new duties as Queen of Spain. " *Oblivisce populum tuum et domum patris tui.*" Elizabeth controlled herself, and set off with her French suite and her Spanish escort, to the sound of trumpets and timbrels, in very bad weather.

She was comforted by the welcome of her new people. At Pampeluna on January 7th, at Tudela on the 14th, at Soria on the 19th, and in the towns and castles where she spent the night, municipal officers, nobility, burghers and populace hailed her with their acclamation as the harbinger of peace, held fêtes in her honour, and made her presents. At Guadalupe, where the King was awaiting her, she made a solemn entrance, mounted on a

80

ELIZABETH OF VALOIS
From a portrait by Pantoja de la Cruz in the Prado

palfrey, under a canopy of cloth of gold borne by twelve *regidores* (town councillors), " clothed in long robes of crimson velvet ".

Philip, without letting her see him, watched her at supper, and bade her hold herself ready to marry him the next day, January 31st. As though the marriage by proxy celebrated by the Bishop of Paris did not strike him as sufficient, he decreed that the Cardinal-Archbishop of Burgos should marry them once more.

" The *onbrifon* (nuptial canopy) was of cloth of gold, which was draped over the shoulder of the King because he had already been married "—one appreciates here the nice distinctions of the Catholic Church—" and held over the head of the Queen. Then, without its being raised, a string of great pearls, rubies and diamonds was placed on their shoulders, so long that it held them fastened and chained together twice around their necks. And so they remained from the Gospel to the end of Mass, each one holding a taper of white wax all the time."

When Mass had been said, Philip escorted his wife to dinner, and then took her to her room, whence he fetched her again in the evening for a ball. He supped in her chamber, whence he withdrew to undress, " and at ten o'clock he returned there to sleep with her until seven o'clock the next morning ". This morning, Mass forgotten, " he dined in private in his own chamber, and the Queen in hers, with the Princess de Bourbon, without any man entering it ".

Though, with characteristic Castilian gravity, he did not show it, Philip enjoyed the pleasure of having a young and pretty wife, who consoled him for his penance with Mary Tudor. From Guadalajara to Alcalá he never left her, and he held her by the hand on their entrance into that university town, whose students regaled them with " verses and prayers in all languages ".

In Madrid, which was not yet the capital, but had prospects of becoming it, " a town about half the size of Melun ", after her passage under a triumphal arch and dances and masquerades, the Queen attended a bull-fight, in the course of which two young pages who had come from France with her " wanted to try their hands and got themselves gored ". Then the royal couple and their train arrived at Toledo, about which the French annalist, de Ruble, speaks with a fine ignorance of Mauresque art and disregard for picturesqueness. This town was, he said, " about the size of Orléans, with badly built houses, most of them of brick, situated on a hill, facing steep cliffs, largely surrounded by the non-navigable River Tagus, along which, above and below the said town, there is very fine and fertile country, so that this is the flower of all Spain " (15).

Into this town, where the Court then resided, Elizabeth made a still more solemn entrance, which the King watched from a window with his son Don Carlos and Charles V's illegitimate son, Don John of Austria. He had occasion to admire the power of endurance of his young Queen, who remained on horseback for nine hours.

The couple declared that they were happy together. Philip wrote to Catherine de Medici about his "infinite contentment", and the young wife that she had such a good husband, and was so happy, that even if the country were " a hundred times duller ", she " would in no way find it so ".

Philip was a good husband, if not a faithful one. " He usually sleeps with her," writes the Dame de Vineuil, in a letter quoted by de Ruble, and never failed to do so " without special reason ". He loved her as much as possible, but he was " of . . . disposition ". The adjective is undecipherable, but it cannot be anything except " amorous ". Of him, as of Henri II, Brantôme might have said that he " liked a change ". Elizabeth, accustomed to the *ménage à trois* of the King, her father, Catherine de Medici and Diane de Poitiers, probably did not mind this so much, young as she was, and in any case she was not humiliated by it. What a difference between the triumphal loves of the Valois, and the discreet and often anonymous liaisons which Charles V and his son never admitted, partly from religious scruples and fear of scandal, but also, perhaps, lest they should expose themselves to feminine intervention in their job as kings !

Philip II's best-known mistress was that Doña Isabel Osorio to whom I have referred above, who called herself his " wife ", perhaps because she was his first love. We do not know at what period to place another mistress of his, Doña Eufrasia de Guzman, maid of honour to his sister, Doña Juana, whom he hastened to marry, when she became pregnant, to the Prince of Ascoli. Nor do we know of what condition was the woman by whom, perhaps during Mary Tudor's lifetime, the King had a child in Brussels, whom he brought up secretly. Whether he was the lover or the unsuccessful suitor of Anna de Mendoza, or whether he never had any relations with her, is a question which it is difficult to answer one way or the other. It remains an open one, despite the discussions of historians, and perhaps it never will be answered.

About Philip's liaisons, or merely passing affairs, with ladies and maids of honour in the palace, and outside it, we get an inkling in the letters of Catherine de Medici's correspondents, and these discreet references are much more convincing than the merely hearsay reports of the Venetian ambassadors. The ambassador of France in Madrid, Sebastien de l'Aubespine, wrote on July 3rd, 1561, to the Queen-Mother : " The King takes his pleasure in the hunting which he has near at hand, and also in other *good acquaintances in this town—not that they make him a bad husband, for he is one of the best in the world.*"

Saint-Sulpice, de l'Aubespine's successor, in a secret letter of October 7th, 1564, sent the French Court a report on a conversation which he had with Ruy Gómez de Silva after Elizabeth's first miscarriage, on August 5th, and her long convalescence. The favourite told him that the Queen's serious illness had increased her husband's affection for her, and " added something about *his past love-affairs, which had come to an end and were no longer carried on inside the household,* so that everything was going as well as one could wish " (16). Philip made some return for his extra-conjugal distractions by renewed consideration for his wife. He immediately increased her Civil List from forty to sixty thousand ecus.

He loved her for her gentleness and her docility. The example of her mother had accustomed Elizabeth to the exercise of these qualities. She came to a country full of prejudices against French morals and with the loftiest ideas about its own. Her *camarera mayor*, the Countess de Ureña, sister of the Duke of Albuquerque, disliked all these foreign ladies and maids of honour, was jealous of their intimacy with the Queen, and, haughty and authoritarian as she was, lost no opportunity of letting them know it.

On the way from Tudela, in Aragon, furious because Elizabeth had given a place in her litter to Louise of Brittany, Countess de Clermont-Lodève, which she had refused herself—perhaps because of some scruple about etiquette—the Countess de Ureña set her lackeys on to the escort and they jostled the bearers of the Demoiselles de Rieux and de Montpensier. When the Queen remonstrated with her that she was annoying two Princesses of the Blood, the *camarera mayor* excused herself with a bad grace.

To avoid such bickerings, and to please her husband, Elizabeth, as soon as she arrived at Toledo, agreed to be housed and served in accordance with the customs of the country. She sent back the chaplains, secretaries, major-domos and grooms in her suite and one of her two doctors, and kept with her only those of her ladies who rendered her the most intimate services, Louise of Brittany and Claude de Valperghe, Dame de Vineuil. They were still too many for the liking of the *camarera mayor*, who took advantage of a dispute between these two favourites to get rid of Louise of Brittany.

Elizabeth lent herself with a good grace to these changes, " being already," wrote the ambassador of France, on April 3rd, 1560, " so much accustomed and almost addicted to the ways of the country that it seems as though she felt no need of any other company and service than that of her own (Spanish) servants ".

She had the knack of accommodating herself to the require- ments of Spanish exclusiveness. She amused herself as best she could. She danced with her maids, played at knuckle-bones, made sweetmeats, dressed dolls, changed and re-changed her costume, made her ladies and maids of honour adorn, mask and disguise themselves in old-time style, and visited churches and convents during Lent. She saw very few men : the ambassador of France ; her step-son, the Infante Don Carlos ; Charles V's illegitimate son, Don John. Once she gave a great ball, " at which there were very few people, which is a thing that suits the King very well, and this pastime lasted more than three hours ". She danced only with her husband. Woe to him who touched the Queen !

She read a little. In the winter of 1560-1 she started sketching, asked Jannet, the great portraitist of the Court of France, for crayons, and learnt painting from an Italian lady. This may have been Sofonisba Anguissola, born in 1535, who enjoyed a con- siderable reputation for portraiture and was summoned to the Court of Spain, where she was a great success both as an artist and as a woman. She married, for the first time, Don Fabrizio de Moncada, whom she accompanied to Sicily.

It was a monotonous life, of which ambassadors' dispatches, some letters, and the private diary kept by Claude de Vineuil— probably for Catherine de Medici's benefit—give us some idea. It must have seemed still more drab to a princess accustomed to the elegances, the fêtes, and, to borrow Brantôme's expression, the " good cheer " of the Court of the Valois. It was varied by stays in the royal residences, at the castle of Valsain (near Segovia), at Aranjuez, at San Ildefonso, at the Pardo.

Here, again, there was little out of the common : Mass in the chapel or in a hermitage, a few walks and rides on horseback. No violent exercise—the King did not like it. He had a delicate constitution. He slept after dinner. His favourite sport was not a good run to hounds across country, but shooting from butts, where the game was driven by huntsmen and villagers on to the weapons of the sportsmen under cover. The King several times had more than a hundred head of deer beaten up in the presence of his wife and his sister, and the Princess " killed one with a cross-bow shot "—just one : not a great proof of skill. But this procession of deer, destined for massacre and escaping it, was, says the writer of the diary, perhaps in jest, " for this country a fine pastime ".

The King had the colts in his paddocks branded with a " P " and an " E ", and took the Queen to watch this being done. Philip's monogram was a contraction of the French " Philippe "— Phle, at least in the letters written in French which he signed. He was very fond of watching dancing. He got many village women to dance for his wife's amusement, and after a bull-fight " which was very fine ", that he attended with her, he had all the girls to dance at the castle in French style and Spanish style. Later he was to make the seminarists at the Escorial dance.

Claude de Vineuil's diary is valuable from more than one point of view. Philip's well-regulated life, his taste for the country and for country pleasures, his walks to the hermitage where he went to hear Mass every day, his interest in his stables—all this is Philip II in the flower of his age. He was thirty-two at the time of his marriage with Elizabeth of Valois. He was forty-one when she died ; and he was already the Philip II of middle and old age.

These royal residences of Charles V and the Catholic Sovereigns were now too animated for this lover of retirement and solitude. He had one built more in keeping with his humour. The Escorial was begun in 1563. Here, eight leagues away from his capital, with a restricted Court, he was to find the calm and tranquillity which were necessary if he was to devote himself to his passion for work. Here, too, by housing a monastery of monks in his palace, he could devote to exercises of devotion and to God such leisure as was left him by the administration of his immense Empire.

NOTE

I think it will be useful here to give some guidance about the money which was current in Spain in the sixteenth century, so that readers of this work may be able to reckon, at least approximately, the revenue and expenditure of Philip II, the cost of his armaments and wars and the extent of his financial embarrassments.

The *maravedi* was the unit of currency in Spain, as the *livre tournois* was in France and the *pound sterling* was in England. It will be convenient, therefore, to reduce the principal currency of the monarchy to terms of this common measure.

The *peso*,   subdivided into 13½ *reales,* was worth 450 maravedis ;
The *escudo (écu)*   ,,   ,, 12 *reales* ,,   ,, 400   ,,
The *ducat*   ,,   ,, 11 *reales* ,,   ,, 375   ,,
     (or, more exactly, 374 maravedis and a fraction).
The *florin* was half a ducat.

Weiss, in *L'Espagne depuis le règne de Philippe II* (which also covers Spain during the reign of Philip II), reckons the peso in French money at 5 francs 20 centimes. This lucky coincidence with the gold exchange of the dollar (5 frs. 20) would, if it were rigorously exact, facilitate the transformation into dollars and cents of the escudo (4 frs. 62), the ducat (4 frs. 33), the florin (2 frs. 165) and the other principal coins current in Spain, Italy, and the Low Countries.[1]

But this estimate in absolute value, or, as it is sometimes called, in weight of money, is only roughly valid, in view of the fact that it does not take account of the variation in the relationship between gold and silver, great as this was after the discovery in 1545, and the exploitation, of the silver mines of Potosi. It does not apply to the whole reign and to all the States of Philip II. At the same time, it is an approximate representation which will help us to follow the parallel course of policy and finance.

One difficulty, which it is to be feared is insoluble, is to establish any relationship between the purchasing power of money in the sixteenth century and in our own time. For purposes of comparison, we should have to know the price of all products, goods and services then and now in Spain, in order to extract a co-efficient of differentiation from them. To my knowledge, no work has appeared in that country comparable with that which Mgr. d'Avenel has published about old France : *Histoire de la propriété, des salaires, etc.*—and in any case the conclusions of this immense investigation are, rightly or wrongly, contested.

The fact is that the market prices of corn, of commodities, of the principal articles of food and maintenance, varied in France from province to province, sometimes with such wide differences that it is impossible to find a standard of measurement. The Spanish monarchy was a much more complex amalgam. Money during the reign of Philip II must be multiplied twice, thrice, four times or even more, if we are to arrive at its equivalent in the money of our own time.

[1] The pre-war gold parity of sterling to francs was 25·22, so that the peso, nominally, may be reckoned at roughly five to the pound.

CHAPTER IV

THE RELIGIOUS UNIFICATION OF SPAIN

AUTODAFES—EXPEDITIONS TO AFRICA—THE MORISCOS

THE Hispanic peninsula, at the centre of this Empire made up of diverse nationalities and countries, was not itself ethnically homogeneous. Among the Spaniards of pure race, especially in the Southern regions, Andalusia, Valencia and Granada, lived Arabs and Berbers, African by origin and Mussulmen by religion, whose ancestors had once conquered almost the whole of Spain and then, driven back by the offensive of the mountaineers of the North, had concentrated by successive retirements in the Kingdom of Granada, whence the Catholic Sovereigns, Ferdinand and Isabel, finally succeeded in dislodging them in 1492.

Once conquered, they had been constrained to adopt the religion of the conquerors, at least in form. Numerous also, in the same regions, were the Jews, merchants and bankers, whom popular hatred and the decrees of princes had compelled to receive baptism at different periods.

What would have become of this disparate State, burdened with a foreign body which might turn hostile, if it had been, like the rest of Christendom in the sixteenth century, exposed to the spirit of controversy, to the zeal for proselytism and the passions of religious parties, ever ready to resort to arms ? But it seemed hermetically sealed against the propagation of the new doctrines. The religion which, for eight centuries, had inspired its struggle against the Mussulmen was so closely united to its patriotism that it formed part of the national consciousness.

Pleasantries and satires at the expense of the loose morals of the clergy and the illiteracy of the monks, such as we find in *La Celestina*, that literary masterpiece of the reign of Ferdinand and Isabel the Catholic (1492), in Torres Naharro's *Propaladia* (1517), and in Tormes's *Lazarillo*, that model of picaresque novels, had no effect upon the integrity of the Faith. The Archbishop of Toledo, Alonso Fonseca; the Grand Inquisitor Manrique, and Charles V himself might find amusement in the *Eulogy of Folly* in which Erasmus made such delightful game of the monks; but they found no laughing matter in the preaching of Luther and Calvin against the Roman Church.

This preaching attacked dogma and reproved the worship of images and relics, aspersed the value of good works, condemned belief in the intercession of the Virgin and the Saints, in Purgatory, in indulgences—everything, in short, in that sum of beliefs and practices which constituted the very basis of Catholicism. There was nothing specifically Spanish about Protestantism. A severe form of worship, the adoration of God in spirit and in truth, was scarcely suited to a people of ardent imagination, responsive above all to the pomp and ceremony of ritual, whose art, even in its most mystical transports, remained sensuous and realistic.

The first Spaniards who embraced these novelties or sympathized with them, the brothers Valdés, Juan Díaz, Miguel Servet, became acquainted with them abroad, where they lived remote from the spirit of their own country. Juan Díaz was killed by his brother, and the grounds for this fratricide are characteristic: as a traitor to his country, to his family, and to his faith. But can one count among Protestants Miguel Servet, that Navarrese of genius, discoverer of the circulation of the blood, whom Calvin burned as an anti-Trinitarian, because he could see no more in Christ than the closest and most perfect incarnation of the Divine essence?

Against the converted Moors and Jews, Moriscos and Marranos, as they were respectively called, who secretly remained faithful to the religion, the ideals and the customs of their ancestors, and against the Old Christians who, attracted by the monotheism of Israel, denied the Trinity and tended towards Judaism, Ferdinand and Isabel the Catholic had instituted, in 1481, an Inquisition to punish relapses and offences. At the time of its foundation, the Inquisition was aimed only at apostates and recognized no other heresy than that of Judaism—the great heresy of Spain in the fifteenth century.

But when Luther and Calvin made their appearance in the following century, the Inquisition found itself quite naturally adapted and armed for combating their followers, like those other apostates: renegade Christians or descendants of renegade Christians. It was surprised, however, at the appearance of such innovations in Spain. It had dealt such shrewd blows at the Judaisants that it flattered itself that it had extirpated the very germ of the heresies which divided Christendom, upset States, and tore peoples asunder.

Seville was doubtless the first city where the doctrines of the reformers crept in and made converts. It was Castile's great river port on the Guadalquivir, and, as the clearing-house of trade with the Indies, it had contacts with every country in Europe. When the Inquisition realized the fact and opened an investigation, the most notorious suspects, Dr. Juan Pérez, five or six other lay persons, men and women, twelve monks of the monastery of San Isidore, including the superiors, and the prior of a monastery at Ecija fled to Geneva, made their way to England, and finally established themselves in Amsterdam.

In 1556 Dr. Juan Pérez published a translation of the New Testament in Spanish, of which many copies, hidden in wine-casks with false bottoms, were sent to Seville. The Inquisition, advised of this smuggling by the Spanish Ambassador in France, Don Francés de Alava, arrested the sender, a man called Julianillo, and the receivers : professors, a doctor, monks, and gentlemen, among them Don Juan Ponce de Leon, brother of Count de Bailen and cousin of the Duke of Arcos, and a noble lady, Doña Juana, wife of the Lord de la Higuera.

Doctor Losada and Blanco, an apostate, were burned. The house of Isabel de Baena, where the conventicles had been held, was razed to the ground. A jealous wife who had followed her husband one night and, instead of an assignation, stumbled upon a meeting for preaching and prayer, revealed this secret of hers to her confessor, who handed it on to the tribunal of the Holy Office.

Great was the wrath of Charles V, now in retirement at Yuste, when he learnt that this perverse doctrine, whose success in Germany he had been unable to prevent, was in course of contaminating his own patrimonial States. Ah, says his historian Sandoval, how he regretted that he had spared Luther ! Of course, he had given him a safe-conduct to come to Worms ; but was he bound to keep his plighted word with an enemy of God ? He wrote to his daughter, Doña Juana, who was acting as Regent in Spain in the absence of his son, to his son himself, and to the members of the Council of the Inquisition, urging them to act with the utmost severity. He reminded his daughter that in Flanders " he had burned alive " those who remained obstinate in error, and had beheaded even those who became reconciled to the Church.

But the Inquisition did not require to be stimulated. The number and the quality of the heretics demanded that it should chastise. It was surprised to find among these perverts many

others were Moriscos, Jews and heretics from France, Burgundy, Flanders and Germany.

That was the end of it. Spanish Protestantism, which had no very deep roots, was extirpated. Henceforth the Inquisition had to deal only with foreigners. Some Frenchmen engaged in business in Catalonia were arrested and executed. Saint-Sulpice, the ambassador of France at Madrid, complained that such proceedings handicapped trade. Philip gave reasons which were mere evasions.

In January, 1563, Cecil, Elizabeth's Secretary of State, protested against the burning of twenty-six Englishmen the previous year. This was perhaps as much for their misdeeds at sea as for their faith. England's maritime development was foreshadowing itself in attacks upon Spain's colonial monopoly.

Valdes and Philip II were born to understand one another. They were both as suspicious as they were merciless. The Grand Inquisitor proceeded against any suspects without distinction of rank. The most outstanding example of his fanatical fury—which in this case, it is true, was accompanied by a personal grudge—was his arrest of Bartholomé Carranza, Archbishop of Toledo, for whose See Valdes had intrigued. The Primate of Spain, a theologian of great learning, who had accompanied Charles V in his progresses and sat on the Council of Trent, was flung into the dungeons of the Inquisition.

The ground of prosecution was the words of consolation which the Archbishop had addressed to Charles V as he was dying. He held the crucifix before the Emperor, and said : " Here is He Who answers for us. There is no more sin. All is forgiven." It was alleged that Carranza had thus professed the Protestant doctrine of justification by faith, and there were also definitions in his catechism—approved though it was by the Council of Trent— which lent themselves to ambiguity.

Carranza appealed to the Pope. But nothing could be less to Philip's liking than this resort to a superior authority—even though it was the Sovereign Pontiff—against the jurisdiction, which was as much political as religious, of the Holy Office. It was something like an infringement of the royal prerogative. The trial lasted seventeen years. Pope Pius V had a great deal of difficulty in getting the Archbishop out of the hands of the Inquisition and having him brought to Rome for Papal judgment. Satisfied though the Pope was of the purity of the Archbishop's faith, he forbore to acquit Carranza, out of deference towards Philip II. Gregory XIII, still more deferential, condemned the Archbishop to five years' suspension and some penances, and forbade the reading of the suspect catechism. Carranza died a few days later, on May 2nd, 1576, absolved, but not acquitted.

Carranza was not the only prelate to be prosecuted. The Archbishops of Granada and Santiago and the Bishops of Lugo and Leon also had to reckon with the Holy Office. The monks and jurists who constituted its formidable tribunals were equally zealous about defending religion, the rights of the King, and the interests of public order. Accordingly the mystical transports of Saint Theresa, Ignatius Loyola, Francisco Borgia and Fray Luis de Leon scared the scrupulous consciences of the Inquisitors, who were devoted to the letter of dogma and disturbed about such super-human aspirations from the point of view both of the Church and of society.

The Spanish episcopate, which had played such a great rôle at the Council of Trent, was more and more hemmed in between the tutelage of the Sovereign and the surveillance of the Holy Office. It lost its independence and its greatness, and the control of religious affairs slipped out of its hands.

Valdes and Philip II were in agreement about carrying on the work of the Inquisition. In 1559 the Grand Inquisitor published the first Index of books whose reading was forbidden. This appeared in Spain in the very same year as Paul IV published the general list of all prohibited works, the Roman Index, which applied to the whole of Christendom (3).

Philip discovered a still more efficacious means of preventing the introduction of bad doctrines. This was to abolish intellectual relations between Spain and the rest of the world. By the pragmat'c sanction of Aranjuez, dated November 22nd of the same year, he forbade all his subjects, of whatever state, condition and quality they might be, ecclesiastics or laymen, seculars or regulars, to go and study in universities, colleges and schools abroad, except at Rome, Naples, and Bologna. He alleged the expenses which they might incur there, the risk of being led astray, and other inconveniences ; and he ordered all those of his subjects who were now studying or residing at these prohibited universities, colleges and schools to return home within four months.

As for those who, contrary to the substance of this decree and the order contained in it, should leave Philip's kingdoms to go and " study and learn, teach, read, reside or dwell in the said universities outside these kingdoms, if they are ecclesiastics, religious, or clerks, they will be considered, of whatever state or condition they may be, as foreigners and deprived of their nationality and the temporalities which they possess in these kingdoms ; and, if

93

they are laymen, they will be subject to the penalty of losing all their property and being banished in perpetuity from these kingdoms ".

This meant closing Spain to the exchange of ideas. Some of Philip's apologists have claimed that she did not suffer intellectually ; but it does not appear that the Holy Office let anything pass at all. One might perhaps with more reason, if irony were permissible in such a connection, praise Philip for having limited the number of places where the Inquisition set up its gibbets. As a matter of fact, it was not out of humanitarianism that he willed this intellectual impoverishment.

For a long time Spain did not produce either a philosopher, or a thinker, or a famous scientist, rich though she was in poets, artists, mystical writers, theologians and casuists. She triumphed in the sphere of vision, of feeling, of imagination ; but what had she to oppose to Bacon, Descartes, Kepler, or Galileo ?

Meanwhile the Inquisition pursued its principal object, the one for which the Catholic Sovereigns had founded it : the surveillance and the punishment of apostates, Moriscos and Marranos. Originally it had to deal only with new Christians, baptized with or without their consent. But logic had condemned the Jews after the Judaisants, and the Moors after the Moriscos.

To dry the impure Mosaic perversion up at its source, Ferdinand and Isabel expelled all non-converted Jews from the Kingdoms of Aragon and Castile. The Moors of the Kingdom of Granada who refused conversion shared the same fate. Those of Valencia had been forcibly baptized by order of the Comuneros, and this was the only measure of those rebels which Charles V ratified. Accordingly the Inquisition had jurisdiction over all the populations of heterogeneous race, whom it was its mission to transform, by virtue of the sacraments, into authentic Spaniards.

It encountered two kinds of obstacles : inside Spain, the mass of converts and the strength of their traditions ; outside, the encouragement which they received from their kinsmen and co-religionists established on the Barbary coasts.

The expulsions ordered by the Catholic Sovereigns had driven back to the other side of the Mediterranean thousands of Moors, who had settled themselves in the ruined towns of Africa, whence they practised piracy at sea to restore their fortunes or avenge themselves. Privateering became organized, extensive, generalized. To protect Spanish commerce, and also to cut off communications between the new Christians of Spain and the Mussulmen of Africa and prevent the latter from concerting disembarkations and raids with the former, the Catholic Sovereigns had been obliged to go and follow up the pirates into their lairs. Isabel, in her Testament, imposed upon her successors the duty of pursuing the conquest of territory in Africa and carrying on the struggle against the Infidels.

After the occupation of Mers-el-Kebir, the best port on the Barbary coast, Cardinal Cisneros, true heir of the Queen's ideas and enthusiasms, struck a great blow aimed at providing a strong base of operations for the enterprises which he contemplated. He put himself at the head of an expedition in person, and in 1509 he entered Oran. In the following year Pedro Navarro occupied Bougie. To overawe Algiers, which was already the market-place and the refuge of all the sea-rovers, he built a fort, the Peñon of Algiers, on an islet at the entrance to the harbour. On Ferdinand's death, in 1516, Spain was mistress of the opposite coast of the Mediterranean from Melilla to Bougie. She had a garrison in Tripoli, and held Tunis in subjection to her.

But out of Asia emerged two intrepid corsairs, the brothers Barbarossa, who, in order to give their raids at sea the support of shore bases, attacked the Spanish citadels and even the Mussulman principalities. They took, lost and retook Algiers, failed at Tlemcen, and occupied Collo, Boné, Constantine, the island of Djerba and even the Kingdom of Tunis.

Kheir-ed-Din, the younger Barbarossa, finally seized the Peñon of Algiers, which was regarded as impregnable. He preserved only the two towers of the fortress, and used the rest of the material to construct a mole which sheltered the town of Algiers against north and north-west winds. He fortified the town ; but, recognizing that he was not yet strong enough to withstand all his enemies, he paid homage for his conquests to the Sultan of Turkey, Suleiman.

Algiers, now the capital of Turkish Barbary and protected by a garrison of Janissaries, went on living only by piracy and for piracy. It grew fat on the spoils of the Christian nations and was the market, the base and the arsenal of all filibusters, abounding in wealth which bold captains had stolen or fought for at sea, and in slaves for whom they raided as far as the coasts of Spain and Italy.

The Sultans, masters of Asia Minor and Egypt, had conquered Rhodes, that last possession of the Knights of Saint John of Jerusalem, and to take it they had constructed a formidable fleet. They dominated the Eastern Mediterranean, and in the Western Mediterranean the Barbary galleys serves them as an advance-guard. Charles V, that last survivor of the great Emperors and the Crusaders of the Middle Ages, made up his mind to strike at the centre of Ottoman maritime power, in order to assure the security of his States of Spain and Italy and clear the African coasts of infidels and pirates.

He had ceded the island of Malta to the Knights expelled from Rhodes, and thence they organized counter-privateering and gave the Barbaresques back blow for blow. Charles V himself, in 1535, disembarked at La Goulette, recovered Tunis from Barbarossa, and restored it to its legitimate native sovereign under his own suzerainty. But, in 1541, he failed in an attack on Algiers, beaten by storm, which wrecked his fleet and left his troops isolated on shore, short of provisions and munitions, under the rain of autumn. This was a disaster, and so great a one that it discouraged him from making any new attack on a town which he thought impregnable.

The Governor of Oran, Count Alcaudete, however, did not despair of reducing Algiers by siege. He occupied Tlemcen and Mascara, in its hinterland, and endeavoured to seize Mostaganem, in order to establish his base of attack on Algiers there. But, left as he was to the resources of his own courage and skill, he failed to take Mostaganem, and was killed during the retreat in 1558—a sad piece of news which it was decided to keep from the dying Charles V.

After the taking, or retaking, of Tripoli, Bougie and the Peñon of Velez by the combined strength of the Janissaries and the corsairs, there was nothing left to Philip, at the date of his accession, but Oran and Mers-el-Kebir, which were more or less hemmed in by the hostile garrison of Mostaganem ; and, quite a long distance away, in the air, the fortress of Tunis. From Algiers and the other ports occupied by the Barbaresques emerged those fast galleys which roamed the Mediterranean in search of prize or surprise. In this great sea highway, from Gibraltar to Sicily, navigation was exposed to so many dangers that it was scarcely any longer possible except in squadrons. The " Lords of the Sea ", the Turkish or Moorish corsairs, boarded almost every isolated Christian ship, killed the crew, and seized the cargo.

Coast-dwellers had scarcely less to fear than mariners. The Cortes of 1559–60 complained to Philip II about the depredations of these sea-rovers on land. " From Perpignan right round to the coast of Portugal, the maritime territories are uncultivated, gone waste, unsuited for working or cultivation, for people dare not live within four or five leagues of the coast, and so the pasture and profit of the said maritime territories diminish, as do Your Majesty's receipts ; and it is a great ignominy for these kingdoms that a single frontier (*frontera*) point like Algiers can do and does such great harm and affront to all Spain " (4). The *procuradores* begged the King to employ the galleys, whose maintenance cost him so much, to defend the pirate-infested coasts of the Mediterranean and the Atlantic, from Perpignan to the Straits of Gibraltar, and from Gibraltar to the estuary of the Guadalquivir and the river port of Seville.

Philip was also moved to act against the Infidels by his duty as a Christian. Perhaps he imagined that he could turn the Moriscos of Granada and Valencia, still secretly attached to their own religion and traditions, into good Catholics, if he cut off their communications with Mussulman Africa, whence they might derive encouragement and hope. But, before he attacked the lairs of the Barbaresques, he decided that it would be a good thing to close the entrance to the Western Mediterranean against supporting squadrons from the Ottoman Empire.

Philip resolved to recover Tripoli, which had been seized by the famous corsair Dragut, the terror of Christian mariners since the death of Kheir-ed-Din, and make it the advanced post of a con- taining line constituted by Tunis, Sicily, and Malta. The expedition was organized in co-operation with the Christian States which had suffered most from depredations by sea and land : Genoa, Florence, Malta, and the Pope. Even private individuals were allowed to take part in it, either by advancing funds, fitting out ships, or sharing the chances of war and booty in person.

The allied fleet consisted of fifty-four warships and thirty-six supply and transport vessels. The former navigated by sail and oars, while the latter, which were big and heavy, navigated by sail only ; but they were armed with cannon, like the galleons, and could take part in a battle. The fleet was manned by eleven thousand to twelve thousand men : Spaniards, Italians, Germans, French, Knights of Malta, Maltese arquebusiers, volunteer foot and horse, and equipped with thirty-six pieces of artillery. It had as its leader the Duke of Medina-Celi, Viceroy of Sicily, who had under his orders the Genoese Gianettino Doria, great-nephew of the great Doria, to command the fleet, and the Spaniard Don Alvaro de Sande to command the army : two lieutenants who did not get on either with him, or with one another.

The armada was concentrated so slowly that it was not ready to sail from Messina until the latter days of October, at the beginning of the bad season. Speed was vital ; and it spent the whole of the month of November at Syracuse. Having lost a couple of thousand men by sickness and desertion at its ports of call, it wasted about a dozen weeks at Malta waiting for the last convoys and belated account and deprive the Christians of their strongholds of Oran and Mers-el-Kebir. He marched against them with a powerful force, but was able to take only the fort of Saint Michael which covered the approaches to Mers-el-Kebir, and had to beat an ignominious retreat. The heroic defence by Don Martín de Cordova, Marquis of Cortes, aroused the utmost enthusiasm throughout Spain, which was further stimulated by the taking of the Peñon of Velez and the blocking of the entrance to the Tetuan River.

The Turks came to the help of the Barbaresques. The Djerba expedition had excited the wrath of the Grand Seigneur against the Spaniards. Hitherto he had had nothing to do with them directly. His counter-stroke, the besieging of Malta, revealed his intention to possess himself of the key to the Western Mediterranean. The Sultan prepared an immense armament to dispossess the knightly Order of sea-rovers of their island headquarters at Malta, and instal an Ottoman garrison and fleet there instead, quite close to Sicily and within striking range of Italy.

All the naval forces of his Empire sailed towards Malta. Dragut and Hassan contributed their contingents of corsairs. Captain-Pasha Piali transported there fifty thousand men, commanded by Suleiman's best general, Mustapha Pasha. The Grand Master of Malta, La Valette, a Frenchman by birth—as the defender of Rhodes, Villiers de l'Isle Adam, had also been—had only seven hundred knights and eight thousand five hundred Maltese to defend the island and its capital, the Town, as it was called.

But one of the bastions of the Town, the isolated fort of Saint Elmo, which was the first to be attacked, put up such a fine defence that it cost the redoubtable Dragut the lives of several thousands of his besiegers. The Castile bastion and Fort Saint Michael, which covered the Town on the land side, were attacked in their turn and battered so furiously by the Turks' heavy artillery that their weak garrisons, including wounded, did not suffice to man the breaches in the ramparts.

The Grand Master, that old man of heroic soul, who went from point to point of resistance in person, appealed to the Catholic Powers for aid in this extreme danger. The Viceroy of Naples, Don Garcia de Toledo, awaited orders from Madrid. Philip, fearing an attack on the coasts of Italy and Spain by the Turks if they were victorious, was afraid of weakening himself and, in accordance with his custom, deferred his decision. Finally the Viceroy put in an appearance and landed ten thousand Spaniards and a few hundred knights and volunteers on the island.

Mustapha, misled about the numbers of these reinforcements,

hastened to re-embark his troops. When he realized the small size of the relieving army, he put some of his men on shore again, but not enough to resist the relievers, who charged them with such success that Mustapha lost several thousand of his men. The victors pursued the Turks into the sea and massacred them there (6).

Suleiman died after this defeat without having succeeded in forcing an entrance into the Western Mediterranean ; but there were enough corsairs left on the African coast to dispute the mastery at sea with the Spaniards, the Genoese, the Tuscans, and the Knights of Malta. The King's three squadrons, those of Spain, Naples, and Sicily, were not strong enough to police the sea and prevent disembarkations. At Valencia, in 1564, Philip II saw with his own eyes an Algiers ship which came pirating right into the harbour. The fact was that the sea-rovers had accomplices on land who welcomed them, guided them, and warned them against possible dangers. To assure the secrecy of maritime operations, it was essential to leave nobody but Christians in good standing near the coasts.

But baptism and the spying of the Inquisition did not succeed in converting converts and descendants of converts into good Catholics. If the New Christians, as they were called, observed the practices of the worship which was imposed upon them superficially, they remained attached to the faith of their ancestors in the depths of their souls. They might be compelled to baptize their children ; but the first thing they did after the ceremony was to remove the trace of the holy oil and have them circumcised. Couples went to church wearing Castilian clothes to get married. On their return home, they threw this borrowed raiment aside and celebrated their wedding to the sound of musical instruments, with the traditional accompaniment of singing and dancing.

The habits of these people, their customs, their usages, had remained the same as they were before the Christian Reconquest. They understood the language of the victors no better than their religion. A Morisco lay dying. The parish priest went to see him, confessed him, gave him Communion ; then he warned him to hold himself ready to receive the last sacrament. " What ! " said the dying man, " three tortures in one day : confession, communion, and extreme unction ! "

There was complete incompatibility of temperament between the two races. The spirit of industry of the vanquished, their zeal for work, their knack of enriching themselves were repugnant to their conquerors, poor but too proud to work. Their use of hot baths was regarded as effeminacy and corruption. After half a to death slowly, cutting them to pieces member by member. Insults alternated with blows. " O Holy Mother of God ! " groaned one victim. " Dog ! " was the reply. " God has no Mother."

These cruelties did nothing to advance the cause of the insurrection. It began with an irreparable defeat, having failed to capture the city of Granada, the old capital of the country, its fortress and its place of arms. Improvised soldiers were incapable of standing up to the old Spanish veterans. The Marquis of Mondéjar took the field, routed the insurgents, penetrated into the interior of the country, occupied strategic points and posted garrisons there. Everything seemed to be lost, despite the indomitable resistance of the titular Moorish King Aben Humeja in the mountains where he had taken refuge. Nevertheless the revolt lasted two years longer.

On the persuasion of Deza, who found Mondéjar too slow and above all too humane, Philip divided the command between the Captain-General and the Marquis of Los Velez. The jealousy and rivalry of these two leaders relaxed the bonds of discipline. The soldiery deserted and resorted to pillage. In Granada, Deza, crazy with rage and fear, had a hundred and fifty Granadine notables whom he had taken as hostages put to death. The excesses of the troops and the barbarity of the Inquisition fanned the flames of the insurrection again just when they seemed to be dying down.

Then Philip concentrated all the forces in the hands of his illegitimate brother, Don John of Austria. This Prince, born in 1547 as the sequel to a passing fancy of Charles V's for a beautiful girl of Ratisbon, Barbara Blomberg, had been brought up in ignorance of his origin by Luis Quijada, the very type of Castilian gentleman, upright, loyal and discreet. It was only by a codicil to his testament that the old Emperor recommended young Jerónimo, as he was called, to Philip's care. The King, eager to do honour to Charles V even for his weaknesses, showed a great affection for this hitherto unknown brother of his. He established a household for him, granted him some of the privileges reserved to Infantes, and in 1568 appointed him Captain-General at sea, with the mission of chastizing the Barbaresques.

Jerónimo, now Don John, showed himself worthy of his birth and his fortune. Charged with subduing the Moors of Granada, whose new King, Aben Bou, was energetic and a focus of enthusiasm, he did not content himself, as Philip would have liked, with playing the generalissimo at Granada and leaving the real control of operations against the insurgents to his lieutenants. The gravity of the situation imposed a more active rôle upon him, and one more in keeping with his effervescent temperament.

Don John marched in person against the Moors, who had fortified the town of Galera, and carried the place by assault, at the cost of great bloodshed. Although this effort weakened his army and the victors had to retire again before the vanquished during the next few days, the Moors were incapable of profiting by this turn of fortune. Aben Bou was assassinated, and the country-side was devastated. From Italy and the Low Countries reinforcements arrived for Don John. The Duke of Alba sent three thousand veteran Walloons. In March, 1571, the last insurgents surrendered.

Philip, always a formalist, asked his Council what punishment the insurgents deserved. The jurists replied that slavery was the proper punishment for their rebellion. The King contented himself with banishment. Even before the end of the war, all the inhabitants of the city of Granada of Moorish race, even though they had not taken part in the struggle, had been assembled in the churches, subjected to census by the royal registrars, split up into groups, and sent into Castile under the escort of soldiers.

This melancholy procession left many of its members on the road to exile. Some of them were killed by the escort. Others were sold as slaves. Many perished of fatigue. Very few reached their journey's end.

Now it was the turn of the other inhabitants of the Kingdom of Granada. The King had made up his mind not to leave a single Morisco in this land of perdition. On October 28th, 1570, Philip decreed that everybody who was not Spaniard and Christian must go. The country was virtually emptied. The exodus of a whole people began. It was true that their numbers had already been enormously diminished by war and massacre, and that captains and soldiers had taken the best-looking Morisco women for themselves or sent them to be sold in the slave-markets of the Balearic islands. But there remained enough men and women to give this violent transplantation, effected to the accompaniment of soldiers' kicks and curses, the character of a migration of primitive tribes fleeing from want and hunger.

Galicia, Castile, and La Mancha were the principal provinces where what was left of the Moriscos were quartered. Care was taken to relegate none of them to the Kingdom of Murcia, which was too near Valencia, where the Moors by race formed a compact body.

We must give Philip II credit for his good intentions. He

It was in order to increase their own power that the Dukes of Burgundy and Charles V had laboured to make one State out of this disparate group of seventeen provinces. Each one of them, under the government of one of the Sovereign's lieutenants, had its own special and independent administration and its own assembly of representatives, who voted ordinary and extraordinary supplies to the Sovereign and expressed their desires and complaints to him.

The first attempt at approximation to one nation took the form of convoking all these provincial assemblies together and uniting them in a general assembly. But this federal Parliament, which the princes imagined they could induce to vote supplies conjointly to meet their pressing needs, instead of having to ask each provincial assembly for its own share, became suspect in their eyes as soon as they realized that it might become a focus of opposition, as in fact happened during troublous times.

Like the good Capetians they were, who knew how much the King of France, their cousin, had gained by the " éscritoire "—in other words, the encroachment of his own system of justice upon ecclesiastical and seignurial jurisdictions—the Dukes of Burgundy established provincial Courts of Justice, to which appeal lay from the decisions of town magistrates and seignurial judges in each province. Charles the Bold instituted a Supreme Court, the Parliament of Malines, to which—without any possible resort to the Parliament of Paris—all judgments delivered by the tribunals of the Seventeen Provinces might be referred.

Charles V was the great organizer of the State. He severed the last feudal links which bound some districts to the Crown of France. In 1529, by the Treaty of Cambrai, he obtained the renunciation by François I and his successors of any rights of suzerainty over Artois, Flanders, and Tournai. To co-operate with him, he created three collateral Councils : the Privy Council, the Council of Finance, and the Council of State : the first two administrative and composed of officials, and the third a political Council, upon which members of the aristocracy sat.

Despite this strong organization of the central authority, the Low Countries continued to enjoy a large measure of autonomy. Each province retained its own States, which voted and collected taxes. The " Joyous Entrance " of Brabant into association with the other sixteen provinces made the obedience of the people of Brabant conditional upon the Duke's observance of his oath to them. Flanders prided itself upon being the freest country in the world.

Its great chartered cities had not forgotten the memory of their struggles against the Counts, and against the Kings of France, the suzerains of those Counts. Holland, Zeeland, and Friesland, in 1477, had secured the grant to them by Marie of Burgundy of the " Great Privilege ", which excluded foreigners from any participation in the administration. The franchise, here and elsewhere, was characterized by that particularist spirit which prohibited a cosmopolitan Sovereign, such as the Spanish monarch, from employing the subjects of his other States in the Low Countries. Hatred of foreigners was, as a Spaniard put it, the original sin of the inhabitants of the Seventeen Provinces.

The aristocracy displayed the same jealous susceptibility. They assisted Charles V in the administration of his immense Empire and in the command of his armies ; but they had no intention of sharing the government of the Low Countries with anybody. They were numerous, popular, and proud. The Venetian ambassador, Badoaro, reckoned twenty-two lords who, between them, enjoyed a revenue of four hundred and fifty thousand écus.

The most famous of them was Lamoral, Count of Egmont, born in 1522, victor over the French at Saint Quentin and Gravelines. The Low Countries' branch of the de Montmorencys was represented by Philip, Count of Hornes, a nonentity, and his brother Florent, Count of Montigny, a clever man. Henry of Brederode, whose father had asserted his claim to the heritage of the old Counts of Holland arms in hand, was a handsome, dissolute gentleman, brave but braggart, violent and drunken.

To the number of these great ones of the land were also to be added John of Glymes, Marquis of Berghes ; Anthony of Lalaing, Count of Hoogstraten ; Philip of Croy, Duke of Aerschot and Prince of Chimay ; the Count of Berlaymont ; John of Ligne, Count of Aremberg ; and Charles of Brimeu, Count of Megen. But *primus inter pares* was William of Nassau, Prince of Orange. He was a descendant of the younger branch of the House of Nassau, which held Dillenburg, Siegen, the Westerwald, and Beilstein in Germany. Through the marriage of Engelberg of Nassau with the heiress of Polanen, this branch of the family had also acquired considerable estates in the Low Countries, among others the town of Breda—which soon became the usual place of residence of the family—the lordship of Gertruidenberg, the countship of Vianden in the Luxemburg, etc.

The properties of this younger branch, divided between Count Henry of Nassau, one of the Emperor Maximilian I's best generals, and William (1487–1559), were again reunited by the death of

René, son of Count Henry, who died in 1544, at the age of twenty-six, without any legitimate child, and designated as his heir William, son of William. In this succession was comprised the principality of Orange, which had reverted to René on the death of his maternal uncle, Philibert of Châlon. The principality was then bounded by the Pontifical territory of the countship of Venaissin and of Avignon. To-day Orange is a county town in the Vaucluse Department of France.

So William, born at Dillenburg in 1533, found himself invested, at the age of eleven, with the lordships of Breda and Châlon, and in 1559, on the death of his father, he added the estates in Germany to them. He was German by birth, but he had received a French education at the Court of Brussels, where he spent his youth. He wrote and spoke French ; it was only to German princes that he wrote in their own language. He was a representative of three nationalities.

There was the same crossing of religious influences in him. His father had embraced the Augsburg confession and had brought his son up in it ; but, in order to enable the boy to assume his inheritances in the Low Countries without resistance, he had sent him, at the age of eleven, to the Court of Brussels, where only the exercise of Catholicism was permitted ; and the little Protestant, dear to the hearts of Charles V and his Chancellor Nicholas Granvelle, seemed as good a churchman to them as he had once been a chapel-goer. Later he became a Lutheran again, and finally he died a Calvinist.

We must not imagine him as a grave and taciturn lord. The name of William the Silent—which is merely " *Taiseux* " translated from Latin into French—simply means that he knew how to keep his mouth shut at the right time. He was—at least at the end of the reign of Charles V and the beginning of that of Philip II— a thorough-going *bon viveur*. He was superbly clad, prodigal with money, and addicted to feasting and " good cheer ". He maintained twenty-four gentlemen and eighteen noble pages in his household. His hospitality was so famous that Philip II begged him to lend him Maître Hermann, his major-domo. The German princes sent their cooks to school with his chef.

On one occasion, in order to reduce his expenses, he dismissed twenty-eight head-cooks. How many did he keep ? In 1556 he was eight hundred thousand florins in debt (several millions in terms of modern currency). It is understandable that, six years later, he was unable to balance his budget. He made his excuses about it in a letter to his brother Ludwig of Nassau : " And it seems to me that we come of a race who are bad managers in the days of our youth." He was then thirty-one, and he dismissed the hope, when they were old, of " being any better than our late lord and father ".

After the death of his first wife, Anne of Egmont, Countess of Buren, he married, in 1561, a Lutheran, Anne of Saxony, who was a dwarf, deformed and odd, but was niece of the Elector of Saxony : a political marriage in which he found no pleasure. When the Electress recommended the future husband, who was still a Catholic, to respect her niece's religion, he replied jokingly that he would not trouble his wife at all about such melancholy matters, but that, " instead of the Holy Scriptures, he would get her to read *Amadis of Gaul* and other amusing books of that kind which dealt with love. . . ." (1).

His Catholicism was only lukewarm ; but still, when the King of France restored the principality of Orange to him by the treaty of Cateau-Cambrésis, he was obliged to take some measures against the Huguenots or Evangelicals who swarmed there thanks to the war, " making marriage, baptism and sepulture after the fashion of Geneva, threatening to treat the Sacrament in the same way, and preaching day and night ". To prevent the Pope from putting the principality under sequestration, he published an edict forbidding all public and private preaching " without express licence, authority and consent of our Governor President and other members of our Council of Parliament ", under penalty of imprisonment and confiscation. But did he ever seriously intend to apply this edict ?

All these aristocrats did not seem to care about anything but pleasures and feasting. They spent all their revenues in this way, and more than their revenues. They ate and drank on the German scale—in other words, nearly to death. When a German did not get drunk at table, the assumption was that he must be ill. After one banquet, so the Prince of Orange wrote himself, Brederode got into such a state that it was feared he would not recover. On the occasion of his marriage with the Princess of Saxony, the Rhinegrave, a German prince, actually did drink himself to death.

What had such a sober man as the King of Spain to fear from these drunkards ? But he judged them wrongly.

The gentry imitated the aristocracy, and ruined themselves in the same way. Debauchery and feasting finished what the war had begun : the impoverishment of these landed proprietors, great and small. They had fought at their own expense, and their peasants, pillaged by the armies, were no longer able to pay their dues and taxes. Badoaro says that the great lords had mortgaged their revenues, some partly, others wholly (2).

Can we suppose that the aristocracy and gentry did not wonder whether it would not be legitimate to indemnify themselves and restore their fortunes, as in Germany, at the expense of those do-nothings of clergy ? The example of secularization so close at hand was very tempting.

The middle classes had gained what the upper classes had lost. The burghers lent the lords money, took up mortgages on their estates, and ended by buying out the seignuries. In their well-protected towns the burghers had not suffered too much from the war between the Kings of France and Spain. The sea and the rivers had enabled them to go on exchanging merchandise between their own country and the rest of the world. Three industries were especially flourishing : linen, wool, and tapestry. Holland sold eight hundred thousand écus' worth of linen. In Ghent, Bruges and other towns, woollen goods were manufactured to the extent of even more considerable sums. In the making of tapestry, a de luxe industry, Belgium was without a rival. From the point of view of representation, its craftsmen were as good as the Italian mosaic-workers.

Antwerp was the great port, the great commercial centre of the Low Countries, and one of the greatest financial markets of Europe, if not actually the greatest, at that time. Since Bruges had become more or less isolated from the sea, it had inherited the trade of that town, formerly the mart of the Hanseatic League. After the discovery of America and that of the route to the Indies, it was to the broad estuary of the Scheldt, upon which Antwerp was situated, that the Spaniards and the Portuguese brought the wealth of the New World and the spices of Asia, and it was there that the peoples of the north came to barter for them.

Antwerp's commerce increased continuously from 1550 to 1566. Printing flourished there. Its bankers made the money that flowed to it work for them. Its Bourse was the rendezvous of governments hard up for money and capitalists in search of lucrative investments. The Fuggers of Augsburg, the Rothschilds of that time, had a branch there. The Kings of England maintained an agent there, Sir Thomas Gresham. Philip II owed twelve millions to one banker, Tucker, alone. One can imagine the bustle, the activity, the taste for display of this city, this port, this financial market.

Like other places, it had its insolvent debtors, its speculators, its panics and its crashes. Antwerp suffered a severe setback in

WILLIAM OF NASSAU

From a portrait by Antonio Moro in the Cassel Gallery

such intention,
the Calvinists.
a native of Pica
had compelled

After many v
speaking republ
weakened by it
Savoy was casti
and the Church
the rule of poli
of Pastors, and
he was its inspi

Unlike Luth
practices and h
Calvin rejected
His *Institution d*
synthesis of an l
and out of it e

The model o
own austere im
disappeared. T
equal among the
or images, corre
ceremonies were
pomp, no specta
soul from its true
only for the pu
transports of lov

The point of
was original sin,
vation. Works
goodness of God
this could only b
to all eternity.

But this hars
congratulated hi
effort, on the c
strength. The f
would have done
itself, accepted
Creator, but as
powerful of attr
for conversion.

1561, when the Sovereigns of France, Spain and England failed to honour their signatures. But the bankers soon recovered from such crises. The common people went on suffering from them. They were " poor and wretched ", says Badoaro.

It is a point to bear in mind, this existence of a class which could barely eke out a living from day to day, below and side by side with merchants and industrialists who kept on getting richer. The countryside had been ruined by friends and foes. Historians have not paid enough attention to this mass of impoverished workmen and peasants ; but its existence constitutes one important factor, among many others which serve to explain the rising in the Low Countries.

All this wealth, with the leisure which it created and the sense of security which it conveyed, helped its possessors to see beyond and above their merely material interests. Literature was held in honour. Chambers of rhetoric and literary societies disputed for prizes in dramatic contests. One of the greatest humanists of the end of the fifteenth century and the beginning of the sixteenth, Erasmus, was a native of Rotterdam. The University of Louvain had five thousand students, and prided itself upon being the Athens of the North.

Education on the one hand, and impoverishment on the other, not to speak of reasons of faith and conscience, provided good soil for the propagation of new religious doctrines. Erasmus contented himself with jeering at the corruption of the clergy. Luther could see no other remedy for it than a breach with Rome and the establishment of a new Church.

The Augustinian monks of a monastery in Antwerp embraced the doctrine of their confrère of Wittemberg in a body. The monastery was razed to the ground ; and three of the monks who persisted in the error of their ways died, one in prison and the other two at the stake. These were the first martyrs, in 1523, of the Reformation in the Low Countries. Unhappily there were to be many others.

Despite Charles V's enthusiasm for getting rid of " this plague ", as he called it, the penetration of the new doctrines never ceased. To keep them out it would have been necessary, as the magistrates of Antwerp pointed out to their Sovereign, to close the Low Countries to the trade of the world. The armies, too, carried the contagion. During his long wars, the Emperor employed in his different States Swiss and lansquenets, who were not Catholics, and sometimes marched accompanied by ministers of the Gospel.

After the death of Edward VI of England, several thousands

Calvin's doctrine spread throughout the Swiss Cantons, Germany and England. It conquered Scotland. In France it absorbed the dissidents of whatever origin and contaminated the Catholic masses. The Church of Geneva was the religious capital of French Protestantism, the seminary of its ministers, and the point of departure of its apostles.

Henri II's attempt to exterminate it was shattered against the solid block of the faithful. In the course of his reign, in spite of persecution and perhaps because of it, the number of the French Protestants kept on growing all the time. Great lords themselves were moved to pity, or even won over by the attraction of the pure Gospel. The first Prince of the Blood, Antoine de Bourbon, King of Navarre, went so far as to mingle with the faithful who, profiting by the King's temporary absence from Paris, in May, 1558, paraded in the Pré-aux-Clercs singing psalms.

It was from France, and often by ministers who spoke French, that the Reformation was introduced into the Low Countries. Calvinism, says Pontus Payen, a contemporary, after having spoiled France, infected the neighbouring regions, " principally the provinces of Flanders, Brabant, Holland, Zeeland, Gelderland and Friesland " (4). The propaganda of the apostles of Geneva insinuated itself, at first discreetly, into towns and countrysides where heresy—or what was left of it—was lying low to escape its persecutors' pitiless Inquisition. It was a soil well prepared by hatred of Rome and Spain.

Here, again, occurred the same phenomenon as in France : the Anabaptist and Lutheran plants sprang up again in Calvinist shoots. " Even many of the lower orders, who, during the wars of the princes (the Protestant princes against Charles V), had been instructed by German preachers in the doctrines of Luther, abandoned them as lightly as they had done the Catholic religion to embrace those of Calvin." Of this facility of conversion Pontus Payen gives the usual explanation. It was because the new Church " was much freer and more in conformity with the desires of the flesh ". He presumably meant that it proscribed the worship of images and relics, the celibacy of priests, confession, the sacrifice of the Mass, and five sacraments out of seven. There were other reasons for its success.

Philip was disturbed to hear of this swarming of heretics. He naturally blamed it on France, which he regarded as the point of departure and the focus of this contagion.

Immediately after the death of Henri II, from the very beginning of the reign of his son, François II, Catherine de Medici, deliberately and for the purpose of preserving her own power, had shown some secret sympathy for the Protestants, whom the Guises, her son's all-powerful Ministers, were persecuting. As Regent during the minority of her second son, Charles IX, she inaugurated a policy of tolerance, and even, looking further ahead, assembled a conference in Paris to re-establish religious unity. She flattered herself that she could bring the faithful of the Roman Church into accord with Calvin's disciples by an ambiguous formula, and achieve a work more enduring than Charles V did through the " Interim of Augsburg ". She succeeded only in provoking one side without satisfying the other.

The result of this attempt was a civil war—the first, but it was not destined to be the only one. The Catholics took up arms and compelled Catherine to declare herself against the Protestants. Convinced by this experience that the Catholics had numbers and strength on their side, she did not revert to the bold generosity of Poissy, but contented herself, on the signing of peace, with issuing the Edict of Amboise, dated March 19th, 1563, which conceded the dissident minority freedom of conscience throughout the kingdom, and freedom of worship in some towns and privileged places.

Philip II watched these experiments in tolerance with impatient wrath. He was afraid of the impression which they would make on the minds of his subjects in the Low Countries. A change of religion in France, wrote the ambassador of France in Spain, would " tend towards the destruction and embroilment of his States ". Elizabeth of Valois, in a letter to her mother, also emphasized her husband's fears. " It concerns him as much as anybody, for, if France were Lutheran (read Calvinist), Flanders and Spain would not be far from it " (5). Even the concessions in the Edict of pacification of Amboise, modest though they were, were more than the Catholic King liked. But Catherine persisted in her policy as a matter of temperament.

The first war of religion possessed the international character of those which followed. Catholics and Huguenots appealed to their co-religionists in all countries. Prince de Condé and Coligny, in order to persuade Elizabeth of England to intervene on their behalf, promised to cede Calais back to her before the expiration of the period fixed by the treaty of Hampton Court. Catherine solicited the help of the King of Spain.

Philip might rejoice to see the French at grips with a foreign nation and a domestic party interested in the progress of heresy in the Low Countries. But his satisfaction did not last long. As soon as Catherine had concluded peace with her external enemies,

Mexico, had made a landfall northwards in a country of luxuriant vegetation, which they called Florida ; cruised along the coasts of what are now the Carolinas ; and even reached the mouth of the Mississippi to the west, but without succeeding in establishing themselves there. English and Portuguese navigators put in an appearance further to the east, but never came back.

The French pushed their explorations further. Verazzano, a Venetian in the service of François I, and Jacques Cartier, a mariner of Saint Malo, made a landfall on the east coast of North America. Cartier circumnavigated Newfoundland in 1534, and in the course of a second voyage went up the Hochelaga River, which he baptized the Saint Lawrence, as far as the site of the present city of Montreal. From a third expedition Cartier never returned.

These waters, in which Basque and Breton sailors may earlier have hunted whales and fished for cod, are designated in a map dating from the reign of Henri II by the name of " Sea of France ". As for the coast, of course badly charted, between the coast of Canada and that of Florida, it was, strictly speaking, *terra nullius*, since nobody had taken possession of it.

Admiral Coligny, one of the leaders of the French Protestant party, decided to found a colony there, which in case of need might serve as a place of refuge for his co-religionists. A captain named Ribaut disembarked in the bay of Port Royal and constructed a fort, which he called Fort Charles in honour of the King of France. But the score of Huguenots whom he left there found themselves dying of hunger, embarked again in an unseaworthy ship, and in August, 1563, were driven on to the coast of England.

In the following year Laudonnière, a close friend of Coligny's, headed a second expedition. He made a landfall in June on the May River (St. John River in Florida), and built a new fort, La Caroline, to the south of Fort Charles, on a triangular island. He would have done better to establish himself on the mainland and clear and sow the soil. His soldiers, having nothing to do, mutinied, seized ships and went pirating as far as the Spanish Antilles. When they came back, Laudonnière had their ringleaders executed. But famine supervened, and the colonists who had landed had only one thought, which was to look for gold. John Hawkins, the famous English navigator, sold these starving people a ship to take them back to France.

At this point, however, in August, 1565, Ribaut made his appearance again with seven ships of large tonnage, carrying about seven hundred men, craftsmen as well as soldiers, and two hundred women. A few days later a fleet was sighted out to sea. They were Spanish vessels. Philip II could not suffer Frenchmen, and above all French heretics, to " install themselves so close to his conquests, so that the very ships coming and going from New Spain would be constrained to pass by them ". By an agreement signed on March 22nd, he had commissioned Captain Pedro Menéndez de Avilés to occupy Florida.

The Queen of Spain warned her mother about her husband's decision. The Duke of Alba claimed this territory which the Spaniards had discovered during the reign of the King Don Fernando (Ferdinand the Catholic) as Spanish, and angrily declared that Philip would use all his resources to take possession of it. The ambassador of Spain in Paris demanded that the Queen-Mother should disavow the Huguenot enterprise. Catherine, stung in her pride, retorted that this territory was " ours, as its name of Bretons' Land already testifies sufficiently ".

As a matter of fact, the Spaniards had no better right than the French to this no-man's-land ; but they were determined, and better prepared, to assert the rights which they arrogated to themselves. Elizabeth instructed Fourquevaux to warn Charles IX and the Queen-Mother that the King and the Duke of Alba had made up their minds to expel the French, " and if they are victorious Your Majesties will hear very sad news of your subjects, whom they will cruelly put to death ".

The thing was already done. Menéndez, who had sailed from Cadiz with a fleet manned by two thousand men, arrived too late to surprise Fort Caroline, where Ribaut had forestalled him. He proceeded to establish himself farther to the south, on the estuary of the Dauphins River, and built Fort Saint Augustine there.

Ribaut embarked all the sound soldiers he had to go and attack him ; but a storm drove his ships on shore, where he landed with only a few hundred survivors. Menéndez, informed of this disaster, made his way through the marshes to Fort Caroline, which he knew was weakly garrisoned, took its remaining defenders by surprise, and butchered them. Only Laudonnière himself, the artist Lemoyne de Morgues, whose sketches illustrate the melancholy history of French Florida, and a few others escaped to the ships anchored inside the May River, and succeeded in making their way to England, where they landed in November 1566, carrying the frightful news.

Meanwhile Ribaut and his comrades, making their way overland to Fort Caroline, where they expected to find Laudonnière, ran into the Spaniards and beat a retreat. They were pursued by the victors, were ambushed or surrendered, and all of them, with the exception of a few Catholics, were killed in cold blood (7).

When Philip heard of this last massacre, he had the audacity to demand from Charles IX punishment of the French admiral, " as a disturber of the peace and the cause of the disorder which had occurred ". Catherine, exasperated by a demand that aggravated the affront which had been laid upon her son, required chastisement of Menéndez, " a fine executioner rather than a good soldier ". She had the humiliation of learning that Philip II, far from reproving this terrible butcher of his in the least, recalled him to Spain only to load him with honours.

A simple gentleman, Dominique de Gourgues, dared to do what Catherine had not the courage to attempt : resort to arms. Sailing from Bordeaux on August 2nd, 1567, with three ships of which the largest was only 250 tons, manned by some two hundred sailors and arquebusiers, de Gourgues surprised the two forts constructed by the Spaniards and the earlier Fort Caroline, and hanged such of their defenders as were not killed in action. A year later, he returned to La Rochelle. Philip II put a price on his head ; and Charles IX was not ashamed to forbid him to appear at Court.

Without any such impetuous taking-up of arms by the Huguenots, events in the Low Countries would have sufficed to avenge the insults offered to the King of France. Before his departure for Spain, Philip had organized the administration of the Low Countries as best he could in accordance with his ideas and interests. Charles V's sister Marie, Queen Dowager of Hungary, longing for rest like her brother, and also not on the best of terms with her nephew, declined to continue the Regency which she had exercised for the past twenty-five years. Christine of Denmark, Duchess Dowager of Lorraine, who had acted as mediator at the congress of Cateau-Cambrésis, put forward her claims to it.

But Philip, fearing lest the marriage of Christine's son, Charles III of Lorraine, with Henri II's daughter might predispose her too much in favour of the Court of France, chose instead an illegitimate daughter of the Emperor's, Margaret, married to the Duke of Parma, Octavio Farnese. Philip had restored Piacenza to the Duke, and he had also taken charge of his and Margaret's son, his own nephew, Alexander, for the purpose of bringing him up in Spain—and also, perhaps, holding him as a hostage for his parent's good behaviour. In order to keep an eye on Margaret and influence her in her policy as Regent, Philip placed beside her the cleverest of his statesmen, the Bishop of Arras, Antoine

Perrenot de Granvelle, the successful negotiator of the peace of Cateau-Cambrésis.

To the posts of governors of the different provinces Philip nominated those of the great lords who had served him best in camp or council. To the Count of Egmont he gave Flanders and Artois ; to William of Nassau, Holland, Zeeland and Utrecht ; to Florent de Montmorency, Lord of Montigny, French Flanders ; to the Count of Aremberg, West Friesland ; to the Marquis of Berghes, Hainault ; to the Count of Mansfeldt, Luxemburg ; to the Count of Megen, Guelderland, etc. ; and to Philip de Montmorency, Count of Hornes, the Admiralty, instead of a province, which he did not want to give him.

To the Council of State Philip added the Prince of Orange and the Count of Egmont, the two most eminent leaders of the aristocracy, to whom he also gave *mercedes* (gifts of money). He imagined that he had provided against everything ; but he was leaving behind him a country exhausted by war, overladen with taxes, and discontented both by its Sovereign's religious fanaticism and by his political pretensions.

When Philip assembled the States-General at Ghent, on August 7th, 1559, in order to take leave of them and invite them to vote him subsidies, Granvelle set forth his requirements and, in his name, declared that the Government would " apply zealously and exactly the edicts and decrees promulgated by the Emperor and renewed by the King for the extirpation of all sects and heresies ". On the same day Philip wrote to the Grand Council of Malines and to the provincial Councils bidding them apply these decrees in all their rigour, without distinction of persons, and threatening to punish any judges who should be lax in their duty through favouritism and connivance. The edicts were not to be read as applicable only to the Anabaptists ; they were applicable—and without mercy—to all " those who may be merely contaminated by the articles and errors introduced and maintained by the said Luther " (8).

It was a solemn undertaking on Philip II's part to pursue Charles V's policy of extermination, without any consideration whether the present time and its difficulties did not counsel some change of system.

Immediately after the conclusion of the peace of Cateau-Cambrésis, Philip had disbanded the bulk of his troops, among others the contingents of the Low Countries. But, perhaps from lack of money, he was in no hurry to embark for Spain or Italy three or four thousand men, the great majority of them Spaniards, divided into two "*tercios*", as these regiments of his were called. The ruling passion of the Belgians at this period, as we know, was hatred of foreigners. They had all the more reason for detesting these soldiers, who, almost always left without pay by a King who was always in debt, went on pillaging and devastating the country as though it were still war-time.

The inhabitants of Walcheren refused to work on the dykes as long as these marauders and robbers were quartered in their island, preferring to be submerged by the sea rather than tyrannized over by this soldiery.• The fighting men of the Low Countries were indignant that the King should not regard them as capable of defending themselves against invasion ; and public opinion went so far as to suspect him of wanting to make use of these mercenaries to reduce the Belgians, despite their franchises, to the condition of the Milanese and the Neapolitans.

Granvelle had said nothing about the departure of the *tercios*, which the whole of the Low Countries demanded ; but, when the States reassembled to reply to his speech from the throne, the deputy for Ghent, who presided over the assembly, begged their Sovereign to withdraw these foreign troops and to close the Councils to entrance by foreigners. Philip, exasperated by this request, is said to have left the hall where the assembly was being held. " Why not demand, too," he asked, " that in my capacity as a Spaniard I should leave the country and renounce any authority over it ? "

This angry scene may not actually have taken place, but the anecdote as a whole symbolizes perfectly the misunderstanding between the prince and his subjects. It is more probable that he held himself in ; and, after reflection, he promised to embark these hated troops of his before the following January 1st. To allay suspicion, he placed them under the command of the Count of Egmont and the Prince of Orange. But he did not keep his promise, and postponed their departure until a year later. It was the first example of those shufflings and breaches of engagements which in the long run alienated the sympathy of his people from him (9).

The lords were also discontented. Even the most favoured of them, such as Egmont and the Prince of Orange, found that the King gave them no real share in the administration. He had nominated them to the Council of State, which transacted important affairs ; but secret instructions from Philip authorized the Regent, in her distribution of offices, charges and benefices, to take the advice only of three Councillors : the Count of Berlaymont, a good soldier who did what he was told ; Viglius der Zuychem ab Atta, a learned Frisian jurisconsult, trained to habits of obedience ; and the Bishop of Arras, Antoine Perrenot de Granvelle. This inner Council, or " *Consulta* ", as it was called, nullified the authority of the Council of State.

Granvelle, with his experience and his gift for affairs, his capacity for work and his keen and profound intelligence, was the natural inspirer of Margaret of Parma and the hidden head of the Government. The " great masters " as Egmont and Orange, with the addition of Hornes, were called, dissatisfied though they were with his function, appreciated his merits. When they found themselves pushed into the background, as the result of the position which he occupied in the foreground, they imputed to him, in the complete good faith of men in opposition, the design of abolishing the franchises of the Low Countries and controlling everything by the royal will alone.

In the Seventeen Provinces there were originally only three bishoprics : Arras, Tournai, and Utrecht, which did not cover the whole territory, although the jurisdiction of the last two was very extensive. The diocese of Utrecht alone, the greatest of all of them, comprised eleven hundred parishes and more than two hundred walled towns. The part of the Low Countries not under the jurisdiction of the local bishoprics was dependent, from the religious point of view, either upon French bishops, such as the Archbishop of Rheims and the Bishops of Metz and Verdun ; or upon German bishops (Trêves, Cologne, Münster, Osnabrück, Minden, Paderborn) ; or upon sovereign bishops or bishops residing in Imperial cities, such as those of Liége and Cambrai.

The result of this state of things was that the bishops of the Low Countries were too few to fulfil their office of shepherds and watchers over their flocks as well as they would have liked, and that the intervention of outside dioceses in internal affairs was liable to provoke conflicts of all kinds. Accordingly Charles V, in the course of his reign, negotiated with the Court of Rome the creation of six new bishoprics.

Philip II thought that this was not enough, and he obtained from Pope Paul IV, on May 12th, 1559, a Bull which instituted fourteen : Antwerp, Bois-le-Duc, Bruges, Ghent, Ypres, Ruremonde, Namur, Saint Omer, Haarlem, Middelbourg, Leeuwarden, Deventer, Groningen, and Malines. This last, raised to an archbishopric, was to be the metropolitan see of the thirteen others.

In order to endow these new bishoprics without adding to the charges on the country, Granvelle proposed, and the King agreed, to add rich abbeys to them. It was not a matter of suppressing these abbeys, or even reducing the number of monks in them, but merely of having their estates administered by priors or provosts and reserving a part of their revenues to the bishop.

This project excited intense opposition in all the provinces. The monks did not want to sacrifice any of their revenues, or to be made responsible in any way to the ordinary (diocesan bishop). The lords were irritated because they had not been consulted. The provincial States of Brabant, nicknamed the Devils of Brabant because of their proverbial pig-headedness, sent a deputation to Philip II to complain that he had violated the article of the " Joyous Entrance " which forbade the Sovereign to alienate the rights of the abbeys.

Philip explained that the article in question did not permit him to confer the benefices upon laymen or even seculars, but did not prevent him from diverting the revenues to bishops—a distinction, it must be admitted, which was a little subtle. As the States of Brabant persisted in their opposition, he abandoned the idea of creating a bishopric of Antwerp for the time being, and concluded on July 30th, 1564, a concordat with the abbots of Brabant which maintained the abbeys of Saint Bernard, Tongerloo and Afflighem in their existing status, but obliged them to contribute a sum of eight thousand florins a year to the maintenance of the Archbishop of Malines and the Bishop of Bois-le-Duc.

Naturally the States imputed the idea of this new ecclesiastical organization to Granvelle. As a matter of fact, the King had not taken him fully into his confidence about the project, and Granvelle's rôle had been limited to that of suggesting a way of maintaining the new bishoprics without burdening the faithful. The actual change was not advantageous to Granvelle himself. He was transferred from the diocese of Arras, diminished by the creation of the new bishoprics, to the new diocese of Malines, and, though he became the Primate of the Low Countries, it was at a financial loss. But public opinion ran strongly against the Minister, whom it accused, quite wrongly, of taking a roundabout way of introducing the Spanish Inquisition into the Low Countries.

The Inquisition of the Low Countries was itself drastic enough. It had claimed at least fifty thousand victims, in a country, it was true, which was exposed to the penetration of heresy by land and sea. But the Inquisition of Spain, even though it had ceased burning, for lack of refractory Moriscos and Judaisants, had a sinister reputation. The secrecy of its procedure invested it with horror. Besides, it was a foreign tribunal, an outside institution, which even the Catholic Flemish detested from national prejudice.

Granvelle, who had been appointed Cardinal in February, 1561, advised the King to reassure public opinion. " It is necessary that Your Majesty should impress clearly upon their minds (the minds of his subjects) that you have never thought of introducing the Inquisition of Spain into these countries, since *this is the honest truth*. . . ." Philip, in a letter to the Regent, dated July 17th, 1562, affirmed that neither the Cardinal nor himself had ever thought of it. In any case, was not the Inquisition of the Low Countries even more drastic than that of Spain ?

But the great lords, jealous of Granvelle, believed—perhaps in good faith—in the suspicions which made him hateful. The Prince of Orange, brought up by one of the sons of Granvelle's chancellor, Jerome, had at first been on cordial terms with the Cardinal, who had persuaded Philip to authorize his marriage with a Lutheran princess, Anne of Saxony, and dissuaded the Pope from putting his principality of Orange, where heretics swarmed, under seques- tration. Orange declared himself so much obliged for Granvelle's good offices " that," he assured him in a letter in 1560, " all my life I shall be at your command as your servant and very good friend ". Less than a year afterwards, Orange forgot his protesta- tions of eternal gratitude. Had not Margaret and her Minister nominated magistrates in Antwerp without consulting him—him, the hereditary Burgrave of the city ?

There was another, and a more serious, grievance which Orange and his colleague on the Council, the Count of Egmont, set forth to Philip in July of the same year. Since His Majesty's departure, they had been " most frequently " summoned only " in connection with matters of little or no importance, while major matters were dealt with by one or two persons without their knowledge. The result was that everybody jeered at them as having titles and nothing else. They would, however, have kept their patience . . . if the Cardinal had not taken it into his head to declare in Council that all the Councillors would be equally responsible for events which might occur. So that they should not have to answer for what was done without their consent, they begged the King to accept their resignations or to order that all affairs should hence- forth be communicated, debated and decided in full Council of State."

At table, where the lords usually deliberated, they drank deeply and talked loftily. In the course of their interminable banquets they proclaimed their discontent. Sometimes they let themselves go in unseemly remarks about the King, but it was especially Granvelle whom they condemned. After drinking enough, they had boyish inspirations. Brederode, always excitable, decided to wear a fox's tail in his hat by way of a plume, intending to signify by this that the Cardinal, that old fox, would not leave the Low Countries without losing his tail. The chambers of rhetoric, those literary societies, made game of Granvelle, and a diplomat out of a job, Simon Renard, a native of the Franche-Comté like him, who had negotiated the English marriage and did not consider himself adequately rewarded, cut Margaret's all-powerful Minister to pieces in anonymous pamphlets which were circulated everywhere.

This opposition, whether flaunting or fugitive, disquieted the Regent. As she was afraid of assembling the States-General, she called a conference in Brussels, in May, 1562, of the knights of the Order of the Golden Fleece, an aristocracy within the aristocracy. Then, disturbed by a meeting which was held at the Prince of Orange's house, by the talk which was communicated to her and by the complaints against Granvelle, she sent Florent de Montmorency, Count of Montigny, to Spain to set forth the country's grievances to the King. He returned in December without securing much satisfaction.

Again during the following year the Prince of Orange, Egmont and Hornes wrote to the King, denouncing Granvelle to him as the person responsible for all the trouble. When Philip invited them to Madrid for the purpose of coming to an understanding with him, they disclaimed any desire to adopt the position of a " party formed against " the Cardinal. As great lords they esteemed that a " simple and brief advertisement " on their part " might suffice to move " His Majesty, and dispose him to employ " this personage in another place where he could serve more fruitfully in accordance with his profession and vocation " (10).

They proceeded to form an alliance with the Marquis of Berghes at a meeting held at Eyndhoven. They could also count upon the pressure applied by the States of Brabant, assembled at Brussels in December for the purpose of voting the subsidy intended for the maintenance of the garrison for a further period of three years. They put the King in the position of having to dismiss Granvelle, that good servant of his.

Philip took six months to reply. He did not want to look like giving way, but give way he must. At the same time as he sent the " great masters " a stiff letter, which implied refusal, he wrote secretly to Granvelle, on February 23rd, 1564, bidding him retire to Burgundy, as though he were going there on his own account to visit his sick mother. Granvelle left within three weeks, and kept his secret so well that as late as the middle of the nineteenth century it was still being asked whether his retirement was voluntary or not. (It was Gachard who finally discovered the King's letter.) The Prince of Orange and the Count of Egmont resumed their seats on the Council.

But the Regent, who had let Granvelle fall because she was jealous of him, soon found that satisfying a few great lords was not enough to allay trouble. The religious problem was much more difficult to solve. Calvinist preachers, animated by an ardent proselytizing spirit, were insinuating themselves into the Low Countries everywhere and winning over to their Church—among what was left of the Lutherans and Anabaptists, and also among the Catholic masses—converts who, like those in France, hated the persecuting power and were no longer resigned to martyrdom. The populace of Valenciennes broke into the prison to free two ministers condemned to the flames.

Granvelle's removal increased the boldness of the Protestants. Precisely in the year 1564, Pontus Payen tells us in his *Memoirs*, the heretics, who hitherto had hidden themselves, were now making overt profession of their faith, " singing openly and publicly Clement Marot's canticles which they call the Psalms of David ". The Anabaptists raised their heads again. The Inquisitor Titelmans denounced seven of their communities at Ypres, Poperinghe, Menin, Armentières, Hondschoote, Tournai and Antwerp.

These Anabaptists of Flanders had as their " sovereign prince " Joachim the Sugarer, whose name sufficiently indicates his social condition and the revolutionary tradition of Münster. There were other places in Flanders which were contaminated : Ghent, for example. Moreover, adds Titelmans, " I do not speak of the Lutherans and Calvinists who are in the country in great numbers and come and go every day to and from England, principally by way of Nieuport." In Antwerp there were so many of the faithful that, to administer the sacrament to all of them, twenty-five to thirty meetings had to held, " inside as well as outside the town ".

If one admits an average of eighty to a hundred of the faithful at each of these meetings for prayer and worship—this is the figure given by Titelmans for Armentières—that would make two thousand five hundred or three thousand communicants in Antwerp altogether. No doubt the English agent exaggerates when, two years later, he reckons forty thousand Protestants in this town, of whom fifteen thousand were Calvinists. But outside this great port they were also numerous, especially in the districts bordering on France. The Inquisitors got tired of hunting them out, prosecuting them and punishing them, as Titelmans's letter shows.

Even among the Catholics many were doubtful about the efficacy, and indeed the legitimacy, of the repression. "Many great personages of that time, good Catholics, whose profession was jurisprudence," Pontus Payen tells us, "refused to take part in criminal proceedings based upon the proclamations" of the late Emperor Charles V, "as it seemed to them a cruel thing to condemn a man to death for his opinions, even though they disapproved of them".

The Prince of Orange, while protesting that he meant to live and die a Catholic, declared in full Council of State that he "could not with a clear conscience approve the excessive power which kings and princes arrogated to themselves of controlling their subjects in their consciences and giving them such a form of worship as seemed good to them" (11). The leaders of the aristocracy and public opinion pronounced themselves so strongly against the blind and furious persecution that Margaret agreed to send the Count of Egmont to Spain, charged with the duty of representing the country's state of feeling to Philip II.

The King gave this envoy a good reception. In the Instructions which he handed to Egmont on his departure, Philip declared that, though "he would lose a hundred thousand lives, if he had them", rather than suffer that there should be any change in religion, at the same time he would permit his sister to assemble, "together with the Council of State, two or three bishops, some theologians, and other counsellors not superior in number to the number of the bishops", to consider whether there were not means of punishing heretics other than those hitherto employed. In the conversations which he had with the Count, he is said to have agreed that Anabaptists who abjured the error of their ways should not be put to death without possibility of pardon.

But Egmont had scarcely returned to the Low Countries when, contrary to the assurances which he carried with him, letters arrived from the King ordering the strict application of the proclamations. In response to the observations addressed to him by Margaret, who was dumbfounded by his change of front, Philip drafted his famous letters from the Wood of Segovia, dated October 17th, 1565. In these letters he commanded her to support the Inquisitors in carrying out their duties, refused to suspend the strictest observance of the proclamations against the Anabaptists, and attributed the ills from which the Low Countries were suffering to the negligence, indifference, and double-dealing of the judges. He announced his intention of dismissing those who were afraid or unwilling to enforce the proclamations, and declared that his decision was "in conformity with the good of religion and of my said countries in those parts, which would be worth nothing without it ".

The most spirited and most resolute members of the nobility met in Brussels in January, 1566, and signed a proclamation against the maintenance of the proclamations and the strengthening of the hands of the Inquisition as tending towards the ruin " of the authority and virtue of the old laws, customs, and ordinances ", and as calculated to incite the people to rebellion and lead to horrible confusion and disorder of all kinds (12).

They swore fidelity and aid to one another " as brothers and faithful comrades ", protesting " that in such and similar cases no crime of rebellion can be alleged, in view of the fact that the source proceeds from a holy zeal and a laudable desire to maintain the glory of God, the majesty of the King, the public peace, and the security of our persons and property ". This declaration was signed by three names : Henry of Brederode, Charles of Mansfeldt, and Ludwig of Nassau, and the nobles of all the provinces were invited to subscribe to this "compromise", as the petition was called. It was circulated throughout the provinces, and received hundreds of signatures : perhaps as many as a thousand. The Prince of Orange, Egmont and Hornes held themselves aloof—not because they had changed their minds about the King's policy, but because they regarded this project of a league as seditious.

With a numerous retinue of nobility, Brederode boldly went to Margaret on April 5th and presented a requisition demanding the suspension of the proclamations and of the Inquisition, in anticipation of such a decision by the King. The Regent promised to moderate the enforcement of the proclamations ; but this did not satisfy the confederates. They returned to the charge, and she gave way.

All these manifestations were accompanied by banquets, at which these distinguished drinkers performed prodigies with goblets. One evening of relaxation after the fatigues of the day, Brederode is said to have hung a wallet around his neck, and, seizing a porringer, to have drunk to the health of the confederates with the toast : " Long live the *Gueux* (beggars) ! " Presumably he meant to convey by this that they would persist in their plans, even if they were reduced to begging like mendicants. In any case, the name " *Gueux* " became a party name.

Warned by his sister about this threatening agitation, Philip, on July 31st, agreed to suppress the Inquisition ; but it went to his heart. On August 9th, in the presence of the Duke of Alba, he signed before a notary a secret protestation against the violence which had been done to his feelings, and reserved to himself the right to punish those who were responsible for it, and especially the authors and promoters of sedition. He excused himself, and almost congratulated himself, for not having had time to consult the Pope about the abolition of the Inquisition. Inasmuch as only the Pope could abolish what a Pope had instituted in the Low Countries, he deemed himself at liberty in his own conscience to go back upon concessions which he had no right to make. So much the better if he could settle religious affairs without resort to force ; but he was quite determined to resort to it if necessary. He would rather lose all his States and a hundred thousand lives, if he had them, than be Sovereign over heretics.

An end to persecution was not enough for the persecuted, who had so long been constrained to dissimulate their faith under pain of death. They proposed to manifest it openly and pray to God in their own language and in their own way. It was the same thing as in France in 1562, when semi-tolerance was conceded. Prayer meetings were held everywhere. Flanders began them, and the other provinces followed suit. Out in the country, or at the gates of towns, hundreds, even thousands of the faithful assembled to listen to the Word of God. The men went armed ; sentries guarded the approaches to these improvised churches under the open sky. The minister climbed a rough pulpit, and spoke at length, without wearying them, to crowds greedy for God's Word (13).

Meanwhile sinister rumours were in circulation. It was known that Philip was raising levies in Germany. In the name of the merchants and the common people, a request was addressed to the nobility, asking for their protection. The leaders of the Gueux met at Saint Trond and promised every possible assistance to the populace and merchants, to the Lutherans and Calvinists, and decided to arm. On July 26th they sent twelve delegates to Margaret, begging her to accept the Prince of Orange and the Counts of Egmont and Hornes as guarantors of security until the con-vocation of the States-General. Margaret was so furious at this insolent request that, so Ludwig of Nassau says, " she nearly died ". But she could find no support among the nobility, except for the Count of Mansfeldt, who had just deserted the camp of the Gueux. She made a few concessions.

Prayer-meetings continued. The Calvinist ministers, who were the most fiery, the most zealous, the most violent against Papistry, attracted the largest congregations. The rigorous logic of their doctrine appealed to the masses. They had been brought up on the teaching of Calvin, or even on his own words. Some of them, the most eminent, were men of education and even of French origin : Jean Taffin, minister of the church of Metz ; Philippe de Marnix de Sainte-Aldegonde ; François de Join (better known under his Latin name of Junius) ; Pellegrin de La Grance, a Provençal gentleman.   In France and in the Low Countries they strove, at the risk of their lives, for the triumph of the pure Gospel and the defeat of superstition and abuses.

The pomp of the Catholic ceremonial, the decoration of altars, the images of Christ bleeding and crowned with thorns, the representation of Saints in their torments and their triumphs—all these enchantments of the imagination and the eyes seemed to these disciples of Calvin a vestige of paganism, a form of idolatry.   They proclaimed the fact very loudly in the presence of the faithful, to whom this worship of images might be a matter of scandal and an occasion of back-sliding ; and, without realizing the consequences, they aroused passions which suddenly exploded.

Without warning, a fanatical populace swarmed into the churches, flung down the Christs and the statues of the saints, tore off the costly vestments of the Virgin, smashed organs, and scattered pyxes and the consecrated Host on the ground.   It committed, so far as that went, no personal violence ; it respected priests, monks, and nuns ; it did not carry off the treasures of the churches.   It destroyed for the sake of destroying, with the wild zeal of iconoclasts.

In Antwerp, where there were several thousand Calvinists, all the churches were sacked.   The Cathedral, a regular museum of the art of the Middle Ages, was left stripped, cold and empty after the passage of the sectaries.   In Flanders, in the course of three or four days, more than four hundred churches were devastated. In Brabant, in Holland, in Zeeland and in other provinces, the work of destruction was no less brutal.   The movement was so sudden, so spontaneous, that the authorities found themselves as powerless " as though it had been a cloudburst, a storm of thunder and lightning, which broke everywhere at the same time " (14).

The " *Beeldstorm* ", as this attack upon images was called, provoked an enormous scandal.   It compromised the cause of the confederates, and all but ruined it.   The Catholic lords, indignant at this profanation, withdrew from the impious league.   Egmont offered his services to the Regent.   The Prince of Orange, who secretly blamed the sectaries but did not dare to declare himself openly against them, became suspect by all parties.

Margaret, with her hands strengthened by this reaction, resorted to arms against the image-breakers and the trouble-makers.   She

put garrisons into the towns. She stormed and punished Valenciennes, which refused to open its gates to her. The few thousands
of men who took up arms for the Calvinists were beaten in the
spring of 1567 in Hainault and at Austruweel, under the walls of
Antwerp.

The rebels were vanquished, and the Low Countries seemed
submissive. But Philip felt that this was not enough to avenge
his authority and God's authority. He made ready for chastisement.

CHAPTER VI

THE "TRIBUNAL OF BLOOD"

PHILIP might have left the responsibility for carrying on the work of pacification to Margaret. The "great masters" would have helped her in it, out of interest in maintaining order and from a sense of loyalty. It would have been better still if he had decided to appear in person in the midst of his subjects in the Low Countries, for the purpose of assuring them that, like Charles V, he regarded them as the equals of the Spaniards. The moment would have been well chosen to exploit in favour of his authority, and of his faith, the reaction of disgust and anger which the fury of the iconoclasts provoked among the Catholic masses.

He had been foreshadowing such a visit for a long time, and now he seemed more than ever decided to pay it. He wrote to Margaret in May, 1566, that such was his intention, and he informed her in July, after deliberation with his Spanish and Belgian councillors, that he would arrive in the spring of 1567 at the latest. When he learnt of the sack of the images, he stated definitely, at the end of September and again at the beginning of October, that he would hasten the preparations for his journey.

Whether there was, or was not, a debate in the Council of State on October 26th or 29th, his Ministers were certainly, as usual, divided in their opinions (1). The partisans of the Prince of Eboli thought it would be a good thing for the King to go himself and re-introduce order into Flemish violence. The Duke of Alba, on the contrary, maintained that, without waiting for the presence of the Sovereign, it was essential to suppress as quickly as possible, to drown in blood, " a revolt which involved the defence of religion, of Divine worship, of churches, of sacraments, of images and of ministers of God ".

This was the feeling of the King, expressed by the man whom he had already chosen as his agent of execution. But, in accordance with his custom, Philip took time for reflection, and meanwhile informed the Regent that he had made up his mind to go to Flanders, with a strong escort. He did not say a word about the Duke of Alba.

He conveyed a strong remonstrance to Pope Pius V, who, doubtful about his intention of leaving Spain, sent the Bishop of Ascoli to him as ambassador extraordinary, in order to repeat his advice that Philip should go in person and pacify the Low Countries. " If he had not already made up his mind, as he had ", to go there, this mission of the Bishop of Ascoli's, " which might give the whole of Christendom a bad opinion of him (Philip) ", " would have been a bad way of persuading him to do so ". At the opening session of the Cortes of Castile, on December 11th, 1566, in the palace at Madrid, over which Philip presided, his secretary Erasso, who read the speech from the throne, said that the expedients employed by the King to pacify the Low Countries had not sufficed, and that it was necessary for His Majesty " to proceed there in person, in order to apply the real and radical remedy which the state of affairs demands ".

Accordingly, the Duke of Alba, as Grand Master of the King's household, warned all the officers and servants under his orders to hold themselves in readiness to start at the end of May or the beginning of June. The Duke of Francavilla, Viceroy of Catalonia, was sent to Barcelona to make preparations for the King's embarkation there, together with the Queen, the Prince of Asturias (Don Carlos) and the Archdukes of Austria, Rudolph and Ernest, then in Madrid.

The Duke of Alba, entering into the spirit of the King's game, prolonged his own stay in Madrid until mid-April. Then he proceeded to Carthagena to embark, and there he received his commission as Captain-General in the Low Countries and the instructions which accompanied it. He complained about the minute orders which were given him, contrary to what was usual in his relations with the Emperor and indeed with the King himself, as though hitherto he had shown himself lacking in his handling of finances and his disciplining of men-at-arms.

During the following months, Philip kept on convincing the world of his firm intention to proceed to Flanders ; but now it was not to be by way of Italy and Germany, which would unduly prolong his journey. He would go by sea, embarking at Corunna, and he charged his ambassadors with the duty of informing Rome, Portugal, the Emperor, France, the Regent of the Low Countries, and Cardinal Granvelle of the fact. In July he caused a statement to be published in Madrid that, despite the attempt of the Cortes to dissuade him, he proposed to start for the Low Countries at the earliest possible moment. That moment never came.

Philip had informed his sister, six months earlier, that he was being preceded to Flanders by the Duke of Alba, who was appointed Captain-General, in order to control the march of the troops, concentrate them near the frontier, " quarter them in places where they would do the least damage and maintain discipline among them ", pending Philip's own arrival in the provinces, " and finally to raise a levy great or small " according to the needs of the moment.

Margaret was none too well pleased with this choice of his, knowing the imperious spirit of the Duke as she did ; and in her reply to Philip she urged the King's early arrival, " as being the sole means of re-establishing the affairs of the Low Countries ". She promised to maintain the " contact " with the Duke of Alba which the King commanded her to keep, " being well assured "— but was she ?—" that Your Majesty would not wish to relieve me of the authority which I exercise in your name to give it to others, since that would not be just and would, besides, have unfortunate consequences for your service ".

What would she have thought if she had known that, in the course of the two interviews at Aranjuez, in which the King bade farewell to his Captain-General, Philip had conferred upon Alba the right to seize men of quality as suspects and inflict exemplary punishment on them ; the right to treat lower-class criminals in the same way ; the right to exact forced levies ; and the right to punish towns and regulate the justice which was to be dispensed there ?

Philip had made ready for Alba the forces required for the execution of his terrible programme. Even before the explosion of the *Beeldstorm*, he had sent Margaret the necessary funds for raising three thousand cavalry and ten thousand infantry in Germany. When he learnt of this outrage against God and the saints, he hurried on his armament in all directions. He would not listen to any further talk about negotiations and compromises, which the Bishop of Ascoli urged, " preferring ", so he conveyed to Pius V, " to expose myself to the risks of war, with all the ills and disadvantages which may result from it, rather than condescend to the least thing which would be contrary to the Catholic Faith itself and the authority of the Holy See ".

He gave orders to Don Garcia de Toledo, his Captain-General at sea, to transport eight thousand men of the veteran Spanish troops who were in garrison in Naples, Sicily and Sardinia to

Lombardy; and to the Duke of Albuquerque, the Governor of the Milanese, to double the effectives of the cavalry in his governorship. He held back a regiment of lansquenets which had been raised for the relief of Malta. With the three thousand recruits whom Alba was taking with him, and the cavalry and infantry whom his sister was awaiting from Germany, Philip could be sure of having the necessary means of punishing the heretics who made trouble and fomented it.

Always short of money as he was, he had employed any means, good or bad, for laying hands on it : *servicio* from the Cortes of Castile ; extraordinary subsidy from the Kingdom of Naples ; loans voluntary and forced ; sale of a playing-cards monopoly ; sale of offices of *regidores* for life ; contributions from the clergy ; raising to the King's profit of the amount of tithe due from the richest " *vecino* " (parishioner) in every one of the parishes of his kingdoms (*escusado*). Thus he procured the six to seven million escudos which he needed.

The Duke of Alba and his men embarked at Carthagena on May 10th, 1567, on board the galleys of Giovanni Andrea Doria. Within a fortnight, having reached Genoa, the Duke assumed command of the forces concentrated in the north of Italy. Alonso de Laloo, secretary of the Count of Hornes, saw these forces at the gates of Brussels three months later. He wrote to the Count of Montigny that they consisted of forty-nine companies (*banderas*) of Spaniards and seventeen hundred Neapolitan cavalry. "The camp numbers more than twenty-four thousand, as there are to be found there any number of useless people and an extraordinary number of women—more than two thousand whores," reports another eye-witness, John of Hornes. According to him there were more than six thousand cavalry, and most of the infantry were mounted.

A Spanish document reckons eight thousand eight hundred infantry and only one thousand two hundred horse. If, as we are entitled to do, we add to these effectives an equivalent number of legitimate wives, prostitutes, camp-followers, and canteen-keepers, we arrive at a figure closely approximating to that which Laloo gives as the personnel of the camp. For the period, in view of the numbers and the quality of the combatants, this was a very strong army (2).

From the Milanese to the Franche-Comté, and from the Franche-Comté to Luxemburg, the southernmost of the Seventeen Provinces, this army had to cross or skirt two sovereign, but friendly, States, Savoy and Lorraine. Here it had a right of free passage, on condition that it did not commit any damage and bought its supplies at current prices (*transitus innoxius*). But these transient troops were so numerous, so mixed in their composition, and so notorious for their habits of marauding and pillaging that the princes and peoples on their line of march took alarm. Philip conveyed assurances to the Dukes of Savoy and Lorraine and to the Swiss cantons.

In France, which was on bad terms with him, excitement ran so high that Catherine enrolled Swiss mercenaries and restored the fortresses on the northern frontier to protect herself against any sudden attack or any attempt to influence her religious policy. The Huguenot leaders were the most zealous in recommending measures of defence and the raising of troops, for they counted upon some frontier incident to embroil the Most Christian Sovereign of France with the Catholic King of Spain, to the advantage of their co-religionists in the Low Countries. But Catherine, who realized the military strength of Spain, was not disposed to challenge it in the interests of the Reformation. She maintained a benevolent neutrality, and even sent supplies to the stages along the line of march.

Then the disappointed French Huguenot leaders started, or resumed, murmuring that the interview between the two Courts at Bayonne had led to a decision to exterminate the Protestants in France and the Low Countries. As a guarantee of Protestant security, they demanded the disbandment of the Swiss, for whose raising they had themselves pressed. They might have given more credit to the Queen-Mother, who, as soon as she had learned of the troubles in the Low Countries, congratulated herself upon her policy of moderation, and, in a letter to Philip, held it up as an example to her son-in-law (3).

Since Margaret had heard of the nomination of the Duke of Alba as Captain-General, she had had her doubts whether his powers would not reduce her own to a nullity. The orders which she received from the King while Alba was on his way to Flanders succeeded in convincing her of the fact. To abolish privileges ; to fill the offices of magistrates by officers of the King ; to construct fortresses ; to confiscate property ; to levy taxes without the consent of the States ; to pardon none of those who had done wrong ; and at the same time to disband the forces which she had raised— all this struck her as extremely difficult of accomplishment.

The Duke of Alba had assuredly been chosen to accomplish this work of violence. She would never have imagined that the King would have sent him to the Low Countries, where Alba was, she said, "so odious that he would suffice by himself to make the whole Spanish nation hated". Accordingly, when he entered Brussels, on August 22nd, 1567, she received him coldly.

The respect which Alba showed her, his protestations that he would obey her in everything, day or night, did not prevent him from acting as master. He refused to stop the enrolment of German mercenaries, which she regarded as unnecessary, or to relieve the city of Brussels, which had behaved itself well during the recent troubles, from having troops billeted in it. She complained to her brother that he had placed her in the position of a supernumerary with the Duke, who did exactly as he liked. The King ought to have ordered her to withdraw on Alba's arrival in the Low Countries, as she had herself already recommended, and not, while she was still there, allowed somebody else to come and display this extra-ordinary authority which was so humiliating for her.

Among the great lords, Egmont, Aerschot and Mansfeldt did not go to meet Alba, but awaited him at the palace in the Regent's room (4). The city of Brussels neither gave him a reception nor paid him any other compliment. Without caring what people thought, Alba bided his time for striking a decisive blow. He proposed to make an example of these " great masters " who for the past seven years had held the rights of the King and the service of God in the balance. He knew that the Prince of Orange, suspicious and wily, would not come back from Germany, whither he had retired on the first news of the approach of a Spanish army, and that the Count of Hoogstraten would not leave Cologne, where a serious wound in the hand gave him a reason, or a pretext, for staying.

As it was essential for Alba to act quickly, he decided to confine himself to striking at two of the leaders of the opposition : the Count of Egmont, who, sure of his innocence, had not left Brussels, and the Count of Hornes, who had left it only to go and com-miserate with the Count of Nuenaar on the death of his sister-in-law. To make sure of Hornes's return, Alba wrote to Nuenaar " that he had always before his eyes the good issue of the affairs of the Count of Hornes, so much so that the King would give him the reward which he deserved " (5). It was soon apparent in what a sinister sense he meant this.

Immediately after Hornes's return, Alba held a council of war to which he summoned him and Egmont, under pretext of showing them the plans of the fortifications of Thionville and Luxemburg. When they left, they were arrested and escorted to prison in Ghent. On the same day the Burgomaster of Antwerp, Straelen, and the secretaries of the Counts of Egmont and Hornes, Backerseele and Laloo, were also arrested and imprisoned. (It has been said that Alba's illegitimate son, Ferdinand de Toledo, whispered into Egmont's ear this day that he should take his best horse and flee with all speed. But it is not likely that the Duke's son should have tried to upset his father's plans out of sheer generosity.)

The Duke of Alba says that nobody raised a hand ; and, indeed, it is probable that the first effect was one of stupefaction. It was in France that the arrests provoked a revolt. The leaders of the Protestant party persuaded themselves that their suspicions and anxieties were justified. They met at the Château de Valery, Prince de Condé's house, and decided to seize the young King and possess themselves of power in order to forestall the wicked designs of which they accused the Queen-Mother. With a few thousand gentlemen whom they mobilized, they set out for the Château de Monceaux, where the Court was on holiday, thinking about nothing but hunting and feasting.

But they did not march so fast that Catherine failed to hear about it. The Constable summoned the Swiss quartered at Château-Thierry, and, under the protection of this heavy infantry, whose pikes the Huguenot cavaliers did not dare to charge, Charles IX reached Paris, where he was more or less besieged. To break the blockade, the Constable, on November 10th, 1567, attacked the Huguenots at Saint Denis, at the gates of the capital, and was mortally wounded. The Huguenots marched to effect contact with their supporters, the Protestants of Germany, and Catherine asked the Duke of Alba for help.

He promised her fourteen hundred horse : four hundred Burgundians and a thousand mounted infantry. He offered her as many troops of the Low Countries, in whom he had no great faith. But he refused her a thousand arquebusiers—Spanish, in this case. He was ready, however, to march to the aid of the Most Christian King with all his Spaniards, five thousand Germans and five hundred cavalry, if His Majesty of France had made up his mind to make an end of the heretics. Cardinal de Lorraine, that poltroon, went so far as to propose to hand over some fortified places to the Duke of Alba ; and the Duke thought that these would be admirable pledges to reimburse him for the expense which Spain might incur in France for the Catholic cause.

The Cardinal is even reported to have gone to the length of saying that, if the King of France and his brothers died, Philip might claim the crown " by virtue of the right of the Queen (Elizabeth of Valois), our mistress ". The Duke was of the same

the Emperor himself had given his daughter to Maximilian. Charles V was the more afraid to let his son-in-law administer the Low Countries, as Maximilian had the reputation of being kindly and tolerant. Charles was determined to exterminate heresy there, and the population might be tempted to appeal against his system of intolerance to the moderating will of a prince of his own blood.

Maximilian, elected Emperor on the death of Ferdinand, was inclined, as much as a matter of policy as by temperament, to compromise with the dissident confessions in Germany : the Lutherans, who were dominant all over the North, and the Calvinists, concentrated in the Palatinate, who formed a very zealous and active minority.

The troubles in the Low Countries disquieted the German princes. They were afraid that these troubles might spread across the frontier, and that the contagion of religious sympathy, the fever of proselytism, might lead to resort to arms, divisions, conflicts, perhaps even civil war, in Germany. " In all sincerity and affection," in the name of the Diet of Fulda and of all the Electors, the Emperor Maximilian recommended his brother-in-law to act " with kindliness and benignity, especially towards the knights of the Golden Fleece imprisoned and proscribed ", rather than " to persevere in the employment of harsh measures ".

Philip protested that " what was being done in the Low Countries was not at all because of religion, but because of manifest disobedience and rebellion, and that whatever was said to the contrary was a calumny of his enemies ". The Emperor, satisfied with this explanation, decided to communicate it to the conference of his commissioners with the deputies of the six Electors which was to be held at Trêves. The Duke of Alba, for his part, also affirmed to an envoy of the Duke of Bavaria that disorders and risings, and not religion, were the cause of his proceedings.

But the King disdained to reply to the Emperor, to the Dukes of Bavaria and Lorraine, and to the reigning and dowager Duchesses of Lorraine, who also wrote to him, in pressing terms, on behalf of the Counts of Egmont and Hornes. Philip was out for their blood, and he commanded, and even begged, the Duke of Alba to expedite their trial. The Duke did the best he could, sometimes spending seven hours a day on the Council of the Troubles ; but he excused himself for not proceeding faster, for it was essential " for the justification of the King before the whole world that the ordinary forms of justice should be observed ".

Public opinion was manifestly so hostile to these proceedings against the rebels and the heretics that the Council of the Troubles not only did not second its president, Alba, but even hampered him so much that he had more difficulty with its members than with the delinquents. This man of war, violent and imperious, was out of his depth in the scruples of these jurists. Juan de Vargas, a person of tarnished reputation, who had left Spain to remove himself from his own country's justice, was the only one of them who lent him a helping hand.

The commissioners whom the Duke dispatched to the provinces laboured to protect the guilty rather than to unearth them. He wrote to the King, in February, 1568, that he had recently received information that secret preaching was being carried on in Antwerp. Since he did not trust the zeal of the Margrave, he had dispatched the Provost of the Court there ; and he had arrested, in an inn, a good number of heretics—who, Alba added with ferocious irony, would never go back to any meeting of that kind again.

A few days later, he cast his net widely. " On Ash Wednesday, he arrested, in all parts of the country, sackers of churches, ministers of consistories, and those who had taken up arms against the King. Nearly five hundred were taken. He ordered that justice should be done to them in accordance with the proclamations." Everywhere he had those who had made trouble rooted out. Nevertheless, the King wrote to him impatiently from Madrid, on April 12th, that he hoped that the business of the punishment (castigo)—obviously of the major culprits—would be finished with before the arrival of his dispatch, and he looked for early news that it was.

But the Duke had a scruple. No doubt, he wrote on April 13th, the sentence on the arrested lords could have been delivered before Easter (April 18th) ; but was Holy Week a suitable time for pronouncing it ? Even to this veteran, this enthusiastic executioner of the royal vengeance, it was repugnant that sentences of death—which, according to the custom of the time, were immediately carried into effect—should be passed during those very days when the Saviour had sacrificed Himself for the salvation of mankind. After Easter, however, Alba promised to make short work of any opposition to his procedure put forward by the defence ; and on the same day he would pronounce sentence upon the absent—the Prince of Orange, the Count of Hoogstraten, etc.

Even when the condemnation of Egmont and Hornes to death was already decided upon, Alba exerted himself to prevent the resort to arms for which the Prince of Orange was making preparations in Germany. He assured Duke Augustus of Saxony, Orange's father-in-law, that, if Orange were found innocent of the offences of which he was accused, his property would be restored to him. Philip conveyed assurances to the same effect to the Emperor and the Elector, in the hope that they would prevent the raising of levies by the Prince of Orange.

But, at this very moment, Philip was protesting in a letter to Chantonnay, his ambassador in Vienna, that, if he had not chosen to proceed with the most scrupulous justice, the matter would have been settled from the very first day ; that nobody could blame him for his conduct ; and that, in any case, he would not have acted otherwise, " even though he should jeopardize his sovereignty over the country and the Heavens should fall on his head ".

It was no easy matter to dispose of William of Nassau, Prince of Orange. The Duke of Alba had made sure of his son, the Count of Buren, and sent him to Spain to be brought up in a monastery there. It was, so Alba declared, for the good of this young lord that he had embarked him in a ship, not as a prisoner, " but at the same time watched in such a way that he cannot escape ". In order to avoid any adverse criticism in Germany, he had conceived it to be his duty to do this as inconspicuously as possible. He had taken the trouble to write to Buren that this enforced journey of his was due to the King's desire that he should be trained so that he could serve Philip well.

In January, 1568, Alba summoned the father himself to appear before him. William of Orange was ready for the summons. He had raised levies in Germany, recruited troopers whom the peace of Longjumeau left without employment, and been joined by some Huguenot gentlemen. The Gueux were defeated at Daelhem, on April 25th ; but Ludwig of Nassau, William of Orange's brother, penetrated into Friesland and, well entrenched at Heyligerlee in a plain protected by lakes, dykes and marshes, awaited the attack of the Spaniards. The Count of Aremberg, that great lord of the King's party, who commanded the Spanish forces, was defeated on May 23rd and perished under arms. All the artillery and the baggage of his army fell into the hands of the Gueux.

On receipt of the news of this disaster, the Duke of Alba, before marching against the invaders of Friesland, brought the Counts of Egmont and Hornes to Brussels to be sentenced there. The sentence, pronounced on June 4th, decreed that, as persons guilty of *lèse-majesté* and rebellion, they should be beheaded by the sword ; that their heads should be affixed aloft in a public place so that everyone might see them ; and that there they should remain until His Excellency the Duke of Alba should otherwise order. Their property, landed or otherwise, rights and dues, fiefs and heritages, of whatever nature or quality, wherever they might be situated, were confiscated to the profit of His Majesty.

When the Count of Egmont heard the sentence, he wrote Philip a letter, couched in an admirable spirit of submission, in which he protested that it had never been his intention to proceed or act against the person or the service of His Majesty, or against " our true, ancient and Catholic religion " ; and he begged the Sovereign to have pity on his poor wife, his children—he had eleven—and his servants, in consideration of his past services. He ended, recommending himself to the mercy of God : " From Brussels, ready to die "—we should probably read : " on the point of death "—" Your Majesty's very humble and loyal vassal and servitor, Lamoral of Egmont " (7).

The scaffold was erected in the market-place opposite the Town Hall. Twenty-two Spanish companies—the whole of Julian Romero's *tercio*—surrounded the place of execution to hold back the populace. Without a single word of Christian resignation, such as the Bishop of Ypres, Rithoven, exhorted him to express— so we learn from Gachard—Egmont laid his head on the block. Hornes was executed after him, and their two heads, planted on pikes with iron bristles, remained exposed for some hours.

Feeling ran high—higher than it had ever run in any other century, reports President Viglius. Everybody pitied the Count of Egmont—even the Spaniards. Spectators broke through the hedge of soldiers and, pressing forward to the scaffold, dipped handkerchiefs in the blood of the two martyrs of Belgian liberties.

The Duke of Alba himself expressed his regret that he had been obliged to act in such a way against these great personages. He recommended to Philip's compassion Egmont's eleven children and the Countess of Egmont, a pious woman whose dowry would not suffice to maintain the family even for a year. Alba expressed himself doubtful whether she had the wherewithal to sup that very evening. Philip II took time for reflection until July 18th, and then said that he recommended the souls of the executed men to God. As for the Countess, he would see whether it was better to fetch her to Spain or leave her in the Low Countries. In any case, he found it just to remedy her needs.

Immediately after these executions, the Duke of Alba pronounced sentence upon the other lords *in contumacia*, and confiscated their property. The sentence on the Prince of Orange enumerated all the offences of which he had been guilty, aggravated by the fact that he owed his fortune less to the heritage of his parents than to the benefits which Charles V had bestowed upon him. Orders were given to the officers of justice to apprehend him and conduct him to Brussels under good guard.

Executions had preceded those of these great personages, and others followed them. As the commissioners charged with carrying out the Duke's orders on Ash Wednesday did not know how to interpret " consistorial ministers ", he explained that by this expression were to be understood " chiefs, superintendents, elders, surveillants, deacons, and finally all those who have in any way taken part in the affairs of the said consistories, such as by having collected money and alms or having had the charge of building and erecting the church "—in short, everybody in any way officially connected with the churches, including any odds and ends.

The arrests effected or ordered numbered eight hundred. It was not possible to execute all those who had offended God and the King. Alba, therefore, proposed to hold some of the richest among the culprits to ransom, though at the same time he was determined to show no quarter to any of those who were most deeply involved.

In Brussels itself, in this same month of June when the Counts of Egmont and Hornes perished, Alba had some notable persons beheaded (and he pretended that he suffered for it in his heart), who had received favours and marks of grace from His Majesty : on Monday, the 1st, in the Place du Sablon, eighteen of those who had been captured at Vilvorde ; on Tuesday, the 2nd, three more, two of whom had been taken under arms at Daelhem ; and then still more, to the number of twenty-three. After the Counts of Egmont and Hornes, the Burgomaster of Antwerp and Egmont's secretary, Backerseele, were dispatched without ceremony.

Then the Duke of Alba hastened to avenge the defeat of Heyligerlee. Setting out from Brussels, he marched towards Friesland with ten thousand Spanish infantry and three thousand horse. He relieved Groningen on July 15th ; and a week later his troops, thirsting for revenge, charged Ludwig of Nassau's army with such fury at Gemmingen, on the left bank of the Ems, that they put the rebels to rout and killed three thousand men. Nassau himself only escaped by swimming the river (8).

Reinforced by two thousand five hundred soldiers whom his son had brought him from Spain, Alba advanced to meet the Prince of Orange and his German relieving army. He made no attempt to prevent Orange from crossing the Meuse near Maestricht and invading the Low Countries. He did not even offer him battle when he had crossed the river. Alba contented himself, clever temporizer that he was, with hanging on Orange's flanks, counting on winter and lack of money to overcome him. This was what happened.

Weakened financially by the raising of his mercenaries, beaten in a few skirmishes, and in despair of inducing the country to revolt for the common cause, the Prince contemplated joining Condé and Coligny, who had taken up arms again and were quartered in the west of France around La Rochelle. In order to prevent him from penetrating into France, Catherine, to the great indignation of Francés de Alava, the ambassador of Spain in Paris, offered him the money he needed to return to Germany. While Orange was hesitating, she worked upon his auxiliary troops with such success that they mutinied and compelled him to recross the Moselle.

The Duke of Alba re-entered Brussels in triumph. As champion of the Catholic faith he received from Pius V a sword and hat ornamented with gold and precious stones. Swollen with pride by his easy victories, he had a statue, made out of the bronze of the guns captured at Gemmingen, erected in the citadel of Antwerp. It represented him in uniform, holding a marshal's baton in his left hand, and with his right hand stretched out towards the town, as though in promise of the blessings of protection and peace. At his feet lay a body with two heads : the nobility and the commonalty of the Low Countries. An inscription engraved on the pedestal commemorated the repression of the troubles, the defeat of the rebels, the re-establishment of religion, the reign of justice, and the return of peace, and celebrated the most faithful Minister of the best of Kings.

Philip was incensed that one of his subjects, however great he might be, should arrogate to himself a glory which belonged of right to the Sovereign. The Flemish gazed with humiliation at a monument which perpetuated the ruin of their liberties. The Duke thought that he was master, and indeed order was re-established ; but his difficulties were only beginning.

Persecution and terror drove merchants, traders, and skilled artisans who were Lutherans or Calvinists out of the Low Countries. Even under Margaret's regime, they had begun to take refuge in Elizabeth of England's dominions, so that they could pray to God in their own way.

Councillor d'Assonleville, who was in close touch with English affairs, recorded in January, 1566, that—

"the country is being depopulated . . . Daily one sees people of this country leaving for England with their families and their tools. In and around London, it is said, there are thirty thousand of these emigrants. The Queen has assigned the newcomers another great and underpopulated city, Norwich, to carry on their trades there, and in this she is thinking of advantaging herself at our expense ; and in truth she is not wrong, for by such means the cloth-trade of England is developed to the destruction of our own."

During the winter of 1565, the English, who hitherto had exported only wool, sent the Low Countries thirty ships laden with cloth, not to speak of what they dispatched by way of Emden.

The arrival of the Duke of Alba quickened both terror and departures. At the beginning he raised no objection to them. But he was not slow to realize that a country cannot be emptied of its traders and its workers without damage even to its masters. England was enriched by the brains and the labour of these *émigrés*. After the execution or holding to ransom of the eight hundred rebels arrested round about Easter, Alba admitted that internal " commerce is beginning to suffer, because foreigners dare not entrust their merchandise to the traders of the country for fear of confiscation. Among these traders themselves there is no more confidence, even between brother and brother or father and son." Prosecutions, investigations, denunciations and general dis-trust hastened the exodus of the Flemish. The number of families which left the Low Countries is estimated at a hundred thousand. That meant half a million persons—a very large number.

So this purveyor to the scaffold wearied of a profession to which he did not feel that he was born, and, on the morrow of the butchery which he had ordered, he recommended to Madrid the grant of a general pardon. " The executions," he declared, " have imprinted so great a terror upon men's minds that they believe it is intended to govern by blood in perpetuity ; and, as long as subjects have that opinion, they cannot love the King."

There was no danger, and there might be great advantage, in making an end of this regime of terror. " These people," Alba said, " are so facile that the clemency of Your Majesty would make them tender their obedience with as good a will as they tender it grudgingly to-day."

But he should not have squeezed this impoverished population dry, whereas he exerted himself to extract money out of it—a great deal of money. The Low Countries had ceased to be the " Black Indies ", which brought in as much as, if not more than, those other Indies which loaded the galleons with the precious metals of the New World. Philip's power had been largely based upon their labour; it was the taxes levied on their commerce and industry which had contributed most to the maintenance of his armies and his fleets. But the troubles had dried up this abundant source of revenue. Margaret had had to resort to her brother for money. This was a very serious change in the state of affairs. Now it was Spain that had to provide for the expenses of these rich provinces which formerly nourished her.

In order to avenge God, Alba had to resort to Spanish assistance even more than Margaret. As soon as he arrived in his sphere of operations, he received two hundred thousand ducats. But he waited in vain for forty-five thousand more. They had been seized by the Queen of England in transit. This was a great deal for the depleted royal treasury; but it was not enough for the regiments encamped as though they were in hostile country.

After the punishment of the rebellion, the Duke's great anxiety was to lighten the burden on his master and procure the money he needed himself. He proposed to make the richest of the culprits, so long as they were not the most guilty, pay ransom; to pay his soldiers out of the proceeds of a lottery, which had already been projected, but whose conditions he changed; to deprive certain towns of their privileges, and to threaten others with the same suppression, in order to make them consent to " just and honest means of finance which will be established by the King ".

Philip agreed to all this; but, as he foresaw that the States would refuse to contribute, " it will be necessary," he said, " to take measures for doing without this consent ". As all these expedients did not suffice, Alba proposed others—the levying of a tax of one-half per cent. on all property, landed estate or other; and the establishment of the *alcavala* as in Spain : a five per cent. tax on transfers of landed property, and a two and a half per cent. tax on all other sales. But this form of taxation was repugnant to the habits of the people of the Low Countries, and, even on the Council of the Troubles, Alba did not meet with the approval which he expected. President Viglius raised a conscientious scruple : it would be necessary to consult a theologian (9).

The Duke was convinced that, after his victories, the States-General would not dare to refuse his demands, and he summoned them in March, 1569—without succeeding in convincing them. They voted, it is true, renewal of the subsidies in the form in which they were already levied, and to Alba himself an extraordinary gift in recognition of his re-establishment of order; but this was all. They refused to vote the *alcavala* as a joint assembly, and

Alba was accordingly reduced to negotiating separately with the deputies of every province in order to persuade them, or constrain them, to pay for two years an annual sum of two million florins— a little less than the estimated amount of the *alcavala*—which they were to be at liberty to levy as they chose and to spend in their own territory. When this agreement expired, the King was to decide whether this compromise contribution was to be continued or the " collection " (as the *alcavala* was called) to be imposed.

Alba was the more impatient about requiring an increased yield of taxation inasmuch as money from Spain was no longer reaching him regularly. Spain's relations with England had worsened in proportion as the Queen grew more confirmed in her Protestantism. The English mariners, who were liable to imprisonment in Spain for heresy and to harrying at sea for infringement of the Spaniards' exclusive commercial monopoly, had only too many reasons to hate these Papists. As privateers or sheer pirates, they often played a part in the war of filibustering which the people of La Rochelle, who had gone over to the Reformation, carried on against the merchant marine of the Catholic King.

Ignoring the colonial pact, adventurers like John Hawkins ran cargoes of black slaves—those tougher substitutes whom Charles V had favoured in view of the exhaustion of the natives—on the coast of America, and disputed traffic in this " ebony ", which they picked up on the African coast, with the licensed purveyors of Spain. He and Drake did even worse.

The depredations of the English, the harshness of the Spanish policing of the seas, and the executions of the Holy Office embittered relations between the two peoples and their governments. In 1564 Elizabeth instructed her ambassador to make representations to Philip II, and herself remonstrated by letter with Margaret, about the acts of violence to which her subjects were exposed. The Duke of Alba's intolerant fury increased reasons for hostility. Elizabeth regarded religious disputes merely with indifference, but she was nevertheless compelled to take account of the indignation of her people against the Council of the Troubles, that " Tribunal of Blood ", whose cruelties were made public by the artisans and merchants of the Low Countries fugitive in England.

She was quite ready to create embarrassments for her Catholic neighbours, whom she knew to be her enemies, and—so long as she had not to untie her purse-strings, for she did not like spending money—to encourage the Prince of Orange, who was preparing to invade the Low Countries, and Condé and Coligny, who were in arms against the King of France. As a sort of representative of the Huguenot party, she had received in England Cardinal de Châtillon, Coligny's brother, an unfrocked and married Cardinal, who issued letters of marque to the privateers of La Rochelle and even to Englishmen eager to harry the Spaniards at sea. The English Channel was a well situated place of ambuscade, and its ports provided markets for the sea-rovers.

It was at Plymouth, where they had put in, that Elizabeth, in December, 1568, seized the Spanish ships which were carrying to Antwerp forty-five thousand ducats, intended for the pay of the Duke of Alba's troops. She set a guard on the house of the ambassador of Spain in London, Don Guerau de Espés, when he protested. She refused to receive Councillor d'Assonleville, whom the Governor of the Low Countries sent her with the same object. By way of reprisal, the Duke of Alba put an embargo on English merchandise and imprisoned English merchants.

Elizabeth gave back blow for blow, though without declaring war. Her subjects, armed for privateering, seized ships and boats, interrupted commerce and fishing. All this accelerated the ruin of the Low Countries. " If a good remedy does not come from God or the King," Arias Montanus, who was working at Antwerp on the Polyglot Bible, wrote in February, 1569, " all commerce in merchandise will be lost and many people will be ruined (*quedan destruidas*). . . . Never is war a good thing, and now less than ever, when affairs of State are such as they are " (10).

A veering in English policy prevented matters from getting worse. Elizabeth, who was following affairs on the Continent very closely, was disturbed over the good relations between France and Spain. The Duke of Alba had sent Charles IX three thousand infantry and two thousand horse, who helped the royal army to defeat the Huguenots at Moncontour, on October 3rd, 1569. Had she not reason to fear lest the Catholic Powers, victorious over the Protestants, might seek to make an end of Protestantism itself by attacking it in its refuge and place of arms, England ?

It seemed to her prudent to abstain from challenging the King of Spain, that powerful monarch, allied to the King of France. She gave Don Guerau de Espés to understand that, if Philip II sent her a negotiator with full powers, she was ready to treat about the restitution of the confiscated money. Using this as a pretext, Alba delegated one of his best lieutenants, Chapin Vitelli, whom he entrusted with the mission of making a close reckoning of the forces upon which the English Catholic party could count on behalf of the imprisoned Mary Stuart. Vitelli returned unimpressed by the resources of the rebels of the north.

Philip sent the Duke full powers to negotiate ; but he was scrupulous about not writing to that thief of an Elizabeth with his own hand. Elizabeth kept the merchandise and vessels which she had seized in her ports, while Philip had no compensation but what little he was able to seize himself. The negotiations dragged on, and it was only at the end of 1570 that an agreement for the mutual restitution of prizes—with one exception—was reached with the English commissioners (11).

Elizabeth's attitude, as well as the solicitations of the German princes and especially of his cousins, the Habsburgs of Vienna, inclined the merciless Sovereign of the Low Countries, for reasons of self-interest or policy, towards clemency. But, slow and unde-cided as usual, he took nine and a half months to decide about that general pardon which the Duke of Alba had recommended to him. Even then, he wrote asking Alba to send him a proposal in due form, together with his reasoned opinion. "It is essential," Philip declared, "for the tranquillity of these States to show them this grace, even from the point of view of the advantage to be derived from it, which will be, as Granvelle says, much greater than the profit of the confiscations."

Although Philip spoke of acting quickly, the exchange of docu-ments between Madrid and Brussels recommenced, and, for one reason or another, it lasted another whole year. Alba, who had recommended clemency in April, 1568, was exasperated by the difficulties of his administration, his lack of funds, the depredations of the English, the antipathy and hatred of his subjects, and the threats from outside. He did not commute a single death sen-tence. Philip, now that he showed himself disposed towards moderation, nominated to the Council of the Troubles a judge of the Court of Valladolid, Jerónimo de Roda, who was even more cruel than Vargas.

The murderous activity of the tribunal increased in proportion. Arrested persons were executed without proof, on mere suspicion. Woe to the suspects if they were rich ! Viglius himself, one of the judges, complained about this thirst for confiscation and blood-shedding. "Almost everybody," he wrote, "despairs of the King's clemency. Criminal proceedings never cease, and already more than eight thousand persons have been proscribed and banished, to whom must be added all those who have paid the last penalty. Let us pray God, Who holds the King's heart in His hands, to incline him towards clemency and pity ! " (12).

Before proclaiming a general pardon, the Duke of Alba pro-posed to expedite judgment upon the Marquis of Berghes and the Lord of Montigny, the one dead of disease in Spain and the other imprisoned in the Alcázar at Segovia. Berghes and Montigny were the two great lords whom Margaret had sent as delegates to her brother to try and persuade him to withdraw the proclamations and moderate his regime of intolerance. It was tantamount to asking the King to yield to the pressure of his people, to deny the religious policy of his father and himself, and to lay aside all his fanaticism and all his pride.

The King gave them a gracious reception on their arrival—Montigny arrived in June, 1566, and Berghes in the middle of August—although in his heart he had already condemned them as bad Catholics. Had they not acted lukewarmly against the Calvinists at Tournai and Valenciennes? A monk of the Order of Hermits of Saint Augustine, Fray Lorenzo de Villavicencio, made a regular job of denouncing all shortcomings towards God and the King to Philip, even shortcomings in zeal, and Philip piously accepted this fanatic's denunciations and his clamour for the death of partisans of tolerance.

According to the monk, Berghes and Montigny were the most wicked gentlemen in the world, ungrateful and perfidious. Berghes had ironically asked the Dean of Saint Gudule's : " Where in the Scriptures do you find that heretics ought to be burned or suffer the penalty of death ? " Montigny had broken fast during Lent at Tournai. He was on good terms with Coligny, d'Andelot and Cardinal de Châtillon, that trinity of heretics, enemies of the Catholic King and Our Holy Mother the Church.

After the sack of the images, Philip was more determined than ever not to let these two backsliders in the faith return to the Low Countries. But he displayed so much " good affection, love and will " towards the Low Countries and " all his subjects and good servitors there " that Montigny was taken in by him. Berghes ought not to have let himself be deceived. Once, when he heard that the King regarded him as " double-faced ", he had replied that he did not know any living soul as double-faced as His Majesty.

Back in France, and a sick man, Berghes was hesitating about rejoining Montigny in Spain when he received a letter in Philip's own hand which decided him to do so. The King received him with consideration on his arrival at Segovia. He lodged him in the castle of Valsain, where he was staying himself, and appointed him his gentleman of the bedchamber, charged with the duty of waking him in the morning and attending him at table on days when he dined in public.

But when Berghes and Montigny, after fulfilling their mission, requested leave to return, Philip kept on putting off their departure, on one pretext or another—for example, that he wanted them to accompany him on that famous journey of his to the Low Countries with which he was entertaining the whole world. They wrote to the Regent of the Low Countries requesting their recall ; and Margaret, impregnated as she was with the duplicity which was in fashion at the Court of Spain, besought the King in an " open " letter, written in French, to let them go, and confidentially advised her brother to detain them.

Berghes, whose state of health was getting worse at Valsain, was reported as needing his native air to assist his recovery. But Philip would not hear of it. It was only when he learnt that Berghes's condition was desperate that he sent Ruy Gómez to see him and tell him—after making sure that his end was approaching—that the King authorized his return to the Low Countries. But Philip expressly told his visitor not to give the sick man anything more than hope of return, if there was any chance of his being cured.

On May 21st Berghes died ; and Philip, as though by way of showing how much he and his Ministers regretted his death, and in how much esteem they held the aristocracy of the Low Countries, paid him the honour of a solemn funeral ceremony. He took good care that Montigny should not escape him, and charged Ruy Gómez and the Duke of Feria with the duty of always keeping an eye on him. Philip kept on lulling Montigny with promises until the news came of the arrest of the Counts of Egmont and Hornes. Then the King immediately ordered Count de Chinchon, the Grand Constable, to imprison Montigny in the Alcázar of Segovia.

This distinguished jailer wrote to the prisoner entrusted to his charge that, in so doing, His Majesty was showing him a great favour. "For," he said, " I have always desired to make myself agreeable to your lordship, and you would not find yourself so well off anywhere else. I am quite sure that the King will soon summon your lordship to load you with all the favours that your services and your zeal deserve." If Chinchon was not a very simple-minded man, we must recognize that this grandee of Spain, like the Duke of Alba and the Regent of the Low Countries, rivalled his master in hypocrisy.

Montigny remained in the Alcázar, under close guard, for three years. By judgment of the Council of the Troubles delivered on March 4th, 1570, he was condemned to death and to execution

156

in public as guilty of *lèse-majesté*, Divine and human. But the requisition confirming his sentence remained unpromulgated. Was it because of that preference for mystery which marked all the policy of Philip II, or because of fear lest the judicial murder of this great lord, devoted to Belgian liberties, should drive the people of the Low Countries to desperation? The King took his time to reflect about the punishment of this outstanding culprit, and even, in the course of a progress which he was making through Andalusia, deferred his decision on the date and method of Montigny's execution until after his own return to the Escorial.

Evidently what concerned Philip most was how to dispatch the condemned man with the least possible publicity. The Council of State, assembled at the Escorial eight months after Montigny's condemnation to death, was unanimously of the opinion that any public execution should be avoided, lest Montigny's family and friends should be given occasion to complain about a judgment delivered against a delinquent detained in Spain, without his being granted opportunity to be heard in his own defence. The majority of the Ministers were in favour of administering him a " mouthful " (*bocado*), or of introducing some other kind of poison into his food or drink which would make him die " little by little ". But the King, who felt that such means were scarcely juridical, pronounced that it would be better to strangle him (*darle un garrote*) in prison, in such an unostentatious way that it might always be assumed that he had died a natural death.

From Segovia, which was too close to the castle of Valsain for any mystery to be staged, the prisoner, in the course of the comings and goings of the Government and the Court, was transferred to Simancas, that gloomy fortress of Old Castile near Valladolid. With its custodian, Eugenio de Peralta, was associated an Andalusian, Alonso de Arellano, who was nominated Mayor of Valladolid, so that, between them, in order to mislead the public, they might concert " dissimulation and secrecy ".

At the outset Peralta allowed Montigny the freedom of the fortress and permitted him to communicate with anybody he liked. Then, on the ground that a note in Latin, which suggested an attempt at escape, had been found in the passage outside Montigny's room, Peralta shut him up in a tower—the one in which Charles V had detained Bishop Carillo, one of the leaders of the *Comuneros*, before hanging him—and kept him so closely imprisoned that he fell sick. A doctor, either an accomplice or a dupe, administered medicaments to him, and let it be known that his fever left no hope of cure. For the salvation of his soul, a

Dominican monk was sent to him, Fray Hernando del Castillo, preacher to the King, a learned and honest man.

This monk conveyed to the unfortunate prisoner the order for his execution. Montigny allowed " some change of countenance " to escape him. But, once this moment of surprise was over, the monk had no difficulty in preparing him for death. Montigny made his confession, received Communion, and signed a profession of his Catholic faith. In it he protested his belief in " all the articles and all the things which the Holy Roman Church teaches and believes through its head the Pope, Vicar of Christ and successor to Saint Peter ", and confessed " the truth of Purgatory and all the other things, in particular, determined by the Council of Trent ".

All Sunday, and during the evening of that day, he prayed and made acts of penitence, reading passages from the *Guia de los Pecadores*, the " Guide to Sinners ", by Fray Luis de Granada, for which he had acquired much taste while he was in prison. Arellano, in accordance with his instructions, left Valladolid on Saturday in time to arrive at Simancas a little after nightfall with a confidential notary and " him who was to perform the execution ".

Arellano let all the holy day of Sunday pass, awaiting midnight before introducing himself and his companions into the condemned man's room. Then he read Montigny the sentence of death, and, in default of a will which would be invalid, permitted him to draw up a list of what was owed to him, " provided," said the instruction, " that he did not speak of the execution which was about to take place, but drafted it as the memorandum of a sick man who felt that he was near death ".

The man condemned to an execution which was disavowed in advance requested that some bequests might be made to his servants and that seven hundred low Masses might be said for the repose of his soul. He handed the monk who attended him a gold ring which served him as a seal, and gave him a little gold chain, of no great value, for his wife, that poor Hélène de Melun who had been widowed after only four months of married life. Peralta and Arellano addressed the usual words of consolation to him. Then the executioner affixed the garrotte to his neck and strangled him—and forthwith disappeared, together with the notary and the Mayor.

The body was carried, in the early hours of October 16th, 1570, into the chapel of the fortress, and clad in the Franciscan habit, in order to hide the marks of strangulation. Peralta immediately informed the King that, despite all the care lavished on the prisoner by two doctors, his state of health had "so much disimproved that he died between three and four o'clock in the morning".

Philip II congratulated himself upon this clever piece of stage-management. "All measures were so well taken," he wrote to the Duke of Alba about a fortnight later, "that so far there is nobody who does not believe that Montigny died a natural death. If Montigny's sentiments were such as he professed externally, according to the testimony of the religious who confessed him, it is to be believed that God will have mercy on his soul." The secretary charged with drafting this letter permitted himself to add that the Devil was clever at giving heretics strength to conceal the error of their ways ; but Philip struck out this addendum, "for," he said, "of the dead one should speak nothing but good" (13).

Nothing, to Philip's way of thinking, could any longer stand in the way of the advantage which he counted upon deriving from a reconciliation with his subjects in the Low Countries. On July 16th, 1571, the Duke of Alba, supported by the Papal Legate, proclaimed in Antwerp, to the sound of trumpets, the general pardon which the King granted to all for the past troubles, with the exception of the most guilty. Pius V, even more generously, absolved "from blame and pain" all those who, within three months, should return to the bosom of the Church.

Here was amnesty at last, and doubtless it must have seemed a blessing to a people who had hitherto been handed over to the arbitrary authority of the Council of the Troubles. Thousands of suspects reconciled themselves to the Church to escape persecution : four thousand two hundred in Bruges, among whom, says the Bishop, there were scarcely a hundred guilty of any grave sin of heresy ; six thousand in Bois-le-Duc ; fourteen thousand in Antwerp.

Nevertheless, the amnesty did not produce the results which were expected of it. Granvelle admitted the fact, and Philip expressed his surprise at it. The reason was that too many persons were excluded from it, and that quite a number even excluded themselves voluntarily. The great lords, still proscribed and deprived of their property, offices, and revenues, and the relations, friends and retainers of those who had died in exile, or on the scaffold, or in the mysterious circumstances of imprisonment, had neither any interest in pacification nor any inclination towards it.

The royal pardon proclaimed forgetfulness of the past ; but it did not open the way to tolerance. It maintained the drastic regime against back-sliders in the faith. The proclamations continued to be enforced ; offences against religion and its ministers to be severely punished ; the magistrates to be constrained to lend their aid to the Inquisition ; and heretics to be handed over by the ecclesiastical judges to the secular arm, and executed within twenty-four hours (14).

All those who had definitely broken with the established Church were therefore driven, if they wanted to avoid punishment, to expatriate themselves, or to live and die with arms in their hands. All obstinate dissidents became so many *émigrés* or rebels, unless they resigned themselves to being martyrs.

But for the Duke of Alba the amnesty was the consecration of his work. He was tired of his administrative job, of his profession as a judge ; and perhaps he felt some remorse for all the blood that he had shed. At last he obtained the King's sanction of his recall. Knowing that his successor had been chosen, if not nominated, he congratulated himself upon escaping " out of this Hell ".

CHAPTER VII

THE DEATHS OF DON CARLOS AND ELIZABETH OF VALOIS

CAN we be surprised that Philip II should have treated his heretical and rebellious subjects of the Low Countries so harshly, when he even arrested and imprisoned his own son, Don Carlos? In 1568, the Prince was his only male child and the heir apparent to his monarchy; yet Philip did not hesitate to deprive him of his liberty and his rights to the crown.

For what reasons did Philip decide to restrain his son's freedom of action, as a preliminary to preventing him from succeeding him? Did he " subordinate his own flesh and his own blood ", as he said, to what he conceived to be his duty as a king? These are problems which history has sought to solve. There is a mystery about this royal family which history has applied itself to penetrating.

Don Carlos, born on July 8th, 1545, was barely twenty-three when he was closely confined under guard in his apartments and later in a tower of the Madrid palace. Our information about his childhood is not extensive; but the dramatic interest of his sad fate only emphasizes how commonplace it was. At the age of six, the Infante had the great sorrow of being separated from his aunt, Doña Juana. At the age of nine, he was entrusted to a very good master, Honorato Juan, and at first showed a taste for study, which was not to last. At the age of eleven, he was taken to see the Emperor, his grandfather, who was on his way to the monastery of Yuste. The boy amused the Emperor by his sallies, and shocked him by his unruliness and his obstinacy about getting his own way.

His governor, Don Garcia de Toledo, and his tutor also complained about his lack of application. Don Garcia de Toledo wrote to Philip II—then in the Low Countries—that it was the same thing with gymnastics and fencing as with his studies. Whatever Don Carlos was required to do, he had to be stimulated by the promise of a reward. " He has hunted sometimes, but I do not let him ride often, because I have found that he is too reckless (*muy descuidado*) to be allowed to do it without danger " (1). But of how many children, who afterwards turned out well and led good lives, might one not say the same ?

What we know about his physical condition as a child deserves more attention. He was born of very young parents—both under nineteen. For some years it was feared that he would be dumb. He was five years old before he began to speak. He stammered a little, and remained somewhat tongue-tied, until he was twenty-one. He was so delicate as a little boy that his father left him in the hands of women until he was twelve. Even when he passed under the control of men, he was still treated gently. We find that at the age of twelve he slept soundly for nine or ten hours, studied for barely two hours in the morning—from nine to eleven—dined, took a siesta and played from eleven to half-past three ; then had his tea, was given a lesson in physical exercise, and went for a walk in the country either before or after supper.

Two hours of study in all per day—obviously not much for a normal child ; but this child was not normal. " He has not a healthy complexion," writes his governor in August, 1557, " and he never has had ; but, as he is not ill, there is no occasion for anxiety about that." The next year, the governor is more optimistic : the boy is enjoying very good health, and may be expected to go on enjoying it, thanks to the regime which he is following.

But here is a curious thing. Charles V recommended the governor to keep his grandson away as much as possible from the company of women (*de la comunicación de las mujeres*). The letter is dated January 10th, 1555. Don Carlos was then in his tenth year. What strange pleasure could this little man find in feminine contacts ? One might conceivably interpret this as meaning that the Emperor was afraid lest women should bring him up too gently and give in to his whims too much ; and, indeed, in the same letter, there is a reference to his unruly temperament and the excessive liberty which he has been allowed. But, at the age of ten, he was no longer " tied to the apron-string ", as they say, and the Venetian ambassador Badoaro, who in 1557 was accredited to Charles V and Philip II in the Low Countries, says in his " Relation " that the Infante must have been very precocious and extremely attracted towards women.

Badoaro also quotes traits of cruelty in his character. When they brought Don Carlos hares which had been caught, his great delight was to see them roasted alive. The Venetian ambassador, who lived in close touch with Philip, was in a good position to keep himself informed, even from a distance. So we cannot be surprised at the anxiety to which letters from Carlos's governor, discreet as they were, began to testify.

He wrote to Charles V, now in retirement at Yuste, asking him to take his grandson to live with him for a while, so that he might make up his mind about the measures which his upbringing required. The governor confessed that his own admonitions and the discipline which he employed were not having the desired effect.

A letter from Doña Juana, Carlos's aunt, four months later, is still more pressing. " It will be rather tiring for Your Majesty to have the prince at Yuste, *but it will be the making of him.* So I beg Your Majesty to be so good as to summon him there at once, for Your Majesty cannot imagine how much it means to us all that you should do us this kindness." But Charles V was no longer in a state of health to render this service, and he died a month later.

The boy must have been troublesome and obstinate indeed if his entourage thus confessed themselves unable to control him. Did he refuse to follow the regime which his governor predicted would do him so much good ? In any case, his health ceased to be as good as it had been. He caught a fever in 1559, the very year when Philip returned to Spain. For two years it weakened him so much that he wasted away from day to day. " The said prince finds himself so afflicted and exhausted to such a point that, if he does not shake off the trouble all this winter, the frank and unanimous opinion of his doctors is that he will fall into a decline, without much hope for the future " (2).

To arrest this wasting-away of his, they advised a change of air. Philip, in October, 1561, sent his son to Alcalá de Henares, with his own illegitimate brother, Don John of Austria, and his nephew the Prince of Parma, Alexander Farnese. The fever disappeared, and Carlos grew visibly fatter. But, in the spring of 1562, he had a fall. One evening, when he was running downstairs to go and meet the gardener's daughter, he slipped, struck his head against the closed door, and gave himself a wound in the skull " as big as a thumbnail ".

The fever returned to him. He was bled several times, in accordance with the therapeutics of the period. An ointment which a Moorish quack employed with great success was tried—without any success. As his condition got worse, the famous surgeon André Vesale, attached to Philip II's service, recommended the operation of trepanning. The patient was not cured. In desperation, it was decided to exhume a Franciscan, Diego de Alcalá, dead a century earlier in the odour of sanctity. Monks brought his bones, which they put as close as possible beside the bed, and covered Don Carlos's head with the shroud. Ten days later, the fever left him.

The people, who were fond of the young prince, and the grandees, who respected him, manifested great joy at this return to life of his—though one cannot see any reason for this general sympathy other than monarchist reverence for the person of the heir apparent and pity for a prince threatened in his springtide.

The following year, the Infante seemed so far restored to health that Philip decided to take him with him to Aragon and have him recognized as his heir by the Cortes. But, on the eve of departure, the Prince fell ill again. The King, who could not put off his journey, left his son at Alcalá, and was away for a period of eight months.

Don Carlos got no better. In an hour of despair on May 19th, 1564, he dictated his testament to the mayor of the Household and Court attached to his person, Doctor Hernán Suárez de Toledo, in whom he had great confidence. Suárez wrote, and the Infante signed at the foot of every page. Manifestations of faith and devotion abound in this document, as though to testify to the orthodoxy of the testator. Certain dispositions are interesting as proof of his patriotism and generosity. He bequeathed ten thousand ducats for the ransoming of prisoners. He created an annuity of three thousand ducats in favour of Count de Alcaudete's brother, Don Martín de Cordoba, who had stoutly defended the fortress of Mers-el-Kebir against an attack by the Moors.

He also made a gift, in token of his high regard, to a girl who was now a nun, or novice, in the convent of Saint John of the Penitence, Mariana de Garcetas. Was this the gardener's daughter, and had she devoted her life to asking God's pardon for their little love-affair?

The testament reads so rationally that Gachard, the great Belgian scholar and the best documented historian of Don Carlos, believes it was dictated by a man of sound mind, who had suffered no ill-effects mentally from his fall. But persons of unsound mind, if we suppose Don Carlos to have been one, have their lucid moments, even when they have not a draughtsman to help them.

This fever-racked youth, infirm as he might be, was the most eligible match in Christendom in the eyes of parents with marriageable daughters. Catherine de Medici, who had married her elder daughter to the reigning King, would have been glad to give her younger daughter to his heir apparent. Cardinal de Lorraine, in the interests of Catholicism and his own family, put forward the claims of his niece, Mary Stuart, widow of the King of France,

François II, and Queen of Presbyterian Scotland. The support of the Spanish forces would provide her with means of withstanding the opposition of the Protestant lords and the pretensions of Elizabeth of England.

The most ardent of the match-makers was the Emperor Maximilian II, Philip's first cousin and brother-in-law, who offered his daughter Anne, in order to tighten the family bond between the Habsburgs of Vienna and Madrid by a new link. He sent his son Rudolph to Spain, in company with Baron Dietrichstein, who was charged with negotiating this marriage. From Valencia, where he had found Philip II, Dietrichstein hastened to send his Court the information which he had picked up by hearsay about the Infante.

" In many things he shows a good understanding ; and in others a child of seven would show as much brains as he does. He wants to know all about everything, and asks any number of questions, but without any discrimination *et in nullum finem*, more as a matter of habit than anything else. As yet nobody has been able to remark any high aspirations in him, or to discover in what direction his interests lie, if it is not towards the pleasures of the table ; *for he eats so much, and so greedily, that it is almost unbelievable, and he has hardly finished before he is ready to begin again.* This excess at table is said to be the cause of his sickly condition."

In other words, he suffered from worms.

Dietrichstein saw the Prince, and the picture which he paints of him, in a letter dated June 29th, 1564—still for Maximilian's benefit —shows that the hearsay came from people who were well informed. Physically, the Infante—

" is not bad-looking . . . his head is nondescript, his brow not very high . . . his chin a little long, his face very pale. Nothing about him reminds one of the blood of the Habsburgs. He is not broad-shouldered, or of much height, and one of his shoulders is a little higher than the other. He is narrow-chested ; he has a little hump on his back, at about the height of the stomach. His left leg is much longer than his right. He is weak on his legs. His voice is thin and mincing. He stammers when he starts talking, and has difficulty in getting his words out ; he pronounces his ' l's ' and his ' r's ' badly ; but, in short, he is able to say what he wants to say and manages to make himself understood well enough."

From the point of view of character, Dietrichstein's estimate is no more favourable. " He is violent, irritable to the point of fury," and so self-willed " that many people are afraid of what he might be capable of doing if he lost control of himself ". Still, since Dietrichstein has to find some good qualities in this possible husband for the Emperor's daughter, as he says frankly, at the risk of appearing tactless, he describes Don Carlos as extremely pious ; fond of trustworthy, virtuous and upright people ; affectionate and grateful to those who serve him well and faithfully ; and hospitable.

Weighing everything together, virtues and defects of body and mind, Dietrichstein concludes without enthusiasm : " Don Carlos is a frail and feeble-minded prince, but, on the other hand, *he is the son of a powerful monarch* " (3).

The ambassadors of Venice, who were not entrusted with the job of marrying the Seignury to the heir apparent to the Spanish monarchy, do not take the trouble to adorn the truth. Paolo Tiepolo, in his " Relation " of 1563, reports that the Prince is short of stature, that his face is plain and disagreeable, that his temperament is melancholic, and that for three years he has " suffered from the quartan fever, sometimes with alienation of mind : a misfortune the more notable in that he seems to have inherited it from his grandfather and his great-grandmother ".

Here is the terrible word out at last. This child was the heir to a hereditary taint. Isabel the Catholic was the daughter of a madwoman, and the mother of another madwoman, Queen Joan the Mad. Charles V, her grandson, was so slow to develop that there were fears about his intellect. This great Sovereign, unquestionably the greatest of the sixteenth century, so shrewd and practical in his genius, fell sometimes into attacks of melancholy, of mystical exaltation, of devotion at once ardent and cruel, which bordered on the neuroses of insanity.

Since Don Carlos's last accident, Tiepolo continues, " he has remained extremely weak and ailing—not that, by nature, he has ever had much health or strength . . ." He has no taste except for doing harm. He amuses himself by ordering persons who appear before him and whom he does not think worth much consideration to be whipped or bastonadoed. " He speaks slowly and with difficulty, and what he says is lacking in continuity."

Dietrichstein says that the Prince has a pretty wit, but the Venetian does not draw the same conclusion from his feeble jokes. Unlike the Spaniards—addicted by nature as they are to mutual admiration—who marvelled at his curiosity, foreigners found his questions meaningless, and his conversation pointless, and saw in them proof of lack of intellect rather than anything else (4).

Philip formed the same opinion as Tiepolo. He gave his son

hard tutoring. He exerted himself, by advice, by discipline, and by orders, to school his violent and impulsive temperament. He gave him as his governor the shrewdest and subtlest of his councillors, Don Ruy Gómez de Silva, Prince of Eboli. Carlos, who was now eighteen, chafed against any kind of control, and he was angry with his father for imposing a kind of tutelage upon him, and with his father's servant for exercising it. The King and his favourite, more convinced than ever that he was incapable of looking after himself, ignored his manifestations of discontent.

The Prince of Eboli explained to the ambassador of France, Saint Sulpice—as Saint Sulpice records in a secret letter to his Court, dated October 7th, 1564—that he was to have charge of the Infante until his marriage, " for after that his wife will take care of him ". The following year, when the ambassador of France pressed Philip II to send Ruy Gómez to Bayonne, the King replied flatly that he would not entrust his son to anybody else but Ruy Gómez, because, if one did not keep an eye on him all the time, there was a danger that he would not be where one had left him when one came back. This fear of Philip II's about his son is worth noting. A mania for playing truant is nowadays regarded as a form of disease.

As Carlos grew up, his lack of self-control, far from diminishing, degenerated into attacks of frenzy. He threatened Cardinal Diego de Espinosa, president of the Council of Castile, with his dagger, because the Cardinal had closed the theatre where his favourite actor, Cisneros, was playing. One day when he was listening, all ears, outside the door of a room where his father had assembled his Ministers in Council, and one of his gentlemen pointed out the impropriety of this indiscreet curiosity to him, he struck him with his fist. He wanted to throw a former favourite of his, Juan Estévez de Lobon, who had fallen into his disfavour, out of the window. He boxed the ears of Don Alonso de Cordoba, a gentleman of his bedchamber, telling him by way of excuse that he had been wanting to do so for the past six months. He also threatened Don Fadrique Enriquez, his major-domo, with his dagger.

These temperamental explosions of Don Carlos may not, after all, have been incompatible with his turning round and showing himself generous. But what are we to think about other brutal actions of his ? We find a mention in his household accounts of sums paid to one Damian Martín, " whose little girls had been whipped by order of His Highness ". And what are we to say about the pleasure he found in cruelty to animals ? Hernán Suárez de Toledo, his confidant, the inspirer of his testament of 1564, reproaches him with going into a stable where there were twenty-three horses and lashing them and slashing at them.

Suárez also speaks of " terrible things ", which, if they had been committed by anybody else, would have led the Holy Office to intervene with the question whether the culprit was a Christian or not. What crime was this which might have drawn down the wrath of the Inquisition ? Gachard was not able to discover what the " terrible things " of which Suárez speaks were. Let us note that it was a question of acts much more serious than not going to confession.

There was an abnormal side to Don Carlos, which was well known and was a subject of amusement. People made fun of him because, at his age, he had no mistress. He explained, by way of defending himself, that he wanted to be as virgin as his wife when he married. But the rumour ran that he was virtuous because his body would not let him be anything else. His father, perhaps for this reason, or for others, refused to listen to the proposal which Maximilian II made to him through Dietrichstein.

Don Carlos had a very keen desire to marry the Archduchess Anne, not for love of her, for he did not know her, but because he was anxious to have his own household and live independently of his father. He wanted to prove that he was fit for marriage. He saw three doctors, took drugs, and after experiment went and boasted to the ambassador about his prowess. But it was only the prowess of " a born half-wit ", if we are to believe Charles IX's cynical representative, Fourquevaux (5).

Thereupon Don Carlos started being a night-bird, a pavement roisterer, as Brantôme puts it. He permitted himself all kinds of insolences, stopping women and kissing them, or abusing them if they resisted. In his accounts are to be found mention of six false beards, and of shirts which he lost when he slept out or burned in his room to wipe out traces of his nocturnal escapades. All these extravagances of his might have passed as venial offences, a prince's pranks, as people say, if, in addition, he had not made his father uneasy.

To escape from the vigilance of which he was the object, in 1565 he contemplated flight. He confided this fine scheme of his to Ruy Gómez, who naturally imparted it to the King and took steps to thwart it. He was ambitious, and complained that his father kept him aloof from public affairs. It has been supposed, though with no proof, that he established relations with the Count of Montigny and the Marquis of Berghes, whom the aristocracy of the Low Countries had sent as deputies to Philip II to beg him to withdraw

Anderson

THE INFANTE DON CARLOS

From a portrait by Alonzo Sanchez Coello in the Prado

the proclamations—in other words the rigorous measures against the heretics. Legend will have it that Don Carlos plotted to flee to the Low Countries and make himself master there as leader of the malcontents.

The truth is much simpler. Affairs in Flanders were so disturbed in 1565 that they almost decided Philip, despite his distaste for leaving Spain, to go there and re-establish order in person. When this intention of his became known, Don Carlos, who was to accompany his father, was highly delighted. What a joy it would be to this restless mortal to go on a journey, quite a long way off! But the King—if he had ever seriously thought of leaving Spain— changed his mind, and, after the sack of the images (*Beeldstorm*), sent the Duke of Alba with an army to chastise these iconoclasts, enemies of God and the King. Don Carlos, disappointed in his hopes, was enraged with the Duke, whom also he threatened with his dagger. " Don't you go to Flanders, or I'll kill you ! "

When there was reason to believe that Philip had definitely abandoned his intention of going to Flanders in person, Don Carlos took his revenge on his father's home-keeping habits, according to Brantôme, by making up a volume entitled : *The Great Journeys of King Philip II.* Every chapter-head of it indicated one of these great journeys : journey from Madrid to the Pardo ; from the Pardo to the Escorial ; from the Escorial to Aranjuez ; from Aranjuez to Toledo. It was the itinerary of the royal residences around Madrid.

Philip had a very keen sense of his duty, and he felt himself responsible towards his peoples and his dynasty. Perhaps he had some scruples about the way in which he had brought the Infante up and trained him. Had he under-estimated his son's capacity and his brains too much ? He tried a different method. He increased Don Carlos's allowance, and made him president of the Council of State and the Council of war. It was a final experiment.

For some little time Don Carlos showed himself well disposed towards it. He exerted himself to understand, or more or less understand, the matters that came under discussion. But soon, if we are to believe what the Bishop of Cuenca, the King's confessor, told the ambassador of Venice, he made a mess of everything and created difficulties in all directions. He spent money wantonly and recklessly. Then Philip relieved him of the functions with which he had invested him. This disgrace completed the exasperation of his naturally irritable temperament.

As the King continued his game of announcing his always imminent departure for the Low Countries, the members of the Cortes of Castile of 1566, who believed that he was acting in good faith, took it into their heads to petition him to leave his son in Spain to govern there during his absence. They had no idea of the mental instability of the Regent for whom they asked. Don Carlos heard of this project with wrath. So they wanted to rob him of his chance of seeing the world, did they?

He took advantage of the fact that the King was away to make his appearance in the midst of the deputies and forbid them to put this request on their list of petitions. As they had also expressed the desire that he should marry, and marry his aunt, Doña Juana, he reproved them heatedly for interfering in a matter in which he proposed to be the sole judge of his own choice. After this imperious declaration of his will, he walked out, leaving the assembly dumb-founded.

In any case, he had made up his mind to get away, either with his father or without him. His hatred of Philip kept on growing. He blamed his own disappointments on him. He was furious that he could neither go to the Low Countries, nor marry the Arch-duchess, nor have a place in the Government. He meditated flight to Italy, and thence making his way to Germany : probably with the idea that, once he was at a distance, he would be able to dictate his own terms.

But he prepared for his departure with all the recklessness of a prince and all the heedlessness of a fool. He negotiated a big loan in Seville. He besought Don John to transport him to Italy aboard a ship of the royal fleet, of which Philip had just given Don John the command-in-chief. He wrote to several great lords to claim their assistance in an enterprise which he had in mind. But the times when the aristocracy could afford to challenge the royal authority were over. Of those to whom he addressed himself, some forwarded the Infante's letter to the King, and others promised their services, but always subject to the King's approval. Don John told the whole story to his brother.

Still more serious revelations came from another direction. On December 27th, 1567, Don Carlos went to confession at the royal monastery of Saint Jerome, outside the walls of Madrid. He requested absolution for his sins, admitting at the same time that he found himself unable to expel from his heart the hatred which he cherished towards a fellow-man. The Hieronymite confessor refused to give him absolution on these conditions, and, when pressed by his penitent, referred him to the monks of the monastery of Atocha, who were good theological consultants, for the solution of this case of conscience.

The Prior in person questioned Don Carlos so cleverly that he led him to confess that the enemy whom he could not forgive was his own father. Philip was immediately informed. The director of postal relays, from whom the Prince demanded horses, hastened to transmit this significant requisition to the King too. Philip realized that the time had come to act. After two weeks of reflection, he left the Escorial and returned to Madrid.

On the night of January 18th, 1568, he assembled Ruy Gómez, the Duke of Feria, the Prior Don Antonio de Toledo, and Luis Quijada at the palace. What he said to them made such a deep impression on them that the echo of it has come down to us. " He spoke as no man had ever spoken before." Doubtless he invoked the interests of his peoples against the Prince, his heir ; the demands of reasons of State against his own flesh and blood.

Then he stood up. Those present followed him. Through long corridors, this silent band, with only the flickering rays of a lantern to light them, advanced upon the Infante's bedchamber. At the King's orders, the French engineer, Louis de Foix, had manipulated the locks so well that the door opened at a touch without a sound. Don Carlos was lying in bed, talking to his gentlemen. Before he had time to move, his terrible visitors were at his bed-side and had seized his still-outstretched arms.

The dread, stern figure of Philip emerged into the light of the room. Startled by this apparition, the Infante flung himself at the foot of his bed. " Your Majesty," he cried, " are you going to kill me ? " The King coldly told him to calm himself, and that everything he did would be for his good. An usher who had brought nails and a hammer with him sealed up the windows. When he had finished, Philip handed over the guarding of the Prince to the Duke of Feria, and prohibited any communication with outside. Then he went out, without looking at his son. He was never to see him again.

A week later, in order to isolate Don Carlos more effectively, Philip confined him in a tower-chamber situated at the end of his apartments. It was lit by only one window, to which bars were fixed, and another window was driven in the wall, with a wooden grating, through which the prisoner was able to hear Mass, which was said in an adjacent little oratory for his benefit.

For the time being Philip had put his son out of harm's way. But how could he hope to safeguard the future ? It has been said that he thought of bringing Don Carlos to trial, or asking the Cortes to disavow him as his heir. Any such means must have been distasteful to an absolute monarch. Besides, would they be efficacious ? Joan the Mad, despite her repugnance for any public activity, had created all kinds of difficulties for her husband, for her father, and for her son. What might one not fear from a turbulent and ambitious prince?

Death was to set all the King's anxieties at rest. Don Carlos, after going on hunger-strike for three days, started gorging himself again, with all the avidity of disease, on food and iced drinks. When the intense heat of summer came, he walked about, almost naked and wearing no shoes, on paving-stones copiously irrigated with very cold water. His own excess and imprudence ended by destroying a body weakened by fever, disappointment, and despair.

Many people have condemned Philip for his harshness. But it must be admitted that he did not take his decision lightheartedly. It was the Infante's plans for flight and his declaration that he hated his father which triumphed over the King's indecision and, so to speak, forced his hand.

It is true that, once Philip's decision was taken, it was, by its very nature, irrevocable. He was incapable of pardoning anybody who had earned his disfavour or deserved punishment, being persuaded—rightly or wrongly—that he never made up his mind, and never condemned, except with good reason. His son could not escape the common law. Philip believed that, consciously or unconsciously, he was guilty; and he cut him out of his life, and perhaps out of his heart. Never would he give him back his freedom.

But, if the King was right to reduce to impotence a son whose reckless temperament and mental disorder threatened to disturb the State, it was a cruel father who consistently refused to see the prisoner, or even to give him the comfort of his blessing when he lay dying and asking for his pardon. Cabrera, Philip III's historiographer, claims that Philip II visited and consoled his son during the earlier days of his confinement, and that, when Don Carlos was dying, Philip glided into the room in the dark, and stretched out his hand over the shoulders of Ruy Gómez and Antonio de Toledo in a gesture of pardon and benediction. But Gachard has demonstrated the unlikelihood of the reports quoted by this official advocate in order to absolve the father from the charge of harshness.

No doubt Philip did not want to precipitate Don Carlos's death; but did he do his best—even at the risk of provoking an outburst of rage—to prevent his son from eating and drinking to excess? One day Don Carlos, having wolfed down an enormous pie containing three partridges, swallowed a quantity of iced water. This excessively cold liquid, introduced into too full a stomach, caused an attack of indigestion, followed by dysentery, which exhausted the glutton and killed him. His accidental death, on July 24th, 1568, served Philip's purpose so well that it could scarcely be accepted as natural.

Pitiless King, pitiless father though he was, Philip made no attempt to exonerate himself for his cruel decision by seeking to inculpate his son in any criminal design. It was not any particular action of the Infante's, he wrote to the Duke of Albuquerque, which led him to put him under arrest, but all the defects of his temperament and his character.

This explanation, which is quite likely, and probably the true one, does not satisfy those questing minds which are intrigued in other ways too by Philip's complex soul. Accordingly they have ransacked his correspondence for any enlightenment, any hint of a confession. But neither in Philip's letters to his sister the Empress and his brother-in-law the Emperor, nor in his reply to his aunt, the Queen of Portugal, have they been able to discover anything more enlightening, or anything more at all, than his declared intention not to release Carlos. Even the famous dispatch to the Pope, for which the learned sighed for centuries because it was unpublished, but which has now been printed long since, failed to reveal any mystery.

The official declarations of the Prince of Eboli to the ambassadors of France and England are also as explicit as possible. He said to the one that His Majesty fully realized that " Don Carlos was even worse constituted in his brain than in his body, and that he would never have a very sound understanding. . . ." " He had lost hope of ever making him a successor fit to govern so many kingdoms." He said to the other : " I confess to you that I have never had to deal with anybody more disordered, more violent and less sociable than the Prince " (6).

The crime of Don Carlos was his physical, intellectual and moral weakness. He never sought to attempt his father's life. He never plotted against the security of the State. His alleged interviews with the delegates of the aristocracy of the Low Countries, the Count of Montigny and the Marquis of Berghes, are very far indeed from being established, and, even if they were, we have no right to deduce from them a formal plan of opposition to the policy of the King.

The accusation of heresy, which Bergenroth had already invoked to explain the long detention of Joan the Mad, has naturally been taken up again in connection with the Prince. As a matter of fact, the orthodoxy of the great-grandson is no more questionable than that of the great-grandmother. His delay in receiving the Easter sacrament, in order to avoid having to accuse himself in the confessional of sins which he still contemplated committing, proves scruples of conscience rather than any impiety. His testament of 1564 abounds in testimonies to Catholic faith and fervour. He requested thousands of Masses, of which one thousand were to be annual and perpetual, for the repose of his soul. He founded a monastery of Franciscans of the Observance, with professorships which he proposed to confine to Old Christians without any admixture of Jewish blood (7).

He asked to be buried clad in the habit of Saint Francis. He never doubted that he owed his early cure to his contact with the bones, or his investment with the shroud, of Fray Diego de Alcalá, and he never ceased pestering the Court of Rome about the beatification of this poor monk. He would not have attached so much virtue to the efficacy of relics and the intercession of saints if he had been at all inclined towards Protestantism, which was so strongly opposed to them. What is still more strange if this were the case, and no less conclusive that it was not the case, is that he should have set the ambassador of Spain in Rome, Don Luis de Requesens, in motion to obtain from the Pope a fragment of the inscription on the Cross and a shred of the holy prepuce (8).

After Don Carlos's arrest, Philip wrote to the Duke of Alba, that everybody in the kingdom regarded the decision which he had taken as so wise (*tan acertado*) that—

" although it causes me such pain and regret as you may imagine, I give thanks to God that it is taken so well since it cannot be excused (?), and this is a proof that His Divine Majesty will be served by it : which is the principal and sole object that determined me to take it, *subordinating my flesh and my blood*. And so you may give to understand to all whom it may concern " (9).

Six months later Don Carlos was dead. If public opinion had not, it appears, been stirred by his imprisonment, it was shaken by this tragic sequel, which nobody outside the King's entourage could have foreseen. On the day of Don Carlos's death, the Keeper of the Seals of the Low Countries, Tisnacq, wrote from Madrid : " Tongues here are very unbridled, more, I should judge, than elsewhere, and the talk is very imprudent." When a high official like Tisnacq, who was bound to be discreet, confessed such a state of mind, it was as good as saying that in Madrid, and elsewhere, high and low did not believe that the Prince's death was natural. They suspected the King of having, by an act of sovereign justice, settled the question of the eventual rights of the heir apparent.

Perhaps, too, they may conceivably have attributed to this

last time at daybreak o
constancy and her affect
wept—to keep back his

When she was dead
Jerome with his brothe
Ruy Gómez. There Ph
ceiving anybody except
once.

The bodies, mother's
carried to the church
shoulders of great lords
posited in the vaults of tl
ceremony, all the people
calling her a Saint ".
the " Princess of Peace "
end of war.

Two years after Eliza
mate wife and a male h
duchess of Austria of on
whom Maximilian had
four sons, of whom the so
succeeded him.

paternal rigour other motives than reasons of State. Later there grew up the legend, immortalized by a great poet, Schiller, hich makes Don Carlos the lover of his step-mother, a bad Catholic, enemy of the strict orthodoxy of his father and accomplice of the rebels of the Low Countries : in a word, a martyr of the rights of passion, of the liberty of peoples, and of religious tolerance.

Even in the sixteenth century itself the imagination of some contemporaries—historians, diplomats, politicians—refused to see a simple coincidence of time in the death of the Queen, Elizabeth of Valois, which occurred about two months after that of Don Carlos —on October 3rd. The suspicion became established, as though it were a case of cause and effect, that the King had avenged his honour in the Spanish way by striking down two culprits.

Of this romantic story of incestuous love in intent, even if no more, the remoter origin is the fact that, during the lifetime of Henry II of France, diplomacy had contemplated the marriage of his elder daughter to the Infante of Spain. But, after the death of Mary Tudor and the conclusion of the peace of Saint Quentin, Philip, in order to strengthen the understanding between the two Courts, took his son's intended fiancée for himself. It has been suggested that the Prince and the Princess resented this substitution.

Don Carlos and Elizabeth of Valois were both about the same age at the time of this alleged disappointment of theirs. But what a difference between this girl, beautiful, well educated, well trained and intelligent as she was, and the poor youth, generous no doubt at moments, and capable of affection, but undermined by fever, livid, stammering, shaken by spasms of violence ! At the age of fourteen she was a woman, although not yet marriageable. At the age of fourteen he was not a man, despite his vicious precociousness.

She treated him tenderly as a kind of younger brother, and he in return displayed a great affection for this step-mother of his, who showed herself a true sister in her gentleness and kindness towards him. Later on, when she realized the discord between the father and the son, she tried to exert a pacifying influence.

With his head too big for his poor body, one shoulder too high and one leg too short, his wan face and his stutter, the Infante, even at the age of twenty, could not inspire any emotion other than pity. Elizabeth appreciated the affection which this prince, who might one day be her king, showed towards her. " The esteem which I have for him," she wrote to the ambassador of France on the day of his arrest, " and the pain which the King feels at having been constrained to put him under restraint as he has, have affected me so much that I am afraid I cannot express my feelings to you

as I should
had done, h;

She coul
if he had be
with touchin
it (desired t
that she had
King, her h
willed that
The French
is in grief ar
the father a
passion.

If he ha
gone and cc
been pleasec
child at this
infidelity ?

No : Eli
poisoned bre
his love-mak
maternity, a
year, on Aug
Clara Isabel
Catherine F

It was in
and death—
births, or ex;
exhausted he
looks and be
matter, of th
nancies, at th
imposed absc
de Medici, w
when she w;
This time El
baby boy, a

Her end
perhaps ever
leave this wo
eternal glory
to her own
brother, Cha

CHAPTER VIII

THE UPS AND DOWNS OF SPANISH POWER

BRIELLE AND LEPANTO

THE death of Elizabeth of Valois had unexpected consequences. The question of the Low Countries came to the fore again.

Immediately after the loss of her elder daughter, Catherine de Medici offered the widowed King of Spain the hand of her younger daughter. But she had the mortification of learning that her son-in-law was seeking, or accepting, as his wife the Archduchess Anne—the very wife whom Catherine intended for Charles IX. It did not satisfy her pride that the Emperor granted her son the hand of Elizabeth of Austria, Anne's younger sister.

Catherine was wrath with the King of Spain, head of the House of Habsburg as Charles V's son, because he decided that the marriage contracts of the two Archduchesses should be signed in Madrid the very same day, and his own immediately before that of the King of France—as though there should be no mistake about the difference in rank and precedence. By way of compensation for these mortifications, great and small, did not Philip owe it to Catherine to marry his sister, Doña Juana, to the Duke of Anjou, with a principality for her dowry, and his nephew, the King of Portugal, to Marguerite of Valois ?

But Philip flatly refused to give Doña Juana and the Low Countries to the Duke of Anjou. He did not seek, however, to dissuade the Queen-Mother of France from establishing her daughter in Portugal. He promised his good offices in this direction. He showed himself " phlegmatic " only when the time came to exert pressure on the Court of Lisbon, where, as the King of Portugal's uncle and a powerful neighbour, he enjoyed great influence.

Catherine complained also that the Spanish Government had not furnished her the smallest aid in men or money since Moncontour. Out of spite, and also from lack of funds for stopping Coligny, who had pushed up the valleys of the Rhone and Saône

178

and entrenched himself with his troops at Châtillon-sur-Loire, within striking distance of Paris, she agreed once more, on August 8th, 1570, to sign peace with the French Protestant rebels.

Then, tired of being fooled by promises, she signified to Madrid that she would renounce the Portuguese marriage. Her own son would find her daughter a husband who would feel greatly honoured and obliged to His Majesty of France. This was the first intimation of Marguerite's betrothal to the Prince of Navarre, the leader of the Huguenots. In default of Catholic alliances, Catherine could put up with Protestants, if it was to her advantage.

Just at this moment attractive proposals were, in fact, being made to her from England. Two of the heads of the Huguenot party, who had taken refuge across the English Channel during this third French civil war, Cardinal de Châtillon and the Vidame de Chartres, were meditating a reconciliation between England and France aimed against the Habsburgs. They presented this project of alliance in the form best calculated to tempt Catherine : a marriage between the Queen of England and the Duke of Anjou, her favourite son.

Elizabeth was thirty-seven, and the Duke was only nineteen ; but this difference in age could not weigh in the balance against the advantages and expectations which the Vidame, a man of vivid imagination, enumerated with superb confidence. " Monseigneur (the Duke of Anjou) "—once he was married to Elizabeth—" could readily, with the forces of the King (of France), the favour of England, and the support of the Prince of Orange, secure the confiscation of Flanders by right of feudality for felony committed." Thus " the House of Austria, which founded the hereditary Empire and the monarchy, would find in a moment two brothers, kings as powerful the one as the other, as a counterpoise to its ambition, leagued with the Protestant princes of Germany, and the two brothers would carry more weight in the Empire than those " who wanted to arrogate all power to themselves " by the ruin of the Ancient Houses of Germany ".

Catherine was dazzled. As for Elizabeth, she let herself be played with, knowing that she could always find a way of backing out whenever she liked. Matrimonial negotiations with the French princes always meant to her—apart from the very feminine pleasure of tickling her vanity—a matter of political calculation. At this moment she had grounds for fearing lest France, freed from the civil war, might unite against her with Catholic Spain.

Mary Stuart, the widow of François II, returned to her Kingdom of Scotland and, left to her own resources, had at first succeeded by her compromises in calming down Scotch Presbyterianism, a form of the Calvinist Church adapted to the temperament and the social structure of the country. But she aroused violent opposition by instigating, or tolerating, the murder of her husband, though for that matter he had insulted her, and marrying, willingly or unwillingly, one of his murderers, Bothwell, though for that matter she was not averse from him. Escaped from the castle where the rebel lords had imprisoned her, and once more vanquished, she fled to England, on May 15th, 1568, sure, as she thought, of finding asylum and support with Elizabeth her cousin. She got nothing from Elizabeth but a prison (1).

Elizabeth, daughter of Henry VIII and Anne Boleyn, never let go again of this fugitive in distress, also a descendant from the head of the Tudor dynasty. Many English Catholics preferred Mary Queen of Scots to Elizabeth, in view of Elizabeth's heresy and the irregularity of her birth, and they regarded Mary Stuart as the legitimate heir of Mary Tudor. Against all right, Elizabeth constituted herself judge of the accusations which the Scots brought against their Sovereign. Alarmed by the number and zeal of Mary Stuart's defenders, Elizabeth made her confinement ever closer and closer.

This hypocritical application of reasons of State, in the name of justice and virtue, and the fury of the Protestants of Scotland and England, which gave it an air of religious persecution, excited keen indignation throughout the Catholic world, and especially in France, the victim's second fatherland. Mary Stuart's errors of passion—for which, as a matter of fact, according to the ideas of the time, she was answerable only to God—were forgotten, and nothing was seen in her but a martyr of her faith. Pope Pius V, by a Bull of February 25th, 1570, which was nailed to the door of the Anglican Bishop of London on May 15th, excommunicated and deposed the English Jezebel as heretic and bastard.

It was to offset the effect of this sentence of deprivation, and to add a reason of self-interest and sentiment to all the other reasons Gallican France might have for repudiating this Pontifical intervention in a " matter of temporalities ", that Elizabeth encouraged the advances of the Queen-Mother of France. Catherine, who did not like Mary Stuart, her former daughter-in-law, and loved the Duke of Anjou above all her other children, had no scruples about urging this son of whom she was uniquely fond to wed the best match in Christendom, whatever prejudices he might have against this coquettish old maid, only too responsive to the compliments and the company of fine young men.

Elizabeth, reassured in the direction of France, could turn to confront her other enemies. Mary Stuart, imprisoned illegally, considered that she had a right to plot. In April, 1571, she sent a Florentine banker, Roberto Ridolfi, to Rome and Spain to beg the Pope and the King for means of getting her out of prison. She offered, as soon as she was free, to marry either the Duke of Norfolk, the leader of the English Catholic party, or Don John of Austria.

Ridolfi, on his way through the Low Countries, made a bad impression on the Duke of Alba, who thought him a great wind-bag (*un gran parlanchin*), only too likely to compromise Norfolk and Mary Stuart by his indiscretions if Queen Elizabeth learnt the secret of his negotiations. This, indeed, was what happened. But Ridolfi made a better impression on Philip II, to whom he set forth the details of the plot.

With the help of Spain, he explained, Norfolk and his friends would have no difficulty in overthrowing Elizabeth and putting Mary Stuart in her place. To seize Elizabeth and kill her, the most favourable time was the months of August and September, when she left London to visit her country residences. Mary and Norfolk, as Mary's husband, would reduce the kingdom to obedience to the Holy See and renew the old treaties of alliance with Castile.

The Pope, well primed by Ridolfi, had conveyed to Philip " that he (the Pope) envisaged this affair as being of the highest importance for the service of God and the good of His Church ". He left the carrying-out of it to Philip and offered him all his aid, being ready, if necessary, poor and ruined as he was, " to devote to this purpose even the chalices (in the churches) and his own vestments ".

In a letter to the Duke of Alba, Philip reported his reply to the Papal Nuncio : " that it did not need many words to persuade him, for his desire to see the projected enterprise carried out was extreme. . . . He would reflect upon it with the hope that God, Whose cause it was, would enlighten him and assist him." Philip added : " The object which it is sought to attain is that the Duke of Norfolk and his adherents should try to kill or capture the Queen Elizabeth, in order to set the Queen of Scots at liberty and transfer the crown of England to her head."

Alba, the King instructed him, was to lend the English Catholics support in this enterprise, even if they failed, though he was not to make open war on Elizabeth, lest the Protestants of Germany, France and elsewhere should intervene. Could Alba put at their disposal the Spanish soldiers whom the English conspirators required? In any case, let him assemble arms, munitions, and artillery.

Philip seemed quite decided, though he envisaged reasons for postponement. He was about to write, he informed Alba, to the ambassador of Spain in London, Don Guerau de Espés, instructing him to exhort Norfolk to persevere in his determination, but to dissuade him from taking up arms before the right moment came. What moment did Philip mean? Meanwhile, the better to keep the secret of the enterprise, he did not propose to commit himself, except in general terms, to Ridolfi, the Nuncio, or the Pope. This discretion of Philip's clearly foreshadowed delays.

An ardent Catholic, but careful to safeguard the rights of kings against the pretensions of the Church, as Charles V had recommended him to do, Philip refused to let Pius V intervene as executor of the sentence of deposition on Elizabeth, lest he should seem to recognize the suzerainty of the Holy See over England and Ireland. Philip was afraid of committing himself too far. Yet the opportunity of rendering a service to God seemed to him so favourable that, on July 14th, 1571, he wrote a marginal note on a dispatch from his Secretary of State to the Duke of Alba. "From what I have already written to you by my own hand, you know how much I have this matter at heart. So I will not say anything further to you about it, being persuaded that you will take the same interest in it yourself."

The Duke of Alba applauded this decision, but he pointed out its dangers. Philip himself, as he informed Alba in a letter of August 4th, had just learnt that the Queen of England had heard about Ridolfi's negotiations, that Mary Stuart was more strictly watched than ever, and that Norfolk was closely guarded. Nevertheless, Philip declared himself resolved to spare nothing which was in his power to carry the enterprise through, "considering himself bound to do so by his duties towards God". Let the Duke, therefore, make his preparations, and be ready to help the conspirators, as soon as they had assembled sufficient forces.

As the objects of their rising, they would avow the setting at liberty of the Queen of Scots, and her crowning as Queen of England. It was for this twofold purpose that Philip would support them. "In truth, his principal object in embracing their cause was the re-establishment of the Catholic religion ; but, if this aim were announced, many inconveniences might arise ; in any case, the restoration of the Catholic faith will be the indubitable result " of the accession of the Queen of Scots to the throne of England. So it was idle to emphasize the fact.

The Duke of Alba was perplexed, as he wrote to the King in reply to Philip's letter of August 4th and his instructions of July 14th. Was it possible for him to help Norfolk, even if Norfolk should fail, without " inevitably " breaking with the neighbouring Protestants ? Another difficulty : the King ordered him to make his preparations for intervention without delay, and at the same time recommended him " to say nothing about it to the Councillors of the country. But he could not do anything whatever except through them and the officers who were under their orders."

Alba had no confidence in any of the originators of the English plot. " For the love of God," he implored Philip, " I beg Your Majesty not to let your great zeal lead you astray in this affair— the most important for the service of God that has arisen since Your Majesty came to the Low Countries (*a la tierra*) ; for it concerns nothing less than the destruction of religion, of which not one stone would be left upon another in Christendom if Your Majesty should be brought to nought." Might it not be possible to come to an understanding with France to dethrone Queen Elizabeth ?

But Philip persisted in his determination. He hoped that God would direct things in such a way that this holy enterprise would have the desired success. " In this cause, which is that of God, there are other and higher considerations which prescribe passing over human disadvantages."

The Duke of Alba had nothing left to do but obey. He did not omit, however, to warn his master that the secret of the enterprise was out. " In Antwerp," Alba wrote on September 5th, " merchants are talking about it quite openly." But Philip remained obstinate. He replied on September 14th that " this matter lies so near to his heart, and he is so far persuaded that God will direct it, as being His own concern, that nothing will induce him to turn aside from it."

Whatever Philip did, Elizabeth would henceforth be his enemy. There was no means of assuring the well-being and the defence of the Low Countries other than the transfer of the crown of England. Still, on the news of Norfolk's arrest, Philip's fever for action declined. He postponed the enterprise to the first favourable occasion. He appears to have abandoned it altogether when he heard of the execution of the English conspirators, and confined himself to hoping that it might please God to change things in such a way that his good intentions might be realized.

Elizabeth made no attempt to save Philip's face. In December, 1571, she expelled his ambassador, Don Guerau de Espés, branding him to the King and the Duke of Alba as " too uncleanly, under-hand and unpleasant " to maintain friendly relations between the two crowns (2).

The Spanish Government had no better success in France.

Catherine, who had not forgiven Philip for failing to impose Marguerite on the Court of Portugal, went ahead with her prepara-tions for her daughter's marriage to Henri de Bourbon, head of the Protestant party and future King of Navarre. She had con-siderable difficulty in winning over the Huguenot leaders, her enemies of yesterday, who had retired to La Rochelle and remained distrustful and distant, to acceptance of this union. The young Prince's mother, a rigid Calvinist, was still less ready to find a suit-able wife for her son in that corrupt Court of the Valois where, so she said, women simply threw themselves at men's heads.

It was an incident in Italian politics that led the Queen of Navarre to change her point of view. Pope Pius V, of his own authority, promoted Cosimo de Medici to the dignity of Grand Duke of Tuscany. The Emperor Maximilian, as suzerain of this State which Charles V had created, and Philip II, who had added the former territory of the republic of Sienna to it, protested against this initiative of the Pope's and this elevation of the Duke. Dis-turbed by these protests, Cosimo sent an agent of his, Fregoso, to Germany, to assure himself of the support of the Protestant princes there in case of need.

From Heidelberg, where he was coldly received by the Elector Palatine, in whose eyes all Papists, and especially those of Italy, were suspect, Fregoso made his way to La Rochelle. There he found Ludwig of Nassau, who was engaged in organizing the " great filibuster " of the La Rochelle privateers and the " Sea Beggars " of the Low Countries against the Spanish merchant marine. In the course of their interviews, the question of uniting France and Tuscany against Philip II was raised.

Charles IX of France, informed of this idea of common action, welcomed it with enthusiasm. He resented the state of subordina-tion in which his mother kept him, and grasped at this opportunity of emancipating himself from it. Catherine de Medici, for reasons different from her son's, found it convenient to favour this enemy of Spain, who was dear to the heart of Jeanne d'Albret, and seemed the only person capable of converting that obstinate Huguenot to her own marriage project.

The Queen-Mother of France and the young King had two mysterious interviews, at Lumigny, on July 14th, 1571, and at Fontainebleau, with Fregoso. In the course of these interviews

Fregoso solicited the support of a French army to deliver the Low Countries from the tyranny of the Duke of Alba. " The King (of France), he affirmed, could count upon Elizabeth and the Protestant princes of Germany, provided that he offered to share the suzerainty of the Seventeen Provinces with England and the Empire. In the presence of his mother, Charles IX replied guardedly that he would be inclined to support this enterprise if he were assured of such support ; but in secret he promised Ludwig to fit out a fleet to strike terror into Philip II " (3).

Coligny, who had become commander-in-chief of the Protestant forces since Condé's death at Jarnac, judged it opportune to seek a reconciliation with the French Court. He was favourably received, two months after her first interview with Fregoso, by the Queen-Mother. With Catherine's support—or even without it— Coligny flattered himself that he could induce the young King, with the resulting glory as a lure, to undertake the conquest of the Low Countries. Haunted by the nightmare of civil war, Coligny dreamt of reconciling the Catholics and the Protestants of France in common action against the King of Spain. Long-range negotiations continued between the Queen-Mother of France and the Queen of Navarre about the clauses of the marriage contract, until at last, in order to get it definitely drafted, Jeanne d'Albret decided to visit the French Court in person.

Pope Pius V was frightened by the prospect of this matrimonial alliance, which threatened to lead to other alliances : perhaps to a coalition against Most Catholic Spain. He was determined to oppose Marguerite of Valois's marriage to the head of the Protestant party by every means in his power ; and he could see but one efficacious way of doing so—namely, persuading Dom Sebastian, King of Portugal, to marry Catherine de Medici's daughter.

Cardinal Alexandrino, the Pope's nephew, whom Pius V had dispatched to Portugal to draw up the plan of operations of the Holy League against the Turks, secured the assent of the young King of Portugal to this French marriage, after a pitched battle with his directors of conscience. Returning in haste to Madrid, the Cardinal persuaded Philip II to agree to it as well. Then Alexandrino set off for France in company with the General of the Jesuits, Francesco Borgia, whose presence guaranteed the intentions of the King of Spain, his Sovereign. He overtook Jeanne d'Albret on her way to Blois ; but he did not carry enough weight of argument to convince her.

Perhaps he might have won Catherine over, if, in addition to the promise of the Crown of Portugal, he could have held out to this ambitious mother the prospect of uniting the Duke of Anjou —whom Elizabeth, on religious pretexts, was obviously not going to marry—to the Princess Dowager of Spain, Doña Juana, or one of the Infantas. But Philip declared explicitly that his sister did not want to marry, and that he was himself not yet ready to marry his daughter, Clara Isabel Eugenia, now aged seven.

The Cardinal-nephew got nothing but fair words. He had to take his leave of the French Court without obtaining from Charles IX the publication, as State law, of the decrees of the Council of Trent, or even the adherence of France to the maritime league against the Turks.

Jeanne d'Albret and Catherine de Medici argued the articles of the marriage contract at length, and ended by signing them, on February 7th, 1572. The interests of the Reformation had finally decided Jeanne d'Albret in favour of this marriage. As though by way of confirmation of her calculations and her expectations, on April 29th a treaty of defensive alliance was concluded between Catholic France and Protestant England.

While Charles IX was letting himself be won over to " fine and glorious enterprises " in Flanders, the Duke of Alba seemed to have made it his business to exasperate the people of the Low Countries. On the day when he received the glad tidings that Philip II, yielding to his insistence, had appointed a successor to him, he wrote to his master that the new Captain-General must be on his guard, in the case of crimes of religion and rebellion, against pardoning a single condemned person.

Alba suffered, alike in his patriotism and his pride, from having to recognize that the revenues of his administration did not suffice for the maintenance of his army, and that he had to impoverish Spain to assure the obedience and defence of the Low Countries. He was only too anxious to hand over the job of discovering new sources of revenue to Medina-Celi. But, inasmuch as Philip, either from lack of funds or from his habit of slowness, was in no hurry to dispatch the new governor, Alba had to reconcile himself to staying where he was and getting all the money he could out of the *alcavala*, since the compromise over its equivalent was, in 1571, coming to an end.

This was no easy matter. Alba learnt, through a letter from Philip's secretary Zayas, that the King was perplexed, " seeing, on the one hand, how much these taxes displease the country, and recognizing, on the other hand, their necessity for the payment of public expenses ". Accordingly, to reconcile the needs of the treasury and the burden on the population, Alba agreed to lower the duties of the *alcavala* on manufactured products intended for exportation, on the national fishing industry, and on material employed for the preparation of cloth, etc. At the same time he declared that these reductions were made provisionally and by way of experiment, and that the King remained entitled to levy the taxes in full.

But the States did not show themselves satisfied with this moderation. The reason, so Alba said, was that they were controlled by " satraps "—such was his name for the principal personages of this national assembly. Apparently Alba failed to understand that, sensitive as they were about the maintenance of the *alcavala*, the States could scarcely feel grateful for concessions which were revocable at any moment. According to his ideas, what influenced them was not the interests of manufacture, or fishing, or anything else of the kind, but simply their regret that they could no longer, as in the past, teach His Majesty a lesson. Let His Majesty yield nothing. As for himself, he was organizing the levying of the five and two and a half per cent. duties, despite the complaints to which they led.

Alba admitted that he encountered opposition even among those who ought to have supported him—in other words, the members of the Council of Finance. Nobody gave him any backing, except his son, Don Fadrique. Ill, aged, and embittered, Alba persisted in challenging an unpopularity whose causes he recognized, but whose consequences he could not foresee.

Don Francés de Alava, the impetuous ambassador of Spain in Paris, who had been relieved of his functions by Philip II at Catherine's instance, proceeded to Flanders and on his way home drew up two memoranda, one to the Secretary of State, Zayas, and the other to the King, directing their attention to the exodus of merchants, with their belongings, from the Low Countries. In Paris there were already four hundred of them, and the number of these *émigrés*, drawn from Brussels, Antwerp, Lille, Douai, Arras and other towns, was steadily increasing.

Half a league from Brussels, de Alava met Noircarmes, President of the Council of Finance, and told him what he had observed. " My lord Don Francés," cried the other excitedly, " there will be more than ten thousand who will leave the country if the Duke of Alba does not take care. . . . We must look for unfortunate results."

But the Duke of Alba, whom de Alava saw on his way through Brussels, did not agree. He claimed that the levying of the five per cent. duty would produce the expected yield, although Noir-

While still protesting his pacific intentions, or allowing his mother to protest them, the King of France pushed forward his maritime preparations for a long-range expedition faster than ever at Nantes and Bordeaux. Philip Strozzi, Colonel-General of the French Infantry, and Baron de la Garde, General of the Galleys, armed merchant vessels as warships and concentrated a powerful fleet.

The King instructed his ambassador at Constantinople, Noailles, Bishop of Acqs (Dax), to inform the Grand Seignior that, at about the end of May, he was dispatching " a sea army of twelve or fifteen thousand men . . . under pretext of guarding my harbours and coasts against depredations, but in fact with the object of keeping the Catholic King in his place and encouraging these Gueux of the Low Countries to be up and doing, as they have been, having taken all Zeeland and shaken Holland considerably ". Some days later, Ludwig of Nassau secretly left Paris, armed with letter of credentials in which Charles IX avowed his undertaking. Ludwig appeared suddenly with a troop of Huguenots before Valenciennes and Mons, which, on May 23rd and 24th, 1572, successively opened their gates to him.

The situation of the Duke of Alba would have been perilous if the English, as well as the French, had come to the aid of the rebels of the north and the invaders from the south. But Elizabeth was afraid of any aggrandizement of France in the Low Countries as a threat to the security of England. She refused to act in concert with Charles IX. She resumed the interrupted commercial relations with Flanders.

The Protestant princes of Germany also showed little zeal for the cause of the Reformation. There was only one frontier, that of France, where William of Nassau could look for support ; and this was reckoning without the Queen-Mother. Catherine did not believe in a French victory over the veteran troops of the King of Spain ; and she was even more afraid of one than of a defeat, since victory in any such successful aggression was calculated to assure its instigators, the Huguenots, a preponderant position in France.

Catherine was already wrath to realize how much influence Coligny was acquiring over her son. She had derived all the benefit she could expect from her reconciliation with the leaders of the Protestant party : a royal crown for her daughter. The death of Queen Jeanne d'Albret of Navarre, that woman with the heart of a man and uncompromising in her faith, on June 9th, 1572, allowed Catherine to hope that the delights of the French Court and the attractions of Marguerite of Valois would triumph easily over the very lukewarm Huguenotry of that very precocious lover of pleasure, her future son-in-law, the Prince of Navarre, now King of Navarre (5).

Coligny was Catherine's great adversary. As leader of the rebels, he had held all the forces of the King of France at bay. Restored to grace and favour, he exposed the kingdom to worse dangers through his spirit of proselytism. As friend or foe, he was equally to be feared.

The Admiral hoped to win Catherine over to belief in success. With the connivance of Charles IX, he kept on recruiting soldiers. But the four thousand men whom he sent, under the command of Genlis, to the relief of Mons were surprised on July 17th by the Spaniards, warned by advices from France, and almost all killed or taken prisoners, together with their leader.

" Fear of the Spanish arms," writes Tavannes, son of an eye-witness, Marshal de Tavannes, " seized the Queen." Charles IX himself wavered between his desire for glory and the test of hard facts. He multiplied pacific protestations in Rome, in Madrid, and in Brussels, and at a solemn audience which he gave the am-bassador extraordinary of Venice, who had been hastily dispatched to urge him to keep the peace. Two councils, one of men of the sword, and the other of men of the cassock, pronounced against any French invasion of Flanders. Catholic opinion condemned a war without legitimate reason against the King of Spain, a neigh-bour and a friend. But Coligny, convinced of Charles IX's tacit assent, kept on raising levies almost openly.

Philip II, like the Duke of Alba, clearly saw the danger of a French invasion, in which Huguenot bands would act as the advance-guard of the royal troops. But he let provocation pass, confining himself to warning Charles IX that his tenderness towards his heretic subjects threatened to compromise the union of the two crowns. Philip procured money by all possible means. Twice he sent five hundred thousand ducats to the Duke of Alba, who owed his infantry fourteen months' pay. He permitted Alba to suspend the levying of the five per cent. duty.

Without withdrawing Medina-Celi's nomination, Philip con-firmed the Duke of Alba as sole and absolute governor as long as he remained in the Low Countries. The Duke was preparing to subdue Zeeland and crush the Gueux, when he learnt of Ludwig of Nassau's entrance into Mons and Valenciennes. He had not a *real* in his treasury, and he judged it dangerous to impose new taxes on the inhabitants. " It seemed to drive him mad with rage (*delirare videtur*)," Granvelle's correspondent Morillon wrote to the Cardinal.

Alba hurried as fast as he could to bar Coligny's way. He concentrated all his forces, left only very weak garrisons in the towns, and with thirty-five thousand men, of whom eleven thousand were Spaniards, marched on Mons and Valenciennes. He captured Valenciennes in his stride and laid siege to Mons. He abandoned Holland to save the rest of the Low Countries.

Salvation came to Alba from a quarter whence he did not expect it. Catherine had definitely made up her mind to get rid of Coligny, who disputed control of her son with her and, in the interests of his own party, was launching the young King of France upon a dangerous adventure by dangling the hope of glory before him. She concerted the murder of this influential rival of hers with the Guises, mortal enemies of Coligny, whom they believed to have been the instigator of the murder of François de Guise, the head of their family. She awaited only the marriage of her daughter before " sounding the tocsin ".

Four days after the marriage of the Protestant King of Navarre and the Most Catholic Marguerite of Valois, a festival of national reconciliation, Coligny was leaving the Louvre, on August 22nd, when he was struck by an arquebus ball, which broke his arm and severed one of his fingers. Charles IX, furious at this attempted assassination, ordered an inquiry in Parliament, which established the culpability of the Guises and promised, if it was carried far enough, to reveal that of the Queen-Mother. The Protestant captains, who had flocked to Paris for the wedding and the enterprise in Flanders, swarmed around the wounded man's house and threatened to exact vengeance for the crime themselves if the King did not see justice done. Some of them talked about leaving Paris, taking Coligny with them.

It was then that into the mind of Catherine, full of boldness and void of any scruple, there came, or was suggested, the idea of making good the attempted murder of the Huguenot leader by the massacre of the whole party. She filled the young King with fears of a new civil war, or even an attack on the Louvre that very night. She reminded him of the rebellions of the past, and revived his resentments. She confessed herself guilty, in order to force him to choose between his own mother and the enemies of religion and the State.

She succeeded, though not without difficulty, in extracting from this man of violent but weak character, capable of the most sudden veerings, an order to put to death all those gentlemen and captains whose services he had accepted. On August 24th, 1572, the day of Saint Bartholomew, at dawn, the Swiss guards began by killing

CATHERINE DE MEDICI
From a portrait by Clouet at Chantilly

the lords whom the King had given quarters in his own palace of the Louvre. Henri de Guise hastened to the de Béthizy mansion to finish off the Admiral. Most of the Protestant leaders were butchered in their beds. A few of them were shot down on the roofs where they took refuge. Only the King of Navarre and Prince de Condé were spared, as being of the Blood Royal ; but it was on condition that they abjured Protestantism.

The populace of Paris extended the order of proscription to all Protestants without distinction of age, sex or social condition. The carnage was interrupted, resumed, went on for several days, overflowed the city. In proportion as the news of the Parisian massacre spread, the Catholics of a number of towns fell upon the Protestants. Meaux, quite close to Paris, opened the cycle of provincial killings on August 26th, and Bordeaux and Toulouse, at the other end of the kingdom, closed it on October 3rd.

When Philip II heard of the bloody execution which had saved the Low Countries, he showed, " contrary to his temperament and custom, more delight than he had ever manifested before over any of the good and fortunate adventures that befell him ". He received the ambassador of France, Jean de Vivonne, Lord of Saint Gouard, in audience, and, at the sight of him, " he started laughing "— perhaps for the only time in his public life. Philip said of Charles IX " that there was no other king who was his peer in valour and wisdom ". He could not succeed in hiding his " great joy " ; but, prudent as he always was, lest he should have to repay the service that had unintentionally been done him, he affected to admire the disinterestedness of this " lofty enterprise ", " sometimes congratulating the son on having such a mother, sometimes the mother on having such a son " (6).

The Prince of Orange recognized what a " knock-down blow " the cause of the Low Countries had been dealt in Paris. " My sole hope," he declared, " was from the side of France." As a matter of fact, at the end of 1572 Elizabeth recalled the English whom she had sent to Zeeland.

Without further anxiety, the Duke of Alba was able to pursue the siege of Mons. He surprised the Prince of Orange, who was advancing to relieve the place, by night, killed part of his infantry and scattered the rest. For fear of leaving a possible avenger of the massacre of Saint Bartholomew alive, the King of France had asked Alba, Diego de Zuñiga, the new ambassador of Spain in Paris, and Philip II himself to exterminate those of his Huguenot subjects who were defending Mons. To shame Charles IX, Alba, on September 21st, accorded the besieged an honourable surrender.

But it was only for the sake of humiliating the King of France that the Duke of Alba showed himself humane for once, as the rebels of the Low Countries were to discover. Malines, which had opened its gates to the Prince of Orange, was given over to be the prey of the soldiers for three days. The army, Alba wrote to the King on October 2nd, " is at this moment engaged in inflicting upon the inhabitants the punishment which God has clearly chosen to give them ". " They deserve, indeed, a chastisement even more severe than that which they are undergoing." The army leaders tried, without complete success, " to preserve the churches, the monasteries, the priests and the councillors of the King ".

The treatment of Malines frightened the defenders of Termonde, who surrendered at discretion. Don Fadrique, glad to have an opportunity of applying his father's methods, had been charged with attacking Zutphen, where the Prince of Orange had left some of his infantry during his retreat. Although he entered the town without much resistance, Alba's son put all the soldiers of the garrison, and even many of the burghers, to the sword, " the Duke having given the order ", as he wrote himself to Philip II on November 19th, not to leave a single man alive and even to set fire to several parts of the town, because he recalled that the burning of Düren had gained the Emperor the conquest of Gelderland in a single day. Some prominent rebels and Frenchmen trapped in the ravelin who defended themselves were hanged by their feet. The horrified provinces of Gelderland and Over-Ijssel submitted.

The Spanish troops on their march towards Holland reached Naerden, a little town reputed to be the crucible of all the Anabaptists. They entered it almost without having to strike a blow, and nevertheless massacred the burghers and the soldiers, letting not one escape. The town was set on fire at two or three points. The Duke wrote triumphantly : " It was the grace of God that they were blinded to the point of attempting resistance in a town which nobody else in the world but themselves would have dreamt of defending, so weak was it. They have thus been able to receive the chastisement which such a wicked population, consisting of such great heretics, richly deserved " (7).

Instead of inspiring terror, this barbarity exasperated the people of Haarlem, who swore to resist to the last extremity, " to escape such murders and sackings ". The Prince of Orange sent four thousand of his best soldiers into the town. The whole population manned the ramparts : men, women, and even monks, who feared the Spaniards even worse than the Gueux, those ravishers of monasteries. The Duke of Alba put the same desperation into his attack. He wrote to Don Fadrique, who was disheartened by the resistance and talked of raising the siege, that he would disown him as his son if he did (8).

The town held out for seven months, until July 12th, 1573, and then, defeated only by starvation, was forced to surrender unconditionally. The French, Walloons and English of its garrison, to the number of two thousand three hundred, were put to death. The leaders of the Germans shared the same fate, and their troops, after having taken oath not to serve the rebel prince again, were driven out stark naked in a direction where they could do no harm. Some burghers were also " chastized ", but the town was not sacked.

Philip, who had no objection to the massacre of rebellious subjects, had developed an interest, since the sack of Malines, in the security of buildings. He was beginning to be worried about the fury of his soldiery, who did not spare even churches or monasteries, and, in place of a rich and flourishing town, an active centre of trade, industry and labour, left only a mass of ruined houses to be restored, to the great harm and even to the shame of the Sovereign. It was this economic and religious consideration which, having saved Louvain from pillage, also spared Haarlem.

But the soldiers were furious at losing this rich prey, which would have indemnified them for arrears of pay and the miseries of the campaign. On July 29th the veteran Spanish companies mutinied, demanded food—we know what a troop of women they had with them—and tried to seize the artillery, the fleet, and the town of Haarlem. To pacify them, the Duke, who had no money to give them, offered to put himself in their hands as guarantor of the arrival of pay. He borrowed in his own name a sum which he distributed to them ; but this concession only increased their demands, and they mutinied again. This time Don Fadrique had the ringleaders hanged, and order was restored for the time being.

It was the first of those great mutinies which several times endangered the Spanish domination in the Low Countries. There was another in November. After the raising of the siege of Alkmaar, the *tercios* refused to install themselves in the quarters which were assigned to them, and the Germans and the Walloons broke camp with flags flying. The sailors, to the number of two thousand, forced their way in to the Duke, demanding the two months' pay which he owed them.

Never in all his military career, he wrote to the King from Grave on November 5th, had he " passed worse days or experienced such great anxieties ". But, witnessing the wretchedness of his soldiers, and a soldier himself to the bottom of his soul, he understood them and almost excused them. " Living has become so dear that, with his month's pay, the soldier can scarcely exist for more than a fortnight, and he has nothing left to buy shoes, powder, matches, etc." At the cost of the utmost efforts, Alba succeeded in providing for the needs of all his army, except the Walloons and Burgundians, almost all of whom he thought it better to disband.

While he was engaged in reducing the northern territory to submission, in Flanders he had been forced to replace the Walloons by the *tercios* of Sicily, in order to prevent fraternization between these French-speaking soldiers of his and the thirty companies whom Charles IX had quartered on the frontiers of Hainault and Artois.

The taking of Haarlem was the last of Alba's great successes. He no longer enjoyed the confidence of his master, who sometimes left him as long as seven weeks without a letter. His violence displeased Philip, and his demands for men and money were a nuisance. Like a raving madman, in order to subdue Holland Alba proposed to destroy by fire all the places which the royal troops could not occupy. Philip himself could understand cruelties which proved both effective and cheap ; but he realized that such means as these would yield no great results and cost him very dearly.

These " Black Indies ", which had formerly helped Spain to bear the expenses of empire, were no longer bringing her in anything, and were, indeed, helping to ruin her. The ever-increasing forces employed in the Low Countries, Spanish, German, and Walloon, mustered fifty-four thousand five hundred infantry and four thousand seven hundred and eighty cavalry, without counting the three thousand men in garrison in the frontier fortresses. The financial resources of the monarchy were being exhausted by the maintenance of this great army.

In proportion as, despite all these powerful means at his disposal, the impotence of the Duke of Alba to reduce the rebel provinces to obedience became better established, everybody started accusing him for his cruelty towards the rebels, his drastic enforcement of the proclamations, and the excesses of his men-at-arms. Secretary Esteban Pratz, employed since the beginning of the troubles in the transaction of criminal affairs, made representations to Philip in April, 1573, about the disorderly behaviour of the troops.

" One sees camp commandants, captains, officers and soldiers killing, ill-treating, violating and dishonouring married women and girls, and ruining poor peasants. . . . Harsh measures have been applied to the nation such as one can find no precedent for in ancient or modern chronicles, by the condemnation to death or banishment of an innumerable multitude of persons."

Even more likely to move the King, as an appeal to his conscience, was the letter in which, on May 13th, François Richardot, Bishop of Arras ; Martin Rithoven, Bishop of Ypres, and Abbot John of Anchin deplored the ills of the Low Countries, the damage which was being done to religion, the loss of so many souls, and the war, which ought to be carried on, if not in a saintly, at least in a Christian, way. The soldiers, those of the country as well as foreigners, lived on pillage and in unbridled licence, addicted to adulteries and shameless sins, and died under arms in great numbers impenitent, running the risk of eternal damnation—an argument which involved the salvation of the King himself, as the prelates fully realized.

" The peasants are exasperated by their violence, and the oppression under which they suffer is driving them to despair." Good Catholics, just because they lived in the same place as heretics, were despoiled of their belongings or robbed of their lives, as was said to have happened at Malines, at Naerden, and elsewhere. The Bishops pointed out to Philip that the excesses and the intolerable licence of the soldiers had often provoked Catholic populations themselves to revolt.

The Duke of Alba, irritated by this unanimous disapproval, crippled with gout—as was his son Fadrique—exhausted after seven years of campaigning, and impoverished to the tune of three hundred thousand escudos, advanced out of his own resources, was in a hurry to be gone from the Low Countries. Accordingly he hastened to hand over his powers to the governor whom the King nominated in his place and in that of his titular successor, the Duke of Medina-Celi. The very next day after the arrival, on November 29th, of Don Luis de Requesens, Grand Commander of Castile and former Governor of the Milanese, Alba thrust these powers into his hands, although Requesens had still to take oath as lieutenant, governor and captain-general for the King. Requesens had been appointed on January 30th, 1573, but did not arrive until November, nine months later. This delay, which was due to the King himself, is characteristic of Philip II's administration (9).

Alba set out for Spain three weeks later. As though he insisted upon liquidating the whole past and leaving a clean slate for his successor, before divesting himself of his office he had the Huguenot Genlis, whom he had been holding prisoner in his suite since his victory near Valenciennes, " secretly " strangled. It was an excess of zeal and cruelty : the very symbol of his way of governing.

In his struggle against the heretics of the Low Countries, Philip did not lose sight of the other struggle which he had to carry on against the Infidel and for the policing of the Mediterranean. As soon as he felt that order was re-established in the north by the Duke of Alba's victories and the proclamation of the amnesty in 1570, he held himself ready to assist Venice, which, threatened by the Sultan, was appealing for help to the Christian princes. As gems out of its sometime diadem of maritime empire, the Republic still retained Crete and Cyprus, two great islands.

Cyprus, situated not far from the mainland of Asia, opposite the Gulf of Alexandretta and the coast of Syria, dominated Turkey's communications with her finest possession in Africa, Egypt. Selim II wanted to conquer this island in order to be the rival in glory at sea of his father, Suleiman the Magnificent, the conqueror of Rhodes. On a trumped-up pretext, he summoned the Seignury of Venice to hand Cyprus over to him, and, on its refusal, declared war.

Venice, with a fleet and troops which she was hard put to it to maintain, impoverished as she was by the loss of the market of Alexandria, could not withstand the attack of this powerful enemy with her own resources. Malta, devoted by vocation to the Holy War, and the Free States of Italy, Genoa, Savoy, Florence, etc., promised her support ; but this could only be on a small scale. The Emperor Maximilian, at peace on land with the Turks, and the King of France, their ally, refused to intervene.

But Pope Pius V took the cause of Christendom in hand, and he had little difficulty in persuading Philip II to follow his example. The representatives of the Catholic States which had decided upon action assembled in Rome, together with those of the Pope and Venice, and in April, 1570, resolved to form a Holy League against the Infidel. Not without objection, it was agreed that this league should be perpetual, and Philip II's brother, Don John of Austria, Charles V's illegitimate son, was appointed commander-in-chief.

But the Turks, who were ready first, disembarked in Cyprus and took Nicosia, after a six weeks' siege. The squadrons of the League, which had only just concentrated in Suda Bay, off Candia, arrived too late to save the fortress. Their leaders were not in agreement. Don John of Austria, who might have assured unanimity of command, was still in Madrid, detained either by his preparations, or by lack of funds, or perhaps by Philip II's usual procrastination. As winter was approaching, the fleet dispersed, and its various groups returned to their respective ports.

The Pope needed all his energy to maintain the links between a coalition which was only too ready to dissolve, but he succeeded in making its members swear to resume operations the following year, in May, 1571. Don John, recognized as generalissimo, started for Barcelona, embarked his *tercios* (commanded by Don Lope de Figucroa and Don Miguel de Moncade), and set sail towards the south of Italy. After a call of several days at Naples, he reached Messina, where he had given the allied forces rendezvous for September 5th.

This was too late to save Famagusta, a port of Cyprus which the Grand Vizier Mustapha took by capitulation on August 2nd, and whose governor, Bragadino, he flayed alive, despite the terms of the surrender. Cyprus was lost ; but the Christians, with a fleet of three hundred sail, manned by eighty thousand soldiers, sailors, and rowers, could still dispute the command of the sea with the Turks.

Spain led the way with a hundred and sixty-four galleys and other well-equipped vessels. Venice followed with a hundred and thirty-four ships, which were not worth as much either in their quality or in their capacity for manœuvre. The Pope had armed twelve galleys, and six frigates. Genoa, Savoy, Florence and Malta came afterwards, with contingents of unequal value. Skilled sailors were in command : the Venetian Veniero ; the Genoese Giovanni Andrea Doria ; and, over the galleys of Naples, the Marquis of Santa Cruz, who now had the opportunity of foreshadowing himself, and later, at the Azores, of revealing himself, as the leading sea-captain of Spain.

It was to a Crusade that Pius V had summoned Catholicism. At Naples he handed over to Don John, through Cardinal Granvelle, the standard of the League, which bore a Christ on the Cross, with the arms of Philip II and Venice interlaced with chains at His feet, as the symbol of an indestructible union, and, over His head, the arms of Don John of Austria, Captain-General of the League. A legate of the Holy Father accompanied the fleet. Before the departure admirals, captains and soldiers one and all made confession and received Communion.

On September 16th, the fleet sailed for Corfu, and thence for Cephalonia, where it moored on October 5th. On the next day but one, October 7th, as it was cruising along the coast of Acarnania, one of its scouts signalled the main body of the Turkish forces, which lay in the Gulf of Lepanto, separated from the open sea by a narrow passage.

Against the advice of the admirals of Genoa and Venice, Don John decided to attack. Of all his squadrons, some of which had become detached on the way, he had left two hundred and eight galleys and sixteen galleasses. The Turks numbered more ships and a hundred and twenty thousand men, fighting men and crews together. But Ali Pasha, whom Selim had invested with the command-in-chief in place of Piali, who had fallen into disgrace, consented to give battle in a restricted area where he could not deploy and sacrificed his advantage in numbers.

He and Don John met in the first onslaught, and the Turkish admiral fell, hit by an arquebus ball. His death and his bad manœuvring, which immobilized half his ships, decided the fortune of the day. The Turks lost two hundred and twenty-four vessels sunk, burned or captured, and thirty thousand combatants killed or taken prisoner, without counting twelve thousand Christian rowers set at liberty by their defeat.

The Bey of Algiers, Euldj Ali, that prince of corsairs, stationed on the Turkish right wing, fell upon the galleys of Malta, all of whose crews perished, except the Prior and two knights. Euldj Ali made the Maltese flagship prisoner, and saved himself from the Turkish rout with the standard of the Order, which he bore in triumph to Constantinople.

The Christians remained masters of the sea ; but their victory cost them eight thousand soldiers and sailors, and they failed to turn it to account. While Pius V, in his enthusiasm, imagined that they were on their way under full sail towards the capital of the Ottoman Empire and Jerusalem, they stopped to besiege a fortress on the island of Saint Maura, only to abandon the siege betimes, and then took the easier course of going into winter quarters.

Venice adorned her palaces with paintings representing the episodes of this naval battle. Colonna made a triumphal entrance into Rome and ascended to the Capitol. Philip II, on receiving the news of this striking success, waited until the end of the Mass which he was hearing before making the chanting of the *Te Deum* resound in thanksgiving. He wrote a letter of praise to his brother, in which, at the same time, he expressed his regret that Don John should have exposed himself unduly : a display of affection which might also be interpreted as a chiding (10).

While the victors were thus glorifying themselves, the Turks were labouring to make good the disaster. Euldj Ali, appointed Captain Pasha, had galleys constructed by forced labour ; and, at the end of a year, he was able to boast of two hundred, better equipped than those lost at Lepanto. For the bows and arbalests of the fighting crews he substituted arquebuses, an arm much surer and more deadly. He was soon in a position to put to sea again with advantage.

The perpetual league was in process of dissolution. The Venetians would have liked to resume operations in the Levant ; but the Spaniards deemed it preferable to go and dislodge the Barbary pirates from the coasts and ports of Africa. Don John was tempted to respond to the appeal of the Albanians and the Mainotes (the Greeks of the Morea) for help against the Turks, and dreamt of making himself king of these liberated Christians with the aid of Pius V. But Philip was of no mind to lend his money and his men to the pursuit of such grandiose ambitions.

Since, however, he could not repudiate the pact which the Venetians invoked, he gave orders to his brother to dispatch twenty-two ships to the help of the Leaguers, but not to stir from Messina himself. It was only at the instance of Gregory XIII, Pius V's successor, that Philip consented to let the Generalissimo of the League start in person. But the new Captain Pasha, Euldj Ali, was a fine manœuvrer, clever at evasion, since he did not want to expose the young Turkish fleet to the risks of an encounter. Don John could not succeed in imposing his own plans on the other squadron leaders, and he returned disappointed to Messina, and thence to Naples, where pleasure and the company of ladies consoled him for the tedium of inactivity.

The following year, after further preparations, it was learned that the Venetians were negotiating with the Grand Seignior through the intermediary of Noailles, Bishop of Dax, the ambassador of France at Constantinople. They resigned themselves to concluding peace, on March 7th, 1573, on humiliating terms : the surrender of Cyprus and the payment of three hundred thousand ducats.

In order to take advantage of the forces which had been concentrated, Don John persuaded the King to employ them against Tunis and Bizerta. After being immobilized for some months through lack of money, he finally procured funds and set sail for Africa in October with two hundred and eight ships and twenty thousand soldiers. Tunis opened its gates to him, and he entered the town without having to strike a blow. He did not allow it to be sacked. As its Sovereign he re-established Muley Hamed, whom his own subjects had expelled. He restored the fortifications of La Goulette, occupied Bizerta, and returned to Italy after a short and glorious campaign of one month.

But it was a success without a sequel. In June of the following year, Euldj Ali disembarked sixty thousand men, recaptured La

Goulette and Tunis, and returned to Constantinople in triumph over the defeat of the Spaniards and the impotence of the League. The Grand Vizier, showing the victorious fleet to the Venetian ambassador, Antonio Badoaro, said to him jestingly : " You shaved our beard at Lepanto, and we have cut off your arm at Tunis. A beard grows again, but never an arm." It was, in jocular vein, the judgment of history itself.

The battle of Lepanto did not break the back of Ottoman naval power, and it is not from this battle, nor as a result of this event, that we must date the beginning of Turkish decadence. The Sultan came out of the struggle the victor. He kept Cyprus, he recovered Tunis and Bizerta, and he definitely expelled Spain from the Eastern Mediterranean, where, in the course of the sixteenth century, she had several times tried to find a fortress and a port. All this part of the African coast reverted to him, and in the Ægean archipelago there was nothing left for him to conquer but one large island, Crete, which one of his successors took from the Venetians a century later.

The Sultan's African possessions in the Western Mediterranean interested him less. They were far away from his sphere of action, and they would have required efforts and expenses disproportionate with his means if he had attempted to conquer their hinterland in order to make them self-supporting. It is by no means sure that Suleiman would have attempted such an enterprise even if he had made himself master of Malta, or that Selim II would have done so if he had won at Lepanto. The Ottoman empire was already immense, and what finally ruined it was not the loss of a fleet, which it was easy to rebuild in a few months, but the necessity of defending such an extensive front of land and sea frontiers with a military caste, the Janissaries, which became reduced in numbers, degenerate and indisciplined.

It sufficed for the Sultan to keep garrisons in the more important of the Barbary ports on the coast opposite Spain, Italy, and even France, a doubtful ally, and to maintain his authority as best he could over their ruling class of bold captains, the *reis* —often renegades—who carried on piracy at sea and raided even in Christian territory for products of the soil, manufactured goods, articles of exchange, and that most precious of all merchandise, men and women destined for the slave markets. Spain, with her annexes of Sicily and Naples, was more especially exposed to their depredations.

Among other proofs that Don John had not freed the seas was the fact that, in September 1575, while he was on his way back

reign and the beginning of Henri III's, the resurrection of the Protestant party and its alliance with the moderate or time-serving Catholics, and finally the divisions in the French royal family made prudence a law for her.

Reassured against any possibility of a French attack, Requesens concentrated all his forces in the north, and on April 14th, at Mooker-Heyden, near Grave, defeated the rebels, whose leaders, Ludwig of Nassau and Duke Christopher, son of the Elector Palatine, were killed in the course of the rout. After this victory the new Governor could afford, without being suspected of weakness, to show himself clement.

He suppressed the Council of the Troubles. He melted down the statue which the Duke of Alba had raised to himself in the citadel of Antwerp with the bronze of the cannon taken at Gemmingen. He consulted the States-General, and offered to withdraw the odious five and two and a half per cent. duties in return for payment of a lump sum down. On June 6th he solemnly published the pardon granted by the King and by the Pope for all acts committed in connection with the recent troubles : breaches of laws Divine and human.

From the royal amnesty two hundred and seventy-eight persons were excepted. The other delinquents could recover all, or part, of their confiscated property by proving that they had always been Catholics. Those who had gone astray, if they reconciled them-selves with the Church, would have their lives spared (1). Those who refused conversion must leave the country.

About any regime of tolerance, more or less qualified, there was not a single word. The utmost concession was the granting of his life, and nothing else, to the heretic who abjured the error of his ways and did not relapse into it again. Nobody had any right to live in the Low Countries except as a Catholic.

Requesens was surprised to find how little enthusiasm Philip II's subjects showed for being laden with such favours. Three months afterwards they were still in no hurry to solicit them. One is sur-prised at his surprise. What had he to offer that was calculated to appeal to material interests or reassure consciences ? The States-General refused to vote subsidies until their liberties and franchises were restored to them.

A still more serious event occurred. The victors of Mooker-Heyden mutinied. They were the best arquebusiers of the army, men capable, so the Captain-General said, of beating enemies ten times superior in number. For more than a year, or longer still, they had drawn no pay. In order to force Requesens to find the necessary funds, they resolved to lay hands on a pledge. They marched straight on Antwerp, the financial capital of the Low Countries.

As was usual in the case of such disorders, the mutineers had deposed their officers and elected one of their own number by direct suffrage, the *Electo mayor*, to assume command and exercise it under the supervision of a soldiers' council. Having forced their way through the gates of Antwerp, they installed the *Electo* in the Town Hall. The garrison of the citadel, who were Spaniards themselves, let them have their way, and were soon acting in connivance with their compatriots.

The burghers showed some disposition to arm and defend themselves. But Requesens, in order to avoid a clash and the sack of the town, went and established his headquarters among the mutineers, to whom he preached patience and philosophy. He negotiated with the merchants to procure means of satisfying his soldiers ; and with the soldiers to induce them to moderate their demands. But the mutineers, living as bailiff's men at the expense of the inhabitants, were in no hurry to come to terms.

The people of Antwerp were reduced to their wits' end and kept in a state of alarm day and night by the parades, the demonstrations, the shouting and the shooting of these dangerous guests of theirs. On one occasion the mutineers snatched a citizen who had wounded one of their comrades in a brawl out of the protection of a Spanish captain and cut him to pieces. On another occasion they removed objects of worship from the churches by main force, erected an altar in a public square, and had Mass said for them in the open air. Requesens stood aside powerless in the midst of all this disorder, fearing, if he left the city, that it would be pillaged, sacked and ruined.

If this was how the Spanish soldiery behaved, in contempt of their own general, as though they were in conquered territory, in a great city like Antwerp, populous and enclosed in its walls, of what violence were they likely to be capable in the open country at the expense of little groups of peasants and people living in isolation ? They succeeded in making the name of Spaniard hateful to all the inhabitants of the Low Countries, whatever language they spoke and to whatever religion they belonged, and they raised the spirit of resistance to fever heat by the hatred which they inspired. The rebels preferred to fall on their ramparts, with arms in their hands, rather than see their houses sacked and their wives and daughters violated, and drag out wretched lives, if their conquerors left them even that much.

Leyden, one of the strong places of Holland, was situated near the mouth of the old Rhine, almost in the centre of the provinces which persisted in revolt. The Spaniards had invested it for the first time in October, 1573. They suspended the siege from March 21st to May 26th, 1574. They resumed it after the battle of Mooker-Heyden.

The death of Ludwig of Nassau shook the courage of the burghers of Leyden. They were on the point of submitting and asking for mercy. But the terrorizing of loyal Antwerp warned them against what back-sliding rebels like themselves had to expect. They were confirmed in their determination to resist to the death. When famine came, their burgomaster, Pieter van der Werf, offered his own body for his fellow-citizens to share in order to prolong the defence.

From outside the Prince of Orange helped them to the best of his power. He kept in communication with the besieged by pigeon-post. When they were at their last gasp, he conceived the idea of cutting the dykes of the Meuse and the Ijssel, and invoking the protective power of the rivers and the sea. On October 3rd a high equinoctial tide, piled up by a violent gale from the north-west, drove back the flow of the rivers, and, making its way into their inland beds, transformed the flat country into an immense lake (2).

The besieging army fell back before this inundation, while the fleet of the Gueux, commanded by Louis de Boisot, sailed up to the town and revictualled it. Leyden had been cut off for a year. In recognition of its heroisim, the Prince of Orange offered it a choice between exemption from taxes in perpetuity or the foundation of a university. Leyden chose the university.

The relief of Leyden strengthened the position of the rebels in the north. Middelbourg, the last town which the Spaniards held in the island of Walcheren, fell into the hands of the Gueux on February 19th, 1574 ; and thus two provinces, Zeeland, on the estuary of the Scheldt, the Meuse and the Rhine, and Holland, between the Zuyder Zee and the North Sea, found themselves almost entirely liberated. They governed themselves, in accordance with their own laws, under the authority of the Prince of Orange, who, once nominated *Stathouder* by Philip II, held himself to be confirmed in his office by right of resistance.

William of Orange remained in arms for the King against the King ; and although, at this period, he still protested his loyalty, he acted as an independent Sovereign. The provincial States and the towns obeyed nobody but him—so far as they were capable of obeying anybody. He was their representative abroad and towards the governors-general. Since it was impossible to subdue Holland and Zeeland by force, the Council of State recommended treating with them—in other words, with the Prince of Orange. Requesens had no option but to accept this recommendation. Negotiations were opened at Breda, on March 3rd, 1575.

The representatives of Requesens proposed that the Protestants should leave the country, but with the right to dispose of their properties after a lapse of seven, eight, or ten years. It was, as the Prince of Orange put it, " a pretty wretched peace ". " You want to uproot us," cried Marnix de Sainte Aldegonde ; " but we are not going to let ourselves be uprooted." The negotiations were adjourned in May. They were resumed in June, with no better success.

The Council of State was almost unanimously in favour of granting the deputies of Holland the withdrawal of the Spanish troops and the convocation of the States-General ; but it denied this representative assembly of the Seventeen Provinces the right to settle the religious question. Refusal to compromise was equal on both sides. Some Protestants talked about prohibiting Catholic worship absolutely in Holland, and the King absolutely refused to tolerate heretical worship anywhere at all in his territory. He was quite prepared to consult the States-General ; but, in conformity with old custom, this was to be only for the purpose of asking their opinion, not for that of receiving their orders, as all the people of the Low Countries were now beginning to demand.

Requesens adopted the position that he could no nothing without instructions from the King. Philip, on August 20th, finally broke the silence which he had preserved for several months. He approved the breaking-off of negotiations with the rebels, hoping that God would open to him " another way, safer and more honourable, of perpetuating religion in these provinces ". He was not surprised at the lack of success in the attempts at peace that had been made, " because he had never expected anything good of such wicked people " (3).

He announced the departure from Santander of a new fleet, whose destination he carefully concealed, as though everybody did not know that he was dispatching it to the Low Countries. On its arrival Requesens vigorously resumed the offensive. His soldiers, wading up to their shoulders, crossed the arms of the sea at low tide and occupied the islands of Zeeland. They had permission to kill everybody.

To these cruelties Sonoy, the Prince of Orange's lieutenant, replied by similar cruelties. He executed priests and monks, and tortured Catholics. The struggle assumed a character of savagery. Any agreement became impossible.

The two adversaries—the two provinces, on the one hand, and the Spaniards, on the other—made ready for a decisive encounter. In July, Holland and Zeeland concluded a treaty of union to resist the common enemy under the government of, and in obedience to, the Prince of Orange, *Stathouder* of the King. The ordinance of Holland of August 27th, to which Zeeland adhered the following year, invested the Prince with supreme authority, with the assistance and under the supervision of a Council (*Landraat*). The Union of Delft, on April 25th, 1576, confirmed the union of the two provinces, and designated the Prince of Orange their head during the war and, so to speak, their Sovereign *ad interim*.

But the continuance of the struggle obliged the States to provide themselves with another protector. The Prince himself, conscious of the insufficiency of their forces, told them frankly that it was necessary either to make peace with the King of Spain or to place themselves in obedience to a powerful monarch. The States decided to solicit the support of the Queen of England, Elizabeth, who was a Protestant and was descended from the old Counts of Holland. These were considerations to which, they said, must be added " the opportunity of commerce ".

The Prince of Orange was rather of opinion that they should address themselves to France. In 1573 he had already offered Charles IX the title, and the responsibilities, of defender and protector of the States. Orange knew how selfish Elizabeth was. She was only too glad, like Catherine de Medici, to create embarrassments for Philip II ; but she was also prejudiced against rebellious subjects, Protestants though they might be. She was pacific by disposition and from a spirit of economy. Above all, she was anxious not to offer the French, who were only too near for her liking as it was, any opportunity of taking advantage of the troubles to extend their influence into the Low Countries. Charles IX of France had just died, and his successor, Henri III, the earlier victor at Jarnac and Moncontour, was regarded as a great captain and might be tempted to play the conqueror.

Elizabeth, as a matter of fact, did not hesitate to come to an understanding with Philip. She signed a treaty with him, on April 16th, 1575, whereby the two contracting parties mutually agreed to sacrifice one another's enemies. Requesens expelled the English Catholics who had gone and sought refuge in the Low Countries, and closed the seminary at Douai, where young English Catholics prepared themselves for the apostolate and for martyrdom. Elizabeth, in her turn, forbade the proscribed of the Low Countries, in other words the Protestants of the Seventeen Provinces, to stay in England under pain of death. She sent an ambassador, Cobham, to Madrid to advise the King of the understanding between Henri III and the Prince of Orange, and she refused the protectorate over them which Holland and Zeeland offered her.

Abandoned by England, and hard pressed by the Spaniards, the rebels were beginning to despair when, fortunately for them, Requesens died, on March 4th, 1576. In the absence of a governor, the Council of State took the direction of affairs in hand. This body, in which natives of the Low Countries were in a majority, recommended that concessions should be made and, in the first place, that the States-General should be summoned to meet.

Philip, after a long silence, foreshadowed in July a reply about the true remedies which were applicable to the ills of the country, but ordered any summoning of the States-General to be postponed. Despite the insistent demands of the Council to know what it was to do, he put off his instructions until the end of August or September. He lost time deliberating when he should have acted, and acted promptly.

In vain did the Council remonstrate with him that " the delay and postponement of remedies have reduced us to such conditions that we are ruined ". The Spanish troops, who had obtained but slender booty at Zierieksee, a little town of Zeeland taken in June, started pillaging the country again to recoup themselves. They marched on Brussels. The States of Brabant, those Brabançon hotheads, attacked the impotent Council of State, and demanded the recall of the foreign troops.

When the mutineers appeared on the hills of Laeken, the burghers of Brussels took to arms and closed the gates of the city. The populace vented their wrath on all Spaniards, whom they chased and beat. A cry was raised : " Death to all traitors ! Death to the Council of State ! " On July 23rd, the Council was shut up in the palace where it sat. The King's most hated officers, Roda, Vargas and Romero, fled and took refuge in the citadel of Antwerp. The Baron of Heze, a friend of the Prince of Orange, declared himself Governor of Brussels and raised troops.

On September 4th a fresh insurrection broke out. The two Councillors of State who were most devoted to the King, the Counts of Berlaymont and Mansfeldt, were imprisoned ; the Council was purged ; Del Rio, one of the most bloodthirsty judges on the Council of the Troubles, was thrown into the dungeons of Treurenberg. The

Prince of Orange, in accord with the States of Brabant, demanded the summoning of the States-General. This was decided upon by a shadow of the former Council of State, sitting under the presidency of the Duke of Aerschot, a faithful subject, but an ardent patriot.

The deputies of the provinces of Brabant, Hainault and Flanders, assembled on September 25th in Brussels, addressed to Philip, in justification of their initiative, a long list of the country's grievances against its Spanish governors. Without awaiting his reply or seeking the King's authorization, they informed him that they were about to resume the Breda conference, hoping, they said, that, after the departure of the Spaniards, Holland and Zeeland would accommodate themselves to the will of His Majesty in all matters of religion.

They were deliberately deceiving themselves. They were representatives of provinces which were Catholic by an immense majority, and they were afraid of the Spaniards. They did, indeed, open negotiations at Ghent with the Prince of Orange, on October 6th ; but they still imposed the same condition : " provided that the Roman religion be exercised and remains as a whole without any innovations whatsoever, and without infringing the obedience due to His Majesty."

As the delegates of the southern provinces claimed that the Catholic religion should be re-established in Holland and Zeeland, where it was prohibited, the delegates of the Prince of Orange demanded the free exercise of Protestant worship in the southern provinces in return. These were irreconcilable theses ; but a new outbreak of Spanish fury submerged incompatibility of doctrine and sentiment.

An army raised by the States, and commanded by the Marquis of Havré and the Count of Egmont, had marched to the deliverance of Antwerp, where the Spaniards occupied the citadel. But the garrison, reinforced by the mutineers from Alost, defeated the liberators, on November 4th. Masters of the town, the Spanish soldiery pillaged, plundered, violated and massacred six to seven thousand burghers, without sparing women, children, or old men. They sacked private houses, warehouses, and banks, and took an enormous amount of booty. One soldier might have twenty thousand écus for his share ; others picked up so much gold that they ornamented their pikes and their swords with it.

Drawn together by their indignation, Catholics and Protestants of the Low Countries, on November 8th, signed a provisional compromise, known as the Pacification of Ghent. It prohibited Protestant worship in fifteen of the provinces, and Catholic worship in the two others, Holland and Zeeland, until the States-General, assembled

But these remedies, merely soporific and too long awaited as they were, lagged behind the ill which it was a question of curing. The States-General had treated it on their own authority by dividing the country between the two Churches, abolishing the proclamations, demanding the departure of the Spanish troops, and swearing not to recognize the new governor until he had sworn to observe all the articles of the Pacification of Ghent.

Immediately after his arrival in Luxemburg, Don John, convinced of his isolation, opened negotiations with the deputies of the States at Marche-en-Famène, near Huy, in the bishopric of Liége, a neutral territory where the bishop and even the representative of the Emperor might play the calming rôle of mediators. This man of war was a bad diplomat, violent and imperious, who bore contradiction impatiently. He confesses in his letters to the King and the Secretaries of State that he nearly replied to a suggestion of the Marquis of Havré by boxing his ears, and that another time he was tempted to seize a candlestick and break it over the head of another deputy, Champagney, Granvelle's brother, but a passionate Belgian patriot.

Appeals to moderation reached Don John from Madrid. Philip II, short of money as usual, was of opinion that it was better not to break off negotiations, but to accept the pacification of Ghent, though it might be put in a different form, and to compromise with the States at the price of some sacrifices, " for in such affairs time and necessity are the best of councillors ". It was essential to conclude peace at any price, and satisfy the Prince of Orange in order to rid the Low Countries of him. Caught between the two fires of the King's conciliatory disposition and the uncompromising attitude of the States, Don John gave way on all points. The Treaty of Marche-en-Famène, signed on February 17th, 1577, left him a governor disarmed in the presence of subjects under arms.

Don John kept on representing to Madrid that the sole means of securing peace was to extend the theatre of war. The two great enemies of the King were the Prince of Orange and Queen Elizabeth. The latter was more to be feared than the former, and she supported him covertly and openly. To get the better of the protégé, it was essential to strike at the protectress.

Why not land the Spanish troops, whose departure from the Low Countries the exigences of State demanded, in England ? Don John reminded his brother of the promises which he had made him. With the *tercios* of the Low Countries, he would require only small reinforcement to undertake with success a conquest " which would render such service to God, would be so glorious for the King, and from which," he added, " I should myself reap such honour and advantage."

But now that he was at a distance, far away from the magnetic influence of personal contact, Philip—who, it was true, had to consider the monarchical chess-board as a whole—brushed aside the idea of carrying out this great design of Don John's. The King tried to soothe his brother's ruffled feelings. " . . . Another and a better opportunity will present itself. Meanwhile it is essential, above all, to settle the affairs of the Low Countries."

Elizabeth was not an easy person to take by surprise. She knew all about Don John's projects and his intrigues with Mary Stuart. She had a spy in his own entourage, among his own intimates. She sent one ambassador to Madrid. She maintained another, Thomas Wilson, in Brussels. She accredited a third, Horsey, Governor of the Isle of Wight, to Don John himself. This ambassador, on the occasion of his first visit to him, went so far as to say that, if the Spaniards put to sea, it would be " to deliver Queen Mary, who was not a prisoner ". " What people say is laughable," replied Don John. The King of Spain was seriously embarrassed in the Levant. If he was recalling his troops from the Low Countries, it was in order to make provision against the aggression of the Turks.

A month later the ambassador returned to the charge and repeated that it was in order to attack England that it was proposed to transport the Spanish troops from the Low Countries by sea. To this Don John replied once more " that he had the King's orders to be of service to the Queen, which was also his own desire, and that he would always be ready to give her proof of it ".

One of the great resources of Elizabeth's diplomacy, whenever she found herself embarrassed and wanted to disarm her adversary, was the offer of her hand. She was not impervious to the appeal to her vanity of adding one more name to the already lengthy list of her suitors. She was always sure of being able to refuse herself afterwards, as she had done once, and was to do again, in the case of the French princes, the Dukes of Anjou and Alençon. Horsey and one of the English Catholics maintained by the King of Spain in the Low Countries made indirect approaches to Mary Stuart's contingent champion about the idea of marriage with their Sovereign.

Don John did not reject this overture, and even lent ear to it, while awaiting whatever instructions about it he might receive from His Majesty of Spain. He nibbled at the bait himself, and was inclined to believe in the sincerity of this game of feminine diplomacy. But he was careful not to commit himself too far.

" . . . If by chance the matter went further," he wrote to Philip, " I would beg Your Majesty to tell me, as one gentleman to another, whether you are of opinion that I ought to follow it up. For, though well I see that by these means a queen and a kingdom might be made submissive to religion and to the service of Your Majesty, not for anything in the world would I do anything contrary to honour ; and let Your Majesty appreciate that, even while I say this, I blush with the shame which I feel at the thought of a negotiation of marriage with a woman whose life and example give so much occasion for talk."

Nevertheless he submitted himself to the will of the King.
On April 6th the King replied—

" that it (the marriage) might be negotiated and concluded in such a form, and with such an intention, that a great service would be done, and a great sacrifice offered, to Our Lord. The submission of this kingdom (England) to the Catholic religion is, in itself, a thing from which so much honour and glory would result that it seems there is nothing which should be neglected to attain this end."

Was it to keep the Queen of England in play, or was it to flatter Don John's vanity, that the King did not brush aside the idea of this marriage ? But, in any case, could he seriously have believed that Elizabeth would yield to his brother's big moustache what she had refused to all the other suitors of whom he now made one ?

Elizabeth demanded, and induced the States-General to demand, that the Spanish army should return to Italy overland ; and Philip, resolutely devoted to the pacification of the Low Countries, yielded again. The treaty of Marche-en-Famène embodied all these concessions, and robbed Don John of the glory which he had promised himself, like a true paladin, of liberating a captive queen and conquering a kingdom.

He was humiliated at the idea of staying on merely as the titular governor, so to speak, of the all-powerful States-General. Accordingly he begged the King to appoint a successor to him, in the person either of the Empress, the widow of Maximilian II, who died on October 12th, 1576 ; or the Duchess of Parma, or the Duchess of Lorraine (5).

Exasperated by his impotence and already troubled by some attacks of fever, Don John dispatched Escovedo, the most confidential of his secretaries, to set forth to Philip the arguments for his recall. Escovedo was a former servant of the Prince of Eboli, who had been transferred to Don John's service and devoted himself to his master's fortunes with a zeal in which pride and an ambition to play a rôle of his own had their part. He had replaced Soto, who had compromised himself by a similar excess of devotion and been transferred by Philip to the military treasury, and he flattered himself that he was cleverer and would be luckier. He was an admirer of this young prince, victor over the Moors, at Lepanto and at Tunis. Knowing that Gregory XIII had inherited Pius V's feelings towards Don John, Escovedo went to Rome and tried to come to an understanding with this Pope about Don John's project of delivering Mary Stuart and dethroning Elizabeth.

Escovedo had accompanied Don John from Italy to Spain, and he remained there for two months after his master's departure for the Low Countries in order to expedite the dispatch of the sinews of war and press the arguments for a landing in England. Finding Philip more and more unresponsive towards this project, Escovedo accused the King of being lacking in initiative and breadth of view. He was even so bold as to reproach Philip, in writing, with being " very disconnected " (*tan descocido*) in his policy. We may, perhaps, be surprised that a monarch so much imbued with a sense of his own greatness as Philip should have contented himself with characterizing this letter of Escovedo's as a " cruel document " (*carta sangriente*).

After his arrival in the Low Countries, Escovedo turned over in his mind the idea, and the possible means, of forming a group in the Council of State in Madrid, of which Don John, recalled to the Court, would be the directing spirit, and which he might inspire with a more energetic foreign policy. Escovedo counted upon Antonio Pérez, a creature like himself of the Prince of Eboli, and Philip II's favourite secretary, to assist him in this design. He wrote freely to Pérez, without taking into account the fact that, if his letters were communicated to the King, they would be bound to turn Philip aside, once and for all, from granting his brother any authority which foreshadowed a diminishing of his own.

Don John's secretary was not afraid to write to his confidant Pérez that his master was anxious to leave the Low Countries— and for what a reason ! " . . . We have no other aim and desire than a chair under a canopy (*silla y cortina*) "—in other words, recognition as an Infante. " Everything else is beside the mark. . . . The appearance of this friend "—Escovedo meant the expedition to England—" having failed us, we are in despair and almost out of our minds ; nothing else means anything to us but disgust and mortification."

Would it not be well to lead the Spanish troops to the support of the King of France, at war with his subjects, in order to spare the nation the dishonour of withdrawing from the Low Countries on the orders of the States-General ? What would be better still, Escovedo wrote to Pérez on February 7th, after mature consideration, would be to recall both Don John and himself to Madrid, where they would arrive " ready to act ".

" So far as you are concerned," Escovedo urged Pérez, " strive to achieve this result, and be assured that, if you succeed in forming a group of His Highness, Los Velez, and Sesa at the Court, with Antonio (Pérez) and Juan (Escovedo) as their acolytes, our point of view cannot fail to prevail in the Council. . . . Yourself and Velez will have good opportunities of deploring the King's excess of work and recommending to him the necessity of taking care of his health, on which the salvation of Christendom depends. I would go so far as to say, without beating about the bush, that, for this reason and in view of the extreme youth of the Prince his son, it would be well that he (Philip) should have someone to share his burden, and that, in appreciation of the wisdom, prudence and fidelity which His Highness (Don John) has displayed in these affairs, it seems that he is the person upon whom this position devolves and the person whom, as the Scriptures say, God has willed, in recompense for the piety of the King, to give him as a staff for his old age " (6).

His old age ! Philip was only fifty-two, and he was to live twenty years longer, always working, always toiling. It was a year later, in 1578, that the Infante who succeeded him, Don Philip, was born. Assuredly it must have angered him that anybody should think him failing in body or mind. It must have enraged him that anybody should propose to provide him with an auxiliary who would wield the reality of power and leave him only the honours of it—him, who all his life long was his own Prime Minister !

Escovedo must have felt very sure of Antonio Pérez to run the risk of saying such things to him. Antonio Pérez, Philip II's Secretary of State, was the son of another Secretary of State, Gonzalo Pérez, a sound man of letters, the translator of the *Odyssey* into Spanish, who had sent him travelling outside Spain and educated him at foreign universities in Italy and Germany. The young man had profited by this extensive education so well that his good father counted upon him to avenge him for the ill will of the Duke of Alba towards himself. This ill will of Alba's may have been due to the fact that Gonzalo Pérez had taken sides with the Prince of Eboli, which was a thing that the Duke, authoritarian and jealous as he was, could never forgive. But, in any case, on Gonzalo's death, his son was recommended by his patron. After some hesitation on the King's part, Antonio Pérez was appointed to take his father's place.

Philip may have hesitated about appointing Antonio Pérez because he found him so unlike those jurists, the best workers on behalf of the monarchical authority, whom Diego de Mendoza, the penetrating historian of the war of Granada, describes as follows : " Their profession was (the observance of) the laws, modesty, discretion, truth ; a way of life completely bound up with respect for old customs ; no paying of visits, no acceptance of presents, no too intimate relationships ; no fine clothes or luxury of any kind " (7).

By contrast with them, he was a very brilliant gentleman, this young Antonio Pérez, Secretary of State. He was fond of scent, rich attire, a home decorated with paintings, adorned with pictures, full of valuable knick-knacks. His house was a museum, which was thrown open to all distinguished visitors by its hospitable, generous master. He knew how to win hearts by fair words and promises ; he lacked the haughty reserve of his race ; he was out to attract and to charm. Accordingly his habits, his expensive and luxurious way of living, did not seem calculated to appeal to this severe King, who liked his servants to be devoted to the point of self-effacement.

But, once Philip took Pérez into his service, the King acquired such a liking for his Secretary's intelligent and expeditious manner of doing his work that he was just as much attracted to him as many other people were. The affection which Philip felt for Pérez had all the marks of a regular passion. This Sovereign, infatuated with his own prestige and ever careful to keep even grandees at a distance, so far forgot himself on one occasion, when Pérez was ill, as to go and inquire for him at his own door. " The King," says Count de Luna, " really loved him, it appears, and he satisfied his passion to such an extent that he carried it to excess."

It was to Pérez, as we have already seen, that Philip, usually so discreet, so close, so enigmatic, revealed his policy of treating the Council of State, that aristocratic body, in such a way as to reduce it to a nullity. What is obvious is that Philip gave him his confidence. What we can infer is that he assigned Pérez the rôle of gleaner of discussions, of reporter of opinions, and in short, to put it brutally, of spy.

Escovedo was an uncommonly bad psychologist to confide in a man who owed everything to the King and who, as a matter of self-interest as well as duty, was bound to tell him everything. Philip regarded it as one of the principal functions of his servants

it was from the heights of these mountains that the Christians set out to reconquer the peninsula. But did he really go so far as to say to Pérez that he and his friends, entrenched on these heights, could thence dictate their own terms to Madrid ? One finds it difficult to believe it ; and, in any case, if he did say so, it was only the outburst of an angry man and, as Pérez put it at the time, " the bragging and bravado of half a dozen worms ".

But Pérez, this odd confidant of Escovedo's, was beginning to get frightened of the reckless sayings and writings of this Southerner of the North. Learning that Escovedo contemplated returning to Spain, still with the idea of exerting pressure on Philip on Don John's behalf, Pérez exhorted him not to stir from the Low Countries. " And so, Señor Escovedo, God preserve us from your coming here, for it would ruin us. I·have already told you how few our friends are. You know it very well. You know also how far the tempera-ment of the brother (the King) is a dangerous temperament." The King, to whom Pérez showed his letter as usual, wrote in the margin : " This document may stand, and everything you say in it is good."

Don John consented to stay in Flanders, and resumed his negotia-tions with the States. He dispatched the Spanish troops overland to Italy, and made his entrance into Brussels. Thence, on May 15th, 1577, he wrote to the Prince of Orange, the man who had to be won over at any price, " to have him consider (that) the opportunity which he had now of living henceforth in peace, wealth, and honour was one of those which were not to be missed, since all this he would certainly find in the clemency and liberality of His Majesty ".

Let the Prince of Orange—

" consider also how unstable and disquieting is a situation which, on the one hand, rests upon dangerous relationships, and, on the other hand, is in opposition with natural reason and laws Divine and human. There are no longer, my lord, either governors or Spaniards to raise their fingers, so it behoves every one of the people of these countries, from the highest to the lowest, to open his eyes and see in what consists his damage or his advantage. Since this depends, in such great part, upon the sole will of Your Lordship, it is assuredly right that you should accommodate yourself to what will be proposed to you at greater length by the Duke of Aerschot and Monsieur de Hierges."

What Philip wanted was that this dangerous adversary of his should withdraw to Germany, leaving his duties and possessions in the Low Countries to his son, the Count of Buren. At a conference held at Gertruydenberg, Don John's envoys offered the Prince of

222

Orange the countship of Charolais, over which his sovereignty would be recognized by the King of France, in exchange for his possessions in Burgundy. But the Prince of Orange found the revenues of the Charolais insufficient, and the negotiations were broken off.

The religious question remained the great obstacle in the way of reconciliation. Don John ordered the governors and councils of justice to prosecute and punish heretics, and the archbishops and bishops to use all their vigilance to protect their flocks from these ravening wolves. But he found, to his great indignation, that the States declared it to be impossible for them to take up arms against Holland and Zeeland, in order to re-establish there the obedience due to the King and the maintenance of the Roman Catholic religion.

" What they want is liberty of conscience." If the King chose to truckle to a demand so unworthy of his title of Catholic King, Don John begged him to find another instrument for this policy of tolerance. He declared, in a letter dated May 23rd, that he was himself incapable of it. Two days later, more irritated than ever by this pretension, he wrote : " I avow to Your Majesty that for my part I would rather die than consent to such a thing, and, if the kingdoms and provinces belonged to me, I would let them be submerged and lost altogether rather than suffer that, in any of their parts, there should be a religion different from that which I profess." Assuredly it was not to this fiery temperament that the responsibility of settling conflicts of ambition and conscience should ever have been entrusted.

The struggle, as it dragged on, increased the pretensions of the Prince of Orange. As long as the war lasted, he was Sovereign *ad interim* in the two provinces and one of the most influential leaders of the States-General in the fifteen others. Once peace were concluded and the country reconciled with Philip II, he would revert to being a mere subject again, and a subject whom his rebellion would render eternally suspect. So he was in no hurry to treat. The Pacification of Ghent had not settled religious questions in such a definite way that the Prince of Orange could find no opportunity of intervening.

It was true that the situation also offered Don John grounds for hope, if he had been capable of patience. Already the religious and political discords which ended by separating the provinces of the north from those of the south were manifesting themselves here and there. Even outside of Holland and Zeeland, the Protestants were openly preaching their doctrine. In the towns the people were rising against the aristocracy. Don John had only to wait. He could have rallied the disaffected nobility and Catholics by a few concessions.

But, instead of looking for glory in the pacification of the Low Countries, he returned by a roundabout route to his cross-Channel projects. He wrote to Pérez, he wrote to the King, that the conquest of England, or of Zeeland, was the only means of breaking the resistance. He did not flatter himself that he could achieve this single-handed, without money, without a fleet, and without an army. The recall of the *tercios* quartered in Italy would provoke a general rising of the people. Recruiting on the spot would raise only soldiers good for service against the King. The best thing would be to replace him by a Regent, the Empress Dowager Mary, widow of Maximilian II, and so make the rebels and their accomplices believe that the Court of Spain was all for peace and induce them to stop arming.

Meanwhile the King should equip a fleet, with Algiers as its declared objective. He, Don John, under pretext of fighting the Barbaresques and the Turks, would return unexpectedly and re-appear in the Low Countries with the combined land and sea forces. It was a highly complicated and very costly project, which, apart from the difficulties of its execution, must have shocked the Government of Madrid, hard up as it was (9).

Inaction weighed upon the young Prince, and the defiance of the opposition humiliated him. He dispatched Escovedo to Spain to represent his case there, and himself left Brussels, where he could not succeed in making himself obeyed. From Malines, which showed itself no more docile, he made his way to Namur and, on July 24th, surprised its citadel, which he proposed to make his headquarters. Philip disapproved of this *coup de force*, which, as might have been foreseen, united " the good and the bad " against the Governor. The more violent, the patriots, as they called themselves, pressed forward measures of defence. On September 23rd William of Nassau reappeared in Brussels.

The King, disgruntled by the turn of affairs in Flanders, was enraged to learn of the disembarkation at Santander, on July 21st, of Escovedo, who, not content with having hypothecated six thousand ducats to construct a keep in his castle, projected further fortifications in the port and in the town. Philip was the more angry with him for arriving without warning, this pressing and importunate solicitor, this zealous and often arrogant advocate of his brother's pretensions.

On the letter in which Antonio Pérez announced this disagreeable news to him, Philip wrote this marginal note : " The blow is on the point of being struck at us. We must be ready for anything, and hasten to get rid of (*despachar*) him before he gets the better of (*mate*) us." It is the double meaning of these two words " *despachar* " and " *mate* " which has led some historians, such as Mignet and Kervyn de Lettenhove, to believe that the King ordered this dangerous mischief-maker to be " dispatched to the next world (*despachar*) ", " before he kills us (*antes que nos mate*) ". If this were so, the King was badly obeyed, for Escovedo was not assassinated until eight months later. It was certainly his indiscretions which led to his being killed, but politics were only the indirect cause of his death (10).

Escovedo's former patron, the Prince of Eboli, had married, in 1553, Ana de Mendoza, only daughter of Count de Melito, of the aristocratic family of the Mendozas. She was born in 1540, and when Eboli died, in 1573, after a dozen years of married life—from 1559, the date of his return to Spain with Philip, to the time of his death—she had had nine children by him. At first she seemed inconsolable, talked of entering religion, and even founded a convent of Carmelites at Pastrana, the chief town of her estates. But she wanted to govern the community and interpret the rules of the order, which Theresa of Avila had reformed and settled, in her own way. After a good deal of wrangling, the nuns left the castle and the Princess returned to Court.

As at Pastrana during the early days of her widowhood, she showed herself quite different from what she was—or what we are led to suppose she was—before : haughty, whimsical, imperious, jealous of her independence and her pleasures. In this country, where, by a tradition handed down from the Moors, ladies went out veiled or in a closed litter, lived in company with their womenfolk, and saw scarcely anybody but their relations, she had become accustomed, presumably during her husband's lifetime, to entertaining people of her own world : grandees, gentlemen, courtiers. Beautiful, though blind in one eye from an accident in her childhood, rich and intelligent, she was very much sought after. Don John, who used to visit her during her husband's lifetime, was pleased, so we are told, to kiss her—in all respect and quite innocently, I imagine —on the good eye which remained to her.

To Antonio Pérez's misfortune and her own, she met the attractive Secretary of State. We know that, on their first meeting, she was amused at the sight of him, dressed up, tricked out, perfumed, rather overdone man of the world that he was ; but she listened to him, and fell under the spell of his charm like so many others. Their *liaison* was known, or at least suspected, when Escovedo returned to Spain.

Mere prudence should have counselled Escovedo to keep on good terms with Pérez, to whom he had written so many compromising letters, and he ought not to have believed his own eyes when he happened to see the lovers "*juntos en la cama o en el estrado en cosas deshonestas*" ("in bed together, or on a couch, in compromising attitudes"). But, either because of his mania for meddling, or from a very keen and quite Spanish sense of honour, he conceived it to be his duty, in his capacity as a former servant of the Prince of Eboli, to protect the dead man's memory against the retrospective stain of posthumous conjugal betrayal. "Here is something no longer to be tolerated," he cried, "and I am obliged to inform the King about it." The Princess replied: "Escovedo, you may tell him, if you like, *que mas quiero el trasero de Antonio Pérez que al Rey*." One may translate *trasero* by a euphemistic equivalent: "that I would rather have the seat of Pérez's trousers than the King himself."

But the lovers, scared by the possibility of a scandal, determined to rid themselves of this indiscreet interloper. Pérez went to the King and, this time without any sparing of Escovedo, reminded Philip of all the proceedings in which he had taken part or even been the prime mover: his negotiations without Philip's sanction with the Court of Rome, and, contrary to his will, in favour of the project of a landing in England; his insistence upon obtaining the title and the privileges of an Infante for Don John; and, above all, his attempt to secure for Don John the rôle of principal Minister on the Council of State and make him Mayor of the Palace to a *Roi fainéant*. Philip, stung in his pride, and fearing some widespread agitation calculated to trouble the public peace and the tranquillity of his States—and incidentally to compromise Don John himself—decided to suppress this bad counsellor of his.

The Council of State was consulted. One of its members, the Marquis of Los Velez—the very man of whom Escovedo had contemplated making use, even though he feared him as a possible rival to his master—declared that if he were asked, with the Host in his mouth, whose life it was more important to sacrifice, that of Juan Escovedo or that of somebody else who was among the most pernicious, he would pronounce that it was Escovedo's.

Pérez, to whom Philip gave orders in writing to dispose of this dangerous subject for him, first tried to poison him, and, having failed in this, proceeded to hire a gang of assassins, who killed Escovedo with a sword-thrust on Easter Monday, March 31st, 1578.

Meanwhile Don John's taking of the citadel of Namur by surprise had closed the ranks of the Seventeen Provinces' coalition against the Spanish administration. The States summoned Don John to lay down his arms, and, on his refusal, declared him deposed, on December 7th, 1577. To resist the Spanish troops, whom he proceeded to recall from Italy, they addressed themselves to Elizabeth ; to the Archduke Mathias, brother of the Emperor Rudolph and cousin of the King of Spain ; and to the Duke of Alençon, brother of the King of France.

The Protestants of the Low Countries would have liked to appeal only to the Protestant Queen. But Elizabeth was lukewarm, and, on occasion, even hostile. The aristocracy sought a counterpoise to the revolutionary movement of the town agitators and the religious reformers, who were allied with the Prince of Orange. One of the leaders of the aristocracy, the Duke of Aerschot, conceived the idea of summoning Mathias, a prince of the House of Austria, to the Low Countries, and then putting him forward for the King of Spain's choice as a prince of his own blood, who would seem better designated than any foreigner for the desirable task of reconciliation.

The Prince of Orange warded off this stroke adroitly. First he tried to let the agitators of Ghent, Hembyze and Rylove, do his work for him. They imprisoned the Duke of Aerschot, the Governor of Flanders, and the principal members of the provincial Council. Compelled by public indignation to trim his sails, Orange ordered them to be set at liberty. But the Prince was luckier in his own dealings with the Archduke Mathias. Orange recognized the Archduke's powers ; but he had them restricted within severe limits, and, by a secret article, he reserved the direction of military affairs to himself. The States-General were compelled by popular pressure to associate Orange, as lieutenant-general, with the Archduke, whom they had appointed governor and captain-general for the King. Henceforth the Archduke was nothing more, as it was said, than " registrar " to the Prince.

In Luxemburg, where he was awaiting the troops from Italy, Don John received a letter from Philip II, dated December 18th, 1577, which informed him of the appointment of Margaret of Parma as Governor of the Low Countries. This was the King's reply to Don John's impetuous occupation of the citadel of Namur ; his departure from Brussels ; his breaking-off of negotiations with the States ; and his recriminations against a policy of peace and compromise which, so Don John had written to his brother from Malines, ran the risk, through the contagion of the example of weakness, of leading to the ruin even of Spanish domination in Italy (11).

Despite Philip, however, the war broke out again. With the Spanish *tercios* and some five thousand soldiers whom the Duke of Guise had disbanded to enable them to join him, Don John marched against the composite troops of the States, and put them to rout at Gembloux, on January 30th, 1578. If he had mustered sufficient forces, he might have pushed on to Brussels and re-entered it as master.

The States, in their dismay, turned towards France and accepted, though without enthusiasm, the offer of help from the Duke of Alençon, Henri III's brother. Alençon was the last of Catherine's sons. Still quite young, this " dark horse ", by his turbulence and his pretensions, had aroused his mother to astonishment, and even to admiration. After the breaking-off of the negotiations between the Duke of Anjou and the Queen of England, he had embraced the idea of marrying Elizabeth himself with delight, despite the fact that she was twenty-one years older than he was. Their difference in religion did not embarrass him in the least. He was quite ready to sacrifice the Mass for a royal crown.

Accordingly the massacre of Saint Bartholomew, which ruined his hopes, administered such a shaking to Alençon that his egotistical soul was moved to pity by it, and he even dared to deplore the murder of the Admiral. During the last months of Charles IX's lifetime, he grouped around him Protestants converted by force on the occasion of Saint Bartholomew's, Catholics who condemned the massacre—the " politicals ", as they were called—and the factious of both religions. He even contemplated a civil war for the purpose of getting himself appointed lieutenant-general to the dying King, and barring the way to France, and to the throne, of the heir presumptive, whom his mother had contrived to get elected as King of Poland.

Imprisoned by Charles IX, held in semi-captivity by Henri III, Charles IX's successor, Alençon fled from the Court in 1575 and in the following year, with the aid of the malcontents and an army of the Protestants of Germany, which the Count Palatine, John Casimir, led under his banner, he imposed upon the King of France, his brother, a peace that granted him a truly royal appanage in the centre of France. Quite unscrupulously, the next year he turned against the Protestants, his allies of yesterday, led the royal army against them, and took and sacked La Charité and Issoire, two of their strongholds.

But, on his return from this victorious campaign, Alençon discovered that the Court was ungrateful to him, and that Henri III had no favour to show him for his Catholic zeal and his devotion. Meanwhile, the Protestant party had found a new leader in the person of Henri de Bourbon, King of Navarre, who, compelled to abjure on the occasion of Saint Bartholomew's and imprisoned—

together with the Duke of Alençon—after the conspiracy of the "politicals", had also fled from the Court, and, once at liberty again, lost no time in reverting to Protestantism.

The Duke of Alençon, now become Duke of Anjou, therefore had only one chance of escaping from his condition as a subject : namely, conquering a principality for himself outside France. On more than one occasion already, as early as 1576, he had been invited to intervene in the Low Countries : in May of that year by the Prince of Orange and the States of Holland and Zeeland ; in October by the more advanced fraction of the States-General. He promised his support ; but the hostility of Elizabeth to the establishment of a French prince in the Low Countries, and the affairs of France, had prevented him from following up this plan.

But he was still thinking about it. While he was marching against Issoire and La Charité, he commissioned his beloved sister, Marguerite of Valois, Queen of Navarre, to go to Spa, under pretext of taking a cure, and sound the intentions of the lords of the Low Countries (12).

In the southern provinces, Catholic by religion, Walloon by race, and French by language, through which Marguerite passed, a section of the nobility was, through hatred of the Spaniards, well disposed towards the French. A brother of the Count of Lalaing, together with four gentlemen " among the principal in Hainault ", offered this clandestine ambassadress their support in handing over Hainault and Artois to her brother. The Lord of Inchy promised to deliver the citadel of Cambrai to him.

The States-General, however, showed themselves less impressed. They addressed themselves directly to Henri III and Catherine de Medici, confining themselves to setting forth the justice of their cause. To the Duke of Anjou's offer of help they merely returned their thanks and postponed any statement of their requirements until a later date.

But the defeat of their troops by Don John at Gembloux made them more ready to treat. The Duke of Anjou gave it to be understood that he was going to enter the Low Countries " in one way or another, as a friend or as an enemy ". The States were, therefore, obliged to accept his support, which was more or less imposed upon them. Negotiations were opened at Saint Ghislain, on April 20th, 1578. The Prince of Orange, who looked for no salvation except from the side of France, pressed for an agreement with the Duke of Anjou.

Henri III and Catherine de Medici had at first declared themselves against any intervention on his part, which threatened to

CHAPTER X

THE GREAT SECESSION

ALEXANDER FARNESE

IT is by no means certain that the death of Don John was a misfortune for Philip II. The new leader of his armies, Alexander Farnese, son of Margaret of Parma, Charles V's daughter, and of Octavio Farnese, one of the Emperor's generals, derived outstanding qualities as a captain, as an administrator, and as a diplomat from this descent of his. He had nothing of a hero of romance about him ; but he was more subtle and more patient than his predecessor, and just as quick to watch his opportunity and grasp it.

In any case, the circumstances were more favourable to Spain at the end of 1578 than they had been in 1576. At the beginning of 1579 the Duke of Anjou and John Casimir abandoned the Low Countries. Religious divergencies, momentarily swept aside by hatred of the Spanish soldiery, were already making their appearance again.

The Pacification of Ghent had proclaimed the union of the Seventeen Provinces and provisionally settled their religious status. Holland and Zeeland, where William of Nassau commanded in the name of the King against the King, had obtained the exclusive exercise of the Reformed worship, and the other fifteen had reserved to themselves that of the Catholic Faith. It was a compromise open to more than one interpretation by the spirit of proselytism.

The Protestants, who monopolized freedom of worship in Holland and Zeeland, in fact claimed the right, careless of the contradiction involved, to arrogate to themselves the same freedom in the other fifteen provinces. In these provinces, where they had gone to ground during the persecution of the Duke of Alba, they resumed praying to God in their own way, and not only behind closed doors either. They made numerous proselytes, especially among the lower orders, to whom everything that came from Spain was hateful, even religion. They were not content with proclaiming their own faith. They wanted to impose it on other people ; and so from being persecuted they changed into being persecutors.

Together with this religious revival, and with the same passions fanning its fire, there occurred another revival, that of the communal spirit, which had been so powerful in the Low Countries during the Middle Ages, but which the Dukes of Burgundy and Charles V had succeeded in suppressing. For the urban administrations, composed of rich merchants, great landlords and officials, who were too docile to royal authority for their liking, the masses tended to substitute magistrates of their own choice.

It was Brussels which seems to have given the signal for this movement. Ghent followed suit, with all the enthusiasm and violence proper to its pure Flemish race. Over the heads of the regular municipal authorities the populace set up a Council of Eighteen, a regular revolutionary " commune ", designed to watch, control and direct these officials of the old order. Two notables, Hembyze and Ryhove, were the leaders of this demagogy. A former Carmelite, converted to Calvinism, Dathenus, was its inspirer and counsellor. In Bruges, in Arras, as in Brussels and Ghent, in most of the towns where the populace gained the upper hand, these mandatories, under the name of notables, clerks of the public, advocates of the nation, acted as masters. The Nassaus favoured this upthrusting from the lower levels of society, because they distrusted the rich classes and the aristocracy, who were more disposed to come to an understanding with the Spaniards.

The tribunes of the people, who dreamt of a political and social upheaval, were naturally of one mind with the religious innovators, who were also in revolutionary throes. The *Beeldstorm* recommenced. Bands of Gueux, setting out from Ghent, smashed images and even burnt monks. Anarchy reigned throughout Flanders. " If the Pacification was signed at Ghent," wrote Hubert Languet, a Protestant, " it was also at Ghent that it was violated."

The Prince of Orange was alarmed by these excesses. Born a Lutheran, brought up a Catholic in Charles V's entourage, a convert to Calvinism by the necessities of the struggle, in the course of his twistings and turnings of conscience he had rid himself of any sectarian spirit. Tolerant and humane, he protected the Catholics of Holland as much as he could. He feared for the stability of the Union, that powerful means of defence against the strength of Spain.

To calm his co-religionists, he decided to give a legal form to their encroachments. On July 22nd, 1578, the Archduke Mathias had solidly established his power in that province by favouring the Protestant propaganda *per fas et nefas*.

The delegates of Holland and Zeeland and four delegates of Gelderland signed at Utrecht, on January 23rd, a special Treaty of Union of the northern provinces. The contracting parties disclaimed any desire to ruin the Pacification of Ghent, and went so far as to claim that they wanted to consolidate it. What they actually did was definitely to prohibit the exercise of any religion other than the Reformed religion in Holland and Zeeland, while at the same time demanding the benefit of the Peace of Religion in the other fifteen provinces—in other words, the right of propaganda against Catholicism.

This Treaty of Union made no reference either to the King, or to the Archduke Mathias, or to the States-General. It took it for granted that the League of Utrecht was an autonomous organization, sufficient unto itself. But, though Ghent rallied to it with enthusiasm, in Holland and Zeeland only two towns, Leyden and Haarlem, adhered to the Union of Utrecht ; and Middelbourg, the capital of Zeeland, repudiated it.

William of Nassau had confined himself to letting things take their course, and as a matter of fact he was not mentioned either in the Utrecht transaction. In order to emphasize his attachment to the national union represented by the States-General, he waited three months before adhering to the particularist, if not separatist, group of the Protestants of the north.

In opposition to the Union of Utrecht, there came into being, on January 6th, the Union of Arras. The Malcontents of the south, after the breach of the Comines Agreement, could see no other recourse against the sectaries of the north than a renewed understanding with Philip II of Spain. Their leader, Valentin de Pardieu, Lord of La Motte, Governor of Gravelines, indignant at the trafficking of the States with Elizabeth for the purpose of getting her support, declared himself for Don John and against the Duke of Anjou. He undertook to hold Gravelines for the King, though at the same time he refused to admit a Spanish garrison—and Philip thanked him for his fidelity. Montigny also put himself, together with his strong places, once more in obedience to the King ; but he, too, would have none but his own soldiers, soldiers of the country, to defend them, and he demanded the recall of the Spanish troops.

At the first indications of this veering of the wind, Alexander Farnese, Don John's successor as Governor, had realized what policy he ought to pursue : lean upon the Catholic Walloon provinces. He kept in touch with La Motte ; he encouraged Montigny. He exerted himself to rally other Catholic lords of the south, such as Aremberg and Lalaing. He persuaded the King, despite his scruples of conscience, to approve—or to let him approve—the Pacification of Ghent, and he agreed himself, much as he disliked doing it, to the departure of the Spanish troops. Philip, all for concession, granted honours and rewards to those who rallied to him.

This clever policy of Farnese's, the loyalist spirit of the Southern provinces which had survived all tests, and the interests of Catholicism decided the States of Hainault and Artois, and the towns of Lille, Douai and Orchies in French Flanders, to conclude, at the Abbey of Saint Vaast, near Arras, on May 17th, a treaty of reconciliation with the King of Spain. It was a consecration of the Union of Arras. By this treaty these provinces and towns protested their fidelity to their Sovereign lord and their indefectible attachment to the Catholic Church. But, to pave the way for the return of the other provinces to obedience, as they desired, they demanded " the ratification of all privileges and the confirmation of the Pacification of Ghent . . . the recall of foreign soldiers, the handing over of fortresses to natives of the country ", and the appointment, within six months, of a Prince of the Blood as Governor-General in place of the Duke of Parma. Philip ended by accepting all these demands.

At the very outset of his administration Farnese had done marvels. He had made sure of those very Walloon provinces where it was to be feared that the Duke of Anjou might find a rallying-point. Without striking a blow, by the exercise of sheer diplomacy, he had once more attached to Spain territories which, by tradition and through affinity of race and language, might be tempted to hand themselves over to France.

He had paved the way to reconciliation with Spain for other sections of the people of the Low Countries too. Between the line-up of the Union of Arras, which had returned to its obedience to Philip, and that of the Union of Utrecht, which persisted in revolt, there was still a great number of provinces and towns that, though hostile to the Spanish administration, were officially subject to the King of Spain in his capacity as Sovereign of the Low Countries. They recognized no authority other than that of the States-General. In fact, through this intermediary, they accepted the control of the Prince of Orange.

It was in this so far undecided region, peopled by Catholics and Protestants, who did not know what master to obey, that the fate of the Low Countries was to be determined. It is not quite correct to say that the Union of Arras and the Union of Utrecht laid the

237

mined to grapple with the leader of the revolt. Montmorency, Croy, Lalaing, almost all the aristocracy, following Melun's and La Motte's example, had made or were preparing to make their submission. The Prince of Orange, in his isolation, seemed more criminal than ever. Cardinal Granvelle, summoned from Rome to Madrid in 1579, had become, since Antonio Pérez's arrest and Philip's journey to Portugal, a kind of Prime Minister to Philip. The Cardinal advised the King to put a price on the head of this irreducible enemy of his. " One might," Granvelle wrote to Philip, " offer a reward of thirty to forty thousand escudos to anyone who kills him or captures him alive. This is what all the princes of Italy do against their rebellious subjects." As Orange was a coward, Granvelle suggested, he might die of fright, or some desperate man might be found in France or Italy who was ready to attempt the job for the sake of the money.

Philip approved the idea, but he was ever a formalist. He must first see whether there was any sentence to be passed on Orange, other than his condemnation for *lèse-majesté* during Alba's administration. By November 30th Philip had made up his mind. Would it not be expedient, he wrote to the Duke of Parma, to take as a model the ban which the Emperor Charles V had pronounced against the Duke of Saxony, John Frederick, and the Landgrave of Hesse, and to put this " criminal ", Orange, who deserved a thousand deaths for all the ill and damage he had done since his first condemnation, outside the law?

The Duke objected that it was not the usage of the country, and that he was afraid lest the step should be badly received ; but he ended by obeying his master's express order. On March 15th, 1580, Philip proclaimed the outlawry of William of Orange. Whoever delivered him dead or alive would receive thirty thousand gold escudos and part of the rebel's property, and he and his family would be ennobled.

To this act of proscription William replied by an " *Apologia* " presented to the States-General on December 13th. It was drawn up by a cleric, Loyseleur, Lord of Villiers and Westhoven, born at Lille, who had first been an advocate in Paris and then, as a refugee in Geneva, had studied theology on the advice of Theodore of Beze. It was less a justification on the part of the rebel than a list of charges against Philip II, often false, but full of passion and here and there of eloquence (3).

Philip's crimes, according to the Prince of Orange, were many. Philip was already married to Doña Isabel Osorio when he espoused the Infanta Maria of Portugal, during the lifetime of this first wife of his, and had two children by her. Don Carlos was the son of Maria of Portugal and a bigamist. His father had had him imprisoned and put to death, " perhaps because he was conscience-stricken at the thought of leaving as his heir one whom he knew to be born in illegitimate marriage ". Philip had poisoned his third wife " and the Emperor of Germany, Maximilian ", his cousin and brother-in-law—in the latter case because he hated Maximilian's liberal and tolerant spirit. During the time of his marriage with Elizabeth of Valois, Philip had had relations with Doña Eufrasia (de Guzman), " who, being pregnant by his act, he constrained the Prince of Ascoli to marry her " and accept the paternity of her bastard.

It was this King, a debauchee, a murderer, and an adulterer, who accused him, William of Orange, because, for good reasons, he had repudiated Anne of Saxony and taken as his wife Charlotte of Bourbon, a Princess of the Blood of France, daughter of the Duke of Montpensier.

Philip had hoped to frighten him. It was a vain hope. William of Orange knew that for some time past Philip had contemplated getting rid of him by poison or assassination, and he put his life in God's hands. He was ready to risk anything and to suffer anything. Willingly would he accept banishment if his departure would serve the public good.

But he united his own cause with that of the Low Countries. He would continue to defend these provinces and their inhabitants, men, women, and children, all those who had put their trust in him. Until his last breath, he proposed to fight for their safety, and to perpetuate and justify the motto of his House : " I will maintain."

But, if William of Orange counted on the help of God, he did not neglect to help himself. The successes of the Duke of Parma drove him to seek aid from outside. He turned towards France again. In June, 1579, he had renewed his connection with the Duke of Anjou.

The moment seemed well chosen. In 1579 Elizabeth of England was forty-six years of age. She had not yet made up her mind to get married, and sometimes she was furious to find herself still an old maid. The English Government was disturbed by the advance of the Spaniards in the Low Countries and Pope Gregory XIII's projects : landings of outlawed Irishmen on the coasts of their island, and attempts to smuggle Jesuit apostles and plotters into England. A new attack of feminine vanity, coinciding with Elizabeth's fear of Papistry, once more brought into the foreground the question of the Queen's marriage to the Duke of Anjou, whose advances she had once entertained, but whose hopes she had hitherto dashed.

This French Prince, who was only twenty-one, might now imagine that, made more amenable by her advancing age, Elizabeth would withhold herself no longer. He went to visit her at Greenwich, and was received as her future husband. She kept him there from August to September, and dispensed him from the formality required by etiquette, so pleased was she by the appearance and the conversation of " her little Italian ", as she called him, or, more affectionately still, " her little frog ".

Sure of the good will of the Queen, the Duke of Anjou could go ahead with his ambitions in the Low Countries without fear of the hostility of England. The intrigues in which his sister, the Queen of Navarre, had engaged during her journey to Spa opened the path for him. Cambrai, an Imperial free city under Philip's protection, guarded the entrance into Flanders. The Lord of Inchy, who had established himself in its citadel in the name of the States, recognized the Duke of Anjou as his Sovereign Lord, on October 25th, 1579. The following year the Count of Rochepot took over the town on Anjou's behalf.

Catherine de Medici and Henri III promised to assist the Duke in his enterprise in Flanders if the English marriage became an accomplished fact. The Queen-Mother of France knew that Philip at this moment was occupied before all else with the settlement of the Portuguese succession and the union with Spain of the last independent State in the peninsula. She proposed to create difficulties for Philip, there and elsewhere, and to compel him, if Elizabeth rejected her suitor once more, to give her son the hand of the Infanta Clara Isabel Eugenia, with the Low Countries as her dowry. To prevent the Duke of Anjou from bedevilling things inside France and plotting against the King of France, Catherine needed to procure him an independent principality outside.

The aid which Catherine gave Anjou in the Low Countries, the claim which she put forward herself to the vacant throne of Portugal, and the expedition to the Azores, with which I shall deal in the next chapter, were all means of concluding a Spanish marriage at the expense of Spain and to the advantage of her son—of her two sons. All Catherine's foreign policy, all her pretended colonial aspirations, were those of a good mother of a family.

The Prince of Orange, without knowing it, served the subtle purposes of this match-maker. But he had a great deal of difficulty in persuading the rebels to resort to the aid of the French prince. Holland and Zeeland would not hear about this " Papist ", who, two years before, had turned against the Huguenots. It was to the Prince of Orange himself that, in April, 1580, they offered their sovereignty, with the title of Count of Holland and Zeeland. He refused the offer ; but, even without a title, he was still the master of these two provinces (4).

Orange summoned the States-General of the Low Countries at Antwerp and advised them to elect some distinguished prince as their Sovereign. There was keen opposition. The deputies of Ghent wanted to elect the Queen of England, a Protestant. Antwerp also declared itself against the Duke of Anjou. But the rest of Flanders, threatened by the Duke of Parma and the Union of Arras, supported the Prince of Orange's proposal. The Flemish deputies, except those of Ghent, proclaimed that, even if they stood alone, they would recognize the Duke of Anjou as their Sovereign.

Nevertheless the States-General hesitated. They distrusted this Valois-Medici. They were afraid of breaking with Philip II without any recourse other than the changeable will of the Duke and the doubtful support of Henri III. Accordingly, to sway the voting, the Prince of Orange was forced to couple his proposal to recognize the Duke of Anjou with clauses which limited the power of the new master and multiplied his obligations. Anjou was to form his household of natives of the Low Countries and appoint not more than one or two Frenchmen to his Council. He was to choose governors on the recommendation of the provinces, and give the command of the army, if he did not command it himself, to a leader acceptable to the States. The King of France was to promise to aid his brother to expel the Spaniards, or otherwise to declare war on Philip II.

A Flemish deputation, with Marnix de Sainte Aldegonde at its head, waited upon Henri III at Plessis-les-Tours. It was well received. The King of France and his mother wanted to make themselves agreeable to the Duke of Anjou. They contemplated making use of him to negotiate peace with the Protestants of the South, who were once more in arms. They had nothing to fear from Philip, who, absorbed by the affairs of Portugal, could reply by no direct attack, and they knew how to act underhandedly, without compromising themselves.

Henri III carefully refrained from formally endorsing the demands of the States. He contented himself with promising to act upon them in a letter to his brother Anjou, which the Duke, for his part, undertook not to turn to account. The Treaty of Plessis-les-Tours, signed on September 19th, 1580, merely declared that the new Sovereign of the Low Countries could count upon the alliance and support of the King of France.

The Duke of Anjou thought that he could. On his return from the south, where he came to terms of peace with the Huguenots at Fleix, he assembled troops and entered Cambrai. He had no doubts about his marriage with Elizabeth. He went back to England. The Queen, blushing like a girl, kissed him on the lips and put a wedding ring on his hand, on November 22nd, 1581. He seemed to have reached the height of his desires : Sovereign of a great country, husband of the Queen of England, heir presumptive to the Crown of France. What more could he want ?

The States-General, assembled at Delft, ratified the Treaty of Plessis-les-Tours on December 30th. This meant a breach with Philip II, and a declaration of independence. Hitherto they could disclaim the reproach of rebellion ; but, after their recognition of the Duke of Anjou as their Sovereign, they could do so no longer, nor did they even try to do so. On April 19th of the next year the States of Holland and Zeeland decided to eliminate the name of the King of Spain from all State documents and measures, and to release all vassals and magistrates from their oath of allegiance to him.

In their turn the States-General, assembled at The Hague, on July 26th, 1581, solemnly declared Philip II deposed. In the name of natural right, which entitled everyone to protect himself against injustice, violence and attacks on liberty of conscience, and in the name of historical right, which regulated the reciprocal obligations of subjects and their prince, and imposed upon the one as upon the others the strict observance of a kind of contract, they declared that they " abjured " the obedience due to Philip II.

It was a great event, and it was a memorable date. The rebels had the audacity to depose their Sovereign and choose a new one for themselves. In justification of their resistance, they alleged their right to defend their property, their lives, their consciences and the ancient liberties of the country. Tyranny without limits had provoked rebellion without scruples.

These revolutionaries were not invoking any new political right. They did not profess that the nation was superior to him who ruled it, or that any magistrate, however highly placed he might be, held all his powers from the nation and from it alone. They drew their inspiration from the past ; they reacted against the present and they had nothing more than the example of their indomitable courage to bequeath to the future.

But what did that matter ? In the midst of monarchies which were absolute, or aspired to be so, buttressed by State Churches, a people had been found to rise against the arbitrary will of kings.

It was an act which transcended the limits of the Low Countries and of the sixteenth century.

The marriage of Elizabeth with the Duke of Anjou, which seemed certain after her bestowal of the wedding ring upon him, soon looked so difficult to bring to a conclusion that Catherine was confirmed in her calculations upon a Spanish marriage. The English demanded that Henri III should sign an offensive and defensive alliance with them before the marriage. The French, who had good reason to distrust them, insisted upon the marriage before the alliance. There was no possibility of compromise. Elizabeth was susceptible, but, when her interests demanded it, her feelings were soon subordinated. She ended by declaring to the Duke that she would remain his friend, but that she could not become his wife.

After three months of assiduous courtship, she dismissed him to the Low Countries, where his subjects were clamouring for him. She did, however, have him transported to Zeeland by an English fleet, with an escort of several great lords, among them the handsome Earl of Leicester, her cousin and her favourite *en titre*, and provided him by way of viaticum with a letter in which she recommended the States-General to treat him as though he were herself.

The Duke of Anjou disembarked at Flushing on February 10th, 1582. It was high time for him to arrive. After two months' siege, the Duke of Parma had possessed himself of the strong place of Tournai. Almost all the aristocracy, except the Prince of Chimay, son of the Duke of Aerschot, and Governor of Brussels, had reconciled themselves with the King of Spain. The Prince of Orange's brother, John of Nassau, *Stathouder* of Gelderland, was on the point of abandoning the struggle and retiring to his hereditary estates in Germany.

The provinces and towns which adhered to the Prince of Orange's party or the States-General were unready to make any advance of money. They refused to raise troops except on the approach of the Walloons or the Spanish generalissimo. William was driven to despair by their indifference towards the common cause.

It was partly in order to supplement their default in good will, as well as their shortcomings in men and money, that he had invited the King of France's brother to the Low Countries. But this foreign protector, left to the resources of his appanage by Henri III, could not provide for all the expenses of war and administration on his own account. The States wrangled with the Duke of Anjou bitterly about the funds necessary for the maintenance of his little Court. They had recognized him as their Sovereign without enthusiasm, and they let him see that they had no intention of giving themselves a master.

To prevent him from nibbling at their liberties, they wanted to put a " good muzzle " on him. Before allowing him to enter Antwerp, where the States were sitting, they made him swear observance of the " Joyous Entrance ", that old charter of Brabant which authorized the revolt of the subjects against the prince if he violated their liberties. Before he was recognized by Gelderland and Friesland, he had to swear to respect their customs and their privileges. At Bruges and at Ghent, on the occasion of his proclamation as Count of Flanders, he took oath to observe the Great Charter, which the men of Ghent had formerly extracted by force from Marie of Burgundy.

The conditions of the Treaty of Plessis-les-Tours were in themselves sufficiently restrictive. It is understandable that the Duke of Anjou should have resented these new demands upon him. From France, even if his own anger did not inspire him, came the advice to put these unruly, crabbed and stingy subjects of his in their place.

Catherine, who since Elizabeth's withdrawal was basing all her hopes on pursuing the Spanish Infanta, bestirred herself to procure enough money to raise ten to twelve thousand French and Swiss infantry and fifteen hundred cavalry, whom she put under the command of Marshal de Biron, an excellent captain. This French army proceeded to camp outside Antwerp. Under pretext of reviewing it, on January 17th, 1583, the Duke of Anjou left the city, escorted by the numerous gentlemen who were lodging there with him ; and the gates, opened for him, were not closed behind him.

The soldiers posted outside crossed the drawbridge, shouting " City won ! Kill, kill ! " ; but they started pillaging, and the city militia had time to arm and draw up the bridge. From the roofs of the houses women and children rained missiles on the assailants, who, caught in front and in rear, took to flight. A few of them succeeded in jumping over the ramparts ; the majority were massacred by the populace or taken prisoners.

In all the towns of the Low Countries where French troops were quartered, they had been ordered to attempt similar surprise attacks. These attacks were successful only at Dunkirk, Termonde and Dixmude. The indignation provoked by this treachery ruined the French cause. The " fury of Antwerp " awakened memories of the Paris massacres. The towns refused to serve as residences to the felon prince. He was obliged to disband his army, at Dunkirk, and to hand over the strong places which he occupied in order to secure the release of the prisoners in Antwerp.

The Duke of Parma profited by this confusion. The forces

which he had at hand were considerable. After the proclamation of the Duke of Anjou as Sovereign of the provinces subject to the States-General, Parma had obtained authorization from the Union of Arras to recall the Spanish and Italian regiments from Italy to the Low Countries, and he had under his orders, including these troops, sixty-two thousand men. He seized the towns which the retreat of the Duke of Anjou left without defence : Eindhoven, Diest, Nieuport, Zutphen, and others. At the same time, in accordance with his custom, he carried on negotiations.

He wrote to the provinces, and begged them to return to their obedience, in order to restore to the country that prosperity which disorder and war were causing it to lose. He entered into conversations with the Duke of Anjou. He tried to win over—or buy over—the town magistrates and the leaders of the party of resistance, among them the Prince of Chimay, whose zeal on behalf of the Protestants had secured his appointment as Governor of Flanders at the end of 1583, and Hembyze, that sometime demagogue, now one no longer.

The people of Ghent, warned by the Prince of Orange and the States that Hembyze was working for the cause of peace and for the King of Spain, rose against him. He was arrested, imprisoned, and later executed. But the Prince of Chimay handed over Bruges, and Parma occupied Ypres after a long siege. Almost all Flemish Flanders reverted to its allegiance to Philip II.

The danger was so imminent that William of Nassau turned towards France once more. It needed courage on his part, after the treachery of Antwerp, to go against public feeling and defy the general disgust. Nevertheless, as a matter of policy, he persisted. To forestall a reconciliation between France and Spain against the rebels, he approached the Duke of Anjou again and solicited the support of Henri III.

" Necessity compels us," he wrote to his brother John of Nassau, that Calvinist sectary, who was hostile to a French alliance. The Duke of Parma could press forward to Antwerp without encountering any resistance. The towns were following their own particularist interests. It was not to be thought of that any help would come from England. So what was to be done ? Either submit to the Spaniards, or call in the French, despite their wrongdoing. Philip was a born persecutor of the Church. Henri III, from jealousy of this powerful neighbour of his, and because of the necessity of handling the Protestant minority in his own kingdom, was the natural ally of the Low Countries (5).

It was the reasoning of a statesman. The States-General took

Orange's advice. At Château-Thierry, whither the Duke of Anjou had retired, negotiations were resumed. This time the King of France seemed resolved to support his brother openly. In their great need, the States consented to cede him two strong places as advanced bases. They even agreed, if the Duke of Anjou should die childless, to allow the Low Countries to become united to the Crown of France.

But the Duke of Anjou was unable to march to their aid. He died, quite young, in June, 1584, of the same disease as Charles IX, phthisis, which his disappointments had aggravated.

Death was a good servant to Philip II. Several assassins, among others the Basque Jaureguy, had been tempted by the reward which he offered, or driven by religious passion, to attempt to put the outlawed Prince of Orange out of the way. Finally, on July 10th, 1584, a native of the Franche-Comté, Balthazar Gerard, a fanatical Catholic, made his way into the house where the Prince was living in Delft, and, as he was leaving his dining-room, shot him in the chest with a pistol. The Prince of Orange fell, mortally wounded. " Oh God," he cried, in French, " have mercy on my soul and on this poor people ! " These were his last words.

So disappeared the man who, for eighteen years, had thwarted the power of Philip II ; the man who founded the dynasty of Orange-Nassau and the Republic of the United Provinces. Protestants have glorified him, and Catholics have found nothing too bad to say about him. The latter refused to see anything but his rebelliousness, the former anything but his devotion to the Protestant cause. But for rebellion there are excuses when it is provoked by a tyranny as abominable as that of the Duke of Alba ; and, if we must speak of religion, it is but fair to recognize that his own, in all its variations, was more tolerant than that of the Calvinists and the Catholics of his time. He had to accept, but he never approved, the violence of his co-religionists and the cruelties which they committed in reprisals for the cruelties of the Catholics. He was a humane man —a great virtue in that century of fury and fanaticism.

His loss seemed irreparable. His son, Maurice, born of his last marriage with Louise de Teligny, daughter of the Admiral, who was later to cut a great figure as a statesman and a soldier, was at this time only fifteen or sixteen years old. The dangers of provincial particularism and the communal spirit looked more daunting than ever now that the conciliator had disappeared. There was no longer any head of the administration, no longer any captain in the field.

Some time before his assassination, William of Orange had appointed Philippe Marnix de Sainte Aldegonde, one of the numerous pastors of French origin and education, as Burgomaster of Antwerp ; and despite Sainte Aldegonde's refusal of it, he had thrust the command of this strong place upon this theologian, diplomat and writer. This governor despite himself found himself invested with a kind of moral authority, as it were, after the murder of the Prince. He was the counsellor of the States-General, and he, too, recommended understanding with France as a necessity.

But, even in this extreme of danger, passions were not disarmed. The Protestants, powerful in the States, forced a decision that, before a fresh appeal was made to France, an embassy should be sent to the Queen of England. Elizabeth declared that she would not intervene except in concert with France. Then resort had to be made to Henri III of France.

He contented himself with giving the deputies a fair welcome. He was afraid of a single-handed attack on Philip II, who was now free from any further anxiety in the direction of Portugal, and he knew that Elizabeth would not permit the annexation of the Low Countries, or any part of them, to the Crown of France. On March 10th he replied to the States that he could not accept their sovereignty, but that he would seek every opportunity to be of service to them, short of making war on the King of Spain.

Relieved of any fear of intervention, and master of Brussels and Malines, which had been surrendered to him, Parma went and laid siege to Antwerp. Marnix de Sainte Aldegonde defended it against him. The city was strongly fortified, and the Scheldt, which served it as a moat, left the way free for support in men, munitions, and supplies. In order to isolate Antwerp, the besiegers flung across the river a boom built on piles, two thousand five hundred feet wide, and sixty feet deep—or even seventy-one feet at high tide—duplicated downstream by a floating bulwark of big ships, and protected at the two ends by forts furnished with men and cannon.

These extraordinary measures of attack were matched by the measures of defence : the launching against the boom of ships turned into floating infernal machines, of which only one reached its goal— but this one split the boom, blew eight hundred men to pieces, and knocked the Duke of Parma senseless ; attempts to cut a dyke and sever communications between the two camps of the besieging army ; frequent and desperate sorties, naval engagements. But the breach in the boom was not wide enough—or else sufficient audacity was lacking—for the relieving fleet of Holland to break a way through it. After thirteen months of siege, Marnix, defeated by starvation, and by nothing else, surrendered, in August, 1585, and was granted honourable terms.

The taking of Antwerp assured the safety of the southern provinces, and gave ground for belief that it might open the way to mastering the northern provinces, the cradle of the revolt. This explains why, when the news was brought to him at night, Philip—usually so undemonstrative—got out of bed, went to the door of the Infanta Clara Isabel Eugenia, that daughter of whom he was so fond, and shouted to her : " Antwerp is ours ! "

After his victories over the French at Saint Quentin, and over the Infidels at Lepanto, what greater triumph could be his than this conquest of the stronghold on the Scheldt, that bastion of the Reformation and of rebellion ?

CHAPTER XI

THE UNION OF SPAIN AND PORTUGAL

HERE we come to the most glorious period of Philip II's reign. He believed himself sure of the submission of the rest of the Low Countries; and he had achieved the unification of the peninsula by adding the crown of Portugal to all his crowns of Spain.

This new kingdom of his, although of limited area in itself, was the head of an immense maritime and colonial empire. To reach the Land of Spices, the Portuguese—unlike the Spaniards, who groped towards it by way of the West, across the " Dark Sea "— had coasted along the African continent, rounded the Cape of Storms, which they baptized Cape of Good Hope, and in 1496 made a landfall in India on the Malabar coast. It was in Asia that they continued to extend their sphere of influence, even after Alvárez Cabral, thanks to wind and wave and a lucky drift, had touched the coast of Brazil in the New World.

Their navigations and conquests in the sixteenth century sub-sequently handed over to them the ports of the Indian Ocean and of India itself, opened the Red Sea and the Persian Gulf to them, and led them to the Moluccas, to China, to Japan, and perhaps even as far as the north coast of Australia.

These were immense territories capable of exploitation, but out of all proportion to the population and the resources of the mother-country. Accordingly the Portuguese made no attempt to people them, as they had done in the case of the Azores, on the meridian of Southern Europe, and of Madeira, nearer to the African coast, but with an Atlantic climate which had little tropical about it.

In their first colonizations towards the Far East they confined themselves, as the English did later, to constructing forts, establish-ing warehouses, and putting garrisons into their principal ports of call. These were at points which commanded straits, and on har-bours giving access to inlets as great as seas : on the Red Sea, on the Persian Gulf, in the Cape Verde islands, at Fernando Po and Annabon, at Saint Helena, at the Cape of Good Hope, at Melinde, at Socotra, at Ormuzd, at Diu, at Goa—this town, situated on an island and well defended by an arm of the sea, was the ideal capital of a maritime Empire ; at Malacca, opposite Sumatra, the largest of the islands of the Indo-Chinese archipelago ; and at Macao, on the confines of China.

In all these parts of the Indian Ocean, the Portuguese admirals and viceroys carried on rude warfare against the Arab flotillas— or Moorish, as they were called—which transported the spices of Calicut to the head of the Red Sea ; and they had barred, or at least very considerably impeded, the commercial maritime route which was continued by caravan routes to the Mediterranean.

They ruined the port of Alexandria, and incidentally impoverished the Venetians, who went there in search of the products of the Far East : pepper, cinnamon, nutmeg, which they re-sold at enormous profits to all the countries of Europe. By force of arms, Portugal held the monopoly of this traffic, permitting neither transhipment nor intermediary, and her capital, Lisbon, took the place of Venice as the great market for spices, with Amsterdam and Antwerp as its clearing-houses.

In the middle of the sixteenth century, Spain and Portugal were the two sole colonial Powers of Christendom. Satisfied with the immense field of exploitation which was secured to each one of them by the famous Bull of demarcation of Pope Alexander VI, dated May 2nd, 1493, and the retroactive treaty signed at Tordesillas on June 7th, 1494, they had no reason whatever to be jealous rivals. Each of them had sufficient territory in which to find elbow-room, colonies and markets in South America without getting in the other's way, and at the extremity of Asia, where Portuguese Indo-China and the Spanish Philippines faced one another, the sea constituted a natural boundary. Any number of matrimonial alliances contributed towards maintaining good relations between Spain and Portugal.

The King of Portugal, Manoel the Fortunate (1495–1521), first cousin of Isabel the Catholic of Castile, had married, as his first and second wives, two of her daughters, and, as his third wife, her grand-daughter Eleonore of Austria, elder sister of Charles V. Manoel's son, John III, married Charles V's younger sister, Catherine of Austria.

Charles V married Isabel of Portugal, Manoel's daughter. He married his daughter, Doña Juana, to John, son of John III, who died before succeeding to the throne ; and his son, the Infante

Philip—who became Philip II—to Maria, daughter of John III and Catherine of Austria.

But these marriages between first cousins and first cousins once removed handed down taints and aggravated them. Madness and hyperæsthesia were not rare in the two families. Isabel the Catholic, the great Isabel, was the daughter of a Portuguese Infanta who went mad, and the mother of another madwoman, Joan the Mad. Don Carlos, born of the Infante Philip (Philip II), Isabel's great-grandson, and of the Portuguese Infanta Maria, her great-grand-daughter, was an unbalanced individual, weak mentally and physically, subject to attacks of morbid frenzy.

The young reigning King of Portugal since 1557, Dom Sebastian, son of Philip II's sister Doña Juana and of the Portuguese Infante John, seems also to have inherited from his ancestors a lack of equilibrium, a pathological sense of exaltation, which his upbringing only succeeded in developing. He had, so the ambassador of France wrote to Catherine de Medici on November 29th, 1569, " very much of the temperament of the late Prince of Spain (Don Carlos, his cousin), being subject to headaches, odd, variable, and terribly obstinate in his opinions ".

The Jesuits, who were entrusted with Sebastian's education, were at this period in all the fervour of a new-born Order. They instilled a passion for crusading into his childish heart. Keen about all physical exercises, but protected against any ·weakness of the flesh either by mental fastidiousness or physical impotence, he sought only an opportunity for making his dreams come true. Accordingly he gave the most favourable reception to a dethroned Sovereign of Morocco, who had come to Europe to solicit the support of Christian princes against the usurping Sheriff, Mouley Abd-el-Malek (El Malucco).

Philip II, who knew the dangers of African warfare, flatly refused his support. But Sebastian embraced this cause with enthusiasm. He saw Morocco conquered, the Cross triumphant, a new dominion added to the empire of Christ. He tried to bring his uncle into line as well ; but, at their interview at Guadalupe, a monastery in Estremadura, the King of Spain showed himself so much concerned with limiting the field of action of the Portuguese, and setting boundaries to any conquests they might make, that the champion of the Faith, highly scandalized, took his leave of a prince so lukewarm and politic.

The Portuguese themselves displayed no more enthusiasm. The aristocracy made the strongest possible representations against the proposed expedition. Even the clergy refused subsidies. With foreign contingents, volunteers and mercenaries—three thousand Germans, six hundred Italians, two thousand Castilians—there was difficulty in raising an army of seventeen thousand men, largely recruited, or even enrolled by force, among farm labourers, artisans and town loafers.

Deaf to all advice, Sebastian, followed by his faithful vassals, set sail for Africa. He wasted a fortnight at Arcila, and gave Mouley time to concentrate thirty thousand infantry and forty thousand cavalry. Thence he made his way overland towards Larache, and, after five days' march under a burning sun, arrived with his jaded troops in the plain of Alcazar-Kebir, where the Moroccans were awaiting him. Battle was joined on August 4th, 1578. The Portuguese nobility did their duty nobly ; the German auxiliaries and the infantry fled. Sebastian refused to retreat. He charged into the heart of the enemy's ranks, and fell under a heap of slain.

It was a disaster for Portugal : the military caste had been decimated, and the King, for obvious reasons, left no direct heir. The crown reverted to his uncle, Cardinal Henry, a weak old man, whose days were already numbered. When he died, who was to succeed him ? Philip II was the nearest heir, and he had unquestionable rights.

But national feeling was hostile to the accession of a Spaniard, and it put up as rivals to him Catherine of Braganza, the Cardinal's niece, and Antonio, Prior of Crato, the illegitimate son of one of his brothers. One party even claimed for the people the right to elect their own king, invoking the legendary laws of Lamego in favour of this thesis and against the King of Castile.

To other claimants—the Duke of Savoy, Emmanuel Philibert, and the Duke of Parma, Ranuccio Farnese, who traced back their descent to King Dom Manoel in the female line—were added two more, who had not been foreseen : Pope Gregory XIII, who, recalling a tribute paid four centuries earlier to one of his predecessors, considered he had something to say about the succession in what he claimed was a vassal State ; and the Queen Dowager of France, Catherine de Medici, whose claims were based on still more frivolous grounds.

Three centuries earlier an outlawed Portuguese Infante, Alfonso, had married in France, in 1235, a richly endowed widow, Mathilde or Mahaut, Countess of Boulogne. But, when he became King in his own country, after the deposition and death of his brother Dom Sancho, Alfonso repudiated her unceremoniously, in order to take as his wife, in 1253, an illegitimate daughter of the King of Castile, who brought him the principality of Algarves as her dowry. By his marriage with Mahaut he had had no children, or at least there was no reason to suppose that he had. This Alfonso III, first excommunicated by one Pope as a bigamist, was rehabilitated by another Pope, on the solicitation of the Portuguese bishops, after the death of his French wife.

It was through this first wife of his, Mahaut, that Catherine now claimed the Portuguese throne. Her ancestors had held the Countship of Boulogne down to her great-grandfather, who ceded it, less the title, to the King of France, Louis XII, against estates in Auvergne and Languedoc. Catherine maintained that Mahaut had had children by Alfonso, who had been set aside from succession in favour of those of his Castilian wife ; and that, on the extinction of the legitimate line after a centuries'-long usurpation, the crown reverted of right to the House of Boulogne, from which she, Catherine, sprang, and of which she was the sole representative.

Cardinal Henry had naturally not thought of this remarkable pretender ; but as the King of France accredited two ambassadors to him, a man of the sword and a man of the Church, to set forth his mother's claims, he added her to the list of claimants.

The King of Spain, the best qualified of all of them, took pains to win over opinion that was hostile to him. He ransomed Dom Sebastian's comrades who had fallen into the hands of the Moors at his own expense. He dispatched Cristóbal de Moura to Lisbon, who, in his capacity as Philip's favourite and himself a Portuguese, could reassure his compatriots better than anybody else about the feelings of the King of Spain. Although Philip refused to let his rights be called in question, he had them set forth and maintained by jurisconsults of the two nations. Two legists, Guardiola Vázquez and Molina, went to Portugal to second the efforts of the ambassadors. Moura scattered money among the nobles with both hands, and assured himself of their adherence.

The Cardinal himself, who at first had been favourable to the House of Braganza, was finally won over in his turn. Just before he died, he summoned the Cortes at Almeirim, and, with his soul on the point of passing, adjured its members to recognize Philip II. Only the representatives of the towns pronounced against the candidature of this foreigner.

When the Cardinal died, on January 31st, 1580, the governors of the five great provinces, acting as a regency council, decided that the question of the succession should be settled by legal trial, just as though it were a civil suit. Of the three candidates to the Crown of Portugal, Antonio was the most popular, Catherine of

Braganza the most suitable, and Philip II the most powerful and the closest by relationship. For him Philip had the majority of the nobility and the clergy, and the will of the dying King. Against him he had national prejudice.

The people and the lower clergy, guided by a very sound instinct, felt that their country was bound to be annihilated by this redoubtable neighbour of theirs. The defenders of independence ranged themselves behind the leader they found to their hands, Antonio of Crato, who, unfortunately, was a man of no ability. Philip was clever, determined, and well armed.

At the same time as he was negotiating at Lisbon, he had taken all necessary steps for fighting. He massed the old regiments of Italy on the Portuguese frontier, and raised the Duke of Alba, the most renowned of his generals, from his disgrace to put him at their head. This army carried Yelves and Olivenza without striking a blow, and marched forward to Setubal, which was regarded as impregnable and proved to be no better defended. Antonio, whom the populace had proclaimed King, attempted to bar the way of the Spanish regiments with his undisciplined bands. He was defeated at the bridge of Alcantara, and compelled to leave Lisbon in a hurry, on August 25th, 1580. The capital fell in the hands of the Duke of Alba, and the rest of the country soon submitted (1).

Philip was awaiting the news of this triumphal march on the frontier. He nearly died at Badajoz, he lost his fourth wife, Anne of Austria ; but still he kept on his way. He travelled with a small escort, and without military display, as a Sovereign proceeding to take possession of a hereditary throne in a country where he recognized neither competitors nor enemies.

The Portuguese Cortes was summoned at Tomar on April 16th, 1581. Philip appeared in the midst of the representatives of the nation in the traditional costume, " clad in brocade ", much against his will, as he wrote to his daughter ; but he had been " told that it was the custom here ". He received the homage of his new subjects, and took oath to respect their laws, customs and usages.

These protestations of obedience did not succeed, any more than the ease of his conquest, in hiding the repugnance of the Portuguese for Philip. This dislike of him appeared in the petitions of the Cortes, which all tended towards reconstituting a national dynasty or guaranteeing the country complete autonomy. The deputies asked that the King should marry a Portuguese princess ; that the heir apparent should be brought up in Portugal ; that this Kingdom should always be kept separate from Castile, and

256

that the Spanish garrisons should be withdrawn from it. We can scarcely be surprised that Philip should have replied evasively to the expression of these desires.

The union of Portugal rounded off the territorial unity of the peninsula. What likelihood was there that he would undo the work which the policy of marriages had been preparing for more than a century, and which he had been given the opportunity to complete? It was an insult to him to imagine that, in order to satisfy the Portuguese spirit of separatism or assure a settlement for one of his sons, he should dismember Spain just when she had reached the apex of her formation and lop off again the part which had hitherto been lacking. Henceforth Portugal could be nothing more than one State united with many other States under the authority of one and the same Sovereign.

But, if Philip never dreamt of untying the link, he was careful that this last comer should not be too conscious of it. His victory had been easy, and the process of adaptation was not made too drastic.

We must, no doubt, pass sentence of condemnation on the violence committed by his armies ; but this was, in the sixteenth century, the inevitable complement of any operation of war. The amnesty which he proclaimed also had too many exceptions. Philip was particularly hard on priests and monks who had taken the rebellious side, as though he held them to be doubly culpable for having fought against their legitimate Sovereign and also the defender of orthodoxy.

It is not a fact, however, that he deliberately humiliated the national pride of the Portuguese. He gave them as their viceroy his nephew, the Archduke Albert, with whom he associated three national lords, Jorge de Almeida, Archbishop of Lisbon ; Pedro de Alcazoba, and Miguel de Moura. The nobility were not despised ; they received titles, favours and revenues on such a scale, it was said, as to make the Castilians jealous.

But, despite these concessions, Philip did not succeed in winning sympathy. The Portuguese soon had occasion to look back with regret to the time when they were an independent people under a national dynasty, devoting their forces and the resources of their diplomacy to maintaining their domination in Africa and in Asia. The Sovereign of the Spains made their army and their fleet serve the purposes of his great designs, and the Portuguese became, like so many other peoples, and perhaps a little more, the victims of his uncompromising Catholicism.

When, through his hatred of rebellion and heresy, Philip forbade the Dutch access to the port of Lisbon in 1583, these hardy mariners went to seek spices directly from India, their country of origin. Once they had found the way there, the Dutch laid the foundations of a colonial empire of their own, side by side with the Portuguese and at their expense. Amsterdam inherited the fortune of Lisbon, as Lisbon had inherited that of Venice.

Philip's first difficulties came from outside. Catherine de Medici had put forward her candidature to the crown of Portugal with the idea at the back of her mind of getting Philip to buy her off. When the Duke of Anjou, called in by the States-General against the Duke of Parma, set off to occupy Cambrai, she had made Anjou sign an undertaking, vague in its terms, but fundamentally quite definite, to " desist entirely " from his enterprises in the Low Countries, if the marriage propositions of his mother could be carried into effect. Catherine took advantage of the complaints of de Tassis to tell this ambassador of Spain " that the true means of confirming friendship between the two Crowns " was the marriage of her son with one of the Infantas, her granddaughters. She thought that Philip might accept this means of settling " the state of things in Flanders and in Portugal ", and she proposed, if he resisted, to exert the necessary pressure upon him (2).

After the Spanish occupation of Lisbon and the whole of Portugal, Dom Antonio, the fallen King, took refuge abroad. But Terceira, the most important island in the archipelago of the Azores, remained faithful to him. Catherine allowed Antonio's partisans to buy vessels and recruit men in France ; and, when the ambassador of Spain complained about this, she replied " frankly " that she had authorized them to do so, and that she had " taken pains " that the King, her son, should see no harm in it. In this way she admitted her own responsibility, while disavowing that of Henri III. This was a difference between herself and the King of Spain about a law-suit which Philip had settled by force to her detriment.

Henri III, who had little taste for adventures, may have kept Count de Vimiosa, Dom Antonio's Constable, waiting " an hour or so " in his mother's room before receiving him, by way of marking his disapproval of the proceedings. But the diligent Catherine raised for Captain Carles, who had agreed with Vimiosa to transport men to the islands, the fifteen hundred écus required for cheering up the troops of Captain Scalin, who was already there. She hurried forward the departure of the reinforcements, knowing that on June 15th the King of Spain had dispatched eight ships and eight or nine hundred men from Lisbon to the Azores. While she supported Dom Antonio, in her letters to him she excused herself for not giving him the title of King, on the ground that the Spaniard might think that she was no longer persisting " in her own right and pretension ".

When de Tassis complained to her again, in September, 1581, that Strozzi, Colonel-General of the French infantry, was raising an army of five thousand men in France to go and attack Philip's possessions, she replied that following up her own rights in Portugal was not doing wrong to anybody or making war on the King of Spain, but preserving her own property, adding " that to this end she would not spare any means she had, since Portugal was hers ".

De Tassis requested Catherine to hand over Dom Antonio— who, for that matter, was not in France, but in England—to Philip. And why should she do that? Dom Antonio was not a subject of Philip's, but of hers.

It was at this same audience of de Tassis, in which she declared herself Queen of Portugal, that she proposed the marriage of the Duke of Anjou with one of the Spanish Infantas. Catherine's personal claims and her matrimonial projects were closely linked. Clearly what she meant was that the Infanta's dowry—a territorial dowry—was to be the price of her own renunciation of her claims in Portugal. As she was too sensible to imagine that Philip II would cede Portugal to his intended son-in-law, a French prince, it followed that the compensation must be sought in the direction of the Low Countries ; nor were the Spaniards likely to have much difficulty in understanding this.

The Count de Brissac was charged with embarking twelve hundred men in Normandy, for the islands. Strozzi, with the bulk of the fleet, was to sail from Guyenne. Catherine made herself responsible for collecting funds. Everything must be ready for the start ; and there was need for haste, for the season was advancing, and the fleet must sail before December 10th. But on December 10th Strozzi was still at Poitiers, waiting for money. The Queen-Mother announced, " much annoyed ", that she was trying to raise some from the clergy and the city of Paris, though with no great hopes. She could obtain nothing from the King of France.

Six months later she was still pressing for the departure of the fleet which was to deprive the Spaniards of the Portuguese archi-pelagos : off the coast of Africa, Madeira and the Cape Verde Islands, where the routes to India and to Brazil crossed ; out in the Atlantic, on the meridian of Portugal, the Azores, an admirable position for spying on and surprising the galleons which every year brought the gold and silver of the New World—in other words, the pay of the armies—to Spain (3). Catherine had, therefore, against his King". More than thirty ships returned to France without having fired a shot. It was worse than a defeat : it was a disgrace.

Public opinion was aroused by the triumphal account which the Spanish admiral published of his victory and his executions. Henri III was moved to indignation by it. Catherine took advantage of his wrath to reinforce the army in the Low Countries, and perhaps to inspire the Duke of Anjou with the idea of possessing himself of Antwerp and other towns of the Low Countries and dictating terms to his disobedient subjects.

The failure of this surprise attack of Anjou's, as we have seen, ruined the French cause in Flanders. Nevertheless, Catherine did not despair of succeeding in Portugal. After the disaster of the Azores she started arming again. She dispatched Aymar de Chastes, a commander of the Order of Malta, to Terceira with two thousand five hundred soldiers, and at the same time she resumed her matrimonial conversations with the Court of Spain. Unhappily for this persistent match-maker, Terceira surrendered on July 26th, 1583, carrying her plans of exchange down with it (5).

The following year, the Duke of Anjou died. By his testament he bequeathed Cambrai, his first and at the end his only conquest, to the King of France, his brother. Henri III, afraid to accept it and ashamed to restore it to Philip II, contemplated renouncing his succession to it. Then Catherine, the natural heiress of her dead son, took the town and appanage of Cambrai under her protection and security. But, lest she should seem to be defying its legitimate possessor, she left the question of its sovereignty in suspense. This was her sole gain from a war carried on without declaration of war, and from a costly process of matrimonial blackmail.

CHAPTER XII

THE APOGEE OF THE REIGN

LETTERS AND THE ARTS

THE territorial unification of the Iberian peninsula marked the apogee of the reign of Philip II. The task of unity, for which the way had been paved by the far-sighted policy of the Catholic Sovereigns and Charles V, was accomplished not by right of conquest, but by legal procedure and by virtue of marriages, without any considerable military effort.

Despite the loss of his wife—the fourth of them—Anne of Austria, and the illness from which he nearly died himself, the victor in this easy conquest showed himself in no way downcast. In the letters which he wrote to the Infantas, Clara Isabel Eugenia and Catherine, during his stay in Portugal, a Philip II appears whom one would not have suspected : full of affection towards his daughters, considerate towards his faithful servants, sensitive to the beauties of Nature, to the broad sweep of the Tagus, the procession of its ships, the noble lines and the gilded hues of the palaces of Lisbon, and to the charm of gardens and the perfume of roses (1).

Fortune smiled upon him even in the Low Countries, where he had succeeded in bringing the Catholic provinces of the south back to their obedience to him, and where he even had great hopes, after the murder of William of Orange and the death of the Duke of Anjou, of reducing the Protestant provinces of the north to submission.

But this was not enough to satisfy his ambition. He had affronts to wipe out, and a dream of glory to make a reality. Philip the Prudent gave place to the great-grandson of Charles the Bold, and the King of Spain to the champion of Catholicism and the Emperor, in all but name, of Christendom.

Out of this passion for greatness, out of this spirit of proselytism, sprang a literature and an art truly national in their inspiration, in which the King and his people were at one. Rough and ready of armour which had belonged to his ancestors and had been mouldering in a corner for centuries, corroded with rust. With cardboard and little strips of iron he transformed a simple morion into a helmet with a visor ; took down a lance and a round shield from his arms-rack ; baptized a farm-horse which had ulcers all over its pasterns with the name of a war-charger, Rocinante ; attached a poor goat-herd, Sancho Panza, to his person with the sonorous title of esquire ; and chose for the lady of his dreams— for there can be no ideal without love—a simple peasant-girl, whom the eyes of his heart saw adorned with all the graces, and whom he promoted to the quality of a noble lady, the imaginary Dulcinea de Toboso.

With his head " stuffed with enchantments, quarrels, challenges, battles, wounds, declarations, love and other extravagances ", this new Amadis took the field to arrest the progress of human perversity in this age of iron, protect damsels, widows and orphans, and succour people in distress. It would take too long to relate all the errors of vision with which he deceived himself, and all the resistance from men and things which he encountered : the inn which he elevated to the dignity of a castle ; the windmills which he took for giants and charged as dangerous enemies ; the common law criminals chained and escorted by archers, whom he set at liberty as victims of the tyranny of judges and the law. He got more blows than he gave, was carried up into the air and dashed to the ground by the wings of the windmill, pommelled by mule-drivers, prosecuted by the Holy Brotherhood, laughed at and robbed by the rascals whom he released.

It was the protest of hard facts against flights of fancy. The good Sancho Panza, always ready to let loose a flood of popular proverbs ; the governess, the priest, the barber, the bachelor— these form, as it were, a kind of classical chorus, which opposes sound common sense to the blindness of generous passion.

The *Lazarillo* of Tormes is the type of picaresque novels, in which Spain appears under another aspect, glorious and poverty-stricken, devoted to the Saints and the Virgin, but indifferent to virtue. She cries famine, the sufficient excuse for her lack of scruples. Here we have an assembly of people " decayed " or decaying, keeping their eyes open for a meal or a bit of bread, beggars stretching out their hands and mumbling prayers outside churches, chanting complaints and litanies in the streets and at the doors of houses ; rogues and vagabonds ; bravoes and cut-purses ; monks selling indulgences and peddling pardons ; hidalgos condemned to the sparest diet by distaste for work and their caste spirit, and reduced, when they cannot live on alms, to stealing as a " point of honour ".

Professional beggars, monks trafficking in sacred things, needy squires : this trio of exploiters of public charity, who recur in all the picaresque novels, make up—together with prostitutes and the usual clientèle of " Courts of Miracles ", fake one-legged men and one-armed men—the reverse side of heroic Spain.

Another prose-writer, who distinguished himself in the sphere of letter-writing—a rarity in Spain—and who foreshadowed the taste for the precious which became so fashionable in the seven-teenth century, was Philip II's Secretary of State, Antonio Pérez. Compelled to flee his master's vengefulness abroad, for reasons into which, perhaps, reason did not enter, he left " Relations " of his misfortunes, and letters about his life in exile down to the date of his death, which are the very stuff of history, written with a refine-ment of art and temperament, and as revealing about his own mind as about that of Philip II.

Under the spur of national spirit, the Spanish historians were less concerned about the Greeks and Romans than about the events and the men of their own period. It was a great period, and its greatness imposed a change of method. Day-to-day jottings-down of details limited in time and space, to one town or to one personage, such as we find reported in the Chronicles, gave place to general views and synthetic writings. Diego de Mendoza wrote in the style of Sallust ; but what he wrote was a history of the revolt of the Moors of the Alpujarras in 1568. Two historiographers, who were conscientious men of learning, Zurita and Ambrosio Moralés, under-took, under the old title of Annals, general Histories of the Crowns of Aragon and Castile, which they were unable to bring to an end. Sandoval, the Moralés' continuator, wrote a well-documented History of the reign of Charles V.

The *Historia de la Orden de San Jerónymo* (Madrid, 1600), by Father José de Sigüenza, written in honour of the Hieronymites, who were so dear to Philip II that he proposed to establish them in the Escorial, is a narrative full of information about the con-struction of the palace, its style and its collections. But Father Juan de Mariana, S.J., was an author of wider scope, honest, un-biassed, and in addition a writer of note. He conceived the idea of writing a *History of Spain* which should make his country's par-ticipation in the general interests of the Christian world known to a Europe that was ignorant of it. He started it and published part of it in Latin ; then he decided to write it in Castilian, and carried it down to the death of Ferdinand the Catholic.

throwing cucumbers or other projectiles. They ran their course without hissing, clamour or uproar."

But they did not enrich him. "Plays," as he admits, "have their own time and their own season. Then came the reign in the theatre of that prodigy of Nature, the great Lope de Vega, who possessed himself of the dramatic monarchy, subjected all actors to his jurisdiction, and filled the whole world with his plays."

Here was the lucky rival of Cervantes and all the other playwrights of the time. "Lope," says Morel-Fatio, "had received from his predecessors a form of drama badly ordered, composite in its style, uncertain in its form, sometimes divided into three acts, sometimes into four, a drama in verse, but in which the distribution of the rhythms was left too much to the caprice of the author. This form of drama he adopted as it was, because the Spanish public had acquired a taste for it ; but, out of the state of confusion and inertia in which it was, he gave it life and balance. Its framework was restricted, and admitted only a limited number of subjects. He introduced into it anything that could provide material for a dramatic situation : the Bible and mythology, the lives of the Saints and ancient history, the chronicles and legends of the Middle Ages, the Italian stories, contemporary events, Spanish life.

"Before his time, the habits and conditions of the personages represented, and their characters, were barely sketched. He observed better and depicted better. He created types, and endowed every social stratum with the language and the bearing proper to it. So far as it was within his power and the extreme rapidity with which he wrote permitted him, he created some characters. The older drama versified poorly and clumsily. He stabilized the use of all the ritual of national poetry, from the old couplets of the *Romancero* to the rarest combinations of lyrical styles borrowed from the Italians " (4).

Out of all these borrowings of his, made from all periods and even from the depths of the ages, Lope de Vega is said to have extracted more than two thousand plays. He was the prince of playwrights, and he was a failure in the other poetical styles. Inferior in epic (*Dragontra, The Lost Jerusalem*) ; interesting to consult only from the point of view of literary history in the didactic style, he occupies the front rank in the lyrical. He was a force of Nature, an inexhaustible source of poetry.

The mystical writers were also to some extent lyrical, since, even when they were raised up to Heaven in their visions, their ecstasies and their meditations, it was themselves that they found in God. They were numerous in Spain, if it is true that we must reckon three thousand of their works, some of which, manuscript or otherwise, are great, beautiful, and noble. What a poetess was Saint Theresa of Avila, who, delirious in the Divine Passion, called upon the Christ, and saw and touched Him ! Saint John of the Cross (*Obras spirituales*) soared upon the wings of dream and lost himself in God.

By virtue of a kind of contradiction, these visionaries showed admirable common sense in dealing with the affairs of this world. Theresa established the convents of the nuns of the Carmelite Order upon the solid foundation of her reforms, and John of the Cross did the same for the monasteries of the monks of that Order. What a marvellous organizer of forces for the defence of the Church and the Papacy was that other knight of the ideal, Ignatius de Loyola !

Saint John of God devoted himself to the apostolate of charity ; and Luis de Granada was a penetrating investigator of souls and their guide out of the way of sin into the path of perfection. Another mystic, Fray Luis de Leon, ranks as the greatest of lyric writers at a time when one can count so many. He left an output of poetry of which one may say that it is the most perfect work upon which Spain can pride herself.

He, too, like Saint Theresa, John of the Cross and Ignatius de Loyola, had to reckon with the Holy Office, which suspected flights of imagination and waywardness of zeal as heresy. Professor of the Greek and Hebrew languages at the university of Salamanca, he was held for five years in the prisons of the Inquisition because he had translated into Spanish the *Song of Songs*, in which orthodoxy refused to see anything other than a symbol of the union of Jesus Christ with His Church, but which ran the risk of seeming, in the eyes of a profane reader, a burning Oriental portrayal of sexual love.

To this Golden Age of literature Philip II did not deserve to give his name. His influence was, so to speak, impersonal. It resembled in no way that of Augustus, of Leo X, or of Louis XIV. He inspired no works. He did not, it appears, either patronize any writers or pension them. One finds no evidence that he helped Cervantes in his distress, when the author of *Don Quixote* returned from the campaigns of Lepanto and Tunis and his captivity in Algiers and tried to make a living for himself and his family by writing plays. It was his own popular vogue, not the favour of the Sovereign, which enriched Lope de Vega. It is by no means certain that Philip approved the transformation of the old mystery plays into stage plays ; it was his people who inspired the evolution of this mode. It is doubtful whether he can have liked the picaresque novels. A good law against the printing of novels of chivalry must have seemed to his imperious temperament a better remedy than the antidote of *Don Quixote*.

Would Philip even have read it if it had appeared during his lifetime ? His bedside books were spiritual works. On the shelves of his monastic cell in the Escorial he had the *Life* and writings of Saint Theresa, the treatises of Luis de Granada, the *Spiritual Exercises* of the Jesuit Father Rodriguez, etc., and any number of missals, rituals, breviaries and other works of devotion. He loved books ; but he does not appear to have had either the time or the taste for reading those which did not aim at edification. He was, no doubt, one of those bibliophiles who are not great readers.

Above all, Philip was a connoisseur and a collector of works of art. The Escorial, the Prado gallery, and the churches of Spain bear witness to this passion of his. In this respect he must be reckoned among the great patrons, in the front rank among the Sovereigns of the Renaissance. He was, as we have already seen, informed enough about painting and sculpture to know the value of a picture or a statue, and appreciate the beauty of a composition. He did not live to see the Golden Age of painting, but he paved the way for it.

Neither Velázquez (1599–1660), nor Zurbarán (1598–1664), nor even Ribera (1588–1656), still less Murillo (1617–82), could find any rivals among the contemporaries of this King who died in 1598 ; but this is not the same thing as saying that they did not owe anything to him. The collections which he assembled in his palace in Madrid and at the Escorial constituted a school of teaching which even dispensed some apprentices from the necessity of making the hitherto obligatory pilgrimage of art to Italy and studying at Rome and elsewhere.

Among the Italian masters, there was one whom Philip admired above all others : Titian, his father's favourite portrait-painter, who also became his own. Philip did not succeed in persuading Titian to come to Spain and settle down there, but he kept on ordering pictures from him. These were not all religious subjects. This great eclectic artist, this pagan of the Renaissance, as devoted to pagan mythology as he was to Christian history, concerned only to achieve perfection of form and colour, would send Philip indifferently " Our Lord's Supper ", " Christ at Prayer in the Garden of Olives ", " Christ at the Tomb ", " The Martyrdom of Saint Laurence ", and sometimes, in the same dispatch, " poesies ", as he called the representation of classical fables in all the marvellousness of their splendid nudity : " Calisto made Pregnant by Jupiter ",

" Acteon surprising Diana at her Bath ", " Venus at her Toilette ", " Love and Music ", and the naked nymph with landscape and satyr, otherwise known as the " Antiope " at the Louvre, and many other fables of the state of nature.

Following " Danæ ", there arrived in England, where Philip had just gone to marry Mary Tudor, " Venus and Adonis " ; Venus with her arms around Adonis's neck to prevent him from going in pursuit of the boar which was to kill him. Danæ displayed herself full-length from in front, and Venus the other way about. This was, so the painter naïvely wrote to the King, " so that the room where they are put may be more pleasant to the eyes ". It does not appear that Philip, then quite young, was shocked by these nudes facing in opposite directions.

But it was not models of this kind that he recommended to the painters of his own country. He required nothing from them but religious paintings. Poetical mythology was an article of foreign importation, and after Titian's death Philip, himself settled down, does not seem to have sought such glorification of the flesh. Spanish painting reverted to its own tradition, which Charles Blanc defines very well : as devoted to religious ideas as it was faithful to reality ; Catholic and colourful. This art was essentially a sacred art. Monasteries and churches absorbed almost the whole of the output of the sixteenth century. At all times the Spaniards have excelled at expressing religious emotion and at introducing a pathetic dynamism into pious pictures.

The painters who flourished during Philip II's reign educated the great painters of the age which followed. Ribalta (school of Valencia), was the master of Ribera, and Juan de Roelas (school of Seville) was that of Zurbarán. They taught them, respectively, to paint monks of all orders and all temperaments, and churchmen. The one borrowed his chiaroscuro from Corregio ; the other brought back its gilded light from Venice.

Francisco Herrera, called the Elder, who disputes with Roelas the glory of having founded the school of Seville, was, says Bertaux, expert in all techniques ; and, while his tavern scenes—the first *bodegones* painted in Spain—have disappeared, as have also his great religious frescoes, there remain in the Seville gallery and at the Louvre, to enable us to estimate his meticulous realism and his bent for impetuous improvization, enormous canvases in which he exaggerates the popular bulkiness of monks, colossal figures brought off with great sweeps of the brush.

But the most powerful and the most original painter was Domenico Theotocópuli, a Cretan, who had studied in Venice and, after settling in Toledo in 1575, became deeply stamped with his Spanish environment in that unique city, whose picturesque site, its Mauresque Alcázar, its Gothic cathedral and its chapel royal of San Juan de los Reyes, with its flowery cloister, made it an open-air museum of art—only a museum, for Toledo had been dispossessed of its rank and its rôle as capital to the profit of Madrid, and was no longer *villa y corte*, the residence of the Kings.

The morose gravity and the nervous sensitiveness of the artist fitted themselves to this past greatness. Despite his Italian training, El Greco, as he was called, had preserved the imprint of the Byzantine genius, the colouring of its fresco-paintings and " its ascetic types ". Accordingly he found himself all prepared to be the natural portrait-painter " of pensive hidalgos, contemporaries of the great mystics and of the Knight of the Rueful Countenance ".

In proportion as he shook himself free of Italian influence, El Greco became less addicted to composition and dispensed with distributing his figures in harmonious groups, which balanced one another and formed pendants to one another. He assembled them and massed them, as in the " Enterment of the Conde de Orgaz ", that great picture in the church of San Tomé in Toledo. He captured and concentrated attention to one figure and one subject. In his famous " Resurrection of Christ ", which is all in elevation, if one may say so, it is towards the rising Christ that all looks, all gestures, all strivings lead. Even the leg of the centurion lying on the ground rises towards the Lord, Who seems to grow in stature as He tends towards Heaven.

The other portrait-painters of Philip II's reign did not penetrate as deeply as El Greco into knowledge of the Spanish soul ; but, by their exact figuration of feature and form, they too help us to understand the personalities of the period. Philip himself, while still an Infante, had been represented by Titian as so handsome that Mary Tudor fell in love with the Prince from this portrait of him. The King would have liked to attach this ideal craftsman to his person, but he could not persuade him at only twenty-four —that was Titian's age in 1559—to leave Venice.

The Flemish Antonio Moro, whom Philip did take with him to Spain or induce to go there afterwards, a disciple of Holbein's, saw and painted his models just as they were, and he added nothing to Nature except by way of reproducing it in all its perfection and emphasising it in all sincerity. He did not linger long in the service of a prince who had too high an idea of his own grandeur to endure the familiarity of any artist. Antonio Moro and his Spanish pupils, Sánchez Coello and Pantoja de la Cruz, represented the family and the great persons of the Court of Philip II " to the life "—with less emphasis in the case of the pupils. Faces of degenerates, these Infantes and Infantas, we have been told— with some exaggeration ; but undoubtedly their pale complexions and their bloodless faces foreshadow degeneracy (5).

Of all the arts, architecture is the one which appeals to the taste of Sovereigns most keenly. Literature, painting and sculpture demand a long apprenticeship, a sustained application and a leisure which politics and affairs do not permit. In the case of building, the most important thing is to give orders. Professional architects are available to draw up the plans and see them carried out. Rare are the Kings capable of writing a fine book or painting a fine picture, and numerous are those who, possessing the necessary resources and also a love of great things, entrust master-craftsmen with translating an idea of strength, of grandeur, of beauty into stone or marble.

Charles V loved building, as we may judge by the Alcázar of Toledo and, better still, by his palace at Granada, standing on the Alhambra hill, which, unfinished and deserted though it is, would be admired, says Bertaux, as the noblest relic of the Renaissance, if it did not mask a marvel " too different from itself ", the Alcázar of the Moorish Kings.

The time which Philip devoted, when he was in quest of the Crown of Portugal, to visiting Merida, the Augusta Emerita of the Romans and the richest city in Roman monuments in Spain, in company with the architect Herrera, bears witness to his passion for the art of stone. On his return to Madrid, Philip founded, in 1582, an Academy of Architecture. The works which he ordered the Spanish disciples of Michelangelo, inspired by the genius of that master, to carry out are also stamped with the national imprint and his own : monuments of austere grandeur ; altar-screens which, in some churches, block the choir right up to the roof ; gigantic statues in plain or painted wood, those triumphs of the Spanish *entalladores* ; sculptures in gilded bronze, a contribution from Italian art ; polychrome marbles sheathed in gold.

Throughout Spain we find this demonstration of grandeur, carried to the *monstruoso*, which is, as it were, an exhibition of the spoils of the Indies. But it is especially to the Escorial that we must go to seek Philip II. For a long time he, like his predecessors, moved from one capital to another of his Spains, in accordance with the needs of politics or respect for tradition : Valladolid, Toledo, Saragossa, Valencia, Barcelona. Later he usually resided in Madrid, which he chose as his capital in 1561.

As his taste for the country and for solitude—a solitude necessarily relative—increased with his years, he made long stays in the neighbourhood of Madrid, in the palaces and hunting-lodges of his predecessors—at the castle of Valsain, or, as it was called, the Wood of Segovia ; at Aranjuez, at the Pardo. But he wanted to have a house of his own, adapted to his own temperament and built according to his own plans. More than a day's march from Madrid, far away from the noise of the city, he chose a deserted spot, at the foot of the Sierra Guardarrama, above the little village of the Escorial, and there he constructed an immense palace with cyclopean walls of bluish stone, a regular parallelogram 675 feet long by 526 feet wide. In honour of Saint Laurence, whose feast-day fell on the date of his victory at Saint Quentin, the edifice was in the form of an immense gridiron, the instrument of torture on which the Blessed Laurence was martyred.

Modesto La Fuente denies that Philip built the Escorial, as the historian Herrara asserts, in reparation for having destroyed a monastery of Saint Laurence at the gates of Saint Quentin on the occasion of his bombardment of that town ; or that he made a vow to build the monastery if he was victorious in the battle—still less that he was condemned to build it by the Pope in expiation of the sack of Saint Quentin. But, in memory of his victory at Saint Quentin and of the feast of Saint Laurence, he named the Escorial palace " San Lorenzo el Real."

Begun in 1563 by Juan Bautista de Toledo, it was finished in 1583 by Juan de Herrera, a pupil of Michelangelo's and a mathematician, in a style which in its rigid lines and the beauty of its pure nudity stands contrasted, says Bertaux, with the light and brilliant geometry of the later phase of Mozarab art. Its church, made in the image of Saint Peter's in Rome, as Michelangelo had conceived it, dominated the assembly of buildings with its towers and its cupola. The church was established at their centre as though to emphasize the master-idea of the whole construction and its constructor. Monks, the Hieronymites, installed there in perpetuity, were to offer God the uninterrupted homage of psalms and prayers.

In the vaults were to repose the royal family of Spain. It was here that Philip had the remains of Charles V conveyed. It was here that he escorted his wives—except Mary Tudor—and his children, before descending into the vaults himself.

The Escorial bore no resemblance to those pleasure-palaces which the Valois had raised in the smiling valleys of the Loire and the Seine, or even to that majestic residence, the setting for fêtes and monarchical pomp, where Louis XIV isolated himself from his people and from Paris. It was, at one and the same time, a country-palace, a monastery, a necropolis ; a Versailles which was not the capital of the Court and an abbey of Saint Denis ; and, through this cohabitation of dead Kings, of the living King, and of monks, the symbol of the alliance of absolute monarchy and the most uncompromising Catholicism.

The House of God, in the middle of the house of the King, is the most monumental and the most highly decorated part of the Royal Monastery of San Lorenzo, as the Escorial came to be called. Its façade, above the wide steps which lead up to it, presents six tall Doric columns, destined to be crowned by colossal statues of the six Kings of Judah. Off the interior, paved with big marble slabs and divided into three aisles by enormous square pillars surmounted by the cupola, open forty-two chapels adorned with fine screens.

The *Capilla mayor* transcends all the others in decoration and magnificence. Its screen, nearly a hundred feet high, is a marvel of paintings, statues and precious marble. On either side of it open oratories in which kneel groups of statues in gilded bronze : to the left, Charles V in armour, draped in his Imperial mantle, with the Empress and their daughters ; to the right, Philip, also in armour, with the three of his wives by whom he had children, and, behind the first of them, the unfortunate Don Carlos. These are the work of the Leonis, Leone and his son Pompeo.

The Custodia, by Jacomo de Trezzo, " is one of the richest jewels in the world, an assemblage of marble, jaspar, agate and porphyry ", " so fine and so translucent ", despite the variety and splendour of the colouring, " that one would say it was enamel and precious stones " (6). The marble Crucifix, by Benvenuto Cellini, on the high altar was a gift from the Grand Duke of Tuscany.

Philip loved music. He had a major and a minor choir, whose costly maintenance provoked complaints from the Cortes. He recruited them for preference in the Low Countries, which produced singers with voices more powerful and less harsh than those of the Spaniards. He was so concerned about filling vacancies as soon as they occurred that he charged his choirmaster Adrian with the duty of going and finding eight choirboys for him there. The letter in which Philip recommended the Duke of Alba to give his envoy any necessary assistance was written two days after that in which he informed Alba of the imprisonment of his son, the unhappy Don Carlos. He tried, but failed, to deprive the Duke represented Charles V and his family among choirs of angels and prophets of the ancient law, transported, like them, in a great soaring of love and faith, with outstretched hands, towards the Holy Trinity, would Philip have recognized himself in this personage of El Greco's muffled in a cloak, midway between the yawning mouth of Hell and a handful of Saints, his patrons ?(8).

Philip was a great collector of books and manuscripts. In 1575 he conveyed to the library of the Escorial four thousand volumes which he had mostly acquired by purchase, or by legacy or as gifts, from the Secretary of State Gonzalo Pérez, from Honorato Juan, the unhappy Don Carlos's tutor ; from the Cardinal-Archbishop of Burgos, Francisco de Mendoza y Bobadilla ; from Arias Mantano, and other men of learning. To this first stock were added, in the following year, the books of Diego Hurtado de Mendoza.

This former ambassador of Charles V's in Venice and to the Council of Trent, the historian of the war of Granada, a great diplomat, a great man of letters and learning and a poet, had assembled, in the course of his duties in Italy and after his disgrace in Spain, about three hundred Greek manuscripts and a number of Arab manuscripts. All these he bequeathed to the King, who had expressed a desire to see them—in other words, to possess them. " It seems to me," Mendoza said—was it without a tinge of irony ?—" that His Majesty has a right to them, since his library in the Escorial is the most sumptuous in the world." The beneficiary paid for this gift by giving the donor authorization to return to Court ; but the old statesman reappeared there only in time to die.

The library was further increased in 1587 by bequest from Antonio Agustín, Bishop of Lerida and later Archbishop of Saragossa. But Philip let the collection of the Italian Cardinal Sirleti, whose heirs asked twenty thousand ducats for it—and it was worth it—escape him ; and so he did those of Cardinal Carbajal and of the historian Zurita. He was less keenly conscious of the value of old Greek originals than Agustín, who esteemed them as much as " pearls, rubies, and diamonds ". Philip collected them in imitation of other Sovereigns, and just because it was the fashion. He had no intention whatever of spending any very large sums on them.

He preferred to keep his money for enormous books of plainchant, on vellum with splendid bindings, worked on and illuminated until they were almost worth their weight in gold, which he loved to see on the music-desk of his choir. He liked to enrich the Escorial

THE ESCORIAL

library at the cheapest possible price. He considered it no less legitimate to procure books for himself without opening his purse-strings than to impose on his subjects by sheer weight of his authority. As soon as he learnt of the death of President Viglius, learned jurisconsult and good man of letters, he hastened to write to the Duke of Alba bidding him keep an eye on this great bibliophile's library.

It was not, perhaps, Christopher Plantin himself, the famous printer of Antwerp, entrusted in his capacity as " Archeographer " with giving his professional imprimatur to the books which should appear, who decided on his own account that two copies of each of them should be sent to Madrid for the King's library. Certainly this levy of Philip's was more justifiable than the seizure as a whole of libraries which had been formed at great expense by private individuals.

Philip was not fond of lending the books which he had procured in all kinds of ways, among which purchase was the least important. Antonio Agustín foresaw that assembling so many good works in the Escorial, if they were not to be communicated to anybody, would do more harm than good. The Escorial, during Philip II's reign, was an almost inaccessible " ocean of books ", into which a hastily prepared index permitted no more than a raid.

Nevertheless Philip's name is justly associated with a work of erudition. Cardinal Cisneros had undertaken the publication at Alcalá de Henares (the ancient Complutum) of an edition of the Old and New Testaments in several languages, the *Biblia Complutense*. But this undertaking, meritorious as it was, lent itself to criticisms which Cisneros's biographer, Hefele, the historian of the Councils, points out unsparingly : the exegesis of the professors of the university of Alcalá was limited to four remarks ; it never indicated variants ; and it did not say on what authority the only version offered to the reader reposed.

The idea of republishing the Polyglot, copies of which it had become almost impossible to find, occurred to Christopher Plantin. The King, whose help and protection he solicited, promised to grant him six thousand ducats in return for six copies on vellum ; and he sent Arias Montanus, the Spaniard who was most learned in Greek and Latin literature, to the Low Countries to direct and supervise the work. It was a question not of a mere reissue, but of a revision of texts and translations and a collection of new manuscripts.

With the help of a staff of linguists, Raphelengien, Plantin's son-in-law, and the brothers Guy and Nicholas Lefèvre de la

Boderie, this great work, a Bible in four languages, Hebrew, Chaldean, Greek and Latin, was finished in five years. To the original five volumes of Cisneros, revised and corrected, were added three others, a grammar, a juxta-linear translation, a dictionary, etc.— an *Apparatus sacer*, as it was called, intended to facilitate understanding and study of the work. On Philip's instance at the Court of Rome, Pope Gregory XIII accorded it his imprimatur, and granted the right of its publication and sale to Plantin alone for a period of twenty years. In recognition of the King's patronage, the Polyglot Bible of Antwerp was designated the *Biblia Regia* (9).

Of all his country residences, the Escorial was the one which Philip liked best, the one to which he preferred to retire, even before it was finished. One can scarcely say that he rested there, or even that he permitted himself innocent amusements there. He hunted and fished—or, rather, he watched other people hunting and fishing, for he lacked either the patience or the strength for these exercises. His Queen, Anne of Austria, and the two Infantes, poor children with nothing to do, amused themselves by watching a flock of sheep being shorn, and laughed at the occasional roguish songs which were sung by farm-labourers to whom they distributed wine.

To add to their entertainment, the King sent for the famous Toledan actor, Cisneros, who staged for their benefit not, indeed, a comedy of cloak and sword or a heroic drama, but two old mystery plays, the " Life of Saint Pelagius," a celebrated " mime " of Antioch, who became converted and shut himself up in a monastery near Jerusalem to do penance there for his success in the theatre ; and the " Martyrdom of Saint Hermenegild ", a Catholic Visigoth prince, whom his father, King Leovigild, a fanatical Arian, put to death for his firm belief in the divinity of Christ (10).

Nor did Philip attend this edifying spectacle on the platform where the Queen and the Infantes sat, but from a window of the palace, far away from the contagion of the amusement. Perhaps, too, he was not eager to have a close-up view of Cisneros, who had once delighted the unhappy Don Carlos.

All Philip's relaxations were of a strictly Christian character. He was passionately fond of dancing, and, even when he renounced this pleasure for himself, he permitted himself at least the sight of it. This form of amusement was so popular that the Church itself did not disdain it. Though it is not possible to affirm that dancing found a place in the ceremonial of worship, certain motets which have the skipping rhythm of rigadoons give us some grounds for believing that this was the case. In any event, the King, who found entertainment in the leapings and gambollings of villagers, bedecked and disguised or not, must have found an even purer joy in watching the young Levites whom the Hieronymites were training for the monastic life pass before his eyes in a kind of sacred farandole, like David dancing before the bow.

He loved to see the altars illuminated. It was a spectacle which he staged in all its magnificence, with bells ringing and organs pealing, for the benefit of his sister, the Empress Dowager Marie, when she returned to take up her residence in Spain. " The whole church," says Father Sepulveda, the historian of the Escorial, " was one vast brasier, so many candles and torches were alight in it " (11).

But all this was only so much innocent amusement and relaxation. The conduct of affairs took up the greater part of Philip's time. When he left Madrid to stay at the Escorial or elsewhere, he took piles of documents with him. He read and made notes even in his litter. Far from the Court, he gave himself up entirely to that passion for work which was the honour and, one may add, the weakness of his life. He even got the Queen—Anne of Austria —and the Infantes to help him. " He wrote and signed," Cabrera tells us, " the Queen sprinkled sand on the letters, and the Infantes carried them to a table where Sebastian de Santoya, the groom of the chamber in charge of documents, a faithful servant of great discretion and well regarded by the King, folded them, made packets of them, and sent them to the secretaries " (12).

The trouble that Philip took was almost incredible. He studied the dispatches of his ambassadors. He covered the margins of reports with remarks. He asked for points to be cleared up, raised objections, cast doubts. Whenever he noticed a particularly interesting point, he made a note of it and fixed it in his mind by writing " *Ojo* " (attention).

His secretaries sent him draft replies, but he went over them himself, suppressing some passages and adding others with his own hand. Amid all the sterile superfluity and the vague phraseology of the Spanish chancellery, the royal hand is to be distinguished by its exactness of expression, its characteristic rectifications, which give both its erasures and its additions a historical value of the first order. In any case, they bear precious testimony to the King's application.

He never stopped reading, writing, ordering, settling. When he went to the Pardo, or to the Escorial, it was not to enjoy a leisure which he had richly earned, but to work harder than ever, sheltered from the fêtes and pleasures of the Court, and from ceremonial duties, in the quiet of the country.

He was as interested in detail as he was in great affairs. His spirit of minute attention appears even in matters which were scarcely within his competence. He decided, for example, that the feast of the Guardian Angels ought to be celebrated on March 1st. He examined the missals printed by Plantin with the utmost care, and pointed errors and slips out to him. Plantin sometimes printed " Paracletus ", sometimes " Paraclitus ". Philip insisted upon knowing which was the correct rendering. His knowledge of the smallest details of worship drove sacristans to despair. " For, if they happened to make a mistake in not placing the ornaments exactly as they ought to be placed, or in substituting one ornament for another, the King did not fail to send and tell them so, and, if they failed to open the church at the proper hour, he could not forgive them."

These were grave defects of valuable qualities. What became of the great interests of the monarchy in the midst of such trivial cares ? When Philip had decided to disgrace Antonio Pérez, just on the eve of setting out for Portugal, he sent to Rome in hot haste for Cardinal Granvelle, whose knowledge of affairs and shrewdness and activity of mind marked him out to act as a kind of Prime Minister during the Sovereign's absence. But, whether he was on the spot or at a distance, Philip always wanted to do everything himself. He wrote too much, Granvelle lamented, and did not know how to let himself be served. He killed himself with work, and failed to realize " what is essential ".

Philip's laboriousness was immense, but it was often sterile, and it was depressing in its effects. He bent under the burden of affairs ; his memory could not stand the strain upon it ; it presented some surprising signs of weakening. He forgot that Schwartzenberg was the Emperor's representative in the Low Countries. He did not recognize Cecil under the name of Lord Burleigh. The rumour gained currency in 1578 in Augsburg, that city of bankers, that he had " lost his reason ". The Papal Nuncio reported to Gregory XIII that there was talk in Madrid about his " lapses " of mind. Henri III asked his ambassador, Saint Gouard, whether it was true that the King of Spain was " very ill and as though his mind were wandering ".

Perhaps this may have been merely an attack of brain fatigue consequent upon the preliminaries to his succession in Portugal, his journey to his new kingdom, his illness, and the deaths of his fourth wife, Anne of Austria, and one of his sons. But at all times, in order to study affairs more closely, he put off dealing with them " from day to day ". This is the eternal complaint of his ambassadors, his governors, his ministers and his army leaders. " If Death hailed from Spain," said the Viceroy of Naples, " I should be sure of living a long time." Philip never could be satisfied that he was sufficiently informed about anything. His inability to make up his mind added to his slowness. " Our master's main decision in all things," Champagney wrote to his brother, Granvelle, in 1565, " is to remain perpetually undecided " (13).

Philip counted delays and postponements as mere nothings ; he even regarded them as a source of strength. "Time and I," he said, " are worth any other two. . . ." In critical circumstances, such as those of 1579, at the time of the Cologne Conference, he left the dispatches of his ambassador, the Duke of Terra Nova, unanswered for eight months. But did his inability to decide what was the best thing to do make any difference to harm being done in any case ?

CHAPTER XIII

ENGLAND AND THE "INVINCIBLE ARMADA"

IT is traditional to exalt, or to attack, Philip II as the born defender of Catholicism, the sworn enemy of heresy; and in one sense it is true that the watchword of his policy, the thought always at the back of his mind, was the triumph of his faith. But if, from the very beginning of his reign, he undertook the task of religious unification and carried it through despite all its risks and perils inside his own States, we must not suppose that at all times he showed the same passion for proselytism outside his frontiers.

The revolt of the Moors of the Alpujarras and the revolt of the Low Countries, the struggle in the Mediterranean against the Turks and the Barbaresques, and his succession to the Crown of Portugal monopolized all Philip's strength and attention for a considerable time. He did not always pretend to the hegemony of the Christian world. For twenty years he endured the aggressions of the French and the English without striking back. He confined himself to standing on the defensive or even simply protesting.

But, after the union of Portugal with Spain, the return of the Walloon provinces to their obedience and the taking of Antwerp, the death of the Duke of Anjou and the assassination of the Prince of Orange—all that sum of effort, success, luck and crime which set his hands free—Philip felt that the time had come to avenge the insults which had been offered to himself and to God. A new era was opening : the era of great hopes and far-flung ideas.

Against the heretical Sovereigns and nations he turned all the resources of his monarchy. From out of the King of Spain emerged the champion of orthodoxy and the pretender to the empire of the world.

He allied himself in France with the Guises, by the Treaty of Joinville, signed on December 31st, 1584, in order to compel Henri III to exclude the heir-presumptive, Henri King of Navarre, the leader of the Protestant party, from his rights of succession. In case of a vacancy of the French throne, Philip contemplated the abrogation of the Salic law and the possible candidature of his own daughter, the Infanta Clara Isabel Eugenia. At the same time he made ready an overwhelming armament to attack heresy in its refuge and citadel, England. This was the great design of Philip's reign. Hitherto he had let the provocations of Protestant England pass. This time he had determined to make an end of her.

In the Low Countries Elizabeth had never stopped harrying him, openly or covertly. Even in time of peace she declared herself hostile to the Spanish domination. It was not that she was angry with the Catholic King for persecuting the Protestants. As a matter of fact, she had never thought of embracing the cause of European Protestantism, as her Ministers, Lord Burghley and Walsingham, pressed her to do. But she was interested in this market for English woollens, which was hampered by the religious persecutions of the Spaniards. She had reason to fear lest, in case of war, the flat shores of Flanders and the wide estuaries of Zeeland might be used to launch an invading fleet and army against her.

Accordingly, as she informed Frederic Perrenot, Lord of Champagney, when Requesens sent him to negotiate the terms of a treaty with her at the beginning of 1576, Elizabeth would never help the Spaniards to establish their footing in the Low Countries. She reproached them with " their haughtiness " and their contempt for her and her people, and accused them of wanting to " hem in " her kingdom.

" She did not want either the French in those parts (the Low Countries) or neighbours as ticklish as the Spaniards, who were already giving her subjects a bad enough reception in Spain, and whom it in no way suited her to have on the coast over there." " And beginning to work herself up very much and let herself go, she said that the Low Countries conducted as they had been in the habit of being by their own inhabitants, and in accordance with their own privileges, would be a much better thing for the King and for herself " (1).

With all her challenges and her changes of front, sometimes for France or against France, sometimes for Spain or against Spain, Elizabeth's policy, which may appear capricious and feminine, was fundamentally clear and coherent, and quite English. Without any thought of religion, in the national interests and in her personal interests she could suffer no powerful neighbours and possible enemies, either Spanish or French, opposite England—nobody except a pacific aristocracy of lords and burghers.

287

But she ought to have acted decisively and made the necessary financial sacrifices. Elizabeth, however, out of a spirit of sheer meanness, could never make up her mind to abandon her close-fistedness in order to constitute this kind of neutral zone about which she dreamt.

At the time of the siege of Antwerp she took alarm. She accepted the sovereignty of the Low Countries which the States-General offered her, on August 6th, 1585. She promised to help the city, which Farnese was investing closely. She dispatched a few thousand soldiers, but they arrived too late ; Antwerp had capitulated. The besiegers, however, were so exhausted and reduced in numbers after their victory that the English could have got the better of the seven or eight thousand surviving Spaniards, if the Queen had given orders to the relieving army to attack them.

She did not do so. She shrank from the expense of a campaign. She was afraid of the triumph of the Calvinists, the most ardent element in the resistance, who were sectaries as opposed to her conception of a Church—the " *via media anglicana* "—as Papism itself.

Until December, 1585—it is true that the need was now less urgent—she kept the leader of the army, that Leicester whom she loved like a cousin, and perhaps a little more, in England. When he disembarked, the States-General hailed Leicester as a saviour and appointed him Governor-General. The Queen, thinking herself compromised by this choice, which Spain might interpret as a declaration of war, signified her disapproval to the elect and his electors. Then she softened and, when she found that Philip was prepared to let this affront pass like so many others, she allowed her favourite to accept the appointment.

Leicester was incompetent. He failed to prevent the Duke of Parma, during the first six months of 1586, from taking Vanloo and Grave and closing the passages across the Meuse against the Protestant auxiliaries from Germany. He did not succeed in possessing himself of Zutphen, on the Ijssel. In an engagement fought with the object of preventing Spanish reinforcements from entering the town, he sacrificed many members of the English nobility, among them Philip Sidney, one of the most renowned poets of the English Renaissance.

The States-General had other reasons for regretting their choice. Leicester proposed to govern in his own way, in contempt of their rights and in the interests of his own retainers. He entrusted the command of a fort outside Zutphen, which his troops had carried, to an untrustworthy Englishman named Yorke ; and he promoted to the post of Governor of Deventer William Stanley, a Papist and former soldier of the Duke of Alba, who had three times sworn fidelity to Elizabeth and was secretly under engagement to serve the King of Spain in the Low Countries.

Against the upper classes, zealous for the rights of the nation, liberal and tolerant, Leicester, like a good demagogue, in order to make himself master, stirred up the Calvinist ministers and the refugees from Flanders and Brabant, who, embittered by persecution and exile, were wrath with the States-General and the town magistrates, and especially Buys and Olden Barnevald, the grand pensioner of Holland, because they tolerated the Catholic Mass on grounds of humanity and also on grounds of policy.

Recalled at the end of 1586 by Elizabeth, who could not do without him for long, her favourite Leicester, on his departure, gave his Papist *protégé* authority to act independently of the leader of the English troops, Sir John Norris. Stanley took advantage of this authority to hand Deventer over to the Spaniards. Yorke, following his example, surrendered the fort at Zutphen to them. Startled by this treachery, the States-General appointed Maurice of Nassau, son of William of Nassau, a young man of twenty who was worthy of his father and of their hopes, as Governor-General *ad interim*, associating with him as his lieutenant Hohenlohe, in command of the German auxiliaries.

The absence of the titular Governor-General, the division and strife between the parties of Leicester and the States-General, and the parsimony of the Queen of England, who allowed her troops to die of starvation, played into the hands of the Duke of Parma. In 1587 he invested Huys, a stronghold of the first importance, quite close to the sea. To act in concert with Philip, who was preparing for invasion of England with the utmost secrecy, Parma needed a port which was not, like Antwerp, watched and at times blockaded by the Dutch fleet. Huys would permit him to keep an eye on Flushing and Ostend, where the English and the Gueux were masters, and to organize means of disembarkation on the English coast.

Leicester had no option except to attempt relief; but he did not succeed in raising the siege, and the Dutch Admiral, Justin of Nassau, declared himself unable to force the passage which linked Huys with the sea. Huys capitulated on August 15th. Leicester blamed his own failure on the States-General and the German and Dutch troops. He flattered himself that he could do better if he was all-powerful.

So he repeated the Duke of Anjou's attack on the towns. At

289   U

Utrecht he abolished the municipal constitution and nominated men of his own choice as magistrates. But he had not the same success at Leyden, the heroic city of the resistance. The plot was discovered, and three of the principal culprits, after being tried and found guilty, were executed on October 26th. Elizabeth's favourite could not be brought to trial himself, but he was nevertheless involved in this condemnation.

The Queen of England, impatient as ever to see her " sweet Robin ", recalled him again in November, 1587. She blamed the successes of the Duke of Parma not on Leicester, but on the States, and she decided to abandon them to their fate. She continued to harry the Spaniards at sea, where expenses were nil and profits were certain. She might have reflected that, after the settlement of the Portuguese succession and the submission of three-quarters of the Low Countries to the Spaniards, such provocation was becoming dangerous.

Philip was organizing his revenge at his leisure. He was in close relations with all Elizabeth's enemies : the Jesuits, then in all the fervour of a new-born order, and the Catholics banished from England, whom Doctor Allen, in the colleges of Douai and Rheims, was preparing for preaching, apostolate, and martyrdom. Philip was corresponding secretly with Mary Stuart, who was still formidable, prisoner though she might be. A close relative of Elizabeth's and her heir, Mary was even, by canonical right, the legitimate Queen of England, since Elizabeth had been declared dethroned by a Bull of Pius V as bastard and heretic.

Mary's misfortunes had aroused the sympathy of the whole of the Catholic world. In France she had the Guises, her first cousins, on her side. In Scotland, where the lords of the congregation had enthroned her young son, James VI, in her place, and even in England, she could count upon numerous partisans among her coreligionists. When she despaired of her liberty and of her son's return to Catholicism, by a secret document she recognized Philip II as her successor on the thrones of Scotland and England (2).

For a long time he contented himself with encouraging plots against Elizabeth covertly. When Pope Gregory XIII pressed him to invade Ireland and establish himself there in order to turn the country into a base of operations against England, Philip refused and he would not even allow the banished Irish to leave the ports of Spain with the object of disembarking in their own island. Ardent Catholics blamed him for his lukewarmness, and criticized him for his indifference. The Nuncio reported to the Court of Rome that Philip was said to suffer from lapses of mind.

The truth was that he was not fond of improvisation. He set the idea of a descent on England aside until he was ready for it. Momentarily carried away though he had been by the plausibility of the Florentine Ridolfi, Mary Stuart's agent, Philip had later let himself be convinced by the Duke of Alba, and still more by facts, that the Duke of Norfolk's plot against Elizabeth was not practicable. More prudent than his brother, and, moreover, always prejudiced against initiatives which did not emanate from himself, Philip was irritated that Don John should have set forth to the Pope his project of leading the *tercios* of the Low Countries to the help of the captive Queen of Scots. Philip was still more incensed that Don John should have come to Spain, contrary to his orders, to submit this project to him.

Philip suffered Elizabeth twice to expel his ambassadors, Don Guerau de Espés and Don Bernardino de Mendoza, as accomplices in disturbances and attempts at assassination in England. He bided his own time : the time when, disembarrassed of Antonio, Prior of Crato, of the Duke of Anjou and of the Prince of Orange, he could turn his attention outside his own States and pursue the sea-rovers, heretics and fomenters of heresy, to their lairs.

After the juridical murder of the Queen of Scots, on February 18th, 1587, Philip pressed forward his preparations for a landing in England. Right was on his side, and he proposed to have might on it as well. In order to leave nothing to chance, he concerted plans with the Catholic princes and parties. His alliance with the French League assured him of Henri III's neutrality. The Duke of Aumale, the Duke of Guise's cousin, seized the fortresses of Picardy and tried to seize Boulogne, which would have provided the Spanish fleet with a port of refuge and refitting opposite the English coast.

In Italy, in order to be surer of the zeal of his feudatories and the support of the free States, Philip solicited from the Emperor Rudolph II the title of Vicar-Imperial. This exposed him to the risk of arousing the jealousy and the suspicions of the Italian princes and the Pope. Accordingly Gregory XIII's successor, Sixtus V, while he praised the idea of the crusade against England, wrangled about the conditions of his support of the crusading Philip II, who lacked sufficient resources to defray all the expenses of the expedition himself—even though he claimed that he alone should reap all the benefit of it.

It was over these points that Philip's ambassador engaged in negotiations with the Court of Rome. The new Pope had put the finances of the Pontifical State in such good order that he could, and did, call himself the richest Sovereign in Christendom. It was not that his revenues were so considerable, but that, by spending less than his revenues, he enriched himself on the difference. Sixtus V extended and exploited the Government pawnbroking establishments so advantageously that he derived very large sums from them, and, despite the number and the beauty of the buildings which he constructed, he found himself in possession of surpluses. He was so proud of his savings, and so avaricious, that, so the ambassador of Spain said, to ask him for any part of this treasure of his was like asking him for his heart's blood.

Only something which was definitely established to be in the interests of religion—and there must be no doubt about its being definitely established—would induce the Pope to touch his hoard. He could not refuse, of course, to contribute towards the crushing of heresy ; but only on condition that this money should not be diverted from its proper object. He consented to grant a million on the day when he heard that Farnese had landed on English soil.

A bad subject at the best for appeals to his generosity, Sixtus V was further vexed by the Spanish pretensions in the country which was to be liberated from heresy. Philip II demanded that the Pope should recognize his rights to the Crown of England. Did not the introduction of such aims of ambition into it change the whole character of the projected struggle ? The Pope found him powerful enough already, this King of the Spains who was his own neighbour as master of the Milanese, the Kingdom of the Two Sicilies, and Sardinia, and was on the point of re-conquering the whole of the Low Countries. Philip's annexation of another kingdom would pave the way for the establishment of a world monarchy, which would be as detrimental to the independence of the Holy See as to the freedom of the Christian world.

The Pope was impulsive and choleric, and he proclaimed his indignation to the Cardinals and to his entourage. He apostrophized the ambassador of Spain, Count de Olivares, another man of violent temperament, but cold in his anger, an enthusiast about his master's greatness, who retorted without much regard for the Pontifical dignity. The disagreement grew so keen that partisans of the expedition had to intervene.

Doctor Allen, whom the Pope had promoted Cardinal on Philip II's representations, wrote to his royal patron that it was superfluous to worry about his investiture with the Crown of England in advance. Once London had been occupied by his troops, it would be time enough for Philip to assert his rights to the Crown, through his relationship with Henry VIII's first wife and with the House of Lancaster. In any case, did not the Bull of Pius V, which deposed Elizabeth as heretic and bastard, name him as the first person to succeed her?

Finally, as a compromise, Sixtus V agreed to the accession of a son of Philip's to the throne of England. This meant no more than the satisfaction of the Pope's *amour-propre*. In 1587 Philip II had only one male child left, Philip, born on April 4th, 1578. As it was not likely that at the age of sixty, sick man as he was, he would remarry for the fifth time, he obtained what he wanted by a roundabout way. If he dethroned Elizabeth, the Infante would become King of England, and, on his father's death, he would inherit the Crowns of Spain and Portugal.

During these diplomatic discussions Philip pushed on with his preparations. He had asked for a plan of campaign from the Marquis of Santa Cruz, Don Alvaro de Bazán, and this great sailor presented him with one which contemplated the employment of one hundred and fifty large ships, three hundred and twenty smaller ones—from fifty to eighty tons—forty galleys and six galleasses, in all five hundred and sixteen vessels, together with two hundred and forty flat-bottomed boats and pinnaces, manned by thirty thousand six hundred sailors and sixty-three thousand eight hundred and ninety soldiers (3).

But Philip, for reasons of economy, reduced the numbers of the fleet; and, heedless of possible conflicts of authority, he gave the Duke of Parma the command-in-chief of all the land forces, leaving the admiral only that of the fleet and its crews. The instructions which Santa Cruz received in September, 1587, enjoined him to go straight to Margate, without turning aside either to the right or to the left, and there, posted on the estuary of the Thames, to cover the passage of the troops whom Farnese was to mass on the beaches of the Low Countries.

Santa Cruz died in February, 1588—killed, so it was said, by a very hard saying of Philip's about his prudence, which Philip interpreted as lack of zeal. The admiral was the only man capable of making the best of an unlucky plan of campaign, which did not include the occupation of a port in Holland or Zeeland in order to keep an eye on the ships of the Gueux and prevent them from joining hands with the English fleet.

Philip had no doubts about success. To the port of Lisbon on the estuary of the Tagus, his armada's point of assembly, flocked ships great and small, built, commandeered or bought in Italy and Spain, one hundred and thirty transport vessels and warships, sailing ships, galleys, Dutch luggers, Portuguese caravels, cutters and pinnaces, dominated from all the height of their forecastles and quarter-decks by the enormous galleons, armed with a formidable artillery. They were divided into ten squadrons, and manned by nineteen thousand two hundred and ninety-five soldiers, eight thousand three hundred and fifty-two sailors and two thousand and eighty-eight rowers.

Parma, on his side, assembled flat-bottomed boats to embark his veteran Spanish regiments, German levies and Walloon recruits. The fleet of Spain, sailing up the English Channel, was to go and meet the flotilla of the Low Countries and, in concert with it, disembark the two armies which they transported at the mouth of the Thames. That would settle with the Queen of England.

But in the year 1587, when the storm was gathering, and even in 1588, when it was on the point of breaking, Elizabeth, disgusted with her difficulties and expenses in the Low Countries, was ready to come to an understanding with the King of Spain. She welcomed the overtures which the Duke of Parma conveyed to her through a rich Italian merchant of Antwerp. It is true that at the same time she authorized Drake, who as early as 1577 had sacked the ports of the Spanish colonies, to undertake fresh raids, in whose profits she would share ; but she recommended him to avoid doing so much damage as might provoke the King of Spain into breaking off relations.

Drake set out in April, 1587, descended on Vigo, where he pillaged the churches ; re-embarked, fell upon Cadiz, and burnt thirty ships and ten thousand tons of merchandise. He withdrew without being pursued, penetrated into the estuary of the Tagus, where the Armada was assembling, and sank one hundred ships ; but, by way of obeying his Sovereign's recommendations, he passed by Lisbon without attacking it. On his return to England he was very badly received by the Queen, and blamed for having done so much harm to the Spanish marine.

It was enough to justify the great maritime preparations of the King of Spain. Was Philip not entitled to arm in order to subdue the rebels of the Low Countries and defend the coasts of the Spanish mainland and colonies against privateering English captains ? Elizabeth did not believe that she was personally threatened. In February, 1588, the English commissioners, the Earl of Derby, Lord Cobham, Sir James Craft, Valentine Dale, doctor in law and sometime ambassador to Vienna, and Doctor Rogers, arrived at Ostend to negotiate. Farnese had entrusted his master's interests to the Count of Aremberg, Champagney,

Richardot, Jacob Maas, and Garnier. But it was he who held the cards and played the game.

The Armada was getting ready to leave Lisbon. It was a question of gaining time. Farnese excelled at this. Before they came to negotiation, where was the best place for the conference to assemble? At Ostend, the English proposed. No, replied the Governor of the Low Countries; the King of Spain could not accept one of his own towns conquered and occupied by rebels and foreigners as the seat of a conference. Dale went back and forth between Ostend and the Duke of Parma's camp—a matter of long journeys and bad lodgings.

Had the Duke's commissioners full powers from the King of Spain? Why raise that point, replied the Duke; what had it got to do with choosing the seat of the conference? Dale maintained that it should be cleared up first, and the Duke that it need not. There were long discussions in which Dale adduced precedents. His contradictor listened to him patiently. Dale was pleased with his own capacity for argument, and flattered by being the centre of so much attention.

In all these conversations Farnese, the great soldier, the great poliorcete, showed himself an excellent comedy actor. Let us not forget that he was, on his father's side, Italian. In this way he gained several months, and during this time he equipped himself. He concentrated ships, constructed flat-bottomed boats, quartered the troops who were dispatched to him from Spain and Italy, and raised levies in Germany and in the Low Countries. Of the one-and-twenty *tercios* which he had at his disposal, he sent a part, twenty-eight thousand soldiers, and some sailors, to Dunkirk, whence he expected to cross over to England on the appearance of the fleet of Spain.

The English commissioners, sluggish though their channels of communication were, heard talk about the armament of the King of Spain. The good Dale questioned Farnese, who said that he had also heard that his master wanted to avenge himself on a certain " Draake ". But what importance could there be in that?

Meanwhile there were circulating in the Low Countries the Bull in which Sixtus V, repeating Pius V's condemnation of her, declared Elizabeth unworthy of the throne, and a pamphlet in English, the " Admonition ", drafted, so it was said, by the English Jesuit Parsons and signed by Cardinal Allen, who charged the usurping Queen with all conceivable crimes and vices. Reports about these documents came to the ears of the Queen's commissioners. Dale went to see Farnese at Bruges and interrogated him. The Duke seemed surprised. He knew nothing about the "Admonition", since he could not read a word of English. As for Sixtus V's Bull, it had nothing to do with him ; he recognized no master except the King of Spain. Elizabeth's ambassadors learnt that the Spanish Armada was leaving Lisbon when it was already in the English Channel.

Philip had made good the damage done by Drake's surprise ; but he could not replace Santa Cruz. The Duke of Medina-Sidonia, one of the greatest lords of Andalusia and the richest of them all, whom he appointed as Santa Cruz's successor, was absolutely ignorant about anything to do with the sea ; and he was quite conscious —and so, still more, was his wife—of his own incapacity. But the King had made it a matter of principle to put a leader at the head of his forces whom the subordinate commanders, his inferiors by birth, would make no difficulties about obeying. Inasmuch as Philip liked to do everything himself, he interpreted the lack of initiative and competence of this former Viceroy of Naples as a disposition to defer to himself in everything. Philip esteemed Medina-Sidonia capable in proportion as he was docile.

The King would accept no excuses whatever. He insisted upon promoting Medina-Sidonia to the job of leader of the Armada. The experience of the Duke's lieutenants, Florez de Valdez, Oquendo, Recalde, and Martin de Bestendona, could not compensate for the weakness in the high command. A duke, even if he was all gold, was no substitute for an admiral of iron.

Philip had wished to leave nothing to chance. From his room —or, to be more exact, from his cell—in the Escorial he looked after everything : arms, munitions, provisions. He went into the smallest details, down to settling the quantity of water with which the crews' wine was to be tempered. But frequently his orders were obeyed in the Spanish manner, which, we are told, is to put off everything *a mañana*, until to-morrow. While Philip was killing himself with work and getting lost in petty details (4), the purveyors, in connivance with the accountants, were delivering damaged supplies, and in short weight as well as bad quality. Medina-Sidonia, when he reached Lisbon, discovered a state of confusion and waste, and had to make fresh requisitions for men, money, and provisions.

By dint of paying attention to the most trivial things, that royal purser Philip lost sight of the most essential things. He was, indeed, anxious about souls rather than about bodies. He took precautions that all the sailors and soldiers should confess and communicate before embarking. He ordered swearing and blasphemy to be punished. He refused to allow prostitutes, the usual companions of armies on campaign, on board the Armada. He placed monks and priests in all the ships to officiate, preach, absolve combatants, and labour after victory for the conversion of the vanquished. The English said afterwards, and perhaps they believed, that the Armada carried chains and instruments of torture intended for the heretics.

The crusade against England was popular. The Spanish people, accustomed by eight centuries of conquest to fighting the Infidels and proud of their rôle in the world, shared Philip II's feelings against the English, whom they detested as heretics and pirates, enemies of God and the King. There were few titled families which did not provide their contingent of recruits. The King, for that matter, had a hand in this himself. One of his best sailors, Don Alonso de Leyva, carried younger sons of the Castilian aristocracy, who had been specially entrusted to his care, on board his ship (5). Simple gentlemen, like Lope de Vega, devoted to literature and study, shouldered the musket to run the risks of battle and the sea. Great lords and foreign princes, such as the Duke of Pastrana, son of the Princess of Eboli ; John de Medici, brother of the Grand Duke of Tuscany ; an Archduke of Austria, a brother of the Duke of Savoy, Amadeo, and more than two hundred other gentlemen enrolled themselves in the army of Spain or in that of the Low Countries.

Expectation ran high throughout the Catholic world, and success was regarded as certain. National pride baptized the immense Armada with the surname of " Invincible ". The standard of the faith was hoisted on the Admiral's flagship on April 25th, and Divine protection was implored by prayers on board the ships and in the churches of Spain. But, in order to complete the preparations, the order for departure had to be postponed for more than a month, until May 30th.

Philip could scarcely be accused of heedlessness. Elizabeth, who had foreseen nothing, could not organize anything either. She placed her land forces under the command of the incompetent Leicester. For all her naval forces she had at her disposal some thirty ships, in addition to which a hundred and fifty small vessels were assembled. She was stingy about powder, about the crews' rations, and about their beer. But the initiative of the nation made good the shortcomings of the government. England was lucky in possessing seamen who were proof against anything : Drake, Hawkins, Frobisher, Raleigh, under the command of the second Lord Howard of Effingham, a sailor himself.

The Ocean declared itself for England. The Spanish fleet had hardly left Lisbon when it was assailed by a violent storm, scattered, and compelled to take refuge in the ports of Galicia. It did not put to sea again until July 22nd, when it steered north. Then an opportunity presented itself which Santa Cruz, despite his orders, would never have let slip. The English fleet, still in course of concentration, had taken refuge at Plymouth at the sight of this immense enemy fleet. Medina-Sidonia's lieutenants were in favour of following it up there and destroying it. But the Spanish Admiral invoked the King's formal order, and kept on his course towards the estuary of the Thames.

The English whom he had spared came and attacked him by night. Their lighter ships, with lower superstructures and easier to handle, sailed close to the heavy galleons of Spain and riddled them with cannon-ball. For four days the English manœuvred around these floating fortresses, and never stopped harrying them until their powder gave out.

Medina-Sidonia, on August 6th, beat a retreat to Calais to have time to think and take breath. But the enemy sail reappeared. During the night Drake launched fire-ships against the Spanish vessels at anchor. At the sight of these blazing hulks, which scattered incendiarism from ship to ship, panic seized the Spanish soldiers, who remembered the siege of Antwerp, and spread to the crews. They cut their cables, abandoned their anchors, and put out to sea. At daybreak this frightened fleet was once more assailed.

The Admiral of the Armada pressed the Duke of Parma to bring up the ships which he had built at Antwerp and concentrated at Nieuport and Dunkirk. The Spanish General was on the point of proceeding to Dunkirk, to embark the twenty-six thousand men of the army of invasion, when he heard of the flight of the Armada. The north-west wind had freshened into a gale. The English had returned to their ports. The Spaniards were left at the mercy of the elements.

In despair, Medina-Sidonia abandoned his enterprise. With the object of getting back to Spain with the rest of his fleet intact, he made up his mind not to face the enemy in that terrible strait of the Pas-de-Calais and the English Channel again, but to bear to the north and circumnavigate Great Britain. It was a bad mistake in calculation. Wind and sea cost him more than that dozen days' battle from July 30th to August 10th.

He lost most of his ships on the reefs of the Orkneys and the Hebrides, or in the dangerous channels off the coast of Scotland.

Their crews were either swallowed up by the waves, or knocked on the head by the coast-dwellers. The wild Catholic Irishry mercilessly massacred their co-religionists whom the fury of the sea cast into their hands. A single man boasted that he had killed eighty shipwrecked men with his own hand. More than fifty ships and eight thousand men disappeared in this disaster. Alonso de Leyva's ship went down, and the flower of the Castilian aristocracy with it.

Elizabeth had profited by a stroke of luck which her lack of foresight did not deserve. But even a successful landing of the troops of the Armada and the troops from Flanders on the banks of the Thames would not, in any case, have ended the struggle. Medina-Sidonia, once his duty as admiral was done, was to have handed over to Farnese, charged with the responsibility for operations on land, a dispatch in which Philip II indicated on what conditions he would leave Elizabeth her Crown : first, the free exercise of the Roman Catholic religion ; second, the restitution of the strong places which the English still held in the Low Countries ; third, an indemnity for all the loss suffered by Spain (6).

It was, naturally, freedom of Catholic worship to which Philip attached the utmost importance, as the first step towards the re-establishment of Catholicism in England. Parma, in any case, was to offer peace at this minimum price only if it seemed to him too difficult to conquer the Kingdom and dethrone the Queen. But could the leader of the invading army have struck an estimate of his chances for and against, even after a victory which opened the gates of London to him?

It is probable that the English levies could not have withstood the Spanish, Italian, and Walloon regiments, commanded by the best military captain of the period. But London was not all England. Elizabeth, even though she were defeated, would never have accepted a peace which would be ruinous to her finances and to her prestige, and would lay her kingdom open to Catholic propaganda under the protection of a foreign army. Indeed, it is unquestionable that she would have held out to the end, and that, with Presbyterian Scotland behind her, and supported by the English Protestants and by loyal and patriotic Catholics, she would have succeeded in containing the Spaniards in the south.

The rebels in the Low Countries would have lost no time, during the absence of Farnese and his best troops, in resuming the offensive and making the most of their advantage. The King of Spain would have had to carry on a twofold war, without the means of carrying it on, in view of the fact that his base of operations was so far away.

The protection of the waves, the valour of the English sailors, and the incompetence of Medina-Sidonia saved Elizabeth from having to stand up to such a test. But the attempt of the Armada was a warning and a lesson. It meant the end of the covert warfare with which Elizabeth had hitherto contented herself, in the form of aiding the revolt in the Low Countries at the cheapest possible price, and authorizing, or even ordering, English raids on the Spanish merchant marine and colonies.

Henceforth she had to commit herself irrevocably. She had to support the activity of the States-General against Philip ; she had to help Henri IV against the French League, that ally of Spain—in short, substitute the counter-offensive, whatever it might cost her, for the defensive. The threat of invasion by sea clearly showed her the necessity of maintaining a powerful and numerous fleet, ready to return blow for blow, in order to ward off any fresh attack.

After the disaster to the Spanish Armada, Elizabeth, led astray by the offers of the Portuguese pretender Antonio and his foreshadowing of an insurrection in Portugal if an English force were landed, dispatched about a hundred ships and some thousands of soldiers from Plymouth, with the object of delivering the country from Philip.

Drake, in command of this fleet, failed in his attempt to take Corunna, on May 4th, 1589, and proceeded to disembark Sir John Norris and the land forces on the coast of Portugal. Norris established himself on the heights of Belem, and Drake moored off the port of Cascaes, ready to attack Lisbon in concert with him. The English, however, after penetrating into the suburbs of the city, were vigorously repulsed. Drake secured the surrender of the fortress of Cascaes and seized some ships laden with wheat. But he and the commander of the English land forces found that, contrary to Dom Antonio's affirmations, the Portuguese populace made no move ; and Drake and Norris returned to England in June, leaving Dom Antonio to his fate. He retired to France in 1595.

In 1591 the English failed in an attempt to surprise the galleons from the Indies, and, surprised themselves by a Spanish fleet emerging from Ferrol, they lost a considerable number of ships. But this defeat of the English, and the losses which they suffered in it, were a poor compensation to Spain for the disaster to the Armada (7).

Philip did his best to resign himself to this disaster ; but it went to his heart that he had "failed to render God the great service" of slaying heresy in its lair. He persisted in his design, and projected a landing in Ireland which would raise her oppressed people and make them take up arms against England. But Elizabeth forestalled him. She armed a hundred and fifty ships, manned by eight thousand soldiers and six thousand sailors, which were reinforced by a Dutch flotilla.

Lord Howard of Effingham, the conqueror of the Armada, entrusted with the command of all the English forces by land and sea, went straight to Cadiz, where the first preparations for the expedition to Ireland were in progress. He disembarked ten thousand English and five thousand Dutch outside the city. The garrison made a sortie to meet the attackers, and were routed. The victors entered the city pell-mell with the vanquished, and, having made themselves masters of it, proceeded to sack it methodically, but in good order.

They emptied the houses, as they despoiled individuals, one by one, but without excess or violence, even letting the women go with the clothes they were wearing. The booty which they took was enormous. Cadiz was the richest city in Spain, the great clearing-house of the trade of the mother-country with the Indies. It is from this sack of Cadiz, in 1596, that we may date the downfall of the maritime greatness of Spain, and the rise of the new masters of the sea, the English and the Dutch.

Exasperated by this bearding of him, which he felt perhaps more deeply than any defeat, Philip II made ready a new fleet, for which Ireland was to serve as a base of operations against England. But this second Armada of his, dispatched in 1597, had no better luck than the first, and it did not get even as far. On the coasts of Spain herself, a storm assailed it and swallowed up its ships, together with their crews and soldiers. The elements declared themselves against Philip once more. His death, which took place the following year, leaves us unable to say whether he bowed down to this form of the judgment of God.

CHAPTER XIV

ANTONIO PÉREZ AND THE LIBERTIES OF ARAGON

THE murder of Escovedo was avenged by the King who had ordered it upon the Minister who had inspired this act of sovereign justice.

As we have already seen, Antonio Pérez, determined to rid himself of an embarrassing witness to his liaison with the Princess of Eboli, had gone to his master, Philip, and denounced Don John's over-zealous secretary as a mischief-maker. Escovedo had returned from the Low Countries to Spain with the object of pressing for Don John's recall, paving the way for the young Prince's entrance to the Council of State, and securing compensation for the abandonment of his plan of a descent on England by the grant of the title and privileges of an Infante to this illegitimate son of Charles V's. For his complicity in these ambitions and pretensions of Don John's, and his own intrigues in Rome against Elizabeth and in favour of the imprisoned Mary Stuart behind Philip's back, Escovedo, Don John's confidential agent, was killed one night, on Philip's orders, by assassins in Pérez's pay.

As soon as the deed was done, the executioners disappeared ; and Philip and his Minister might hope that, without undue inquiry, the crime would be attributed to persons unknown and consigned to the files of unsolved murder mysteries. But public opinion immediately singled Pérez out as the instigator of it. Pérez's enemies—for this flaunting, influential Secretary of State had many—neither sought nor even tried to seek any excuses for the deed of which they accused him.

Another of the King's private secretaries, Mateo Vázquez de Leca, influenced either by jealousy, or by the strict obligation which the King laid upon all his servants to keep him informed about everything, regardless of personal considerations, hastened to report to Philip the " suspicions which spread more and more widely among the people against the said secretary (Pérez) because of the death of the other ". It was, so popular rumour ran, " one of his (Escovedo's) great friends who had had him killed, and that on account of a woman ".

The voice of the people proclaimed the truth. Here was Philip informed of what it said ; and the question arose in his mind, and for his conscience, whether the arguments which had been used to induce him to punish Escovedo were the real ones, or at least the only ones. To find this out, Philip proceeded in his own way, which was slow, and might seem tortuous. He passed the defamatory communication on to the person defamed.

Antonio Pérez and the Princess of Eboli burst out into angry protests and threats against their denunciator. The Princess, who found herself doubly insulted, addressed a proud and almost insolent remonstrance to the King, in which she required him both as King and as gentleman to proceed against the enemies of her honour and her house. Philip went on with his own game.

He reassured Vázquez, who feared, or pretended to fear, for his life. He allowed Vázquez to recommend Escovedo's widow and children to lay information against Antonio Pérez before the President of the Council of Castile. At the same time, Philip wrote to Antonio Pérez assuring him, on his word as a *caballero* (gentleman), that he would not fail him. " As long as I live, there is nothing to fear ; for, though others may change, believe that I do not change. If you have observed me in this respect, I think that you will have seen for yourself that I am not given to change." When Pérez informed Philip how much regret the death of his protector, the Marquis of los Velez, had caused him, and also how much alarm, Philip calmed Pérez's fears. " I will not fail you. Of that be well assured. Bear up stoutly, then, against this grief and anxiety of yours. You can do so, since you still have me."

It was a promise as ambiguous as the responses of the Oracles, as Pérez was to discover a little later. It would have sufficed for Philip to prohibit Mateo Vázquez from carrying his inquiries any further ; but he did not do so. In place of the Marquis of los Velez, Philip appointed the Count de Barafas, an adversary of Pérez's, to the Council of State. He charged the Grand Inquisitor, Cardinal Quiroga ; the President of the Council of Castile, Pezos ; Diego de Chaves, his own confessor ; the ambassador of Germany, Khevenhuller, and other persons besides with the duty of intervening and negotiating an understanding between his two secretaries. Pérez, relying upon Philip's royal word, and the Princess, haughty, vindictive, and high-spirited, would agree to no understanding.

Is it quite certain that Philip was not speculating upon this uncompromising attitude of theirs? In his suspicious mind, the idea was taking deeper and deeper root that, under pretext of punishing a plot, he had been induced to cover up an amorous liaison.

Philip kept Pérez in play. He informed his secretary of his intention to appoint him ambassador to Venice. But on March 30th, 1579, the first anniversary of Escovedo's assassination, Philip wrote to Cardinal Granvelle, who was living in Rome without employment, and bade him come to Madrid with all speed. "The sooner you do so, the better I shall be pleased" (1).

On the very day of Granvelle's arrival, July 28th, Philip went on working with Pérez. At ten o'clock at night he sent his secretary some Italian documents. He assured him by letter that he would deal with Perez's difference with Vázquez before returning to the Escorial. As a matter of fact, Philip did not fail to do so. At eleven o'clock the Mayor of the Palace, Alvaro Garcia de Toledo, presented himself at Pérez's house and escorted him to his own quarters. At the same hour the Princess of Eboli was arrested in her house and escorted to the Tower of Pinto (2).

Philip wrote to the President of the Council of Castile that, as all efforts to effect a reconciliation between his two secretaries had proved unavailing, he had given orders to lay hands on Pérez and the Princess, in order to prevent them from putting into execution the plan, which they had several times threatened, of having Vázquez killed. No charge was brought against Pérez, but he was kept under observation. The King's confessor and the Archbishop of Toledo assured Pérez's wife, Juana Coello, and assured Pérez himself, that Philip had taken this step only in order to forestall more serious consequences for Pérez.

Pérez was given his own house as his prison. At the end of eight months, his guards were withdrawn. He was given liberty to go to Mass, to take exercise, and to receive visits, though he was expressly prohibited from paying any. During the King's journey in Portugal, and in Philip's absence, Pérez continued to discharge his duties as Secretary of State. "Nothing in his charge was changed."

But Pérez got tired of being suspect and held in semi-captivity, while at the same time invested with the highest functions. He petitioned the King, he sent his own wife to him, to beg Philip to reconcile this contradiction. On his side Pezos, the President of the Council of Castile, a scrupulous jurist and an honest man, demanded insistently that the Princess and Pérez should be tried and condemned if they were guilty, or released if they were innocent.

Philip was more than ever confirmed in his suspicion of them. Very secretly, he had an inquiry into the murder of Escovedo opened by Rodrigo Vázquez de Arce, President of the Council of Finance, whose harshness, combined with his sugary manners, had earned him the nickname of " Garlic Jam " (*ajo confitado*). The result of this inquiry was devastating for Pérez, whom witnesses and testimony worthy of credence convicted of venality, passion for gambling, love of luxury, and prodigality, and also of scandalous intimacy with the Princess of Eboli. De Arce gave it as his belief that Escovedo had been killed because he had discovered this liaison and threatened to denounce it.

The King, who had the depositions communicated to him as they were taken, did not choose to strike at the two culprits simultaneously, as though by way of distinguishing between their crimes and the reasons for their punishments. He had had the Princess transferred from the Tower of Pinto to San Torcaz, where she fell ill, and he permitted her, in March, 1581, to return to residence in her castle at Pastrana. But in 1582, dissatisfied with her behaviour, her feasts and extravagance, Philip deprived her of the custody of her children and the administration of their property.

He still went on keeping Pérez in play. Settlement of his account was not pressing ; on the contrary, it was essential to have time " to verify and clarify further the charges which were being unearthed " against Pérez. It was decided to subject his papers to a domiciliary visit (*juicio de visita*). This investigation threw into relief the large gifts which Pérez had received from abroad, and tended to show that he had given away secrets of State and, in the course of deciphering dispatches, had altered or modified the sense of them.

In the *Relaciones* which he published in his defence after his flight abroad, Pérez claimed that he had shown the King's confessor letters from Philip which ordered him to truncate and falsify documents. Diego de Chaves recommended him to say nothing about them, " since all this (the inquiry) was only a matter of form ". Pérez, accordingly, kept silent. As the reward for his obedience, he had the surprise of learning that he was relieved of his duties for a period of ten years, and condemned to pay a fine of thirty thousand ducats. On the promulgation of this decree, on January 23rd, 1585, he was arrested and escorted to the fortress of Turulgano.

Hitherto Pérez had been treated considerately enough. But fear lest he should take refuge in Aragon, that country of franchises, where he would be protected against arbitrary exercise of the royal will, transformed his detention into close confinement.

He was forbidden to see his wife or his children. His property was confiscated. Juana Coello, that devoted wife of his, was invited to hand over all his private papers. She stoutly refused to do so, and the prisoner had to send her a note written in his own blood before she could be brought to obey.

Once the papers were surrendered, the King, who seemed to find pleasure in leading public opinion astray, had Pérez brought back to Madrid and permitted him to return to residence in one of his finest houses. There Pérez spent fourteen months, and was visited by all Madrid society. He was allowed to go out freely for the ceremonies of Holy Week, " to the great astonishment and surprise of everybody, since nobody could understand the cause of this chopping and changing ".

Meanwhile Rodrigo Vázquez de Arce, promoted to President of the Council of Justice, was secretly continuing his inquiry. During the session of the Aragonese Cortes at Monzon, whither he accompanied the King, de Arce obtained a conclusive deposition from Enriquez, one of Escovedo's assassins. The relatives of the victim, who had hitherto been prevented from pursuing proceedings against the instigator of the crime, were authorized to resume them ; and Pérez, as the object of these proceedings, was imprisoned in the fortress of Pinto. It is true that he was brought back to Madrid two months later ; but this was only to enable him to stand his trial, a secret trial or *proceso de Cámara*, as it was called, on the charge of corruption.

The end of this long-drawn-out procedure was the strangest and the most dramatic episode in it. Vázquez asked Pérez whether he was the instigator of Escovedo's murder. Pérez denied it. Then Philip's confessor, Diego de Chaves, intervened and enjoined the accused to tell the truth. The right of kings over the lives of their subjects was incontestable. The King had ordered Escovedo's execution. Pérez had obeyed. There was no crime in admitting that one had obeyed orders. But Pérez objected that the King had forbidden him to confess that this murder had taken place at his orders.

In fact, what concerned Philip was not learning once more, and from Pérez's lips, that he had condemned Escovedo to death, but learning why he had condemned him. Was it with good reason, or without ? Had Pérez represented to his Sovereign, as a faithful servant, that the safety of the State was involved in getting rid of an agent of criminal intrigues ; or had Pérez only wanted to eliminate a witness to his intimate relations with the Princess of Eboli, who threatened to divulge them ? Had he, the

King, legitimately struck at a guilty person ; or had he unintentionally, by an act of authority, covered up an amorous liaison ?

What a case of conscience, if Philip had been duped—and if, as some historians suppose, he had himself been a rejected suitor of the Princess, what a blow to his pride ! So we cannot be too much surprised, strange as the fact may seem, that, after the confessor, the President of the tribunal himself, Rodrigo Vázquez de Arce, should have visited Pérez and read him an autograph letter, dated January 4th, 1590, in which the King allowed the hidden motives of his own conduct and the mystery of this long prosecution of Pérez to appear.

"You may tell Antonio Pérez on my behalf, showing him this letter if necessary, that he knows very well the knowledge I have that it was he who had Escovedo put to death and the reasons which he gave me for acting in this way. And because, for my own satisfaction and that of my conscience, it is requisite to know whether these reasons were sufficient or not, I order him to disclose them and render a full account of them, that he may set forth and prove the truth of those (reasons) which he declared to me. . . ."

The prisoner obviously had good grounds for remaining silent. He refused to explain himself on all these points, and appealed from His Majesty to His Majesty himself.

Then the licentiate Juan Gómez, Vázquez's assessor on the Council of Justice, had Pérez fettered, and, when he persisted in his silence, put to "the question". After eight days of the rack, Pérez, with his power of resistance broken by torture, agreed to speak. He explained Escovedo's death on the grounds which he had already given, but alleged that, as his papers had been seized and the death went back a dozen years, he had no means of establishing proof of the fact. His torture was suspended from that day, "to be continued and renewed whenever the lords judges deem it opportune " (3).

Antonio Pérez had only one means of escaping death left open to him—flight. His friends—for friends he still had, and very devoted ones : the Aragonese ensign, Gil de Mesa ; a student of the same country, Gil Pérez, and a Genoese, Mayorini—made preparations for it. During the night of Ash Wednesday, April 18th, Antonio Pérez made his way out of his prison, and he and his comrades mounted horses that were standing ready for them, left Madrid at full gallop, covered thirty leagues without a break, and crossed the frontier of Aragon.

Here was a sanctuary where the implacable severity of Philip II could no longer touch Pérez. Here a more liberal legal system, laws more humane, and restrictions on arbitrary power guaranteed him life and liberty. This explains why, as he reached this hospitable soil, he hailed it with joy : " Aragon, Aragon ! " and knelt down and kissed it devotedly over and over again.

Philip was only all the harder on Pérez's accomplice. Fearing lest she, too, should make her escape from Pastrana, in May, 1590, the King had all its doors, windows and skylights barred, cut off all the Princess's communications with outside, and transformed her apartments into a sombre prison, with little air and almost no light—a " dungeon of death ", as his prisoner said. She died there on February 2nd, 1592, at the age of fifty-two, after one-and-twenty months of this cruel seclusion (4).

The Kingdom of Aragon, which had the same Sovereign as Castile, had made up its mind to preserve its full independence. Separated from the neighbouring State by a customs barrier, it lived its own life, with its own laws, judges, administration and customs. Its Cortes was the strongest buttress of this particularist spirit. The Aragonese nobility had not, as in Castile, deserted the national assembly. They were even represented there by two " arms " or orders : the aristocracy (*ricos hombres*) and the simple nobles (*infanzones*), both of whom, though they were themselves exempt from taxes, helped the town communities to resist the fiscal demands of the Sovereign.

But the essential safeguard of public liberties in Aragon, and the one which did this country the most honour, was, as I have already remarked, the institution of the *Justicia mayor*, the supreme magistrate, placed alongside and above all seignurial, ecclesiastical and royal jurisdictions. In his delivery of his own judgment, from which there was no appeal, in case of any conflict of jurisdiction, he might come into conflict with the King ; but he had no interest in deliberately challenging the Sovereign. He was appointed by the Sovereign for life, and for a long time chosen from among the members of the family—doubtless deferential—of the Lanuzas, of the order of *infanzones*. Since the imprisonment, and perhaps the poisoning, of the *Justicia mayor* Martin Díaz de Aux by order of Alfonso V, in 1439, no law prevented the *Justicia mayor* from holding other royal offices, civil or military.

When we find that Juan Lanuza the second, *Justicia* under Ferdinand the Catholic, was at the same time Admiral and Viceroy of Sicily, we can scarcely imagine that this officer of the King's was the born enemy of his master. In fact, Ferdinand and Charles V, with the assent of the Cortes and without the *Justicia* raising any objection, introduced the gendarmerie of the Holy Brotherhood into Aragon to suppress brigandage and hunt down highway robbers and murderers, even into the castles where the lords were pleased to give them refuge. Indeed, the jurist Blancas, in his *Commentarii rerum aragonensium*, excuses the poverty of his narrative about Juan de Lanuza in these characteristic terms : " All these times were entirely peaceful ; to tell the truth, all the actions of King Ferdinand and of Charles V rendered this magistrature (the *Justicia mayor*) otiose."

The office of *Justicia* was, for that matter, suspect by the Cortes, which took its precautions against any courtier-like complaisance, or any personal prejudice, on the part of the *Justicia*. The Cortes left it to drawing by lot to choose his lieutenants in the exercise of his responsibilities, instead of letting him choose them himself, as was the original system. It instituted Inquirers, authorized to receive complaints from the lowest in the land against the supreme judge and his assessors, and entrusted to a political grand jury of seventeen deputies, drawn by lot, the investigation of such complaints, with power to deliver judgment upon them, if necessary, within forty days at latest.

But the *Justicia*, under the twofold control of the King and the Cortes though he was, still disposed of two potent means of action : *firmas* and *manifestación*. *Firmas* were letters of safe-keeping, delivered to anybody who demanded them, which put him and his property under protection against any judgment contrary to the *fueros* (local statute law or privileges). *Manifestación* was the recourse to the supreme magistrate of any prisoner who feared, or even professed to fear, any violence on the part of his judges or of his jailers (5).

As soon as he was advised of any such complaint, the *Justicia* ordered the complainant to be handed over to him, and transferred him to the prison of " *los Manifestados* ". If the complainant's jailors refused to hand him over, the *Justicia* went and fetched him in person, with sufficient forces for the purpose. His intervention did not interrupt the normal course of justice or in any way affect the validity of the prosecution ; but, until sentence was pronounced, it put the accused under protection against any bad treatment.

The Inquisition was the sole tribunal common to the two Crowns of Castile and Aragon, and the only jurisdiction against which the Aragonese could not invoke the apparatus of legal formalities.

It was in this country, jealous of its rights and on its guard against any possible encroachment upon them by the King of Castile, that Antonio Pérez, sometime Secretary of State to Philip II, came to seek sanctuary. In this land of liberties, legal procedure had to be conducted in due form ; there was no place, as in the neighbouring kingdom, for extraordinary tribunals and secret investigations. Here Pérez's tribulations caused his crime to be overlooked and aroused keen sympathy for him. He inspired it as a victim of that arbitrary regime which the Castilian Government was accused of seeking to introduce into Aragon.

Philip, as a matter of fact, had no such intention. Even in this affair, which involved his dignity and also, perhaps, a case of conscience, he observed legal form as far as he could. He could scarcely forgo his revenge on Pérez ; he would have made himself the laughing-stock of Europe if he had let himself be defied in one of his own States by one of his own subjects. In the subtleties of Aragonese procedure, Philip sought for means of reaching the fugitive without violating the law.

His Crown Attorney obtained from the *Justicia mayor* a warrant for the arrest of Pérez wherever he might be found, notwithstanding the local privileges, as a person accused of crimes against the security of the State. It is true that the same magistrate, at the same time, granted the accused the privilege of *manifestación*, had him escorted to Saragossa, and lodged him in the prison under his own jurisdiction.

Then Pérez, driven to desperation by his enemy's persistence, hesitated no longer about confessing that he had had Escovedo killed ; but he proved that he had committed the murder on the orders of his master. Great was the scandalization of Aragon, where the spirit of liberty detested acts of sovereign justice. In face of the general indignation, the Crown Attorney withdrew his demand for prosecution.

Philip was a tenacious person. An old law put officials at the mercy of the Sovereign, since they were regarded as his own agents and, as such, were deprived of the guarantees which protected other citizens. Philip claimed that, on this ground, his former Secretary of State belonged to him, and he was free to deal with him as he chose. Pérez objected that this Aragonese law did not apply to him at all, inasmuch as he was not an Aragonese, had never held office in Aragon, and had never served Philip except in his capacity as King of Castile. The *Justicia* found himself compelled to accept the validity of this objection.

Since juridical means were exhausted, it seemed that there was nothing left for Pérez's persecutor except to resort to force ;

but this was the last means to which a man so formalist by temperament as Philip would elect to resort. The intervention of the Inquisition still offered a chance worth trying. Here there was no juridical opposition to be feared ; in matters of faith, the franchises were regarded as null and of no effect. Under pretext that Pérez contemplated taking refuge in Béarn, that land of heretics, Molina de Medrano, Inquisitor of Saragossa, opened an inquiry and interrogated the servants of the suspect.

Their replies were extorted with the utmost artistry from the point of view of extracting some ground of accusation from them. It appeared that, in the anguish of his dreadful torture, Pérez had so far forgotten himself as to groan : " Oh, there cannot be any God at all ! " and that, in the ravings of his desperation, he had emitted other similar blasphemies. It was the King's own confessor, Diego de Chaves, who was charged by the supreme council with the duty of pronouncing upon these cries wrung from Pérez by pain. Naturally de Chaves declared them in the highest degree criminal, detestable and heretical. The tribunal of Saragossa received orders to arrest the culprit.

Against this dreadful jurisdiction the laws of Aragon were of no avail. The *Justicia*, summoned haughtily and with menace, was compelled to hand over his *manifestado* to the agents of the Holy Office, who escorted Pérez to the dungeons of the Aljafería. There was no further appeal except to the populace ; but the populace declared themselves forcibly against an illegality surrounded with all the appearance of right. From the very beginning of the crisis, members of the aristocracy and the nobility, such as Diego de Heredia and Martin de Lanuza, had openly taken sides with the man whom they regarded as a victim of Castilian tyranny. The burghers and the artisans of Saragossa showed the same sentiments.

Pérez had realized what powerful strength and support he might find in public opinion. He laboured to develop the sympathy which his misfortunes inspired. Against his enemies he opened a campaign of pamphlets and popular songs. In these States of Philip II's, which we are tempted to imagine as the domain of silence, a single man created a formidable agitation by his satirical writings. In his *Pasquinade of Hell*, Pérez held his adversaries up to contempt and hatred, and posed as the victim of violence and injustice. So, when his life seemed in danger, the appeals of his friends awakened a powerful echo. The populace of Saragossa took up arms. Assailed in the Aljafería by a raging mob, the Inquisitors were compelled to relinquish their prey.

On the news of the rising, Philip concentrated troops on the frontier of Aragon ; but he hesitated to employ them. He let it be understood that he would pardon his subjects if Pérez was returned to the prisons of the Holy Office. In Saragossa itself, once the first fury had died down, people began to calculate the consequences of the insurrection. The *Justicia*, the members of the Deputation, and the jurisconsults advised obedience. Even Pérez's most ardent supporters were inclined to yield. Pérez realized that he was lost if he fell into the hands of the Inquisitors again. He appealed to the pity of his adherents and excited the wrath of the populace by every means in his power.

On September 24th, when the constituted authorities, *Justicia*, deputies, jurists and town councillors were proceeding with all due ceremony, in sign of submission to Philip, to the handing-over of the prisoner, the procession was attacked by the artisans and the retainers of the lords. The Inquisitors and the magistrates took to flight ; the prison was stormed : and Pérez, set at liberty, hid himself in Saragossa until he was able to cross the frontier and take refuge in France.

Philip II had been outrageously challenged. He gave orders to Vargas, the commander of the Castilian troops, to advance into Aragon. The new *Justicia*, Don Juan de Lanuza, who was young and impulsive, let himself be carried away to the extent of proclaiming the Constitution violated and issuing a call to arms. This summons found small echo in the kingdom, which did not share Saragossa's enthusiasm for the cause of a proscribed Castilian. Lanuza had great difficulty in assembling even a few thousand soldiers.

Vargas advanced as far as the capital itself without having to strike a blow. He quartered his troops there, and, satisfied with the order which reigned everywhere, wrote to his master advising clemency. The resistance had been so mild, so poorly organized, that even those who had taken part in it did not regard themselves as deeply compromised. The *Justicia* and his friends, counting on pardon, ended by returning to Saragossa.

Meanwhile the King kept his own counsel. He listened to all opinions without revealing his own intentions. Suddenly Philip made up his mind. One day when a gentleman, Gómez Velázquez, had come to ask a favour of him, he recalled him just as he was leaving the audience, handed him a letter, and ordered him to carry it to Vargas without delay. Velázquez went out, pledged a gold chain for a travelling cloak, leapt on horseback, and rode full speed for Saragossa.

The letter was in the King's own hand. "On receipt of this note, you will arrest Don Juan de Lanuza, *Justicia* of Aragon; and let me hear of his death at the same time as his arrest." Vargas could do nothing but obey. The head of the supreme magistrate of Aragon fell, on December 20th, 1593, in the presence of the soldiers under arms, without a single inhabitant of Saragossa being present at his execution. Other executions followed. Diego de Heredia and Martin de Lanuza were also decapitated, and Count de Aranda and the Duke of Villahermosa perished in prison.

These were the chief, and almost the sole, victims of the repression. Philip did not show himself cruel towards smaller fry; the royal tribunals condemned only five or six persons to death. It was not the same with the Inquisition, which showed itself merciless in avenging affronts to itself. The King almost had to threaten it with violence to impose an amnesty upon it.

Philip II treated the institutions of Aragon no less moderately than the men of Aragon. It is a mistake to suppose that he suppressed all Aragonese liberties. Undoubtedly he introduced changes intended to strengthen the royal authority, but his requirements were relatively modest. He was careful not to act like a conqueror imposing his will by force of arms. It was to the Cortes that Philip addressed himself to obtain the reforms which he wanted. The pitiful failure of the insurrection gave him an authority over that assembly which he was able to turn to the very best advantage.

Aragon retained her separate Government, her particular system of administration and justice, and her own Cortes and the permanent commission which, under the name of Deputation, sat during the intervals between the sessions of the Cortes. It is true that the mode of deliberation of the Cortes was modified. Whereas previously unanimity was required to represent the vote of an order, henceforth a majority in each " arm " sufficed. The powers of the Deputation were diminished. It lost the right to dispose of the funds of the kingdom and to assemble the national forces. Policing in general and the maintenance of public order became the responsibility of the King.

The reform of justice was more fundamental. The *Justicia* ceased to be irremovable. This meant depriving his office of the best guarantee of his independence; but was it possible, after the insurrection of Saragossa, that Philip should tolerate this power which rivalled his own? The Sovereign intervened also in the nomination of the *Justicia's* lieutenants, and in the choice of the seventeen Inquirers, charged with the duty of judging the supreme magistrate and his assessors in case of need. The *Justicia* thus found himself completely in the hands of the King, who appointed him and could dismiss him, and, on occasion, nominated his judges and his supplanters. To eliminate any fresh cause of conflict, extradition between Aragon and Castile was made the rule. The castle of the Aljafería received a royal garrison.

It does not appear, therefore, that Philip abused his victory. The royal authority was consolidated, abuses were abolished, and some privileges were suppressed. But, while the Sovereign assured himself of means of making his will prevail in his States, he touched neither legislation, nor the franchises of the towns, nor the rights of classes, nor the national representation. Aragon kept her own government and a large measure of autonomy.

Possibly the state of affairs in France explained this consideration on Philip's part.

CHAPTER XV

PHILIP II'S PRETENSIONS TO THE CROWN OF FRANCE

PHILIP had missed England, but a more attractive prey presented itself in France. For long enough, without striking back, he had suffered the open or covert attacks of the Valois. Never had his patience seemed so great as at the time of the Duke of Anjou's enterprise in the Low Countries and Catherine de Medici's intervention in Portugal, when she tried to constrain Philip to give his daughter's hand, with all or part of these patrimonial States of his as her dowry, to that unjust aggressor, Anjou.

The death of the Duke of Anjou left something better than merely affronts to be avenged. It raised the question of the vacancy on the throne of France which would occur sooner or later. Henri III had no child, and, after ten years of unfruitful marriage, no likelihood of having one. In accordance with the Salic law, the fundamental law of the French dynasty, which excluded women from the succession, however closely related they might be to the last occupant of the throne, the heir presumptive was Henri of Bourbon, King of Navarre and first Prince of the Blood. He was opposed by the mass of his future subjects on the ground of religion.

Born a Catholic, but nurtured by his mother, Jeanne d'Albret, in the creed of the Reformation, converted by force to Catholicism at the time of the massacre of Saint Bartholomew, Henri of Navarre had reverted to Protestantism as soon as he regained his freedom. The Catholic majority were moved to wrath and fear at the idea that some day they might have for their King a heretic, a twice relapsed apostate, whom they contemplated as a persecutor after their own measure.

It was upon the bitterness of religious passions that the King of Spain counted to abolish the dynastic law and, when the time came, put forward the candidature to the throne of France of his daughter, the Infanta Clara Isabel Eugenia, daughter of Henri II's

315

elder sister. About 1582 Philip had entered into relations with the Guises, the leaders of the French Catholic party : an understanding which the death of the Duke of Anjou transformed into a formal and definite agreement.

In 1585, or, to be more exact, on December 31st, 1584, at the château of Joinville, in Champagne, Philip's representatives, Jean Baptiste de Tassis and Juan Moreo, concluded with Guise, Mayenne and Cardinal de Bourbon an offensive and defensive alliance " for the sole teaching, defence and conservation of the Catholic, Apostolic and Roman religion ", and the complete extirpation of all heresies in France and in the Low Countries. The heretical Bourbons were to be excluded from the French throne, Cardinal de Bourbon to be called to the succession to Henri III, and Cambrai, the solitary conquest of the Duke of Anjou, to be restored to its legitimate Sovereign. To these ends Philip II granted a subsidy of fifty thousand écus a month, and, in order to expedite arming, he deposited a whole year's contribution during the first six months.

The French nation had not awaited the marching orders of the Catholic princes to band together against the heir presumptive. In Paris a movement in opposition to him occurred spontaneously. Priests, a gentleman of Auvergne, advocates, attorneys, and merchants formed the first nucleus of the resistance to Henri of Navarre. They recruited adherents among the priests and monks of Paris, among the professors of the Sorbonne, and in the querulous, needy circles of lawyers' clerks and university students. Their propaganda had less success in business and legal circles, among civil servants and in the upper middle classes, which were both prudent and loyalist.

From Paris emissaries set forth to endoctrinate the great provincial cities, Bourges, Orléans, Lyons, Marseilles and Toulouse. They enrolled numbers of inhabitants and prepared the municipal levies for supporting the initiative of dissident governors.

Three months after the pact of Joinville, the Guises took up arms. By the Treaty of Nemours, signed on July 7th, 1585, they imposed upon Henri III abrogation of all the edicts of tolerance, suppression of freedom of conscience and worship, and proscription of all Protestants, high and low.

Philip was acting in his accustomed way, or rather making ready to do so. Hitherto he had put off offering his second daughter, Catherine, in marriage to the Duke of Savoy, but he had not discouraged the Duke from aspiring to her hand, lest the Duke should turn his eyes towards Christine of Lorraine, Catherine de Medici's granddaughter, or towards a Florentine or Mantuan princess. But, once the Duke of Anjou was dead and the French Catholic princes had taken up arms against the heretic pretender, Philip hastened to conclude a family alliance with a prince whose States, straddled across the Alps, marked him out either to cover the Milanese or to intervene in France.

On August 26th, 1584, Charles Emmanuel of Savoy was able to make the announcement of his great marriage, which filled him with so much pride and hope that Philip found himself obliged to recommend him to be more measured in his transports. But at Saragossa, whither the Duke betook himself for the wedding, he had all the honours that he could possibly desire.

The King rode out of the town to meet him, escorted by mounted archers of the Burgundian Guard and by the Spanish Guard, and accompanied by all the great lords present at Court. When Philip caught sight of him, he dismounted with the aid of his Master of the Horse ; and as the Duke, who had leapt from the saddle himself, bowed to kiss the King's hand, Philip stretched out his arms to him and kissed him on both cheeks, saying to him : " My son, you are very welcome."

The King set the Duke at his right hand for their entrance into Saragossa, and stamped the importance which he attached to this union by brilliant festivals : dances at the palace on this first meeting of the bridal pair ; illuminations that night and the following nights ; on the day of the wedding, procession of the Court from the palace to the cathedral, in triumphal array of gala attire and all magnificence ; Mass with full ceremonial celebrated by the Archbishop of Saragossa, to the accompaniment of the singing of the royal choir, including a special motet composed by the choir-master George de la Hale, orchestrated for hautboys, organs, and other musical instruments ; nuptial banquet, on March 11th, 1585, to the sound of tambours, trumpets and timbrels ; and finally, in order to associate the populace with the dynastic rejoicing, tourneys, tilting-matches, and bull-fights and single-stick combats, those national amusements (1).

Charles Emmanuel had every possible gratification of his glory, except one : Spanish pride would not suffer that his bride should condescend to the rank of Duchess. She remained Her Highness, and her husband had to honour and serve her as though she were, in fact, Queen of Spain. But the bridal pair were so much in love with one another that their mutual affection salved any wounds to amour-propre.

The Duke, as a practical politician, suffered less on this account than from his realization of the fact that his wife, though she brought him a dowry of five hundred thousand écus, seemed to bring him no other hope whatever. He could not extract a single word from his father-in-law which entitled him to foresee the elevation of his duchy into a kingdom, or at least an aggrandizement of his ducal territory. He had only the vague assurance that, when he had children by the Infanta, he " would then know the great interest " of His Majesty " in the well-being and increase of fortune of his descendants ". It was a maxim of Philip II's that one obtains more from people by promises than by favours (2).

Sixtus V also took up his stand against the heretical Bourbons. To support the cause of the Leaguers, he issued his famous Bull of deprivation, dated September 9th, 1585, which declared the heir presumptive deprived of all his rights to the Crown of France, robbed him of that of Navarre, and released his subjects from their oath of allegiance.

But the Parliament of Paris, brought back to ideas of tolerance by its Gallican objections to Pontifical theocracy, protested against the Edict of July, confirming the treaty of Nemours, which put the Protestants outside the law. The Parliament turned upon this Pope, " so far removed from the modesty of previous Popes ", and contemptuously invited him " to show by what right he claims, in the transfer of kingdoms established and ordered by God before the name of the Pope was known in the world, to give away that which is not his, to take from another that which legitimately belongs to him, to stir up vassals and subjects against their lords and sovereign princes, and to disturb the foundations of all justice and political order ".

Henri III claimed to be just as good a Catholic as the Leaguers. Bitterly humiliated by having to obey the orders of his subjects in arms, he applied the programme of extermination to which they had made him swear without any zeal. After the defeat of his favourite the Duke of Joyeuse at Coutras by the King of Navarre, on October 20th, 1587, and the victory of the Duke of Guise over a reinforcing army of foreign Protestants on November 24th, the King of France, more pained by the victory of the latter than by the defeat of the former, granted honourable terms to these Swiss and German invaders, instead of massacring them mercilessly, as the ardent Catholics wanted him to do. He even provisioned and paid them so that they might recross the frontier more quickly.

The Leaguers, exasperated by these concessions on the King's part, intensified their propaganda and prepared for a *coup de force* in Paris. Henri III, warned by his spies, summoned two Swiss regiments in his pay which he kept in barracks at Lagny, and posted them, together with his French guards, in the public squares and at the strategic points of the capital. This was the signal for insurrection. Barricades were thrown up in all directions and hemmed in the soldiers. The King, fearing lest he should be made a prisoner in his own palace of the Louvre, fled from the city.

Despite the urgings of his mother, Catherine de Medici, whom he had left behind to negotiate with Guise and the municipality, he refused to return. He agreed only to summon the States-General at Blois, in order to obtain means of resuming the struggle against the Protestants from them. But the Three Orders, while enjoining him to re-establish unity of faith by force of arms, refused him money, those sinews of war. Meanwhile the Duke of Savoy, that ambitious princeling, assured of the connivance of his father-in-law, Philip II, had invaded the marquisate of Saluces, the last of the French possessions on the other side of the Alps.

Guise kept on defying and threatening the King. Henri III, seized with panic, had him assassinated in his study and had the Duke's brother, Cardinal de Guise, stabbed to death with halberds. He ordered the arrest of Cardinal de Bourbon, the League's candidate for the succession to him, whom he kept prisoner ; the Guises' mother, the Dowager Duchess of Nemours, though her he hastened to set free again ; the murdered men's half-brother, the Duke of Nemours, and the provost of the guilds of Paris.

Henri III imagined that he had killed the League along with its leaders ; and the ambassador of the King of Spain in Paris, Mendoza, thought so too—so far were these men, accustomed to the discipline of a monarchical State, incapable of understanding the resiliency of the soul of a people. The example of the Low Countries should at least have convinced Philip II's representative of the persistent strength of religious passions.

On the news of the murders and arrests at Blois, the populace of Paris rose, on December 26th, broke open the King's armouries, and destroyed his effigies. The faculty of theology of the University of Paris, the Sorbonne, whose authority in matters of dogma had the force of law, even outside France, struck Henri III's name out of the canon of Mass, and released his subjects from their oath of allegiance. The great cities rose in revolt and forswore the Sovereign, following the example of Paris, and recognized Cardinal de Bourbon as King, under the name of Charles X.

The Duke of Guise's younger brother, Mayenne, hastened to Paris on February 12th, and, fortified by the popularity of his family, had the administration of affairs entrusted to a general council of the Union of Catholics, consisting of members of the

Three Orders, with himself as the head of it. The Parliament, obliged to yield to public feeling, appointed him chief executive and leader of the army, with the title of Lieutenant-General of the State and Crown of France.

After this general revolt, which left Henri III only Tours, Blois, Beaugency and Angers in the valley of the Loire, and Bordeaux farther away, the only course open to him to resist attack by the League was to come to an understanding with the King of Navarre. This was what he did. Then, with Protestant reinforcements, Swiss auxiliaries, and the loyalist nobility, he marched on Paris at the head of a fine army of thirty thousand men.

Henri III was just flattering himself upon re-entering his capital by force or surrender, when he was stabbed in the stomach by a Jacobin fanatic, Brother Jacques Clément. As he lay dying, he received Henri of Navarre, kissed him, and blessed him as his legitimate heir, at the same time making him swear to become a Catholic. He ordered the great lords present to swear allegiance to Henri of Navarre. That day there was no protest ; but the next day the royalist leaders, more mindful of the interests of religion, invited the new King to have himself instructed, in other words converted, within six months. Henri of Navarre, now Henri IV of France, evaded any promise subject to a time-limit, which would have humiliated him without convincing anybody of his sincerity.

At the outset Henri IV was very fortunate. He defeated Mayenne at Arques, subjected Touraine, Anjou, and Maine, and proceeded to undertake the conquest of Normandy, where he left the Leaguers nothing but the city of Rouen. In order to bar Mayenne's way into this province, he laid siege to the fortress of Dreux, which commanded the passage of the Eure.

Startled by these rapid successes, the Lieutenant-General invoked the aid of the Spaniards. The Duke of Parma sent him five hundred arquebusiers and twelve hundred Walloon lancers, commanded by the Count of Egmont. They arrived just in time to get beaten at Ivry, on March 14th, 1590. This was the first time that Philip II had openly supported the League. Determined though he was not to let it be destroyed, this formalist prince nevertheless thought it his duty to justify his intervention in France by " the imminent danger of the Holy Catholic Church ".

In a declaration published a week before the battle of Ivry, Philip begged and required all the Catholic Christian princes to join with him " for the extirpation of heresy and the deliverance of the Most Christian King of France, Charles X ". He protested

THE INFANTA CLARA ISABELLA EUGENIA
From a portrait by Alonzo Sanchez Coello in the Prado

" before God and His angels " that the preparations which he was making tended " to no other end than the exaltation of the Holy Catholic Church Apostolic and Roman, the repose of good Catholics in obedience to their legitimate princes, the entire extirpation of all kinds of heresies, and the peace and concord of the Christian princes ".

Philip declared himself ready to devote to this holy cause all his resources and even his life. The next day, he ordered the Archbishop of Toledo, the Grand Inquisitor, to draw up a list of holders of benefices in his kingdom who were to contribute, as though this were a crusade, to the maintenance of the two armies intended for the help of the Kingdom of France (3).

Two months after his victory at Ivry, Henri IV besieged Paris. He had only twelve or thirteen thousand soldiers, and he was besieging a city of two hundred and twenty thousand inhabitants, defended by fifty thousand men of the train-bands and a garrison of six hundred French arquebusiers, twelve hundred German lansquenets, and five hundred Swiss from the old Catholic cantons. But the Governor of Paris, the young Duke of Nemours, who had escaped from captivity, like most regular soldiers had a prejudice against burghers and artisans turned soldiers. He did not attempt to risk them outside against the victors of Arques and Ivry, and kept them inside the ramparts. They were only watch-dogs, Pigaffeta, an Italian captain, said jeeringly ; but they kept the house well guarded.

After a hazardous attempt to force the entrenchments of the Faubourg Saint Martin, on May 12th, Henri IV renounced his plan of carrying by assault ramparts and barricades which were defended by the entire population. He decided to starve Paris out, and transformed the siege into a blockade. The city council and the military leaders had assembled supplies hastily and without foresight. There was just enough, with the help of rationing, to last a month.

In June wheat began to give out. The ambassador of Spain, Bernardino de Mendoza, distributed a hundred and twenty écus' worth of bread every day. The Papal legate, Caetani, gave his plate to pay the troops. Things went so far that even church ornaments were sold, and such sacred vessels as were not indispensable for worship and treasures of gold and silver ware were melted down. The municipality ordered visits to the monasteries, and made large requisitions from the monks' reserves.

Enormous coppers were installed in the streets here and there, in which boiled a mixture of oats and bran. It was the soup of starving people, cooked, so it was said, in the cauldrons of Spain. Wine, of which there was an abundance at the beginning of the siege, ended by giving out too. The people fell upon horses, donkeys, rats, cats and dogs, and fed themselves with grass, fat and tallow. Bread—and what bread !—ceased to be anything but a treat for the rich. The skin and bones of animals, ground down and turned into flour, served as food. People even dared to dig up the bones of the dead from the charnel-house of the Innocents cemetery in order to grind them down and obtain something from them to deceive the pangs of hunger.

But a band of fanatics were determined to hold out to the end. These were the Sixteen, members of the committees of the sixteen wards of Paris, who spied on royalist agents and kept their eyes on the upper parliamentary classes and the rich burghers, among whom signs of weariness and disgust at privation and vile sources of nourishment were manifesting themselves. The preachers of this faction occupied the pulpits twice a day, foreshadowing help from Spain and promising Paradise to those who died of hunger. Thanks to the fierce obstinacy of these priests and laymen, Paris held out for four months on one month's supplies of food.

It was only on formal orders from Philip II that the Duke of Parma made up his mind to deplete his forces in the Low Countries and suspend the struggle against Maurice of Nassau. Then, with the Spanish army, he joined the Duke of Mayenne, who had assembled a few thousand men, at Meaux. Henri IV, tempted by the hope of defeating the great captain of the time in pitched battle, raised the siege of Paris and marched to meet the Spaniards.

But Parma manœuvred to unblockade the city without risking a decisive engagement. He marched past Clayes, established his camp between the Marne and a marsh, and covered his front behind entrenchments. The position was so strong that the royalists did not dare to attack. On the eighth day, the Spanish general feinted that he was going to give battle. While Henri IV was making his dispositions to meet him, two of Parma's regiments crossed the Marne on a pontoon bridge, and, under cover from the royalist army and before its eyes, attacked and took Lagny, on September 7th. Master of the two banks of the Marne, Parma could communicate freely with the besieged and provision them. Paris was saved.

Thirteen thousand persons had died of hunger, and thirty thousand perished of burning fever after the horrors of the siege. So the preachers laid the heroic city waste. " Let the sufferings of the famine be remembered," said Panigarola, Bishop of Asti, one of the Legate's attachés. "There was neither flesh, nor fish, nor milk, nor fruit, nor vegetables. I might almost say that there was neither sun, sky, nor air. . . . Let them speak now of the siege of Bethulia, of the siege of Jerusalem ; let them speak of Titus and of Sennacherib ! This was a miracle." It was a miracle of fanaticism.

Even before he had rendered this great service, Philip II claimed his reward—even during the lifetime of Charles X, who died a prisoner on May 9th, 1590. Philip's ambassador in Paris, Bernardino de Mendoza, kept on protesting that his master, old and ailing as he was, and sufficiently provided with kingdoms in any case, had no interest in that of France. Yet, at the same time, he was setting the preachers and the Sixteen in motion to bring pressure to bear on the Council-General and make it offer Philip the title of Protector.

Mayenne, who was beginning to think about himself, and those of his councillors, like Jeannin and Villeroy, whom religious passion did not blind, had accepted and even solicited Spanish assistance ; but they did not want to pay for it at the price of national independence. Moderate and patriotic Leaguers, determined as they might be to oppose the accession of the heir presumptive as a heretic, with all their hearts desired his conversion, which, by making dynastic right and religious right coincide, would free them from the necessity of appealing abroad.

This solution found an echo even in Italy. The Republic of Venice, which saw the best counterpoise to Spanish hegemony in the restoration of the French monarchy, had hastened, in November, 1589, to recognize the new King of France, even though he was a heretic. The Court of Madrid made strong representations to the Seignury. The Papal Nuncio left Venice ; but Sixtus V ordered this over-zealous prelate to return to his post. The Pope himself, reversing his uncompromising attitude of 1585, desired to find in Henri IV an obstacle to Philip II's ambition.

"The Republic of Venice," Sixtus V told Badoaro, charged with the duty of excusing the Seignury's initiative to him, "has a fine opportunity of persuading the Navarrese to reconcile himself with the Pope ; then the Pope will load him with favours, and we shall all embrace him." This declaration, and the audience which the Pope gave to the Duke of Luxemburg-Piney, delegated to him by the Catholic royalists, created a scandal.

In Paris the zealots waxed indignant against this politic Pope. They conveyed to him, in respectful but explicit terms, that he could by no means absolve the King of Navarre, as though the keys of Saint Peter had no power to open the Kingdom of Heaven, or a kingdom on earth, even to a relapsed apostate. Philip inspired preaching against the Pope. A Spanish Jesuit permitted himself to accuse him from the pulpit. "Not only does the Republic of Venice favour the heretics, but . . . silence, silence ! " he added, putting his finger to his lips, "the Pope himself protects them."

The ambassadors of Spain in Rome, the Duke of Sesa and Count de Olivares, denounced to their Sovereign, on July 31st, 1590, the indifference of the Pontiff towards the League and his relations with the Navarrese. They proposed, in order to make an end of these bad practices of the Pope's, to frighten him by recalling the Spanish embassy from Rome, or hit him in his most sensitive spot, his avarice, by stopping the dispatch of funds from Spain to Rome. In audiences on August 6th and 7th, they strongly represented to the Pope the danger of sending a Legate to the princes and the royalist lords in the camp of the heretic. Their dispatches spoke so outrageously about the Pope and the Roman Court that the good Modesto La Fuente does not dare to quote them. They even suggested assembling a Council to bring this scandalous Pontiff to his senses (4).

Encouraged by this quarrel, Mayenne, in accord with the Legate Caetani, replied to Mendoza " that the Pope would not find it good that any other than His Holiness should be declared Protector of the Catholic religion in France."

After the death of Charles X, which was closely followed by that of Sixtus V, and the deliverance of Paris by the Duke of Parma, Philip showed his hand more clearly. The agents of Spain began to treat the Salic law as a French prepossession, and to put forward the rights of the Infanta Clara Isabel Eugenia to the throne of France.

Mayenne, who was in need of money, was obliged to make concessions to Philip. On the demand of the frightened Parisians, Mayenne, in February, 1591, allowed twelve hundred Spaniards and Neapolitans to be garrisoned in the city. Meaux also received a Spanish detachment. Together with the soldiers, in order better to watch over Philip's interests, arrived Jean Baptiste de Tassis and Diego de Ibarra, who succeeded Bernardino de Mendoza as ambassadors. The Duke of Parma also demanded that Mayenne should hand over to him the fortress of La Fère, to serve as a stage-point between the frontier of the Low Countries and the French capital.

When, at the beginning of 1592, Henri IV besieged Rouen, Philip II, solicited to break the blockade of the town, charged the

Duke of Parma with the duty of making known to the leaders of the League his "intentions to the Crown of France". Conferences took place at La Fère, and Mayenne allowed Jeannin to draw up the draft of a treaty which bound him, in return for the deliverance of Rouen and on some other conditions, to summon the States-General for the purpose of electing the Spanish Infanta as Queen of France.

Parma broke the blockade of the city, which Marshal de Biron and Henri IV were besieging ; but he was hemmed in himself, by a return of the French army to the offensive, between the English Channel and the Seine. He succeeded in crossing the river on a pontoon bridge and beat a retreat.

He had been seriously wounded a month earlier before the little fortress of Caudebec, and returned to the Low Countries to be treated there for his wound, the healing of which was retarded by his state of exhaustion. Parma needed all his physical strength to subdue the northern part of the Low Countries, which his preparations for a descent on England and his two campaigns in France had enabled to take breath and organize an offensive.

Five provinces irreducible in their rebelliousness, Holland, Zeeland, Friesland, Utrecht and Gelderland, each had their own States, which delegated representatives to the States-General, the supreme council of the resistance. Their link of union was a loose one, but the necessities of defence, in spite of disagreements, assured unity of action and command. Other causes also contributed in this direction, among them the recruitment of the States from among the town burghers since the disappearance, the downfall or the defection of the local aristocracy. Holland, the richest of the provinces and the one which made the largest contribution to the war expenses, played a preponderant rôle in the federal Union.

This Republic already had a leader, Maurice of Nassau, son of William of Nassau, who had won the sympathy of the States for himself. After the departure of Leicester, in 1587, they had appointed him Governor and Captain-General. Maurice was, besides, *Stathouder*—in other words, lieutenant-governor—in Holland and Zeeland, with all the powers belonging to a representative of the King. In 1590, on the death of the Count of Moeursel and Nieuwanaer, he became *Stathouder* of Gelderland, Utrecht and Over-Ijssel, which last he had to bring into subjection.

Still quite young, reserved, taciturn and distant, Maurice had hitherto shown no very decided taste except for mathematics. This scientific discipline developed in him a systematization of war different from that of the generals of the period. He conceived war as a study whose elements were ground, men and circumstances. With one of his cousins, William Louis of Nassau, lieutenant-governor of Friesland, and a great connoisseur of the classics, he delved deep into the composition of the legion and the phalanx of antiquity.

The army of the States was small in numbers : twenty thousand infantry, two thousand cavalry ; but well armed, well equipped, and regularly paid. Maurice exercised it, made it flexible, and divided it up into mobile groups. He taught it to march either in close ranks or in open order. He utilized the canals and river channels for the transport of munitions, and of a powerful artillery, better than anybody had ever done before. He succeeded in massing his fire to the best effect for opening breaches and affecting the morale of the besieged.

During the Duke of Parma's first expedition to France, Maurice of Nassau had drawn up his plan of campaign. It was essential for him, above all, to bar access by his enemies to Zeeland and Holland, those two citadels of the resistance. The Rhine, when it leaves Germany, divides into several branches, one of which, the Wahal, runs from east to west until it joins the Meuse ; while another runs north towards the Zuyder Zee. These were two enormous barriers across which the Spaniards held the bridge-heads : Nimingen on the Wahal, Zutphen and Deventer on the Ijssel.

Maurice of Nassau took Breda, on March 3rd, 1590, which, with Bergen-op-Zoom, covered the approaches to them. He forced Zutphen and Deventer to surrender at the cannon's mouth. He showed the Spaniards that he disposed of heavy artillery, and that he knew how to conduct a siege. In his three campaigns of 1590, 1591, and 1592, he carried Steenwyck, which was the key to Friesland ; possessed himself of the crossing of the Wahal at Nimingen, and pushed forward as far as Hulst, at the gates of Flanders and Antwerp. He had liberated three more provinces, and assured and aggrandized the sphere of domination of the Union of Utrecht.

For all these losses, Philip had nobody but himself to thank. He had weakened the forces at his disposal in the Low Countries in order to intervene in France. But he could never forgive his lieutenants for failures for which he was himself responsible. He accepted the accusations against the Duke of Parma which were made to him by Moreo, Champagney, and the other agents, recognized or unrecognized, whom he maintained in Flanders.

Parma, according to these reports, was a bad administrator of the King's funds. He kept a mistress, whose retainers cost a lot of money. He left the royal seal lying about in his bedroom at the disposal of a servant of his, half an idiot, who lent it to all sorts and conditions of people. He surrounded himself with foreigners and nobody else. In short, he did just what he liked.

Philip, moreover, almost reproached Parma with being ill, and showed some bad temper when his general proposed to go to Spa in order to take a rest cure and a course of the waters there. But, always prudent and secretive, Philip was careful not to let his dissatisfaction appear on the surface. When Farnese complained about the calumnies against him and proposed to justify himself, Philip wrote to him on September 11th, 1592 :

"As for your request that the imputations of which you are the subject should be communicated to you, he would be very bold who would permit himself to come and tell me about you things different from what I believe of you and promise myself of you, after the numerous proofs that I have, and hope to have more every day, of your support and your good services in the affairs which mean the most to me. Therefore be assured in this respect."

On October 17th, Philip assured Parma once more of "the great satisfaction" with which he regarded him (5).

For several months past, however, Philip had made up his mind to recall Parma. The previous January, he entrusted Don Juan Pacheco, Marquis of Cerralvo, and then in June, after Cerralvo's death, Don Pedro Enriquez de Azebado, Count of Fuentes, with a letter to Parma inviting him to return to Madrid for some time. In case Farnese should refuse to do so, the King's mandatory was to reveal his own commission as lieutenant-general of the army, and order all Spanish camp commandants, captains and officers to carry out whatever he might command.

Farnese had left Brussels when Fuentes arrived there. He was making ready to enter France for the third time, when the disease which had so long been undermining him struck him down. He died at Arras on December 3rd, 1592, knowing nothing of the disgrace into which he was doomed to fall.

Philip reckoned, no doubt, that the accession of his daughter to the throne of France would much more than compensate him for the loss, which in any case he did not regard as permanent, of some provinces of the Low Countries. Was not the Infanta Clara Isabel Eugenia, elder daughter of Henri II's elder daughter, the legitimate and direct heir of her deceased uncle, Henri III ? The Salic law, which, by excluding women from succession to the throne, opposed her just rights, was nothing more than a French prepossession.

Philip talked about his daughter as though there were no other relatives as well qualified, and perhaps better qualified. Of Henri III's sister, Marguerite of Valois, wife of the heretical Pretender, though she was an ardent Catholic and had declared herself for the League against her brother and her husband, Philip took no more account than as though she did not exist.

Marguerite, however, was closer in relationship than the Infanta, her niece once removed. But she had no party behind her, and, having emerged from the dangers in which, through her behaviour, or misbehaviour, she had nearly lost her life, she thought herself lucky to be alive out of harm's way, as a voluntary or involuntary recluse, in a remote château in Auvergne. There were other claimants who did not let themselves so easily be forgotten, among them Charles, Duke of Lorraine, married to Henri II's younger daughter, Claude of Valois.

By her the Duke of Lorraine had had a son, Henri, Marquis of Pont-à-Mousson, who, by virtue of the right of representation, could substitute himself for his mother, and, in his capacity as a male, might appear to the partisans of the Salic law to have a better title than the Infanta, a girl. His father may have hoped that the Guises, as a younger branch of the House of Lorraine, would help him to realize this dream of family greatness ; but he soon found that these cousins of his, the young Duke of Guise and particularly Mayenne, were pursuing only their own advantage in the rivalries of the League. He did not even succeed in possessing himself of Champagne, which would have doubled the area of his State.

Another male claimant, son of a daughter of François I's, was more energetic and more tenacious. This was Charles Emmanuel, Duke of Savoy, Philip II's son-in-law. Immediately after the death of Henri III, he requested the Parliament of Grenoble to recognize him as King of France, " as being the nearest who can claim to be so ", to the exclusion of the heretical and heresy-fomenting Bourbons. At the least he cherished the ambition to found—together with Geneva, which he proposed to conquer—a Kingdom of the Allobroges, and he even dreamt of reconstituting the former Kingdom of Arles.

Philip II was not entirely opposed to the idea of dismembering the Kingdom of France to satisfy the claimants and provide for himself among them. In case of the maintenance of the Salic law, could he not claim Burgundy for himself, as great-grandson of

Marie of Burgundy, daughter of Charles the Bold, unjustly despoiled by Louis XI, as well as Provence, in his capacity as successor to the Counts of Barcelona ; and Brittany for his daughter, as descendant of Queen Claude of France, Duchess of Brittany, if it was established that the former Duchy was the family possession of the Valois and not an integral part of the domain of the Crown ?

It was true that here Philip would have to reckon with the Duke of Mercœur, who claimed Brittany too, in his wife's title, as heiress of the rights of the family of Penthièvre. But Philip had no objection to acting with Mercœur for the moment against Henri IV, being sure that, after their joint victory, he would be able to thrust this competitor of his aside or indemnify him.

Meanwhile Philip put forward the candidature of his daughter to the Crown of France. About the legitimacy of his daughter's claims he had not the least doubt. This was a civil law suit which any competent tribunal could not fail to decide in his favour. There remained the objection of the Salic law, which his legists would be able to meet by weight of documents and arguments. No doubt, if Philip liked, he could invoke the services which he had rendered, and was still rendering, to Catholic France ; but, independently of any merits of his own, the rights of the Infanta were peremptory.

After the death of Charles X and the deliverance of Paris by Farnese, Philip conceived the idea of referring the matter of succession and election to the Parliament of Paris, as the supreme court of justice. One thinks of him as a man of the law, judging everything by contracts and certified documents, without concerning himself in the least with the preferences and repugnances of the French national soul. He imagined, perhaps, that the majority of the Leaguers were, like the Sixteen and a few fanatical theologians, ready to throw themselves into his arms ; but he was deceiving himself.

Mayenne's principal councillor, Villeroy, declared that the Spaniard was so hated that the people were almost forgetting their secular hatred of the English. The Bishop of Asti, Panigarola, relates that, after the deliverance of Paris, the League nobility laughed " openly " at the Duke of Parma's army, because it had failed to take the little fortress of Corbeil. When Philip sent money, " he was spending it without profit, and the French jeered at him even while they used it ; if he sent troops, the whole of France took umbrage ". A pamphlet, the *Anti-Espagnol*, whose title sufficiently indicates its source and spirit, expressed not only the declared hatred of the royalists, but also the covert antipathy of the moderate

Leaguers. Apart from a small number of fanatical sectaries and hangers-on who were ready to surrender or sell the kingdom to Philip II, the Catholic majority endured the Spanish tutelage with no liking for it.

The Duke of Parma had foreseen that any attempt to secure the accession of the Infanta would lead to " a thousandfold of difficulties ". " Without an obvious miracle," he wrote to Philip on January 18th, 1592, " there is no hope whatever of any success in obtaining what is wanted."

After many postponements, Mayenne resigned himself to summoning the States-General in Paris in order to give France a Sovereign. Philip flattered himself that he would obtain recognition of the rights of his daughter from the deputies. Now that Farnese was dead, the Count of Mansfeldt, invested with the command of the Spanish troops, marched on Noyon, which barred the valley of the Oise and the road to Paris, and captured it after a desperate resistance. The Spanish garrison which he established there assured him a new halting-place within thirty leagues of the French capital. An ambassador-extraordinary, the Duke of Feria, proceeded to Paris in company with a legist, Don Iñigo de Mendoza, the one provided with arguments, good or bad, and the other with money, and the two of them together in a position either to convince or to corrupt.

Sixtus V's successors—very different from that authoritarian Pope, badly disposed towards the King of Spain—Urban VIII, Gregory XIV and Innocent IX, in their short tenures of the Pontifical throne between 1590 and 1592, had supported the Leaguers, and consequently helped Philip, with men and money. Clement VIII, the next Pope, was disturbed by Henri IV's progress and trembled for the future of French Catholicism. He exhorted the great lords and the Catholic cities of France to band themselves together against this heretical tyrant. To back up his recommendations, the Pope dispatched to Paris as Legate the Cardinal Archbishop of Piacenza, Philip Sega, who was regarded as one of the finest diplomats of the Roman Court, that school of diplomacy.

The States-General of France opened their sessions on January 26th, 1593, at the Louvre. Feria was received in solemn audience, on April 2nd, with almost royal honours. Emphatically, in the Spanish way, he magnified the services which his master had rendered to the Kings of France since the beginning of the troubles, and drew a contrast between Philip's good offices and disinterested zeal and the French aggression against him in Portugal and in the Low Countries. Feria enumerated all the support in men which

Philip had sent to François II, Charles IX, and Henri III, the deliverance of Paris and Rouen, the six millions in gold which he had expended, and the collaboration of Spanish diplomacy at the Court of Rome to hasten the summoning and assembly of the States-General.

The deputies listened not without distaste to the " reproach and exprobation " of the Spanish ambassador to France. The letter which Philip addressed to them was no less tactless. He invited them not to separate before electing a king as Catholic as the circumstances demanded. After beginning in a tone which smacked of the master, Philip continued in that of a creditor demanding the repayment of a debt. " There is good reason, moreover, why you should know your own profit on this occasion and recognize in my respect all that I deserve from your kingdom, by giving me satisfaction, which, though it should be only for your own good and advantage, I shall nevertheless receive with great contentment."

But Cardinal de Pellevé, whom the Three Orders had chosen to speak in their name, ultra-Leaguer though he was, did not fail to retort that France had rendered no less great services to Spain, as far back as the most remote times. Clovis had conquered and killed the King of the Visigoths, Alaric, defender of the Arian heresy. Childebert, heir to his father's piety, had even entered Spain to combat Amalaric, who persisted in the same error. Charles Martel had arrested the victorious march of the Arabs, already masters of Africa and Spain, at Poitiers.

" What are we to say of Charlemagne, and how did he gain the titles of great, blessed and invincible, if it was not that, having fought with good fortune for the faith, he constrained the Saracens, already established in Spain, to stay within their own borders and leave the Catholics of this country in peace and repose ? " Pellevé did not forget Bertrand Du Guesclin, Constable of France, who overthrew Pedro the Cruel and put the reigning dynasty of the Trastamares on the throne of Castile.

" There are to be found, too, many other testimonies to the good will and friendship of our Kings towards the Kings of Spain." All this amounted to recalling that France was not behindhand in good works, and hinting that Spain had received in advance the price of her efforts on behalf of French Catholicism.

But, having made these reservations of patriotic dignity, the Cardinal proceeded to exalt the House of Austria. If the princes of Lorraine, " like new Macchabees ", had liberally expended their blood and their money for the faith ; if Pope Clement VIII had " extended us the humanity of his aid from day to day ", King

331

Philip surpassed all these defenders of the faith. Accordingly the orator promised Philip, in recompense of his zeal, " all the duty of good will and affection " that he could hope for from the French Catholics, and, on earth and in Heaven, an immortal glory.

" When, to reward him for so many labours endured in the cause of religion, he is introduced by Divine goodness into the celestial tabernacles, not only will a thousand million angels, servants of the Most High, go to meet him, but also an infinity of people whom he has rescued from error, from infidelity, and from the sin of heresy will come with joy and gladness, bearing in armsfull the sheaves of their merits." Might one not say that, in holding up his palms to Heaven, the orator of the States seemed to be trying to turn Philip aside from seeking his reward on earth ?

The Spaniards were not in luck. To the letter in which Mayenne invited the Catholic royalists to unite with the Leaguers against Henri IV, the royalists replied, " with the leave and permission of their King and natural prince ", by an offer to the Catholics of the Holy Union to enter " into conference and communication about the proper means of allaying the troubles and conserving the Catholic religion and the State ". It was a formal overture for peace ; and the States, urged on by public opinion, were obliged to respond to it, with the reservation that their delegates would not enter into relations, direct or indirect, with the King of Navarre, but would content themselves with setting forth the reasons why the French should not recognize a heretic as their King.

Feria was powerless to prevent all this. Three days after his solemn reception, on April 5th, the assembly at the Louvre conveyed to the Catholic royalists its desire to expedite the date of the conference they had proposed. It was decided to hold it at Suresnes, and deputies were appointed on both sides.

The mass of the Parisians were tired of the war. On the day when the twelve representatives of the States left the town to proceed to the seat of the conference, a great crowd assembled at the Porte Neuve, shouting at the top of their voices : " Peace ! Blessed be those who seek it and ensue it ! Accursed be those who do not, and to the Devil with them ! " In the surrounding villages the inhabitants went down on their knees as the delegates passed, and with clasped hands begged them to give them peace. It was a manifestation of general weariness and wretchedness.

The serious discussions began on May 5th. The orators of the two parties, the Leaguer Archbishop of Lyons, Pierre d'Epinac, and the Royalist Archbishop of Bourges, Renaud de Beaune, set

forth the reasons against and for the admission of a heretic claimant.
It was then that, in a master-stroke of policy, in which some persist
in seeing an inspiration of the Holy Spirit, Henri IV, on May 17th,
announced his desire to be instructed in the Catholic religion.
France had such a need of peace that she embraced this promise
of his to become converted as her salvation. Epinac might say
what he liked, and the Legate might do what he liked, but the mass
of the people persisted in believing in the sincerity—humanly speaking so opportune—of Henri's return to the traditional Church (6).

By way of rejoinder, Philip's ambassadors pressed on with the
question of the election. Mayenne transmitted their demand, in
which they set forth the Infanta's rights. It was the sole remedy
for the prevailing miseries, the solution indicated by His Holiness
and His Catholic Majesty, and the crowning of the task to which
good Catholics had devoted themselves. Then the Spanish jurist,
Don Iñigo de Mendoza, in a long discourse in Latin, overwhelmed
the partisans of the Salic law under the mass of his arguments. He
proved superabundantly that, instead of going back to the first
King of France, Pharamond, the Salic law had not been applied
earlier than Louis X the Headstrong. But what did that matter
to men anxious about safeguarding French nationality?

The States did not show themselves disposed to choose the
Infanta without conditions. They asked whether Philip would
marry his daughter to a French prince. De Tassis, more adroit
than Feria, suggested to them, on June 13th, that, if they did not
want to reverse the exclusion of women, they should elect the
Archduke Ernest of Austria. He was a son and grandson of Emperors, brother of the reigning Emperor Rudolph, who had no
children, and nephew of the Archduke Ferdinand (of the Tyrol),
who had only daughters, ineligible to succeed. "All this in time
would fall to Ernest."

What a claimant and what hopes : the Imperial Crown, and
almost all the dominions of the House of Austria ! But, apart
from a few desperately credulous fanatics, could Leaguers in whom
any light of common sense remained believe that Philip, from love
of his daughter, would restore the Empire of Charlemagne for the
benefit of France ?

The States objected that their laws and customs prevented
them from recognizing a " German " as King. Imprudently, they
added that, if the King of Spain were agreeable to choice being
made of a French prince and gave him his daughter in marriage,
Philip would put them under infinite obligations to him. The
Spanish ambassadors ought to have grasped at this opportunity as

333

it flew. But they were too proud to admit that the Infanta should reign only by virtue of her marriage with an elected French prince.

They asked to be allowed to make a fresh proposal. At a solemn session at which all the princes of the League were present, on June 21, the Spanish ambassadors declared that, if the States forthwith made " Sovereigns proprietory of this Crown *in solidium,* as it is said, Her Serene Highness the Infanta and that one of the French princes, including all the House of Lorraine, whom Her Majesty may choose, he (Philip) will be bound from this hour and henceforth to marry her to him." The Legate, who felt that the hour was decisive, had himself carried to the assembly, shivering with fever though he was, and lent all the weight of his authority to this proposal.

But this half-concession satisfied nobody. It was bound to displease Mayenne, who, since he could not be the King of Spain's son-in-law, had no interest in favouring any arrangement in which the advantages he was to gain himself were not carefully stipulated in advance. Mayenne's confidant, the Archbishop of Lyons, took occasion to inform the Spaniards that the States considered that to elect a Queen, " being yet uncertain of a King ", would amount fundamentally to a violation of the Salic law. Besides, they could not admit that the King of Spain should reserve himself the right to give them a King, for " to constitute a King over them depended on their own power and authority, and not on any foreign prince ". The Spaniards replied that the Infanta could not set out from Spain for France " without an honourable quality ", and that they could not leave the French at liberty to accept her or reject her.

Into this deadlock burst the decree of the Parliament of June 28th, pronouncing that, through the mouth of one of the Presidents of the Court, " iterative remonstrances shall be made to M. le Duc de Mayenne . . . that he employ the authority which has been entrusted to him to prevent that, under pretext of religion, this Kingdom, which *does not depend upon any other than God and recognizes no other lord, whoever he may be, in this world so far as its temporality is concerned,* should be occupied by foreigners." This amounted to condemning both ultramontane pretensions and Spanish ambitions at one and the same time.

Public opinion had found its mouthpiece. It went over to the royalists. The declaration of the Archbishop of Bourges, the announcement of Henri IV's conversion, had disposed of the last scruples of the moderate Leaguers. The States no longer had the necessary authority to go against the decree of the Parliament in favour of the Salic law and hereditary right. They explained to Philip's representatives that it would be " not only out of order, but even perilous for religion and for the State, to create and establish a King ".

The Legate hoped to effect a change of mind by a fresh concession. He took it upon himself to announce that the French prince for whom Philip intended his daughter was the young Duke of Guise, the son, dear to the Parisians, of the hero of the barricades. But nobody, not even the person principally concerned, took this expedient of diplomacy on its last legs seriously.

On July 25th, 1593, Henri IV abjured Protestantism. On February 27th, 1594, he was crowned at Chartres. The French people, reassured about their faith, hastened to return to the paths of obedience. Paris opened its gates to Henri IV on March 22nd. Victor without a struggle, he granted the foreign garrisons, who had not dared to stir, their lives and the right to withdraw with their arms and baggage. From a window of the Porte Saint Denis he watched them leaving his capital. As they passed by, Henri IV saluted Feria, Ibarra and Tassis, marching in the midst of the Spanish battalions, humiliated participants in this national victory.

In Rome Henri IV pursued his reconciliation with the Roman Church. Clement VIII objected to the absolution given the King at Saint Denis by the French bishops as a Gallican infringement of his own rights, since, in a matter of this importance, only Saint Peter's successor had the right to loose or bind. After Barrère's plan to assassinate him, and the attempt on his life by young Jean Châtel, a former pupil of the Jesuits, Henri IV was himself convinced that only Pontifical pardon, by cleansing him from the stain of heresy and rehabilitating him in the eyes of all Catholics, would deprive would-be regicides of any excuse for striking at him as a tyrant.

Philip II's efforts at Rome, his prayers, and even, so it was said, his threat to prevent the arrival of corn from Sicily and starve out the Romans, did not succeed in turning the Pontiff aside from a decision which conjured away the risk of a breach with France, paved the way for the general pacification of Christendom, and liberated the Roman Court from its hateful tutelage to the Spanish Government. Even the decree of expulsion against the Jesuit Order, pronounced by the Parliament of Paris, only retarded a design of the Pope's which was at once generous, Christian, and politic.

On September 17th, 1595, the proxies of the King of France, du Perron, Bishop of Evreux, and d'Ossat prostrated themselves at the feet of the Pope, denied the absolution at Saint Denis, and implored the only true absolution, that of the Sovereign Pontiff. Clement VIII took up a rod and touched the shoulders of the two kneeling penitents with it.

It meant the reconciliation of monarchist France with the Roman Church, and a bad defeat for the King of Spain, who could no longer invoke the argument of religious unworthiness against the Navarrese. But Philip did not despair of dismembering the kingdom which his daughter had failed to win. He continued, as before, to support the League leaders in revolt and the princes in arms against the King of France : Mayenne in Burgundy, Nemours and Saint Sorlin in the Lyonnais, Joyeuse in Languedoc, Mercœur in Brittany, and other lords of less importance.

Philip did not succeed in keeping in alliance with him the Duke of Lorraine, Charles III, who, tired of a struggle without profit to him, in which he knew very well that he had no chance of winning either the Crown of France for his son, the Marquis of Pont-à-Mousson, or Champagne for Lorraine, was the first to retire from it. But Philip could count upon the self-interested attachment of his son-in-law, the Duke of Savoy, the ambitious Charles Emmanuel. The Duke's desire to retain the marquisate of Saluces, and even to make additions to it in Provence and Dauphiné, kept him united to Philip's fortunes.

It remained for Henri IV, converted, crowned at Chartres, and recognized by the majority of his subjects, to pursue the conquest of his kingdom at the point of the sword. As soon as he was assured of Pontifical absolution, he declared war on Spain, as though by way of emphasizing that his greatest, if not his sole, enemy was the foreign Sovereign who kept on exploiting the religious zeal of the last of the Leaguers for the benefit of his own ambition.

Henri IV launched into the Franche-Comté the Lorraine troops whom he had taken into his own pay. The Constable of Castile, Velasco, governor of the Milanese, crossed the Alps with three thousand horse and fifteen thousand foot to clear the province. He let himself be persuaded by Mayenne to cross the Saône and occupy Dijon, which Marshal de Biron was threatening. Henri IV hurried up, and pushed ahead with a few squadrons of horse. He charged the Spanish advance-guard so furiously that Velasco could not bring himself to believe that the King of France would risk himself, like any mere scout, unless he had a whole army behind him. Velasco, despite Mayenne's urgings, refused to give battle to Henri IV.

This encounter, on June 5th, 1595, was a hot one, but not a

very serious one. There were no more than some sixty dead on both sides. Its consequences, however, were important. Velasco recrossed the Saône and abandoned the Leaguers to their fate. Mayenne, furious at this desertion, left the Spanish army and henceforth thought only of making his peace with the King of France.

Henri IV invaded the Franche-Comté and raided it. But he was obliged to let go his prey through the intervention of the Protestant cantons, its allies, and on September 22nd he renewed the agreement which guaranteed the neutrality of this Spanish province.

In the north Henri IV succeeded only in capturing Ham. The new governor of the Low Countries, the Count of Fuentes, a great lord and a great captain, had reorganized the Spanish army, which, being neither paid nor fed, was dispersed by marauding, decimated by sickness, and enervated by indiscipline. With this admirable infantry which, once it was taken in hand and regularly paid, soon learnt how to obey again, Fuentes besieged Doullens, one of the bulwarks of the French frontier. He routed a relieving army, killing almost all its infantry and six hundred gentlemen, and a week later gave the town, with its garrison and its inhabitants, up as a prey to his soldiery.

From Doullens Fuentes marched on Cambrai, entered it without striking a blow, thanks to the complicity of the populace, and forced the citadel to surrender. Even after the submission of Mayenne and of Joyeuse, Governor of Languedoc for the League, the King of France was hard put to it to resist the force, no less than the intrigues, of the formidable King of Spain.

The Governor of Provence, d'Epernon, whom Henri IV had recalled for his violence and his extortion, treated with Philip II against " the Prince of Béarn ". Two ardent Leaguers, the consul Casaulx and the provost Louis d'Aix, plotted to hand Marseilles over to Philip. His son-in-law, the Duke of Savoy, maintained himself in the Maurienne despite all the efforts of Lesdiguières, leader of the Protestant party, and governor for the King of France, in Dauphiné. One of Philip's lieutenants established himself strongly south of the Loire, without paying too much attention to the Duke of Mercœur, the one of all the leaders of the League who was the last to submit.

Happily for Henri IV, the young Duke of Guise, who had gone over to his cause and to whom Henri had extended his confidence, forced d'Epernon to make his submission. In Marseilles Liberta, one of the captains of the local militia, raised the populace and chased the two petty tyrants who were oppressing them out of the city.

But Spain was hard to defeat. She had the first army in the world, and a leader worthy to command it. Ardres did not even make any attempt to resist Fuentes when he advanced on the fortress. Protestant Germany and England looked askance at the new convert to Catholicism. Elizabeth offered to defend Calais, but only on condition that the King of France ceded it to her. Henri IV refused ; he would rather have seen it in the hands of the Spaniards. It was only with difficulty that he obtained from his former ally Elizabeth aid to the extent of two thousand men and twenty thousand écus, to be repaid in five months. The Dutch, more generous, advanced him four hundred and fifty thousand florins and promised to co-ordinate their operations with his the following year.

With this money and the auxiliaries whom he had at his disposal, Henri IV contemplated recapturing Arras, and chose the city of Amiens as his base of attack on it. But the Spanish Governor of Doullens, Hernán Tello Carrero, informed that Amiens was badly defended, possessed himself by surprise, on March 11th, 1597, of this fortress, which barred the Somme valley and covered Paris. The King of France reeled under the blow. His capital was threatened, and the pacification of his kingdom compromised.

But, if Henri IV was easily disheartened, he pulled himself together quickly. He marched upon Amiens with all the forces at his disposal and bombarded it with forty-five cannon. Cardinal Albert, Philip's nephew, whom Philip had appointed Governor-General of the Low Countries, advanced to relieve the city, but he suffered severe losses from the French artillery and was forced to beat a retreat. The besieged had nothing to do but surrender, and on September 25th, Amiens was granted a capitulation with the honours of war. The siege had lasted six months.

France was tired after her great efforts, and Spain was at the end of her resources. The Pope, disquieted by the exhaustion of the two great Catholic Powers, and by the development of the Protestant Powers by land and sea, had already, in 1595, sent his nephew, Cardinal Giovanni Francesco Aldobrandini, to recommend the cause of peace to the Catholic King. It took the recapture of Amiens by the French and a sense of his approaching death to convince Philip II of the vanity of his ambitions.

Bonaventura Calatagirone, General of the Franciscans, had better success with him than Aldobrandini, and, under the auspices of the Papacy, negotiations were opened at Vervins. France was represented by Pomponne de Bellièvre, Lord of Sillery, and Spain by Jean Richardot, a native of the Franche-Comté, Jean Baptiste de Tassis, and Verreichen.

The treaty of peace, " long disputed, often in deadlock, sometimes despaired of ", was finally signed at Vervins on May 2nd, 1598. It re-established the *status quo* of Cateau-Cambrésis. The King of France recovered his lost towns : Ardres, Doullens, Calais, etc. He agreed that the treaty should contain a declaration of the pretensions of Philip II and his heirs to the heritage of the House of Burgundy ; but Philip on his side agreed " to prosecute them by way of peace and justice, not by force of arms ".

As it was not likely that the Parliament of Paris would hand Burgundy back by judicial award, Philip's reassertion of his claims was equivalent to a renunciation. Of the provinces of which Louis XI had deprived the heiress of Charles the Bold, the King of Spain kept only the countship of Charolais, under the suzerainty of the King of France.

The two Kings were in agreement that their allies should be included in the treaty. But Charles Emmanuel refused to give back the marquisate of Saluces, and the negotiators decided to defer this point and submit it to the arbitration of the Pope. Henri IV's allies, the English and the Dutch, had too much interest in continuing the war on land and sea to make peace. They declined the King of France's offer of mediation, and even qualified it as treachery.

Philip had not given up hope of bringing back into obedience to him the northern provinces, Holland, Zeeland, Utrecht, Friesland, Groningen, Gelderland, Zutphen and Over-Ijssel, which had been definitely freed by Maurice of Nassau and constituted into a State independent *de facto*, if not *de jure*. Philip had convinced himself that direct government by the Court of Madrid wounded the particularist spirit of the Flemish and Walloon populations. He imagined that this was the only obstacle to the reunion of the Belgians and the Dutch under the Spanish Crown.

In order to forestall a fresh revolt in the provinces which had submitted, and pave the way for the return to their obedience of those which persisted in revolt, Philip decided to constitute the Low Countries, the Franche-Comté, and the Charolais into an autonomous principality. He proposed to transfer its sovereignty to his favourite daughter, the Infanta Clara Isabel Eugenia, to the husband whom he intended for her, the Archduke Albert of Austria, her cousin, and to their children, if they had any. But would they have any ? Many people thought not.

In Philip II's intention, the separation of the Low Countries and Spain was to be only provisional. All the dispositions taken in his letters patent of May 6th, 1598, tended in this direction. If the succession fell into the female line, the heiress could marry only the King of Spain or his heir apparent.

As though Philip were going out of his way to put difficulties, or rather impossibilities, in the path of making an end of the secession of the Low Countries, he compelled the new Sovereigns to forbid their subjects trade with the Indies and the exercise of any religion other than the Catholic. These were two reasons, among many others, for which the Dutch, Calvinists in great majority, who were showing themselves bold mariners and enemies of the colonial monopoly of Spain and Portugal, would never consent to renounce their independence.

The King of Spain could not resign himself to letting them go. Philip was supposed to withdraw the Spanish troops from the new State; but, by secret articles, which did not become known until the nineteenth century, he reserved to himself the right to maintain garrisons in a certain number of fortresses (7).

Through all the shortcomings in these dispositions of his, the future married couple and their descendants were to be deprived of all rights to the possession of the Low Countries.

The Archduke Albert summoned the States-General of the provinces still submissive to Spain, and presented to them the letters patent which conferred the sovereignty of the Low Countries upon himself and the Infanta. After some difficulties, raised by Brabant, agreement was reached. The Archduke, in his own name and that of the Infanta, accepted the seventeen articles drawn up by the States. He was to marry the Infanta. The foreign soldiers were to be employed in the pay of the King of Spain and only on the frontier. The provinces were re-established in their rights and privileges, and administration was to be reserved to natives of the country.

Albert doffed his Cardinal's hat and title, and set off for Spain to marry the Infanta. He had written to the representatives of the rebel provinces, and to Maurice of Nassau, informing them of the change that had taken place in the government of the Low Countries and of his desire to make peace with them. He received no reply whatever.

When the Archduke arrived in Spain, Philip II was dead.

CHAPTER XVI

THE END OF THE REIGN

OUT of Philip's immense effort to win the mastery of the world Spain emerged exhausted. Her exclusive exaltation of the warrior virtues, her hereditary contempt for work, which were the characteristic features of the nation at this period, led to the ruin of the country and the monarchy.

Charles V had left his son a heavy load of debt, which was still further increased by the renewal of hostilities in Italy and in France after the denunciation of the truce of Vaucelles. From the budget estimates of Spain quoted by Don Modesto La Fuente, which do not include Italy, the Low Countries, or the Indies, it appears that from March 18th, 1557, to the end of the year, the Spanish Government needed, for its ordinary expenditure, 393,750,000 maravedis, and that the receipts which it had at its disposal to cover them had fallen to 220,392,000 maravedis. The deficit amounted to 173,358,000 maravedis. It was a little less than half the expenditure, and a little more than four-fifths of the revenue.

Accordingly we can appreciate the necessity for the expedients proposed by the Council of Finance (*Hacienda*) on March 17th, 1557, during the earliest days of Philip's reign : sale of a thousand titles of nobility ; sale of municipal offices of *regidor* and jurat ; sale of letters of legitimization and of nobility to the sons of priests ; alienation of perpetual jurisdiction over towns and vassals to lords. One could become a noble for five thousand ducats ; and the need was so pressing that the Council was in favour of overlooking the unworthiness of candidates and of introducing into the privileged class descendants of Jews and Moors, and men whose parents had worn the San Benito and figured in *autos-da-fé*. At the time this was a much bolder step than legitimatizing the adulterous bastard of a priest.

As long as the war went on, Spain's financial straits were terrible. Philip would have had to accept peace with France if Henri II had not been in even more of a hurry to make it. In his need of money, instead of merely levying his "fifth" on the precious cargoes imported from America, Philip put an embargo on all the cargoes of the galleons—as, for that matter, he had a right to do, though the right had not been used before, on payment to the merchants of interest on the values impounded.

Nothing could be more significant than Philip's own confession. "All the ordinary revenues," he wrote in 1559, "are mortgaged ; to free them it would take twenty millions of ducats, so that there can be no thought of doing so. There are owing, besides, seven millions of ducats to the bankers of Antwerp, to the merchants of Seville, and others."

The debt was about five and a half times the whole revenues of the monarchy : five million escudos (5,333,333 ducats). The sources of these revenues the Venetian Michael Suriano, on his return from his embassy to Brussels in 1559, divides as follows : Spain, one million and a half ; the Indies, half a million ; Naples, one million ; Milan and Sicily, one million ; the Low Countries, one million. At the rate of seven per cent—the ordinary rate for loans, says the Venetian ambassador, Leonardo Donato—on a debt of twenty-seven millions of ducats there would be an interest of 1,890,000 ducats to be added to the annual deficit (1).

The peace of Cateau-Cambrésis enabled Philip II to re-establish financial equilibrium. It is true that the expedition to the island of Djerba, the relief of Malta, the expeditions against the Barbaresques, the campaigns against the Moors, the first troubles in the Low Countries and the Duke of Alba's army of execution involved heavy expenditure. But the end of operations of war in Italy and on the French north-east frontier left Philip time to breathe.

Expenditure was largely met out of borrowing. Pope Pius V helped towards the cost of the holy wars. In 1567 he granted the King of Spain, for the punishment of the iconoclasts in the Low Countries, the right to levy tithe himself in all the parishes of Spain on the richest *vecino* (inhabitant), who was thus " excused " from paying it to the ecclesiastical collector—hence the name of *escusado* given to this concession.

At the time of his elevation to the Pontificate, Pius V, on account of abuses, had suspended the Bull of the *Cruzada*, which authorized the sale, to the King's profit, of dispensations from fasting and eating " eggs, cheese and milk foods on vigils, during Lent and every Friday throughout the year ", and a multitude of spiritual graces, such, for example, as the power to rescue such-and-such a soul from Purgatory. But in 1571, at the time of the formation of the Holy League, the Pope re-established this venal body of indulgences.

Of the improvement in the financial position we may judge by the statement of the budget of the Spanish Monarchy made to the Senate of Venice by the Venetian ambassador, Leonardo Donato. He had lived in Madrid during his mission in 1569, but his statement was not drawn up until 1573, as we may infer from his allusions to the year 1572. Donato details receipts and expenditure article by article, according to information which had been given him by competent persons, probably treasury officials. The budget is probably that of 1571, or a provisional draft of that of 1572. So we may assume from the small returns (350,000 escudos) from the *Cruzada*, only just re-established by Pius V, which produced as much as a million escudos when it was fully in operation.

Revenues, not including those of the Indies, amounted to 5,585,000 escudos (5,952,000 ducats), and ordinary expenditure to two millions. While Donato cannot exactly estimate the figure of the debt, which was somewhere between thirty-two and forty-five millions, he can at least inform us that 2,200,000 escudos (2,346,666 ducats) had to be paid to creditors in interest *every year*. After deduction of expenses and arrears, there remained to the King 1,400,000 escudos (1,493,333 ducats), to provide for " any needs which might present themselves ".

In anticipation of them, Philip ought to have reduced his household and administrative expenses ; but he did not even think of it. At the time of his penury in 1559 he had raised the income of his young Queen, Elizabeth of Valois, from 60,000 to 80,000 ducats. How could he cut anything out of this sum at the time of his fourth marriage with Anne of Austria ? His civil list absorbed 415,000 ducats out of a budget of about six millions.

Great buildings are costly. In 1563 Philip began the construction of the Escorial, which, including the church, in twenty-two years swallowed up three and a half millions of ducats, half the annual revenues of the monarchy (2). This was an average of 150,000 ducats, which had to be added every year to the cost of maintaining his Court and his Guard and of his personal needs. All this had to be met from the modest surplus of 1571.

Receipts diminished at the same time as expenses increased. After the repression of the revolt, the Kingdom of Granada was ruined. The Low Countries revolted, ceased to bring in anything, and cost a great deal.

But what really overwhelmed Philip financially was the way in which events succeeded one another and grew out of one another. Once it had started, the war in the Low Countries was never-ending. After his annexation of Portugal, there were all his great endeavours to overthrow Elizabeth and Protestantism, and to conquer France or dismember her.

In the budget which Morosini reports during his embassy to Spain in 1578–81, receipts, including those from Portugal, had risen to 12,472,000 ducats, but expenditure exceeded fourteen millions. The Low Countries were definitely struck off the list of States which contributed towards the expenses of the Monarchy. Morosini does not regard the situation as desperate ; but the expedients of which he speaks, such as borrowing, increases of taxation, levying of subsidies, sale of offices in the Indies, and, above all, the clearing of persons condemned by the Holy Office from any stain, in return for a money payment, prove that it was far from sound.

Spain was not rich enough to pay for all her glory. It was long believed that the gold and silver mines of the New World paid the costs of Philip's policy of magnificence. But the very frequent mutinies of the troops left without pay constitute sufficient proof that the produce of the mines did not even cover ordinary war expenses. And what were these expenses by comparison with those of Philip's dreams of greatness : triumph of Catholicism and of the Spanish hegemony, religious unity and the empire of the world ? The creation of powerful fleets and the maintenance of armies ever stronger in numbers, even the recruiting and payment of agents abroad, were a very costly business.

The historians of the eighteenth century supplemented documentary deficiencies by fantastic approximations. Weiss declares that they estimated at two milliards of piastres—nominally about four hundred million pounds—the sums which entered Spain from the discovery of America up to 1595.

Alexander Humboldt, in his *Political Essay on the Kingdom of New Spain*, scales down these flights of imagination very sharply, and adduces figures which are based on definite data, even though conjecture is not entirely absent from them. He asserts that, on a yearly average, from 1492 to 1500 the value of precious metals imported into Spain was two and a half million piastres (nominally half a million pounds), and from 1500 to 1545 three million piastres (nominally 600,000 pounds). The discovery of the silver mines of Potosi and the treatment of ore by mercury raised the output, between 1545 and 1600, to eleven million piastres (nominally 2,200,000 pounds).

According to Humboldt's calculations, therefore, during the forty-two years of Philip II's reign, from 1557 to 1598, Spain received only about 450 million piastres. It is true that Humboldt probably counts only the *quinto*, the one-fifth tax which the treasury levied on precious metals imported (3).

344

Don Modesto La Fuente, our contemporary, a conscientious and fully documented historian, does not desire to keep on boring his readers with all the figures which he has at his disposal about the revenues from the New World. We have to content ourselves with what this despoiler of archives is prepared to vouchsafe to us. To be done once and for all with dull financial details, La Fuente declares, according to official data, that Philip II drew annually from America more than 450,000 millions of maravedis, or more exactly, 451,212,031 maravedis, in other words, 1,002,694 pesos at 450 maravedis to the peso, or 1,128,030 escudos at 400 maravedis to the escudo, or 1,203,233 ducats, otherwise nominally about two hundred thousand pounds.

" It was," comments La Fuente, " a considerable sum, in view of the value of money and the price of commodities at that period." But, even if we add this average revenue from the Indies to the 1,400,000 escudos of budget surplus reported by Leonardo Donato, we arrive only at the annual figure of 2,528,030 escudos. It was not enough to buy world monarchy.

From the day when the Low Countries started being in a state of perpetual war against the King of Spain, the balance of the budget was permanently upset. It was the Low Countries, as Suriano rightly reckons, which were " the treasury of the King of Spain ". The seventeen provinces whose commerce and industry made wealth flow to them from other parts of the world—these were the real Indies which for so long maintained the enterprises of Charles V in his wars in France, Italy and Germany, " and which preserved and defended his States, his dignity, and his reputation" (4). He was able to draw from them, within the space of a few years, twenty-nine millions in gold.

It was also these " Black Indies ", as this country of coal was called, from which Philip II, at the beginning of his reign, drew a part of his expenses in his war against France. Their share of taxes was not their sole contribution to the cost of his monarchy. In 1558, at the time of Philip's extreme penury on the eve of the treaty of Cateau-Cambrésis, they granted him a large loan. They voted him —with a bad grace, it is true, but in any case they voted him—an annual subsidy, payable for nine years, of 800,000 florins (400,000 ducats).

Holland, so Ranke (5) asserts, contributed on her own account 300,000 florins (150,000 ducats) to an extraordinary levy which the other provinces must obviously have paid too—for Holland was always the most backward of all in this respect—and which must therefore have totalled more than a million and a half. It must be borne in mind that, before 1592, no extraordinary aid could be obtained from the Kingdom of Aragon ; that Sicily, after consenting to raise her *servicio* from 200,000 to a quarter of a million, refused to go any further ; that the Milanese, though it twice increased its monthly subsidy, refused to grant a third increase, proposed by the governor, the Duke of Terra Nova, and that, while in 1584 it contributed 1,180,000 scudi, this sum was almost entirely absorbed by the 1,166,696 escudos expended on the spot for the maintenance of the troops in garrison in the Milanese.

To avoid provoking trouble elsewhere, Philip exploited the Low Countries, Castile and Sicily as much as he could. One can imagine his embarrassment when, instead of receiving money from Margaret of Parma, and the governors who succeeded this Regent of his in the Low Countries, he was obliged to dispatch funds to them. The revenues of the New World could not meet the deficiency of those of the Low Countries. As early as 1575 a cry of despair escaped Philip. " The disarray of the finances is irremediable. I am forty-eight. What an old age awaits me ! Old age is upon me, and I do not know how I shall live to-morrow. I do not even know how I live to-day, with all the distress which these anxieties give me."

It seems paradoxical to ask whether, under this needy King, the Spanish population was not reduced to poverty. Nevertheless, the Venetian ambassador Leonardo Donato presents, in 1572, a picture of Castile, the most exploited of all Philip's kingdoms, which has nothing sombre about it. Let us bear in mind that Spain had never been ravaged, like the north of France and various parts of Italy, by hostile armies. She had no experience of invasion and the miseries which accompanied it : pillaging, incendiarism, devastation more ruinous than any excess of taxation.

The titled aristocracy and the nobility, Donato reports, were laden with debts and mortgages ; but they had such vast estates, and so many rights of jurisdiction to exercise, that they had enough left to live on a lavish scale. Simple gentlemen were distributed among such a large number of cities and towns that they did not suffer any embarrassment. This observer, who on his own confession never left Madrid, knew nothing about that class of hidalgos which figures so largely in the picaresque novels, who would not work, because they held that work dishonoured them, and who could find no other employment than that of squires in great houses, unless they swindled and stole, lest they should die of hunger, " as a point of honour ".

The merchants were enriched by the trade and business which they carried on with the Indies, as we may judge from the loans which they made to the King. The artisans profited largely by the rise in the status of craftsmen. The peasants, as a result of the area of estates left uncultivated and the shortage of workers, took the lands of the great proprietors over to farm on advantageous terms, and in some districts, such as Andalusia, even succeeded in buying them.

Spain, that land of plain living, was sufficient to herself. To feed and clothe herself, without any occasion to look abroad, she produced wheat, wine, oil, silk and wool. She even had a surplus of oil, which she sold to England for the preparation of cloth, and she exported salt to the Low Countries and to the northern lands for the curing of fish. What she lacked was flax and hemp for body-linen. But did her dour people really need shirts?

Even if this picture is correct—and the ambassador admits that he speaks only from hearsay—the exhaustion of the royal finances, or, as it was euphemistically called, "the embarrassment of the treasury", and the perpetually renewed borrowings were bound in the long run to have their repercussion upon the prosperity of the country.

The economic prepossessions of the time contributed towards this. A false idea of that period, which has not yet completely disappeared, was that all the profits of colonial exploitation ought to be reserved to the motherland. Castile, which had discovered and conquered the New World, proscribed the commercial competition of foreign nations, including, except by special licence, even that of Aragon and Catalonia. She prohibited the natives, and even the colonists, from manufacturing the same merchandise, or growing the same crops, as Spain. If she allowed the vine and the olive to be cultivated in Chile and Peru, very far away in South America, it was only subject to formal prohibition against the transportation of wine and oil to Panama and other exporting ports, where they might be embarked clandestinely and sent to Spain to compete with similar produce of Spanish soil.

The motherland assumed the responsibility of providing her subjects in America with manufactured articles and other products which she thought they wanted, or even thought they ought to want. But, for fear of risks, she abandoned the less advantageous transactions to private enterprise, and she granted the right to trade with the Indies to any shipowner who requested it. She derived considerable revenues from these privileges, and she imposed considerable precautions to safeguard the interests of the treasury.

The concessionaire, before departure, had to declare the nature and the value of his cargo; and the captains had to carry long bills

347

of lading, in which every detail of it was enumerated. On return there were similar formalities, and even more. Since gold and silver were the principal merchandise imported, none of these precious metals must be allowed to escape. The King took the *quinto* (fifth) for his own share, and imposed customs duties on what was left to the merchant.

In order to avoid fraud and render this jealous supervision more complete, Seville, first replaced by San Lucar and later by Cadiz, was the sole port of Spain where ships coming from the American ports, Porto Bello, Carthagena, Vera Cruz, were allowed to unload ; and they were forbidden to call elsewhere, at any island or mainland- either on the outward voyage or the homeward. The *Casa de Con, tratación* (Chamber of Commerce of the Indies) was the obligatory intermediary between the Indies and Castile. Everything was subject to its supervision. Not an article left for the Indies which was not declared to the *Casa de Contratación* ; not a product arrived from the Indies which was not bonded by the *Casa de Contratación*. The Council of the Indies, created in 1524 by Charles V, dispatched the royal decisions and orders from Madrid.

From Cadiz, during Philip II's reign, every year two squadrons set forth, the fleet and the galleons, as they were called, in all upwards of a hundred ships, each armed with thirty to thirty-four cannon and manned by a crew of a hundred and twenty men, which maintained the shuttle of exchange between Spain and America, either on their own account, or with the aid of the merchant vessels which they convoyed. All these rules, designed to assure the strict application of the colonial trade monopoly, hampered the development of commerce and the mercantile marine.

At least this American market might have been used to further the growth of Spanish markets. But nothing of the kind was done. The merchants of Seville, who, by arrangement with the State, provided for the needs of the colonies and had secured a monopoly in supplying them, were still in Philip II's time accepting, in exchange for the manufactured goods which they sent them, indigo, sugar, tanned hides, tobacco, cocoa, bark, and " a quantity of other articles of Peru and New Spain which were sought after in all the markets of Europe ". But the Spanish importers tended more and more to require payment in precious metals. Gold and silver were the merchandise which attracted them most, and in the end the only merchandise which attracted them at all.

Spanish commerce was hard hit as a result. It lost a part, perhaps the most lucrative part in a declining volume of trade, of its exports to other European countries. The steady flow of silver, after the discovery of the mines of Potosi and the treatment of ore with mercury, was still more harmful to national production. There developed a situation, paradoxical only in appearance, in which Spain, far from being capable of supplying this external market that she had jealously reserved as a monopoly for herself, ceased to supply even her own needs.

It is a phenomenon common to all times that gold and silver, when they are in superabundance, lose their purchasing power, and that food and commodities become dearer in proportion. High cost of living is a function of low cost of currency. The cost of labour and raw materials closed many a Spanish workshop.

The neighbouring countries, which were poorer and produced more cheaply, finished off the ruin of Spanish manufacture. The Genoese especially, who had secured payment in the form of commercial privileges for the loans which they had granted to Charles V, threw quantities of merchandise on the Spanish market. The manufacturers of Cuenca, Segovia, and Toledo, unable to withstand this competition, ceased to supply America, to which they had been the principal providers. The monopolists of Seville were obliged to buy outside Spain the manufactured goods which they sent to the New World. They were reduced to being no more than shipping-agents for foreign merchants. The gold and silver which they received from overseas largely slipped out of their hands and passed across the land frontiers. The prosperity which Donato mentions, if it was ever as real as he believed, diminished and even disappeared (6).

The Cortes of Castile was especially concerned about the high cost of living. In order to re-establish the former purchasing power of the currency, the Cortes proposed at one time prohibiting the export of Spanish products to America, and at another time authorizing the import of foreign products into Spain : different means tending towards the same end, which in the first case was that of preventing prices from rising, and in the second case forcing them to fall. The heroic remedy, which did not occur to anybody, would have been to restrict the output of the mines.

The embargo on the exportation outside the Kingdom of Spain of crops or cattle, cloth, carded or spun wool, and crude or manufactured silk, and the enactment which imposed the death penalty on Spanish manufacturers who sold leather goods of any kind to France or elsewhere, were as detrimental to agriculture as they were to industry. Even inside the peninsula, restrictions of all kinds prevented the free circulation of products of the soil and of labour. The Basque provinces and the Kingdom of Aragon were regarded as foreign countries and defended themselves behind customs barriers.

It is true that the *bandoleros* remedied the abuses of protectionism. These smugglers and brigands, precursors of free trade without knowing it, were popular with the people and highly esteemed by them. Cervantes was not far from regarding the *bandoleros* as a kind of knights-errant, more useful and less ridiculous than Don Quixote. The Barcelonese, who gave an enthusiastic reception to Cervantes's hero, declared themselves great friends of Roque Guinart, a leader of *bandoleros*. Even between the different States of the Crown of Castile there was nothing analogous with what some centuries later was called a *Zollverein*.

With the resources which he had at his disposal, Philip II, if he had renounced his ambition of laying down the law to the world, could have turned the Spanish tracks into roads and canalized the Spanish rivers, not one of which was navigable, with the exception of the Guadalquivir from its mouth as far up as Seville—and even in this case the port of the Indies had to be removed first to San Lucar and then to Cadiz, outside the estuary. But the King could find no money except for his wars and his works of magnificence, such as the Escorial.

It was a great event, in which policy played its part, when, in 1581, after the union of Portugal and Castile, Philip commissioned an Italian engineer, Antonelli, to improve the course of the Tagus. In 1588 seven large boats descended the river from Toledo to Lisbon in a fortnight. But Antonelli died, and his plan of joining the Tagus to the Douro by way of the Manzanares and the Jaranne did not survive him. Perhaps it would have been abandoned in any case, through Philip's lack of money or his lack of zeal for undertakings without glory.

When Philip planted twenty thousand trees at Aranjuez, it was to build Armadas, not to encourage agriculture. One of the scourges of agriculture was the Mesta. This was a powerful association of big sheep-breeders, organized for centuries past for the purpose of controlling the migration of the flocks, which went up from the plains of Castile to the mountains of Galicia and Leon in summer, and came down again at the beginning of the cold weather. Everywhere the animals went, they turned aside right and left from the road, knocked down the farmers' fences, grazed on young shoots and even tore them up by the roots. Out of respect for vested interests, or in order to protect one of the sources of Spanish wealth, Philip refused to allow landowners to protect their property by means of hedges and ditches.

But, in order to keep the towns supplied with corn, Philip did not hesitate to prohibit the peasant-farmer " from kneading himself

350

the bread to supply his own needs ", and this under penalties, severe enough in any case, which at the third offence might go so far as banishment for life and confiscation of property. The measure, which did not do the townsmen much good, did the countrymen so much harm that, in 1594, it was found necessary to allow those who grew corn to keep half of it for their own consumption.

It was also on the productive classes that the burden of taxes (*pechos*) weighed most heavily. The number of persons exempt from taxes was considerable. Let us grant that the earlier Sovereigns may not have liked to reduce the hidalgos who had helped them to reconquer Spain, or their descendants, to the condition of being taxable and workable at their lord's discretion. But these Sovereigns also granted the same dispensation to retainers and favourites, or, through need of money, sold it to rich men, former subjects of the Moors, who had been won back with the soil and had never fought in their lives.

The nobility, of old or recent origin, apart from this precious privilege, could not have their houses, horses, mules or arms distrained upon for debt ; nor could they be put to the torture, except for the crime of *lèse-majesté* Divine and human.

We can understand, therefore, that *hidalguía* was a condition much sought after. Many *pecheros* petitioned to obtain it. Merchants who had made their fortunes secured its privileges in a roundabout way. They constituted a *majorat*, an indivisible property which escaped taxation, in favour of one of their children (7).

The census of 1541 estimated the number of *pecheros* in Castile at 781,642, and the number of hidalgos at 111,158. We must obviously interpret these figures as meaning households, not heads. If we multiply them by four, as is usual, we arrive at 3,126,568 taxable persons, and 446,632 exempt, in all 3,573,200 souls. With the increase in the sales of *hidalguía* under Philip II, the proportion of taxable to non-taxable, which in 1541 had been seven to one, was altered to the detriment of the treasury and the taxable.

The clergy also were exempt from taxation, though they contributed by so-called free gifts, or helped the needs of the State indirectly through sales under the Bull of the *Cruzada* and the surrender of the *escusado*. But the piety of the faithful indemnified the clergy largely for sacrifices which in any case were not in proportion to their revenues. In 1563 the Cortes held in Madrid—following the example of those held in Valladolid in 1522 and 1523 and in Madrid in 1534—denounced the quantity of properties in mortmain which had fallen into the hands of " the churches and the monasteries through donations, sales, heritages and successions ", involving a crushing burden on other owners.

The Cortes petitioned the King to instruct his councillors, pending the assent of Rome being obtained, to order the churches, cathedrals, colleges, and monasteries of religious not to buy landed property, and, if they had acquired it in any way, to sell it within a year ; if they failed to do so, the justices were immediately to tax the said property, and the Council was to be at liberty to sell it to anybody who chose to buy it. But to this petition Philip replied that it was not desirable to introduce innovations into such matters or to restrain donations and increments in which, he felt, conscience probably played a part.

The monasteries and convents, sanctuaries of the ardent piety of the period, and sometimes carefree refuges for idleness, were populous with men and women, and Spain was depopulated. The wars in Europe, the lure of adventure in America, the temptations of glory and gain, added to contempt for the pleasures of this world and passion for those of the next, emptied the fields and the towns. The population of Spain, which was about ten million souls at the time of Philip's accession (8), had fallen by 1594 to 8,206,791.

The Cortes perceived the evil, but it does not appear to have had the courage to advise Philip to adopt the right remedy. Though it had dared to tell Charles V that his endless wars were ruining the country, it did not show itself so bold in the case of his son. These States-General of the Castilian monarchy, reduced to the thirty-six procuradores of the towns, possessed no authority. The King summoned them, because he was a traditionalist by temperament, but it was a mere matter of form. Never was the Cortes assembled so often as during his reign, and never was less account taken of its views. Its sessions lasted several years. The Cortes of 1575 sat until 1578, that of 1579 until 1582, that of 1588 until 1592, and that of 1593 until 1598.

The Cortes suffered, like all other institutions, from the length of time that Philip took about everything. He was no more respectful of its advice on that account. One may ask what reason Philip had for keeping the assembly sitting when he paid so little attention to it. To its complaints, to its requests, he replied most frequently in an evasive way : " We shall order it to be looked into and see what it is expedient to decide and decree." Most of Philip's promises were neither more definite nor more compromising. It was rarely that he gave satisfaction to the grievances of the nation ; but it was rarely also that he flatly rejected any proposal for reform. Philip's refusals, like his commitments, were wrapped up in one of those

352

PHILIP II.
From a portrait by Pantoja de la Cruz in the Escorial

vague, indeterminable formulæ which permitted him to postpone and do nothing. " We shall see."

There was, however, one point on which the Cortes and the King were in agreement. When the Cortes asked for sumptuary laws and the prohibition of articles of luxury manufactured abroad, Philip hastened to subscribe to its proposals. In economic matters he and it had the same prejudices. The Cortes conscientiously sought a remedy for financial embarrassment and the distress of the nation in the repression of luxury and other expedients of the same kind.

With much better reason the Cortes attacked the extension of property held in mortmain, but in this case without success. The Church offered the State a field so easily capable of being exploited under the form of tithe, forced loans, the *Cruzada* and the *escusado*, that Philip, like Charles V, had no interest in restricting this field.

Nevertheless, timid though it was, the Cortes accentuated its remonstrances as Philip's reign went on and the population became more and more exhausted. As early as 1570 the Cortes prayed the King to consult it about the imposition of taxes. In 1580 it opposed the appointment of more civil servants. At the time of the annexation of Portugal, in the same year, it denounced the excesses committed by the troops on their march. It complained in 1585 of the duration of its sessions and the slowness of the King in satisfying its wishes, whenever Philip did happen to satisfy them.

The Cortes protested sharply this time, and again in 1588, against the imposition of new taxes without its consent. Tired of sitting for four years, from 1588 to 1592, without any result, it recommended the King to abstain from deciding everything for himself. The last Cortes of Philip's reign, which assembled in 1593 and sat until 1598, without claiming the right to participate in the legislative power, begged that it might be consulted about the laws and pragmatic sanctions in course of preparation, so that it might express its views. It requested, incidentally, the same right for the Council of State. To all these requests came Philip's eternal reply : " We shall see."

Philip's need of money dominated everything. There was no vested interest whatever, there was no tradition whatever, which could prevail against this necessity of his. Philip's Government extorted the utmost possible yield from agreed taxes, and established new taxes on its own authority. In vain the Cortes protested against this abuse. The King contented himself with replying that he would see, and went on with the illegal levying of taxes just the same.

Philip mortgaged and burdened the future to procure himself the resources necessary for the present. His sale of patents of nobility, by multiplying the number of privileged persons, increased the load on the *pecheros* more and more. No scruple stopped the hard-up monarch ; Philip acted as though he was absolute master of the fortunes of his subjects. The *Casa de Contratación* of Seville bonded the gold and silver which the merchants obtained from America in its warehouses. On occasion Philip drew upon this reserve, helped himself to what he found there, and regarded himself as cleared by paying interest on an equivalent sum.

As happens at all such periods of deficit, people with advice to give away flocked to Madrid. Everybody had a remedy to offer. The Council of the *Hacienda* was inundated with memoranda whose authors, known and unknown, posed as saviours of the State. Adepts of alchemy talked about transmuting copper and the basest of metals into gold. These dreams found some credit with the King. Philip spent some thousands of ducats on ridiculous experiments.

Other outsiders, more modest—and less listened to—proposed a recasting of taxation, and others again suggested means of squeezing the taxpayer without making him squeal too much. It was from the Church that Simon Pedro Abril contemplated seeking the funds necessary for the repayment of the debt. To leave bishoprics and other benefices vacant for a certain length of time, on the death of the existing incumbents, would suffice to assure the King an annual revenue of a million ducats, which could be devoted to amortization.

These project-mongers, these " *arbitristas* ", as they were called, were far from being regarded favourably by the nation. It distrusted them as auxiliaries of the treasury. It watched the threat of new taxes looming up over the horizon with alarm, for it had given up hoping for any relief. He was not, perhaps, entirely a figment of the imagination, that *arbitrista* of whom Cervantes speaks, who contemplated introducing one day of fasting a month, together with a gift to the treasury of all the savings made at the expense of everybody's stomach.

Philip II may have seemed, thanks to the mines of America, to be the richest monarch in Christendom ; but all this gold melted in his hands. His compromised credit was headed towards bankruptcy. He took a final step. Under pretext that his creditors refused to make him any fresh advances and were exacting enormous interest from him, he declared himself, on November 20th, 1596, obliged to suspend the service of all the mortgages which he had granted on different departments of the public revenues. " The money which was derived from them would be put in his own coffers."

This measure, which deprived the merchants, from whom the King had borrowed vast sums, of their interest and even of their security, caused profound perturbation in the financial centres of

Spain, Italy and Germany. Many people were ruined ; but Philip soon found that one cannot damage public credit with impunity. When his coffers were once more empty, he had to resign himself to recalling the bankers and submitting to their onerous terms. The Genoese showed themselves particularly exacting ; it was only at the price of numerous concessions that they consented to lend Philip eight millions more at a high rate of interest.

In order to fulfil these ruinous commitments of his, Philip was obliged to raise the scale of taxation still higher. He was even reduced to soliciting from door to door a free gift of eight millions, which a contemporary historian justly describes as " alms ".

Realistic literature, like official documents, reveals in a glaring light the spectacle of a people who could not always eat when they were hungry. Distress was widespread at every level of the social scale, among the hidalgos no less than among the lower orders of society. Proverbs, in their brutal wisdom, tell us clearly enough how the Spanish people, glutted with greatness and glory, suffered from lack of nourishment.

What painful calculations are betrayed by this vulgar comparison : " There are more days than sausages " ; and what anxieties are revealed by the cynical statement : " The day's work, but not the daily bread " ! We may note that in *Don Quixote*—and there is no mockery about it—Sancho Panza speaks of acorns as a usual, and even pleasant, article of diet, so much so that his wife, wishing to make the duchess, their protectress, " an agreeable present ", sends her several dozen acorns carefully picked. All hail to the nourishing oak !

Philip's Government exhausted the substance of the nation to its very marrow. War and poverty mowed down nearly two million souls. The ungrateful soil of Spain needed men. For lack of workers, its desert areas spread. A journey in Spain presented all the chances, the risks and the inconveniences of an exploring expedition. Inns were rare, and no comfort was to be found in them. One had to carry provisions, and often camp in the open air. Taxes, customs duties, the difficulties of communication and the struggle for the empire of the world had destroyed the country's wealth.

Accordingly Philip found malcontents, if not opponents, even in Castile, the most domesticated, but also the most exploited, kingdom of his monarchy. The Cardinal Archbishop of Seville, advised by his confessors, informed the King of the unpleasant things that his subjects had to say about him. To this Philip retorted that " since they had their tongues free, it was right that they should have their hands tied ".

355

There were, indeed, at the time of the trouble in Aragon, some meetings in the city of Avila of hidalgos, who in speech and song advertised the discontent, even of persons exempt from taxes, with Philip's voluntary, or involuntary, loan of eight millions. The King dispatched a mayor of the Household and Court, Pareja, who arrested some of these privileged persons and, with great ceremony, executed their leader, Don Diego de Bracamonte, " a caballero of illustrious family and zealous for the public good (9) ".

But Philip, after an inquiry carried out by Cabrera de Cordoba —later Philip III's historiographer—condemned this excess of rigour. He conferred military orders on two of the brothers of the executed man, reversed the confiscation of his property, and disgraced the zealous executioner, who died of the shame of his disgrace. The King, who all his life long was a man with a taste for mystery, undoubtedly found it tactless that the resistance of the privileged classes to fiscal demands should be broadcast to public opinion in this way.

The Cortes itself emphasized the impoverishment of the people in its remonstrances during the closing years of Philip's reign. " How can one engage in commerce," the *procuradores* protested in 1594, " when one is forced to pay three hundred ducats in taxes on a capital of a thousand ducats ? . . . In the regions where 30,000 *arrobes* of worsted were formerly worked, scarcely 6,000 are now consumed. (The *arrobe* was a measure of twenty-five pounds weight.) It results from this, as well as from the tax imposed on wool, that the number of flocks is also diminishing. Agriculture and the raising of cattle, industry and commerce are ruined ; there is now not one region of the kingdom which does not lack inhabitants ; any number of houses closed and uninhabited are to be seen ; *in short, the kingdom is perishing*."

This was the lamentable end of a great reign, the consequence of an effort disproportionate with the resources of the country. " Spain, a fountain of pride in a valley of wretchedness "—this phrase of an English observer well sums up the ambitions, and the results, of Philip II's policy.

The last days of Philip II were clouded. Illness overwhelmed him—but how much more anxiety about the future ! He thought of his poor heir, the Infante Philip, to whom he was bequeathing his immense States ; and, father though he was, he could cherish no illusions about his son's intellectual capacity.

When Philip felt his end approaching, he had himself carried to the Escorial. It was a dreadful journey. His body was nothing but one great sore. It took him six days to cover seven leagues.

Philip showed himself a great Christian at the last. Despite his terrible suffering, he faced death bravely.   He insisted upon having his coffin placed beside his bed.   He had a crown of gold put on a skull.   It was his own future image that he wanted to have before his eyes ; it was the degradation of the flesh that he contemplated.

He desired that he might touch the scourge that his father, the Emperor, had used to discipline himself, which still bore the traces of a blood that was dear and precious to him.   He settled the order of the procession and the ceremony which were to be observed at his own burial.   Philip II died, on September 12th, 1598, with his eyes fixed on the Crucifix (10).

History has shown itself severe towards this Prince.   If Spaniards, at least until recent years, have made Philip an object of worship, most foreigners have reviled his despotism, his cruelty, his intolerance.   Few voices have been raised in his favour ; and tactless pleaders have done more harm than good to his cause.

How could it be otherwise ?   Philip had alienated the nations which, in the following centuries, fashioned and inspired public opinion : Holland, England, and France.   Every one of them had a grievance to avenge : Holland, her long martyrdom in the war of independence ;   England, a dreadful assault on her religious liberties ;   France, disorders in which her prosperity and her greatness all but foundered.

In proportion as they developed outside his clutches, and Spain declined under the destructive principles of his policy, these nations realized ever more clearly with what a burden Philip II's oppressive system had threatened their future.   Their hatred naturally went out against this man, who seemed to them the enemy of progress and the instrument of decadence.   They might, perhaps, have pardoned a conqueror who pushed them forward, even with sword in hand ; they could preserve only a hateful memory of a Sovereign who sought to imprison them by violence in the errors of the past.

On the fabric of facts, indignation and fear wrought a sombre woof.   The growth of a legend was favoured by the secrecy with which Philip II loved to surround all his actions.   The mysterious death of Montigny, for example, served, even more than the public murder of the Prince of Orange, to justify any possible suspicions of him.   Criminal causes were assigned to the most natural events : Don Carlos and Elizabeth of Valois were transformed into victims of jealousy and despotism.   Philip came to be regarded as a man without a heart or bowels of compassion, " whose smile and whose dagger were very close neighbours ".

But, at the same time as he became more hateful, Philip grew in the imagination of mankind.   It reached the point of representing him as a gigantic figure of darkness, a kind of genie of evil, released to stay the progress of religious freedom and political freedom. Philip personified all the vices, all the errors, all the cruelties. Hatred of him, rage against him, were concentrated into one supreme insult : " the Devil of the South ".

Philip II was neither so black, nor so great, as he has been painted. We must, of course, resist any temptation to rehabilitate him. He was intolerant ; he was cruel. His dissimulation repels us, his casuistry revolts us, his acts of vengeance, carried out in cold blood, make us shudder. One could more easily pardon furious outbursts of passion than those cold resentments of his.

But, in short, Philip II did his job as a king. If he had a false idea of his duties, he devoted all his time, all his labours, his whole life, to this mistaken idea of his. Philip kept always before his eyes the greatness of his country and of his race. He did not hesitate, in order to safeguard the future of his monarchy, to sacrifice his own son. If he exhausted his country, he assured it, for half a century, of preponderance in Europe, and, for much longer, of renown for grandeur and strength. How many countries have paid more dearly for a glory more ephemeral !

Still, Philip II was not a great king. He did not understand his own time. He did not even understand his own people. He imagined that he could rule a nation of soldiers from a desk in his study, and that he could succeed in mastering Europe by chaining her to the doctrines of the past. He was a man who fussed with documents, incapable of dominating a century which was as prompt in action as it was in thought.

BIBLIOGRAPHY AND NOTES

A BRIEF BIBLIOGRAPHY

The Bibliography of Philip II, the son and heir of Charles V, is that of the second half, and even a little more, of the history of Christendom in the sixteenth century. Accordingly public and personal archives, and also collections in private hands, still contain an enormous mass of unpublished material; but they have been sufficiently explored, and in part exploited, to give us a general view of the personalities and the events of his reign. Nevertheless, despite all this ransacking and publication, the character of the King remains enigmatic, and presents itself as admirable material for defendants and prosecutors.

Even among printed sources and documents, one must resign himself to making a choice.

The *Actas de las Cortes de Castilla*, publication of which was begun by the Spanish Chamber of Deputies in 1877, embrace in their thirteen first volumes the whole reign of Philip II from 1563 onwards.

In the great *Colección de Documentos inéditos para la historia de España* (still in course of publication), out of upwards of a hundred volumes already published many refer to the reign of Philip II. Volume XXX contains a table of contents of the preceding volumes.

I may specially mention:

The *Correspondencia del duque de Alba con Felipe II y otros personajes sobre la conquista de Portugal en 1580*, Vol. 32.

The *Correspondencia de Felipe II con sus Embajadores en la Corte de Inglaterra* (1558–84), Vols. 87, 89, 90, 91, 92.

The *Correspondencia de los principes de Alemania con Felipe II y de los Embajadores de Este en la Corte de Viena* (1556–98), Vols. 98, 101, 103, 110.

Weiss, *Papiers d'Etat du Cardinal Granvelle*, 1841–2, 9 vols. (*Collection des Documents inédits relatifs à l'Histoire de France.*)

Poullet and Piot, *Correspondance du Cardinal de Granvelle faisant suite aux Papiers d'Etat*, published by the Belgian Government in the *Collection des Chroniques belges inédites*, Brussels, 1877–96, 12 vols.

Gachard, *Précis de la Correspondance de Philippe II sur les affaires des Pays-Bas*, Brussels, 1848–79, 5 vols.

Groen van Prinsterer, *Archives et Correspondance inédites de la Maison de Nassau*, 1st series (1552–84), 8 vols., Leyden, 1841–7; 2nd series (1584–1688), 5 vols., Utrecht, 1857–61.

Kervyn de Lettenhove, *Relations politiques des Pays-Bas et de l'Angleterre sous Philippe II* (1555–79), 11 vols., 1882–1900.

Stevenson, Crosby and Butler, *Calendar of State Papers, Foreign Series, of the Reign of Elizabeth* (1558–82), 16 vols., in course of publication, 1863–1910.

H. de la Ferrière and Baguenault de Puchesse, *Lettres de Catherine de Médicis*, 10 vols. and a supplement, 1880–1909 (*Coll. Doc. inédits*).

Berger de Xivrey and Guadet, *Lettres missives de Henri IV*, 9 vols., 1843–72 (*Coll. Doc. inédits*).

On the manuscript dispatches of the Spanish ambassadors in France and the dispatches of the French ambassadors in Spain, which are to be found in Paris, in the Archives Nationales and the Bibliothèque Nationale respectively, consult Forneron, *Histoire de Philippe II*, Vol. I, pp. 395–7. I may mention also :

Dépêches de Sebastien de l'Aubespine, ambassador of France in Spain under Philip II, *Revue d'Histoire diplomatique*, XIII and XIV, 1899–1900.

L'Abbé Douais (afterwards Bishop of Beauvais), *Dépêches de M. de Fourquevaux, ambassadeur du roi Charles IX en Espagne* (1565–72), 3 vols., 1896–1904.

Muller and Diegerick, *Documents concernant les relations entre le duc d'Anjou et les Pays-Bas* (1576–84), The Hague and Amsterdam, 5 vols., 1889–99.

Teulet, *Relations politique de la France et de l'Espagne avec l'Ecosse au XVIᵉ siècle*, 5 vols., Paris, 1862.

Gachard, *Relations des Ambassadeurs vénitiens sur Charles-Quint et Philippe II*, Brussels, 1855.

Alberi, *Relazioni degli ambasciatori veneti al Senato*, 15 vols., 1839–63.

Du Mont, *Corps universel diplomatique du droit des Gens*, Amsterdam and The Hague, 8 vols., 1726–31.

The works of certain contemporaries have a documentary value :

Diego de Mendoza, *La guerra de Granada*, Madrid, Rioadenagra.

Alfred Morel-Fatio, *L'Espagne au XVIᵉ et au XVIIᵉ siècles, Documents historiques et littéraires*, Heilbronn, Paris, Madrid, 1878.

Antonio Pérez, *Las Obras y Relaciones*, Geneva, 1644.

Antonio de Herrera, *Historia general del Mundo de XLVI años del tiempo de Felipe II*, Madrid, 3 vols., 1601–12.

Luis Cabrera de Cordoba (historiographer of Philip III), *Historia de Felipe II* (edn. " published by royal command "), Madrid, 4 vols., 1876–7.

Books at Second Hand.—One may ignore the imaginative historians Leti and Watson. Bratli has published a good, though sometimes tendencious, biliographical study on Philip II : Copenhagen, 1902, of which a French translation still more complete has appeared, Paris, 1912. After him, I may mention some other works, which are important or have appeared since :

Don Modesto La Fuente, *Historia general de España*, Vols. IX, X, XI, Barcelona, 1889.

Don Vicente de la Fuente, *Historia eclesiástica de España*, Vol. V, Madrid, 1875.

W. Prescott, *History of the Reign of Philip the Second, King of Spain*, London, 1859, 3 vols. (uncompleted).

Forneron, *Histoire de Philippe II*, Paris, 4 vols., 1881–2.

Martin A. S. Hume, *Philip II of Spain* (with a bibliography), London, 1897.

Gachard, *Don Carlos et Philippe II*, Brussels, 1863.

De Mouy, *Don Carlos*, Paris, 1863.

Marquis de Pidal, *Philippe II, Antonio Pérez, et le royaume d'Aragon* (translated from the Spanish by Magnabal), Paris, 2 vols., 1866.

Mignet, *Antonio Pérez et Philippe II*, 2nd edn., Paris, 1866.

Gaspar Muro, *La Princess d'Eboli* (translated from the Spanish by Weil), Paris, 1878.

Philippson, *Ein ministerium unter Philipp II, Kardinal Granvella am Spanischen Hofe* (1579–86), Berlin, 1895.

Lothrop Motley, *The Rise of the Dutch Republic*, London, 1859.

Th. Juste, *Histoire du soulèvement des Pays-Bas sous Philippe II*, Paris, undated.

Kervyn de Lettenhove, *Les Huguenots et les Gueux*, Bruges, 6 vols., 1883–5.

Froude, *History of England, from the fall of Wolsey to the defeat of the Spanish Armada*, London, 12 vols., 1887.

Grammont, *Histoire d'Alger sous la domination turque* (1515–1830), Paris, 1887.

Jean H. Mariéjol, *Catherine de Médicis*, 3rd edn., 1922 ; by the same, *Marguerite de Valois*, 1928 (English translation, *A Daughter of the Medicis*, Harper & Brothers, New York and London, 1929).

De Törne, D. *Juan d'Autriche et le projet de conquête de l'Angleterre*, Paris, 1928.

Ranke, *L'Espagne sous Charles Quint, Philippe II et Philippe III* (translated from the German by Haiber), Paris, 1873.

Weiss, *L'Espagne depuis le règne de Philippe II jusqu' à l'avènement des Bourbons*, Paris, 2 vols., 1844.

Gounon-Loubens, *Essai sur l'administration de la Castille*, Paris, 1860.

L. Febvre, *Philippe II et la Franche-Comté, La Crise de 1569. Etude d'histoire politique, religieuse, et sociale*, Paris, 1911.

Menéndez Pelayo, *Historia de los Heterodoxos españoles*, Madrid, 1880.

R. Altamira y Crevea, *Historia de España y de la civilización española*, Barcelona, Vol. III, 1906.

Ticknor, *History of Spanish Literature* (translated from the English by Magnabal), Vols. II and III, Paris, 1870–2.

Fitz-Maurice Kelly, *History of Spanish Literature* (French translation), revised and augmented edn., Paris, 1913.

Max Rooses, *Christophe Plantin, Imprimeur Anversois*, Antwerp, 1882.

André Michel, *Histoire générale de l'art* (in course of publication), Vol. IV, 2nd part, Paris, 1911 ; Vol. V, 2nd part, 1913.

Paul Lefort, *Le peinture espagnole*, Paris.

Hymans, *Antonio Moro, son œuvre et son temps*, Brussels, 1910.

Maurice Barrès and Paul Lafond, *Le Greco*, Paris, 1911.

Camille Mauclair, *L'âpre et splendide Espagne*, Paris, 1931.

Combarieu, *Histoire de la Musique*, Paris, 3 vols., 1913–19.

Henri Collet, *Le Mysticisme musical espagnol au XVI⁶ siècle*, Paris, 1913.

Louis Bertrand, *Philippe II à l'Escorial*, Paris, 1929.

Jean Cassou, *La vie de Philippe II*, Paris, 1927.

David Loth, *Philip II of Spain*, New York, 1932.

Other works will be found mentioned in the notes.

NOTES

CHAPTER I

(1) Regarding Philip's childhood, see D. Modesto La Fuente, *Historia de España*, IX, p. 82, note, and p. 83, note. In connection with Villalobos, see Mariéjol, *L'Espagne sous Ferdinand et Isabelle*, p. 239. The quotations from Varro occur in Fragments of the Works of M. Terentius Varro, entitled *Logistorici Hebdomades*, edited by Ch. Chappuis, Paris, 1868, pp. 11 and 12. See also Sepulveda, *De Caroli Quinti Gestis*, Opera, 1780, II, p. 189. Prescott, I, p. 51, in the French translation by Renson and Ithier, 1860. D. Vicente de la Fuente, *Historia Eclesiástica*, V, p. 221. Gachard, *Relations des Ambassadeurs vénitiens sur Charles-Quint et Philippe II*, Brussels, 1885, p. 42, note. Dr. W. Maurenbrecher, *Die Lehrjahre Philipp' II von Spanien*, Historisches Taschenbuch, Sechste Folge, Zweiter Jahrgang, Leipzig, 1883, pp. 271–346. For Charles V's Augsburg " Instructions " to Philip, January 18th, 1548, see text and translation in *Papiers d'Etat du Cardinal Granvelle*, III, pp. 267 *et seq.*

(2) Regarding Philip's relations with Doña Isabel Osorio, see Cabrera, *Historia de Felipe el Prudente*, Madrid, 1576–7, III, p. 367, and Du Mont, *Corps Diplomatique*, V, Part I, p. 390.

(3) This litter was the same as the *lettica* which the good Sylvestre Bonnard records that he used from Monte Allegro to Girgenti (Sicily) as late as November 30th, 1859 : " a carriage without wheels, or, if you like, a litter, a chair carried by two mules, one in front and the other behind. The use of it is very old." (Anatole France, *Le Crime de Sylvestre Bonnard*, Calmann-Levy, p. 65.)

(4) In connection with Charles V's plans in Genoa, Doria's opposition to them, and Philip's passage through Genoa, see Chap. XVI of Edouard Petit's *André Doria*, Paris, 1887.

(5) Granvelle, *Papiers d'Etat*, IV, p. 112. Regarding Philip's being unhorsed, see Prescott, I, p. 69. For his letter to Charles V about his marriage to Mary Tudor, see Mignet, *Charles-Quint*, p. 76.

(6) Froude, V, pp. 312 and 355.

(7) La Fuente, IX, p. 106, note 1.

(8) Froude, V, p. 534. In connection with the Marck conference, see Pierre de Vaissière's chapter in his monograph on Charles de Marillac. See also Prescott, I, pp. 135–6, and Froude, V, pp. 478 and 535, note, regarding Philip in England.

CHAPTER II

(1) Gachard, *Relations des Ambassadeurs vénitiens*, pp. 50–1 (cf. 55–60), and 124–5.

(2) Duruy, *Le Cardinal Carafa*, p. 81.

(3) Prescott, p. 194, note 3.

(4) La Fuente, IX, pp. 178–9. See also La Fuente, p. 117, regarding the Pope's summons to Philip.

(5) Froude, *History of England*, VI, pp. 44–5. See Froude also, pp. 69–70, for the surrender of Calais. For the battle of Gravelines, see Prescott, I, p. 251.

(6) Record of the outrages committed by the English, Flemish, Spanish and

German soldiers at Saint Quentin, according to a document in the Escorial quoted by La Fuente, IX, p. 158.

(7) Gachard, *Relations des Ambassadeurs vénitiens*, pp. 278 and 280.

(8) *Les Papiers d'Etat du Cardinal Granvelle*, V, pp. 168–584 (documents relating to the peace of Cateau-Cambrésis). See also De Crue, *Anne duc de Montmorency*, Paris, 1889, p. 220 ; cf. de Ruble, *Le Traité de Cateau-Cambrésis*, p. 32, and Romier, *Les Origines des Guerres de Religion*, II, Chap. I.

(9) Froude, VI, p. 176. See Froude also for Philip's dispatch to Count de Feria, p. 143.

(10) *Commentaires de Blaise de Montluc*, edited by de Ruble, II, p. 318.

CHAPTER III

(1) De Ruble, *Le Traité de Cateau-Cambrésis*, pp. 244–5. In connection with the date, see note 4, p. 214.

(2) Mariéjol, *Ferdinand et Isabelle*, pp. 188–94.

(3) " Relation " of Leonardo Donato, 1573, in Appendix to IV, *Historia de Felipe II*, by Cabrera, p. 448.

(4) Du Mont, *Corps Diplomatique*, V, Part I, pp. 333–5. See Du Mont also in connection with the cession of Sienna, pp. 10–11.

(5) Febvre, *Philippe II et la Franche-Comté*, p. 58.

(6) Mariéjol, *Ferdinand et Isabelle*, pp. 104–5. See also Lavisse and Rambaud, *Histoire générale*, V, p. 973.

(7) Gams, *Series episcoporum quotquot innotuerunt, India occidentalis*. G. González Davila, *Teatro de las Grandezas de la villa de Mexico*, Madrid, 1623, p. 471, reckons six archbishops and thirty-two bishoprics, seventy thousand parishes, five hundred monasteries, and more than thirty thousand religious ; but he was writing a quarter of a century after the death of Philip II, and the figures of churches and monks at the end of the sixteenth century must probably be reduced. Regarding the transportation of negroes, see Vicente de la Fuente, *Historia Eclesiástica*, V, p. 316.

(8) Albert Girard, *La rivalité commerciale et maritime entre Seville et Cadix*, Paris, 1932. In connection with the organization of a protective armada, see Haring, *Trade between Spain and the Indies at the time of the Habsburgs*, pp. 68–71.

(9) " Relation " by Morosini, Venetian ambassador (1578–91), published in Appendix to Cabrera, IV, p. 491.

(10) Weiss, pp. 104, 198, and 205. The Viceroy of Valencia resided in the towns of Valencia, Cagliari (Sardinia), and Palma (Balearics). Cf. *Diario de Camillo Borghese* (1594), published by A. Morel-Fatio, *L'Espagne au XVIe and XVIIe siècles*, 1878, pp. 180–7. Regarding the Council of War, see Ranke, pp. 163–4.

(11) Gachard, " Relation " of Antonio Tiepolo, 1567, p. 150. For Michael Suriano's " Relation ", see Gachard, *Correspondance*, p. 130. For Philip's statement to Pérez, see *Las Obras y Relaciones de Antonio Pérez*, ed. of 1631, pp. 449–50, quoted by Gachard, *Correspondance de Philippe II sur les affaires des Pays-Bas*, I, Intro., pp. liv–lv, Brussels, 1848.

(12) Vicente de la Fuente, V, pp. 79–80 and 139. Cf. Mariéjol, *Ferdinand et Isabelle*, p. 293. For Morosini's " Relation ", see Cabrera, Appendix, IV, p. 488.

(13) Antonio Rodriguez Villa, *Etiquetas de la Casa de Austria*. For the muster-

roll, see Gachard, pp. 251 *et seq.* For the contrasted expenditure of Ferdinand and Isabel, see Mariéjol, pp. 258–9.

(14) *Relación del Viaje hecho por Felipe II en 1585* . . . *escrita por Enrique Cock, notario apostólico y archero de la Guardia del Cuerpo Real*, edited by Morel Fatio anp Antonio Rodriguez Villa, Madrid, 1876, pp. 90–1. Cf. Morel Fatio, *Etudes sur Espagne*, 1st series, pp. 263–4.

(15) De Ruble, *Le Traité de Cateau-Cambrésis*, pp. 258–61, 264 *et seq.* (from an anonymous and unpublished account, preserved in Vol. 4815 of the French archives), 249, 269–70 and the references, 273, 276–9.

(16) Gachard, *Don Carlos*, pp. 242, note 4, and 243, note.

CHAPTER IV

(1) Mariéjol, *Ferdinand et Isabelle*, p. 48. See also Vicente de la Fuente, V, pp. 239–41, 245 and 259, and 137. Modesto La Fuente, IX, pp. 137 and 193.

(2) Regnier de la Planche, *De L'Etat de la France sous François II*, Panthéon littéraire edn., p. 219.

(3) Philippson, *Le Contre-Réforme*, p. 203.

(4) Modesto La Fuente, p. 199.

(5) Monchicourt, *L'expédition espagnole de 1560 contre l'Île de Djerba*, Paris, 1913 (thesis), pp. 88–9, 91–3, 107–8, 110, 130–2, 134–5. Cf. Gramont, *Histoire d'Alger*, p. 93, who gives the Spanish losses as ten thousand, not fifteen thousand, as Monchicourt says.

(6) Vertet, *Histoire des chevaliers hospétaliers de Saint-Jean de Jerusalem, aujourd'hui les Chevaliers de Malte*, Paris, 1726, III, map and plan of Malta ; the siege, pp. 445–92, and IV, 1–79. Calderon de la Barca, *Gloriosa defensa de Malta*, Madrid, 1796.

(7) Vicente de la Fuente, V, p. 145. For Mondéjar, see Modesto La Fuente, pp. 289–90, and 290, note. The Captain-General, Don Iñigo de Mendoza, was Count of Tendilla, but on the death of his father, the Marquis of Mondéjar, President of the Council of Castile, which occurred about this time, he assumed his title.

(8) Mariéjol, Lavisse and Rambaud's *Histoire générale*, V, Part II, pp. 57–8. See also pp. 61–2.

CHAPTER V

(1) Groen van Prinsterer, *Archives de la Maison de Nassau*, 2nd edn., p. 123. In connection with the Nassaus, pp. 59–69, and in connection with William, p. 195. See also p. 107.

(2) Gachard, *Relations*, pp. 82 and 87.

(3) In connection with the inauguration of the Inquisition and the Edicts, see Charles Paillard, *Considérations sur les causes générales des troubles des Pays-Bas au XVIᵉ siècle*, Brussels, 1874, pp. 120–7.

(4) Pontus Payen, *Memóires*, edited by Henne, p. 6.

(5) Mariéjol, *Catherine de Médicis*, pp. 108, note 4 (October 30th, 1561), and 108, note 5 (Elizabeth's reply to a letter from her mother, July, 1561). On the interpretation of the Edicts, see pp. 137–40.

(6) In connection with this meeting, see the texts, which seem conclusive, in Mariéjol, *Catherine de Médicis*, pp. 152–4.

(7) Eugenio Ruidiaz y Caravia, *La Florida y su conquista por Pedro Menéndez de Avilés*, Madrid, 1893, 2 vols. Ch. de la Roncière, *La Floride française*, Paris, 1928. The agreement with Menéndez is quoted in Gaffarel, *La Floride française*, Paris, 1876, pp. 162–3. See also *Catherine de Médicis*, p. 157 and note 4.

(8) Lothrop Motley, pp. 161 and 267. See also La Fuente, IX, pp. 175–6.

(9) Correspondence between the King and the Regent of the Low Countries relating to the *tercios*, in Paillard, *Considérations*, pp. 16–17.

(10) Gachard, *Correspondance de Philippe II*, I, Intro., pp. xciii–ci ; I, pp. 195, 202, 207, 202–3 (letter from Margaret of June 14th, 1562). For the marriage of William of Orange and Anne of Saxony, see Groen van Prinsterer, I, p. 68.

(11) Pontus Payen, *Mémoires*, I, pp. 16 and 70–1. For Gachard's discovery of the King's secret letter to Granvelle, see *Correspondance*, I, Intro., p. clxxxv ; and for Titelmans's letter to Margaret of Parma (Ypres, November 4th, 1561), II, p. 484. See also Motley, I, p. 413, of Guizot's translation.

(12) Groen van Prinsterer, II, pp. 3–4. See also Gachard, *Correspondance*, I, pp. 346–7, and 362, and Intro., lcxxx, note.

(13) See Kervyn de Lettenhove, *Les Huguenots et les Gueux*, I, p. 330, in connection with the meeting at Bondues, near Tournai. For the letters between Philip and Margaret, see Gachard, *Correspondance*, I, pp. 443 and 446.

(14) Le Petit, quoted by Groen, II, p. 217.

CHAPTER VI

(1) Gachard, *Don Carlos*, pp. 362–3, quotes Strada and Cabrera ; but he does not himself believe in this discussion of October 26th or 29th, of which he could find no trace in the Archives of Simancas (I, Intro., pp. cli–clii). The division of opinion, however, is unquestionable.

(2) The Spanish document is to be found in *Colección de Documentos inéditos para la historia de España*, Vol. IV, quoted by La Fuente, IX, pp. 258–9. For John of Hornes's report, see Gachard, *Correspondance*, I, p. 565. Figures relating to military effectives, as well as to financial reckonings, should always be accepted with reserve.

For the letters, see Gachard, *Correspondance*, I, pp. 487 (letter from Philip II to the Grand Commander of Castile, Don Luis de Requesens, ambassador in Rome, November 26th, 1566) ; 386, Intro., cliv–clvi, 505, 446 (letter written from the Wood of Segovia to the ambassador in Rome, August 12th, 1566) ; 564, and II, p. 29 ; *Don Carlos*, pp. 405–6, 425, 428–9 (regarding the preparations for Philip's departure), and 407, note 3.

(3) Mariéjol, *Catherine de Médicis*, p. 158.

(4) It is usually stated that the great lords went to meet Alba, but on this point there is a piece of testimony to the contrary which cannot be regarded as suspect, that of Miguel de Mendivil, *contador* of artillery in the Duke's army, Gachard, *Correspondance*, I, p. 567 (letter to the King of August 29th, 1567). For Margaret's letters to Philip, see I, pp. 556 (letter of July 12th), 566, 567, and 570.

(5) Kervyn de Lettenhove, *Les Huguenots et les Gueux*, II, p. 52. Alba had multiplied his testimonies of affection for Hornes in an interview with his secretary, Alonso de Laloo, as Laloo wrote on August 17th to Montigny, Gachard, *Correspondance*, I, pp. 563–4.

(6) Mariéjol, *Catherine de Médicis*, p. 164. For the letters in connection with

Spanish aid to France, see Gachard, *Correspondance*, I, pp. 591 (letter from Alba to the King, October 26th, 1567) and 593 (letter from Philip to Alba, November 1st, 1567).

(7) Kervyn de Lettenhove, II, p. 120. See the text of the sentence on Egmont according to the Archives of Simancas, La Fuente, IX, pp. 271–2, note. In connection with the earlier proceedings of the Council of the Troubles, see Gachard, *Correspondance*, I, pp. 575–6 (letters to the King and Requesens, September 13th, 1567), and 584 ; II, 14–15, 16, note 1 ; 18 (letter from the King to Alba), 20, 22, 23, 27 (letter from the King to Chantonnay, his ambassador in Vienna ; also 7 and 14. See also La Fuente, IX, pp. 265 and 275. Easter in 1568 fell on April 18th.

(8) La Fuente, IX, p. 327. See also p. 275, and Kervyn de Lettenhove, II, p. 125.

(9) Gachard, *Correspondance*, II, p. 146. See also I, Intro., pp. cciv–ccv (cf. 392), 575 and 590 ; II, 23–4 and 29.

(10) *Documentos inéditos*, XLI, p. 146, quoted by Kervyn de Lettenhove, II, p. 386.

(11) Froude, IX, p. 158. See also VIII, p. 42, and IX, p. 114 ; and Gachard, *Correspondance*, II, pp. 163 (letter from Alba of December 1st, 1570) and 678.

(12) Kervyn de Lettenhove, II, p. 228. See also pp. 220 ; and Gachard, *Correspondance*, II, pp. 63 and 220–1.

(13) Gachard, *Correspondance*, II, p. 162. Regarding Fray Lorenzo de Villavicencio, II, Intro., pp. xxii *et seq*. See also Gachard, *Don Carlos*, pp. 340 and note, 342, and 353. Regarding the death of Berghes, see autograph note from the King to the Prince of Eboli, May 16th, 1567, *Correspondance*, II, p. 535. In connection with Chinchon, see Kervyn de Lettenhove, *Les Huguenots et les Gueux*, II, p. 61, with the relevant notes and references. Regarding Montigny's death, *Correspondance*, II, pp. 125, 160–1, 157–9 (letter from Fray Hernando de Castillo) and declaration made by Florent de Montmorency, Lord of Montigny, and written in his own hand, in the fortress of Simancas, October 14th, 1570) ; 160–1.

(14) Kervyn de Lettenhove, II, pp. 168, 250 and 257. Gachard, *Correspondance*, II, 150–1, 683, 685, 687, and, for the revenues of the great rebels of the Low Countries, 115–16.

CHAPTER VII

(1) Letter of August 27th, 1557, quoted by Gachard, *Don Carlos*, I, p. 25. There are similar complaints in a letter of April 13th, 1558. See also p. 9,

(2) Gachard, *Don Carlos*, p. 67, note 1. For Doña Juana's letter to Charles V. see p. 53.

(3) Gachard, *Don Carlos*, pp. 146–9.

(4) Gachard, *Don Carlos*, pp. 152–3.

(5) Dietrichstein to the Emperor, June 5th, 1567, and Fourquevaux to Charles IX, June 30th, Gachard, *Don Carlos*, p. 419 and notes. See also pp. 155, note 4, 156, 270–1, 286 ; II, pp. 394–5.

(6) Gachard, *Don Carlos*, II, pp. 509–511. Regarding Don Carlos's imprisonment, pp. 581–2.

(7) La Fuente, IX, p. 309.

NOTES

(8) De Mouy, *Don Carlos*, 1888 edn., p. 94, note 2, which quotes a letter seen by Eugene Plon.

(9) Gachard, *Correspondance*, II, p. 10.

(10) Mariéjol, *Catherine de Médicis*, p. 179.

CHAPTER VIII

(1) Mariéjol, *Catherine de Médicis*, p. 181, and for the references, note 3 on that page. For the Vidame de Chartres's letter, see pp. 181–2.

(2) Gachard, *Correspondance*, p. 212, note 1 (letters from Elizabeth to the King of Spain and the Duke of Alba). For the progress of the English plot, see II, pp. 185, 187, 188, 191–2, 195–6, 197–9, 203, 211. These vacillations of Philip's partly explain Prosper Merimée's very harsh judgment of him, specifically in connection with these letters of his to the Governor of the Low Countries : " he was the weakest and most muddled head of his immense empire " (letter to Mme. Delassert, *Revue de Paris*, May 1st, 1931, p. 347). In connection with the bad relations between France and Spain in 1571, see a letter from Alba to the King, July 7th, 1571 (Gachard, *Correspondance*, II, p. 181).

(3) Mariéjol, *Catherine de Médicis*, p. 184.

(4) Gachard, *Correspondance*, II, p. 228. See also pp. 208–9 and 213 (letters from Alba to the King, November 4th and December 23rd, 1571), and 215–17 for Francés de Alava's memoranda.

(5) Mariéjol, *Marguerite de Valois*, English translation, *A Daughter of the Valois*, p. 31. See also *Catherine de Médicis*, p. 186.

(6) Letter from Saint Gouard of September 12th and 19th, 1572, Groen van Prinsterer, *Archives de La Maison de Nassau*, 1st series, supplement, 1847, pp. 125 and 127. *Catherine de Médicis*, p. 193.

(7) Gachard, *Correspondance*, II, pp. 300–1. See p. 283. For the Prince of Orange's statement, see Kervyn de Lettenhove, III, p. 69. Regarding the sack of Malines, see the letter from Secretary Estaban Prats to the King, November 30th, 1572, Gachard, *Correspondance*, II, p. 299.

(8) La Fuente, IX, p. 352.

(9) Gachard, *Correspondance*, II, pp. 431–2. See also pp. 351, 357–8, 387, 397, 437, 449–50.

(10) La Fuente, X, p. 59. See also pp. 42–3 and 54–5, and Grammont, *Histoire d'Alger*, p. 108.

(11) See the story of the captive in *Don Quixote*, that very poignant description of the population of Christian prisoners in Algiers.

(12) Weiss, I, p. 98.

CHAPTER IX

(1) Decisions of the King, modified, with his authorization, by Requesens, Gachard, *Correspondance*, III, p. 33, and Appendix, pp. 486–92.

(2) Groen van Prinsterer, *Archives*, IV, p. 47, and V, pp. 38 and 67. Since the legal year, before the Gregorian reform of the calendar in 1583, was twelve days in advance of the solar year, October 3rd fell on September 20th, the day of a high equinoctial tide. See also p. 121.

(3) Gachard, *Correspondance*, III, p. 356.

(4) Bréquigny, *Histoire des révolutions de Gênes*, Paris, 1750, II, p. 153. Modesto La Fuente, *Historia*, X, p. 84. For Lippomano's opinion of Don John, see Alberi,

Relazioni, 2nd series, II, pp. 289–92, quoted by Gachard, *Correspondance*, V, Intro., pp. xii, notes 3 and 4, and xxi.

(5) Letter from Escovedo to Philip, February 9th, 1577, Gachard, *Correspondance*, V, p. 181. For the earlier letters regarding a descent on England, see pp. 155, 159, 180 (cf. Kervyn de Lettenhove, IV, pp. 373–4), 185, 164–5, 134, 184, 288.

(6) Philip's son, Don Ferdinand, born on December 4th, 1571, who died in 1578, was six years old in February, 1577, La Fuente, X, p. 310, note 1. Mignet, *Antonio Pérez et Philippe II*, 2nd edn., pp. 44–5. See also p. 35, and Gachard, *Correspondance*, V, p. 187.

(7) Mariéjol, *Ferdinand et Isabelle*, pp. 36–7.

(8) Mignet, p. 54. See also p. 49, and Gachard, *Correspondance*, V, p. 191.

(9) Letter from Don John to the King, May 29th, 1577, Gachard, *Correspondance*, V, p. 373. See also pp. 196–7, 198–201, 344–5, 353–5, 357 and 364 ; Mignet, 432 and 54, and Kervyn de Lettenhove, IV, p. 401.

(10) The passage reads in full : " *Ya nos llega el alcance cerca ; menester sera prevenirnos bien de todo y darnos mucha priesa a despacharle antes que nos mate.*" Mignet, p. 75 and note. Kervyn de Lettenhove, IV, p. 452.

(11) Gachard, V, p. 435. See also Mignet, p. 88.

(12) Regarding the negotiation of Marguerite of Valois in the Low Countries, see Mariéjol, Chap. V of *Marguerite de Valois* (English edn., *A Daughter of the Valois*).

(13) Kervyn de Lettenhove, IV, p. 255. See also p. 573.

CHAPTER X

(1) Groen van Prinsterer, *Archives*, VI, p. 389. See also p. 463.

(2) Kervyn de Lettenhove, V, p. 421. See also pp. 243, 244–5, 350–1, and note 4.

(3) Du Mont, *Corps Diplomatique*, V, pp. 384 *et seq.* and 368. Regarding Villiers, see Groen, III, p. 102. See also Groen van Prinsterer, VII, p. 166.

(4) Lothrop Motley, French translation, IV, pp. 412–13.

(5) Groen van Prinsterer, VII, p. 340.

CHAPTER XI

(1) *Colección de Documentos inéditos*, Vol. XXXI, correspondence of the Duke of Alba with Philip II.

(2) Mariéjol, *Catherine de Médicis*, p. 331.

(3) Mariéjol, *Catherine de Médicis*, pp. 347 *et seq.*

(4) Mariéjol, *Catherine de Médicis*, p. 349.

(5) Cabrera, *Historia de Felipe II*, deals at length with the submission of the islands of the archipelago and Aymar de Chastes's failure, III, pp. 30 *et seq.*

CHAPTER XII

(1) *Lettres de Philippe II a ses filles . . . écrites pendant son séjour en Portugal* (1581–3), Gachard, Paris, 1884. Cf. Mariéjol, Lavisse and Rambaud's *Histoire générale*, V, p. 91. See also pp. 97–8.

(2) Graux, *Essai sur les origines du Fonds grec de l'Escorial*, p. 13, Paris, 1880,

46th publication of the École des Hautes-Études. Regarding the character of the knowledge of antiquity in Spain, see pp. 19 *et seq.*

(3) Ticknor, *Spanish Literature*, II, p. 111, note 2, in Magnabal's French translation. See also III, pp. 43 and 51. Regarding Lope de Rueda's company, the actor Cisneros and Don Carlos, see De Mouy, *Don Carlos*, p. 121.

(4) Morel Fatio, in his article " Spain " in the *Grande Encyclopédie*, Vol. XVI, p. 338.

(5) Henri Hymans, *Antonio Moro, son œuvre e son temps*, Brussels, 1910. For Fray Luis de Leon, see Ticknor, II, p. 136. Regarding Titian, see letter quoted by Lafenestre, *Le Titien*, p. 249. Titian's " Love and Music " should be thus styled, and not " Venus and the Organist ", as a Catalogue says. Octavio Farnese, sword at side, " improvises on the organ at his mistress's bedside, and, as he plays, he turns half around to look at the naked woman . . ." (Camille Mauclair, *L'Apre et splendide Espagne*, p. 35). See also Bertaux, *Les Arts en Espagne*, 1927 ; Paul Lefort, *La peinture espagnole*, and Maurice Barrès and Paul Lafond, *Le Greco*, Paris, 1911.

(6) Louis Bertrand, *Philippe II à l'Escorial*, p. 191.

(7) Paul Lafond, *Jérome Bosch*.

(8) See Chap. V in Camille Mauclair's *L'Apre et splendide Espagne* : " A spiritual peak : the enigma of El Greco."

(9) Regarding the printing of the Polyglot Bible of Antwerp, see *Elogio histórico del doctor Benito Arias Montano*, by Don Tomás González Carvajal, Vol. VII, of the *Memorias de la Real Academia de historia de Madrid*, pp. 1–199 ; and Max Rooses, *Christophe Plantin*, Antwerp, 1882, pp. 118 and 309. See also Graux, pp. 167–72, 272, 58–9, 35 (cf. 276), and Ticknor, II, p. 60, note 1.

(10) Karl Justi, *Philipp II als Kunstfreund, Zeitschrift für bilbende Kunst*, XVI, 1881, pp. 351–2.

(11) Louis Bertrand, *Philippe II à l'Escorial*, pp. 189–90.

(12) Ex Cabrera, II, p. 198.

(13) Gachard, *Don Carlos*, II, pp. 254–5. See also *Correspondance*, I, Intro., p.l, and Van der Hammen, quoted by Gachard, *Correspondance*, p. 224, note 2 ; Kervyn de Lettenhove, VI, p. 62.

CHAPTER XIII

(1) Gachard, *Correspondance*, III, pp. 203 *et seq.*
(2) Froude, XII, p. 175.
(3) Hume, p. 808.
(4) Kervyn de Lettenhove, VI, p. 63.
(5) Froude, XII, pp. 454–5.
(6) Hume, p. 211. See also La Fuente, X, p. 188.
(7) La Fuente, X, p. 301. See also p. 293.

CHAPTER XIV

(1) Mignet, *Antonio Pérez*, 2nd edn., p. 135. See also p. 123, notes 1 and 2.
(2) Muro, *La Princesse d'Eboli*, p. 134.
(3) Pidal, I, p. 118. See also p. 204, and Mignet, pp. 192–3, and 193, note 1.
(4) Muro, p. 383.
(5) Mariéjol, *Ferdinand et Isabelle*, p. 189.

CHAPTER XV

(1) Enrique Cock, *Jornada de Taragona*, pp. 41 *et seq.*

(2) Italo Raillion, *Storia di Carlo Emanuele I, Duca di Savoia*, Milan, 1896, p. 227 and note.

(3) Mariéjol, in Lavisse's *Histoire de France*, VI, Part I, p. 313. Cf. Antonio de Herrera, *Historia de los sucesos de Francia* (1585–94), Madrid, 1598.

(4) Modesto La Fuente, X, pp. 208–9. Henri de l'Espinois, *La Ligue et les Papes*, Paris, 1886, p. 437. See also Mariéjol, in Lavisse's *Histoire de France*, VI, Part I, pp. 322 and 329–31.

(5) Gachard, *Correspondance*, II, Intro., p. lxxxvi.

(6) Mariéjol, in Lavisse's *Histoire de France*, VI, Part I, p. 375. See also 337–8, 356, 366, 369–70, 371 ; and Gachard, *Correspondance*, Intro. to the letters to the Infantes, p. 12, note.

(7) Gachard, *Correspondance*, II, Intro., p. xcviii.

CHAPTER XVI

(1) " Relation " quoted in Appendix in Cabrera, IV, p. 425. The same figures, or not far short of them, are given in Modes to La Fuente, X, p. 282 : five million ducats = four million, six hundred and eighty-seven thousand escudos. See also La Fuente, IX, p. 179. For the financial straits of the kingdom at the time of the peace of Cateau-Cambrésis ; cf. Forneron, I, p. 103.

(2) This is the figure given by the " master-foreman ", Fray Antonio de Villacastin, Louis Bertrand, *Philippe II à l'Escorial*, pp. 153–4.

(3) Weiss, *L'Espagne depuis le règne de Philippe II jusqu'à l'avènement des Bourbons*, Paris, 1844, II, pp. 114–15. Weiss assimilates the piastre to the peso, which according to him was worth 5 frs. 20. Elsewhere, however, he reckons the piastre at 5 frs. For Morosini's " Relation ", see Appendix in Cabrera, IV, p. 504.

(4) Gachard, *Relations des Ambassadeurs vénitiens*, pp. 103–4.

(5) Ranke, *Spain under Charles V, Philip II and Philip III* (French translation, 2nd edn., 1873), p. 373.

(6) Albert Girard, *Le commerce français à Seville et Cadix au temps des Habsbourgs. Contribution a l'étude du commerce étranger en Espagne aux XVIe et XVIIe siècles*, Paris, 1932 (thesis).

(7) Weiss, II, p. 133. See also pp. 101, 116, 133, 211, 263, 265–6.

(8) Badoaro says three millions, but this is an incredible figure—probably that of Castile alone, and even then merely a round number. See La Fuente, IX, p. 215. Sometimes not merely four, but five or even six heads are reckoned to a household.

(9) Cabrera, III, p. 304. Alberi, *Relazioni*, 1st series, V, p. 488.

(10). See a very fine chapter of Louis Bertrand's, " How a King dies ", pp. 229 *et seq.* in his *Philippe II à l'Escorial*, Paris, 1929.

INDEX

INDEX

INDEX

377

INDEX

INDEX

Philip II (*continued*)—
appearance, 34 ; resists Pope Paul IV, 35–6 ; invades Picardy, 39 ; successful diplomacy, 43–8 ; marries Elizabeth of Valois, 49 ; his monarchy, 50–7 ; colonial possessions, 60–5 ; his thirteen councils, 69 ; method of government, 70–3 ; love of music, 78, 277 ; patronage of art, 272–3 ; of architecture, 275 ; mistresses of, 82 ; pastimes, 23, 84–5 ; religious fanaticism and *autodafes*, 87–93 ; campaigns against Turks, 96–100, 199–203 ; and Moriscos, 101–6 ; colonial clash with France, 120–2 ; persecutes Low Countries' Protestants, 129–34 ; and Council of the Troubles, 142 ; clash with Elizabeth, 153 ; execution of Montigny, 158 ; relations with Don Carlos, 161–74 ; and Zeeland rising, 189–96 ; seeks to reconcile Low Countries, 214–38 ; proscribes William of Orange, 240 ; deposed by Low Countries, 244 ; conquest of Portugal, 251–7 ; and the Armada, 286–97 ; second Armada, 301 ; and Antonio Pérez, 302–11 ; modifies Aragon's constitution, 313–14 ; claim to French crown, 329–34 ; war with Henri IV, 336–9 ; death of, 340, 357 ; character of, 283, 284, 357, 358
Philip, the Infante, 72, 293, 356
Philippines, the, 64
Piali Pasha, 98–9, 100, 200
Piracy, Moorish, 96–101
Pius IV, Pope, 56
Pius V, Pope, 57, 136, 149, 159, 180, 185, 198, 293, 342, 343
Pizarro, 60–1
Plantin, Christopher, 281, 284
Plessis-les-Tours, Treaty of, 243, 244, 246
Plymouth, 298, 300
Pole, Cardinal, 29
Polyglot Bible, the, 153, 281, 282
Population of Spain, 352
Portugal, 178, 251–8, 300
Potosi, mines of, 61, 86, 349
Proclamation of Brussels, 131
Protestantism in Spain, 88–92

Quiroga, Cardinal, 303

Reformation, the, 113, 116
Renaissance in Spain, 264–82
Renard, Simon, 31, 128
Renneberg, Count of, 238
Repartimientos, system of, 62
Requesens, Berenguer de, 99
Requesens, Luis de, 75, 174, 197, 204–10, 287
Rhodes, 95–6
Ribalta, 273, 279
Ribaut, Captain, 120–2
Ribera, Juan de, 106, 272, 273
Ridolfi, Roberto, 181, 291
Rochepot, Count of, 242
Roda, Jerónimo, 154, 210
Rodriguez, Fr., 272
Roelas, Juan de, 273
Rome, sieges of, 10, 37–8
Rotterdam, 113
Rouen, siege of, 324
Rudolf II, Emperor, 57, 291, 333
Rueda, Lope de, 269
Ryhove, 233, 235

Saint Aldegonde, Marnix de, 133, 208, 243, 248–9
St. Bartholomew, massacre of, 192, 193
St. Ghislain, 229
St. Quentin, battle of, 41, 276
Saint-Sulpice, 83, 92, 167
Saint Trond, 132
Saint Vaast, treaty of, 237
Salic Law, the, 142, 287, 315, 327
Saluces, 336, 339
Sande, Alvaro de, 97
Sandoval, 27, 89, 267
Santa Cruz, Marquis of, 199, 261
Santander, 221, 224, 293
Saragossa, 311, 312, 317
Savoy, Emmanuel Philibert of, 31, 40, 254
Savoy, Charles Emmanuel of, 317, 328, 336
Savoy-Piedmont, 18, 44, 48
Schiller, 175
"Sea Beggars", the, 184, 188
Sebastian, King of Portugal, 185, 253, 254, 268
Segovia, 130, 155, 157, 276
Selim II, Sultan, 198
Sempere, 268
Sepulveda, Fr., 283
Servet, Miguel, 88
Sesa, Duke of, 57, 322
Seso, Carlos de, 91
Setubal, 256
Seville, 64, 89, 91, 97, 269, 349
Sicily, 54
Sidney, Sir Philip, 288
Sigüenza, José de, 267
Siliceo, Juan Martínez, 11, 12, 15
Sixteen, the, 322, 323
Sixtus V, Pope, 291, 295, 318, 323
Suriano, Michael, 34, 71
South America, Spanish conquest of, 60, 61
slavery in, 61–2
Stanley, William, 289
States-General of France, 319, 330–5
States-General of the Low Countries, 23, 32, 42, 123, 151, 205, 208, 210, 211, 243, 244, 247
Steenwyck, 326
Strozzi, Philip, 190, 259–61
Suleiman, Sultan, 17, 95, 98, 100, 118

Tassis, Jean Baptiste de, 258, 259, 316, 324, 333, 335, 339
Tavera, Cardinal, 15, 16
Taxation, Spanish, 150, 151, 351, 353
Teligny, Admiral, 248
Terciera, 258, 262
Tercios, the, 58, 67, 124
Termonde, 194
Theresa, St., 93, 271
Thermes, Marshal de, 43
Thionville, 43, 48, 140
Three Bishoprics, the, 25, 49
Three Orders, the, 319, 331
Tibaldi, Pellegrino, 278
Tiepolo, Paolo, 166
Titelmans, Inquisitor, 129
Titian, 13, 272, 274
Tlemcen, 95
Toledo, 81, 102, 274, 349
Toledo, Garcia de, 100, 137, 161, 212, 304
Tomar, 256
Tordesillas, treaty of, 252
Tournai, 58, 108, 129, 245
Trent, Council of, 17, 54, 57, 92

379

INDEX

Trèves, 144
Trezzo, Jacomo de, 277
Tripoli, 65, 95
Tunis, 65, 95, 202
Tuscany, 56

Utrecht, Union of, 236, 326

Valdés, Fernando, 90
Valdez, Florez de, 296
Valencia, 53, 101, 165, 269, 275
Valenciennes, 129, 134, 155, 190, 238
Valladolid, 9, 90, 157, 275, 351
Valois, Elizabeth of, 48, 49, 79–85, 117, 118, 141, 175–7, 241
Valois, Marguerite de, 178, 184–6, 190, 229, 328
Vargas, Juan de, 55, 142, 145, 154
Vaucelles, Truce of, 32, 35, 341
Vázquez, Mateo, 302, 304
Vega, Lope de, 67, 270, 297
Velasquez, 272
Veneziano, Hassan, 203
Vervins, Treaty of, 339
Vimiosa, Count de, 258, 261
Vineuil, Claude de, 83–5
Vitelli, Chapin, 153
Vivonne, Jean de, 193

Walcheren, 124, 189, 207

Werf, Pieter van der, 207
West Indies, the, 60, 64
Weyden, Roger van der, 279
William of Orange, at Cateau-Cambrésis, 44, 49; origins, education and religion, 110–11; character, 110, 233, 248; marriages, 111; as councillor of state, 123, 127, 128, 130; and the "Sea Beggars", 188; founds Leyden University, 207; treats with Requesens, 208; unites Holland and Zeeland, 209; and Don John of Austria, 222–3; initiates Peace of Religion, 234; ratifies Treaty of Comines, 235; proscription and apologia, 240; offered sovereignty of Holland and Zeeland, 243; assassination, 248

Yelves, 256
Ypres, 107, 129, 247
Yuste, 33, 42, 89, 161, 268

Zayas, 72, 186, 187
Zeeland and Holland, Union of, 209
Zieriekseе, 189, 210
Zuccari, Federigo, 278
Zuñiga, Diego de, 193
Zurbarán, 272, 273
Zutphen, 189, 194, 247, 288, 289, 326, 339
Zwichem, Viglius de, 44, 124, 147, 154